CIVIC HERALDRY

By the same author
THE ROMANCE OF HERALDRY
SHAKESPEARE'S HERALDRY

CIVIC HERALDRY
OF ENGLAND & WALES

by

C. WILFRID SCOTT-GILES, O.B.E., M.A.

Sometime Exhibitioner of
Sidney Sussex College, Cambridge.
Member of the Heraldry Society.
Secretary of the Institution of
Municipal Engineers

Illustrated by the Author

BENJAMIN BLOM, INC.
Publishers New York 1972

Framingham State College
Framingham, Massachusetts

First published London, 1933
Revised edition 1953
Reissued 1972 by
Benjamin Blom, Inc.
New York, N.Y. 10025

Library of Congress
Catalog Card Number 71-184280

Printed in the
United States of America

TO THE PRESIDENT AND MEMBERS
OF THE INSTITUTION
OF MUNICIPAL ENGINEERS

PREFACE TO THE FIRST EDITION

HERALDRY is my pastime; with local government my daily duties are connected. Of the union of these two interests this book is the outcome. It has been compiled gradually, by noting down the insignia of counties and towns displayed on documents or in public buildings, and by searching out their history and significance. The difficulty I experienced in obtaining much of the information showed that it was not readily available, and that there was room for a book which should not only record civic arms and other devices in simple terms, but also give explanations thereof.

Where a local authority has in modern times obtained a grant of arms, the significance of the various emblems is generally ascertainable; but there is a large number of authorities whose arms are of ancient origin, or who, lacking arms, use some locally assumed device; and I have found that in many of these cases the origin and meaning of the arms or insignia are not known even by local officials. In others, my inquiries have led to a search of the town records and the unearthing of some forgotten report or minute concerning the adoption of the device and the reasons therefor. In a few cases I have been able to supply information rather than to receive it.

The book is thus a compilation from local records, supplemented by information derived from the College of Arms and from other sources, including Fox-Davies's *Book of Public Arms* and other books.

So far as I am aware, there is no other book devoted exclusively to the heraldry (including both arms and unauthorized devices) of English local authorities, and giving not only a general survey and description of civic insignia, but also, so far as possible, their meaning. To the general reader, descriptions and illustrations of arms are of little interest unless accompanied by the story or significance which lies behind them, and it is this that I have been at pains to record. The five heads in the arms of Reading evoke no more than a passing interest, until we learn that they probably recall the thousand-year-old crime of a jealous stepmother. Dunstable's ale-warmer arouses curiosity which is only satisfied when it is traced to the device of a pile, horseshoe, and ring adopted by an old religious house.

A distinction has been drawn between genuine coats of arms—that is, those granted by the Kings-of-Arms, who have jurisdiction over armorial matters in England and Wales—and devices adopted by local authorities without reference to the Heralds' College. The latter sometimes have the form and appearance of arms, but are, in fact, only unauthorized local insignia. They largely outnumber true coats of arms, and because they have not the status of arms, and are not recorded at the Heralds' College, have generally been neglected by students of heraldry. Nevertheless many of them are of great interest for their references to the history and character of the county or town which they represent and for this reason, and also because they may in time be recast in heraldic forms and established as true coats of arms, I have judged them well worthy of inclusion in this book. Of some 580 local authorities whose insignia are here recorded, approximately 320 are using devices of local adoption.[1]

I have to acknowledge my indebtedness to many clerks, engineers and surveyors, librarians, and other officials and members of local authorities for their willing compliance with my request for information.

My thanks are also due to Mr J. D. Heaton-Armstrong,[2] Chester Herald, for much valuable advice and information; to my sister, Miss Phyllis Giles, for tracing the source of some of the mottoes; and to my wife for undertaking some of the drawings which were beyond my skill, and for assistance in checking.

C. W. S.-G.

May 1933.

---

[1] In the second edition the insignia of 715 authorities are recorded, only 210 being of local adoption.
[2] Now Sir John Heaton-Armstrong.

PREFACE TO THE SECOND EDITION

DURING the period of nearly twenty years which has passed since this book was first published, some 240 local authorities in England and Wales have obtained grants of arms, while a number of others have been granted crests or supporters as additions to the arms they already bore. These have been included in this revised and enlarged edition, which thus contains a record of the heraldic insignia granted or confirmed to local authorities to 31st December 1952. Local councils bearing arms by authority on that date numbered:

County Councils	55
Municipal Corporations	313
Urban Districts	103
Rural Districts	28
Development Corporations	6
	505

As in the first edition, a number of devices adopted by local councils without heraldic authority have been included.

I have taken the opportunity of this revision to alter the arrangement of the book by grouping local authorities in their geographical counties, thereby bringing together insignia which have in common county emblems such as the roses of York and Lancaster, the Cheshire wheatsheaves, the Kentish horse, and the Sussex martlets.

Some friends who are versed in heraldry would have had me describe armorial bearings in the heraldic language used by the Kings-of-Arms in their official blazons. I have decided against this, since most readers would have difficulty in following such descriptions, even with the illustrations before them. I have, however, used rather more heraldic terms (e.g. the names of colours) than in the first edition, and on page 45 I have given some notes on the method of describing arms.

While thanking all those who have readily responded to my request for information, I have particularly to mention Mr H. Ellis Tomlinson and Mr R. Bretton, fellow students of civic heraldry, who have placed at my disposal notes on armorial bearings in the design of which they have been concerned.

C. W. S.-G.

January 1953.

CONTENTS

PREFACE TO THE FIRST EDITION vii
PREFACE TO THE SECOND EDITION ix

PART I

CHAP.		PAGE
I.	SOURCES OF CIVIC HERALDRY	3
II.	ROYAL AND KINDRED EMBLEMS	10
III.	FEUDAL AND FAMILY EMBLEMS	19
IV.	RELIGIOUS AND ECCLESIASTICAL EMBLEMS	22
V.	CASTLES, GATES, AND BRIDGES	26
VI.	THE SEA, RIVERS, AND SPRINGS	28
VII.	FOREST AND MOORLAND	32
VIII.	INDUSTRY	33
IX.	REBUSES	37
X.	HISTORY, TRADITION, AND LEARNING	39
XI.	MOTTOES	41

PART II

A DESCRIPTION OF THE ARMORIAL BEARINGS OF LOCAL AUTHORITIES
IN ENGLAND AND WALES

* denotes authorities whose arms, etc., are illustrated.

	PAGE		PAGE		PAGE
ANGLESEY		BUCKINGHAMSHIRE		LAMPETER B.C. . . .	68
ANGLESEY C.C.* . .	47	BUCKINGHAMSHIRE C.C.* .	58	CARMARTHENSHIRE	
BEAUMARIS B.C. . .	47	AYLESBURY B.C.* . .	59	CARMARTHENSHIRE C.C.* .	69
BEDFORDSHIRE		BUCKINGHAM B.C.* . .	59	CARMARTHEN B.C.* . .	69
BEDFORDSHIRE C.C.* .	48	HIGH WYCOMBE B.C.* .	60	KIDWELLY B.C. . .	70
BEDFORD B.C.* . .	48	SLOUGH B.C.* . . .	60	LLANDOVERY B.C. . .	70
DUNSTABLE B.C.* . .	49	ETON U.D.C.* . . .	61	LLANELLY B.C. . .	70
LUTON B.C.* . . .	50	NEWPORT PAGNELL U.D.C.*	61	AMMANFORD U.D.C.* .	70
LEIGHTON BUZZARD U.D.C.*	50	CAERNARVONSHIRE		CARMARTHEN R.D.C.* .	71
BERKSHIRE		CAERNARVONSHIRE C.C.* .	62	CHESHIRE	
BERKSHIRE C.C.* . .	51	BANGOR CITY C.* . .	63	CHESHIRE C.C.* . .	72
READING C.B.C.* . .	52	CAERNARVON B.C. . .	63	CHESTER CITY and C.B.C.* .	73
ABINGDON B.C.* . .	52	CONWAY B.C. . .	63	BIRKENHEAD C.B.C.* .	74
MAIDENHEAD B.C.* . .	53	PWLLHELI B.C. . .	63	STOCKPORT C.B.C.* .	74
NEWBURY B.C.* . .	53	LLANDUDNO U.D.C. . .	63	WALLASEY C.B.C.* .	75
NEW WINDSOR B.C.* .	54	CAMBRIDGESHIRE		ALTRINCHAM B.C.* .	76
WALLINGFORD B.C. . .	54	CAMBRIDGESHIRE C.C.* .	64	BEBINGTON B.C.* .	77
WOKINGHAM B.C. . .	54	ISLE OF ELY C.C.* . .	65	CONGLETON B.C.* .	77
BRACKNELL DEVELOPMENT		CAMBRIDGE CITY C.* .	66	CREWE B.C. . .	78
CORPORATION * . .	55	WISBECH B.C.* . .	66	DUKINFIELD B.C.* .	78
BRECONSHIRE		CARDIGANSHIRE		HYDE B.C.* . .	79
BRECONSHIRE C.C.* .	56	CARDIGANSHIRE C.C.* .	67	MACCLESFIELD B.C.* .	79
BRECKNOCK B.C.* . .	56	ABERYSTWYTH B.C.* .	67	SALE B.C.* . . .	80
YSTRADGYNLAIS R.D.C.* .	57	CARDIGAN B.C. . .	68	STALYBRIDGE B.C.* .	81

CONTENTS

CHESHIRE (continued)

	PAGE
BOWDON U.D.C.*	81
BREDBURY AND ROMILEY U.D.C.	82
CHEADLE AND GATLEY U.D.C.*	82
HALE U.D.C.	83
HAZEL GROVE AND BRAMHALL U.D.C.*	83
KNUTSFORD U.D.C.	83
NANTWICH U.D.C.*	83
NORTHWICH U.D.C.	83
SANDBACH U.D.C.	83
WILMSLOW U.D.C.*	83
CONGLETON R.D.C.*	84

CORNWALL

CORNWALL C.C.*	85
TRURO CITY C.*	86
BODMIN B.C.	86
FALMOUTH B.C.	86
FOWEY B.C.	87
HELSTON B.C.	87
LAUNCESTON B.C.*	87
LISKEARD B.C.	87
LOSTWITHIEL B.C.	87
PENRYN B.C.	87
PENZANCE B.C.*	87
ST IVES B.C.*	89
SALTASH B.C.*	89
BUDE-STRATTON U.D.C.*	89
NEWQUAY U.D.C.*	90
ST AUSTELL U.D.C.	90

CUMBERLAND

CUMBERLAND C.C.*	91
CARLISLE CITY and C.B.C.*	92
WHITEHAVEN B.C.	92
WORKINGTON B.C.*	93
KESWICK U.D.C.	93
PENRITH U.D.C.*	94

DENBIGHSHIRE

DENBIGHSHIRE C.C.	95
COLWYN BAY B.C.*	95
DENBIGH B.C.	96
RUTHIN B.C.	96
WREXHAM B.C.*	96
WREXHAM R.D.C.*	96

DERBYSHIRE

DERBYSHIRE C.C.*	97
DERBY C.B.C.*	98
BUXTON B.C.*	98
CHESTERFIELD B.C.*	98
GLOSSOP B.C.*	99
ILKESTON B.C.*	99
BELPER U.D.C.	99
LONG EATON U.D.C.	100
MATLOCK U.D.C.	100
NEW MILLS U.D.C.	100
SWADLINCOTE U.D.C.*	100
WIRKSWORTH U.D.C.	100
BLACKWELL R.D.C.*	100
SHARDLOW R.D.C.*	101

DEVONSHIRE

DEVON C.C.*	102
EXETER CITY and C.B.C.*	103
PLYMOUTH CITY and C.B.C.*	104
BARNSTAPLE B.C.*	104
BIDEFORD B.C.*	105
DARTMOUTH B.C.*	105
GREAT TORRINGTON B.C.*	106
HONITON B.C.	106
OKEHAMPTON B.C.	106
SOUTH MOLTON B.C.	106
TIVERTON B.C.	106
TORQUAY B.C.*	107
TOTNES B.C.*	107
ASHBURTON U.D.C.	107
AXMINSTER U.D.C.*	108
EXMOUTH U.D.C.*	108
ILFRACOMBE U.D.C.*	109
NEWTON ABBOT U.D.C.*	109
PAIGNTON U.D.C.*	110
SIDMOUTH U.D.C.*	110
TAVISTOCK U.D.C.*	111
TEIGNMOUTH U.D.C.*	111

DORSET

DORSET C.C.*	112
BLANDFORD FORUM B.C.*	112
BRIDPORT B.C.*	113
DORCHESTER B.C.*	113
LYME REGIS B.C.*	114
POOLE B.C.*	114
SHAFTESBURY B.C.*	114
WAREHAM B.C.*	115
WEYMOUTH AND MELCOMBE REGIS B.C.*	115

DURHAM

DURHAM C.C.*	116
DURHAM CITY C.*	116
DARLINGTON C.B.C.	117
GATESHEAD C.B.C.*	117
SOUTH SHIELDS C.B.C.	117
SUNDERLAND C.B.C.*	118
WEST HARTLEPOOL C.B.C.*	119
HARTLEPOOL B.C.	119
JARROW B.C.*	119
STOCKTON-ON-TEES B.C.*	120
BARNARD CASTLE U.D.C.	121
BILLINGHAM U.D.C.	121
BISHOP AUCKLAND U.D.C.	121
FELLING U.D.C.	121
HEBBURN U.D.C.	121
HOUGHTON-LE-SPRING U.D.C.	121
SEAHAM U.D.C.*	122
SHILDON U.D.C.	122
SPENNYMOOR U.D.C.*	122
WASHINGTON U.D.C.*	123
SUNDERLAND R.D.C.*	123

ESSEX

ESSEX C.C.*	124
EAST HAM C.B.C.*	125
SOUTHEND-ON-SEA C.B.C.*	125
WEST HAM C.B.C.*	126
BARKING B.C.*	126
CHELMSFORD B.C.*	127
CHINGFORD B.C.*	128
COLCHESTER B.C.*	128
DAGENHAM B.C.*	129
HARWICH B.C.*	130
ILFORD B.C.*	130
LEYTON B.C.*	131
MALDON B.C.*	132
ROMFORD B.C.*	132
SAFFRON WALDEN B.C.	133
WALTHAMSTOW B.C.*	133
WANSTEAD AND WOODFORD B.C.*	134
BRAINTREE AND BOCKING U.D.C.*	135
BRENTWOOD U.D.C.*	136
CHIGWELL U.D.C.*	136
CLACTON U.D.C.*	136
HORNCHURCH U.D.C.*.	137
RAYLEIGH U.D.C.	137
WALTHAM HOLY CROSS U.D.C.	138
BASILDON DEVELOPMENT CORPORATION *	138
HARLOW DEVELOPMENT CORPORATION *	139

FLINTSHIRE

FLINTSHIRE C.C.*	140
FLINT B.C.	140
PRESTATYN U.D.C.	140

GLAMORGAN

GLAMORGAN C.C.*	141
CARDIFF CITY and C.B.C.*	142
MERTHYR TYDFIL C.B.C.*	143
SWANSEA C.B.C.*	143
BARRY B.C.*	144
COWBRIDGE B.C.*	145
NEATH B.C.	145
PORT TALBOT B.C.*	145
BRIDGEND B.C.*	146
PENARTH U.D.C.	146

GLOUCESTERSHIRE

GLOUCESTERSHIRE C.C.*	147
BRISTOL CITY and C.B.C.*	148
GLOUCESTER CITY and C.B.C.*	149
CHELTENHAM B.C.*	150
TEWKESBURY B.C.	151
CIRENCESTER U.D.C.*	151
KINGSWOOD U.D.C.*	151
DURSLEY R.D.C.*	152

HAMPSHIRE

HAMPSHIRE C.C.*	153
BOURNEMOUTH C.B.C.*	153
PORTSMOUTH CITY and C.B.C.*	154
SOUTHAMPTON C.B.C.*	154
WINCHESTER CITY C.*	155
ALDERSHOT B.C.*	155
ANDOVER B.C.*	156
BASINGSTOKE B.C.	157
CHRISTCHURCH B.C.	157
EASTLEIGH B.C.*	157
GOSPORT B.C.	158
LYMINGTON B.C.	158
ROMSEY B.C.	158
FAREHAM U.D.C.*	158

CONTENTS

	PAGE
FARNBOROUGH U.D.C.*	158
HAVANT AND WATERLOO U.D.C.	159
PETERSFIELD U.D.C.*	159

HEREFORDSHIRE

HEREFORDSHIRE C.C.*	160
HEREFORD CITY C.*	160
LEOMINSTER B.C.*	162

HERTFORDSHIRE

HERTFORDSHIRE C.C.*	163
HEMEL HEMPSTEAD B.C.	163
HERTFORD B.C.*	164
ST ALBANS CITY C.*	165
WATFORD B.C.*	165
BALDOCK U.D.C.*	166
BERKHAMSTED U.D.C.*	166
BISHOP'S STORTFORD U.D.C.*	167
CHESHUNT U.D.C.*	167
EAST BARNET U.D.C.	168
HARPENDEN U.D.C.*	168
HITCHIN U.D.C.*	168
LETCHWORTH U.D.C.*	169
ROYSTON U.D.C.*	169
HATFIELD R.D.C.*	170
HERTFORD R.D.C.*	171
HEMEL HEMPSTEAD DEVELOPMENT CORPORATION *	171
STEVENAGE DEVELOPMENT CORPORATION *	172

HUNTINGDONSHIRE

HUNTINGDONSHIRE C.C.*	173
GODMANCHESTER B.C.	174
HUNTINGDON B.C.	174
ST IVES B.C.*	174

ISLE OF WIGHT

ISLE OF WIGHT C.C.*	175
NEWPORT B.C.	175
RYDE B.C.*	176
VENTNOR U.D.C.	176

KENT

KENT C.C.*	177
CANTERBURY CITY and C.B.C.*	178
BECKENHAM B.C.*	178
BEXLEY B.C.*	179
BROMLEY B.C.*	180
CHATHAM B.C.*.	180
DARTFORD B.C.*	181
DEAL B.C.*	182
DOVER B.C.*	182
ERITH B.C.*	183
FAVERSHAM B.C.*	183
FOLKESTONE B.C.	184
GILLINGHAM B.C.*	184
GRAVESEND B.C.*	184
HYTHE B.C.	184
LYDD B.C.*	185
MAIDSTONE B.C.*	185
MARGATE B.C.*.	186
NEW ROMNEY B.C.*	187
QUEENBOROUGH B.C.	187
RAMSGATE B.C.*	187

	PAGE
ROCHESTER CITY C.*	188
SANDWICH B.C.*	188
TENTERDEN B.C.*	188
TUNBRIDGE WELLS B.C.*	189
ASHFORD U.D.C.*	189
CRAYFORD U.D.C.*	190
HERNE BAY U.D.C.*	190
SEVENOAKS U.D.C.	191
SHEERNESS U.D.C.	191
SITTINGBOURNE AND MILTON U.D.C.*	191
TONBRIDGE U.D.C.*	191
DARTFORD R.D.C.*	192

LANCASHIRE

LANCASHIRE C.C.*	193
BARROW-IN-FURNESS C.B.C.*	194
BLACKBURN C.B.C.*	194
BLACKPOOL C.B.C.*	195
BOLTON C.B.C.*	196
BOOTLE C.B.C.*	197
BURNLEY C.B.C.*	197
BURY C.B.C.*	198
LIVERPOOL CITY and C.B.C.*	198
MANCHESTER CITY and C.B.C.*	199
OLDHAM C.B.C.*	200
PRESTON C.B.C.*	201
ROCHDALE C.B.C.*	201
ST HELENS C.B.C.*	202
SALFORD CITY and C.B.C.*.	202
SOUTHPORT C.B.C.*	203
WARRINGTON C.B.C.*.	204
WIGAN C.B.C.*	205
ACCRINGTON B.C.*	206
ASHTON-UNDER-LYNE B.C.*	207
BACUP B.C.*	207
CHORLEY B.C.*	207
CLITHEROE B.C.*	208
COLNE B.C.*	209
CROSBY B.C.*	209
DARWEN B.C.*	210
ECCLES B.C.*	211
FARNWORTH B.C.*	211
FLEETWOOD B.C.*	212
HASLINGDEN B.C.*	213
HEYWOOD B.C.*	213
LANCASTER CITY C.*	214
LEIGH B.C.*	215
LYTHAM ST ANNES B.C.*	215
MIDDLETON B.C.*	216
MORECAMBE AND HEYSHAM B.C.*	216
MOSSLEY B.C.*	216
NELSON B.C.*	217
PRESTWICH B.C.*	217
RADCLIFFE B.C.*	218
RAWTENSTALL B.C.*	219
STRETFORD B.C.*	220
SWINTON AND PENDLEBURY B.C.*	221
WIDNES B.C.*	221
ABRAM U.D.C.	222
ASHTON-IN-MAKERFIELD U.D.C.	222
ASPULL U.D.C.	222
ATHERTON U.D.C.*	222

	PAGE
AUDENSHAW U.D.C.*	223
BRIERFIELD U.D.C.*	223
CLAYTON-LE-MOORS U.D.C.	223
CROMPTON U.D.C.	223
DENTON U.D.C.*	223
DROYLSDEN U.D.C.*	224
FAILSWORTH U.D.C.*	224
HAYDOCK U.D.C.	225
HINDLEY U.D.C.	225
HORWICH U.D.C.	225
HUYTON-WITH-ROBY U.D.C.	225
KIRKHAM U.D.C.*	225
LEYLAND U.D.C.*	226
LITTLE LEVER U.D.C.*	226
POULTON-LE-FYLDE U.D.C.*	227
PREESALL U.D.C.*	227
RISHTON U.D.C.	228
STANDISH-WITH-LANGTREE U.D.C.	228
THORNTON CLEVELEYS U.D.C.*	228
TYLDESLEY-WITH-SHAKERLEY U.D.C.*	228
URMSTON U.D.C.*	229
WALTON-LE-DALE U.D.C.*	230
CHORLEY R.D.C.*	230
GARSTANG R.D.C.*	230
PRESTON R.D.C.*	231
WHISTON R.D.C.	231

LEICESTERSHIRE

LEICESTERSHIRE C.C.*	232
LEICESTER CITY and C.B.C.*	233
LOUGHBOROUGH B.C.*	234
HINCKLEY U.D.C.*	234
MARKET HARBOROUGH U.D.C.	235
MELTON MOWBRAY U.D.C.	235

LINCOLNSHIRE

HOLLAND C.C.*	236
KESTEVEN C.C.*	236
LINDSEY C.C.*	237
GRIMSBY C.B.C.*	237
LINCOLN CITY and C.B.C.*	238
BOSTON B.C.*	238
CLEETHORPES B.C.*	239
GRANTHAM B.C.*	240
LOUTH B.C.*	241
SCUNTHORPE B.C.*	241
STAMFORD B.C.*	241
GAINSBOROUGH U.D.C.*	241
SLEAFORD U.D.C.*	242
SPALDING U.D.C.*	242
GAINSBOROUGH R.D.C.*	243
GLANFORD BRIGG R.D.C.*	244
SOUTH KESTEVEN R.D.C.*	244
CORBY DEVELOPMENT CORPORATION	244

LONDON

LONDON C.C.*	245
LONDON CITY CORPORATION*	245
BATTERSEA B.C.*	246
BERMONDSEY B.C.*	247
BETHNAL GREEN B.C..	248
CAMBERWELL B.C.*	248
CHELSEA B.C.*	248

CONTENTS

LONDON (continued)

	PAGE
DEPTFORD B.C.	249
FINSBURY B.C.*	249
FULHAM B.C.*	250
GREENWICH B.C.*	250
HACKNEY B.C.*	251
HAMMERSMITH B.C.*	252
HAMPSTEAD B.C.*	253
HOLBORN B.C.*	253
ISLINGTON B.C.*	254
KENSINGTON B.C.*	255
LAMBETH B.C.*	255
LEWISHAM B.C.*	256
PADDINGTON B.C.*	257
POPLAR B.C.	257
ST MARYLEBONE B.C.*	257
ST PANCRAS B.C.*	258
SHOREDITCH B.C.*	259
SOUTHWARK B.C.*	259
STEPNEY B.C.*	259
STOKE NEWINGTON B.C.*	261
WANDSWORTH B.C.*	261
WESTMINSTER CITY C.*	262
WOOLWICH B.C.*	263
METROPOLITAN WATER BOARD *	263
PORT OF LONDON AUTHORITY *	264

MERIONETH

	PAGE
MERIONETH C.C.*	266
BARMOUTH U.D.C.*	266

MIDDLESEX

	PAGE
MIDDLESEX C.C.*	267
ACTON B.C.*	267
BRENTFORD AND CHISWICK B.C.*	268
EALING B.C.*	269
EDMONTON B.C.*	269
FINCHLEY B.C.*	270
HENDON B.C.*	271
HESTON AND ISLEWORTH B.C.*	272
HORNSEY B.C.*	273
SOUTHALL B.C.*	273
SOUTHGATE B.C.*	274
TOTTENHAM B.C.*	275
TWICKENHAM B.C.*	276
WEMBLEY B.C.*	276
WILLESDEN B.C.*	277
WOOD GREEN B.C.*	278
ENFIELD U.D.C.*	279
FELTHAM U.D.C.*	279
FRIERN BARNET U.D.C.*	280
HARROW U.D.C.*	281
HAYES AND HARLINGTON U.D.C.*	281
RUISLIP-NORTHWOOD U.D.C.*	282
STAINES U.D.C.*	283
SUNBURY-ON-THAMES U.D.C.*	284
UXBRIDGE U.D.C.*	284

MONMOUTHSHIRE

	PAGE
MONMOUTHSHIRE C.C.*	285
NEWPORT C.B.C.*	286
ABERGAVENNY B.C.*	286
MONMOUTH B.C.*	287
BLAENAVON U.D.C.*	287

MONTGOMERYSHIRE

	PAGE
MONTGOMERYSHIRE C.C.*	288
LLANFYLLIN B.C.	289
LLANIDLOES B.C.	289
MONTGOMERY B.C.	289
WELSHPOOL B.C.	289

NORFOLK

	PAGE
NORFOLK C.C.*	290
NORWICH CITY and C.B.C.*	290
GREAT YARMOUTH C.B.C.*	291
KING'S LYNN B.C.*	291
THETFORD B.C.	292
DISS U.D.C.	292
EAST DEREHAM U.D.C.	292
NORTH WALSHAM U.D.C.*	292
SWAFFHAM U.D.C.	292

NORTHAMPTONSHIRE

	PAGE
NORTHAMPTONSHIRE C.C.*	293
SOKE OF PETERBOROUGH C.C.*	294
NORTHAMPTON C.B.C.*	294
PETERBOROUGH CITY C.*	295
BRACKLEY B.C.*	295
DAVENTRY B.C.	295
HIGHAM FERRERS B.C.	295
KETTERING B.C.*	295
WELLINGBOROUGH U.D.C.*	296
NORTHAMPTON R.D.C.*	297

NORTHUMBERLAND

	PAGE
NORTHUMBERLAND C.C.*	298
NEWCASTLE-UPON-TYNE CITY and C.B.C.*	299
TYNEMOUTH C.B.C.*	300
BERWICK-UPON-TWEED B.C.*	300
BLYTH B.C.*	301
MORPETH B.C.*	301
WALLSEND B.C.*	302

NOTTINGHAMSHIRE

	PAGE
NOTTINGHAMSHIRE C.C.*	303
NOTTINGHAM CITY and C.B.C.*	304
EAST RETFORD B.C.*	305
MANSFIELD B.C.*	305
NEWARK-ON-TRENT B.C.*	306
WORKSOP B.C.*	307
ARNOLD U.D.C.*	308
EASTWOOD U.D.C.*	308
HUCKNALL U.D.C.*	309
WORKSOP R.D.C.*	309

OXFORDSHIRE

	PAGE
OXFORDSHIRE C.C.*	310
OXFORD CITY and C.B.C.*	311
BANBURY B.C.*	311
CHIPPING NORTON B.C.	312
HENLEY-UPON-THAMES B.C.	312
WOODSTOCK B.C.*	313
WITNEY U.D.C.	313

PEMBROKESHIRE

	PAGE
PEMBROKESHIRE C.C.*	314
HAVERFORDWEST B.C.	315
PEMBROKE B.C.*	315
TENBY B.C.*	316

RADNORSHIRE

	PAGE
RADNORSHIRE C.C.*	317
LLANDRINDOD WELLS U.D.C.	317

RUTLAND

	PAGE
RUTLAND C.C.*	318

SHROPSHIRE

	PAGE
SALOP C.C.*	319
BISHOP'S CASTLE B.C.	319
BRIDGNORTH B.C.	319
LUDLOW B.C.*	320
OSWESTRY B.C.*	320
SHREWSBURY B.C.*	321
WENLOCK B.C.	321
WELLINGTON U.D.C.*	321

SOMERSET

	PAGE
SOMERSET C.C.*	322
BATH CITY and C.B.C.*	322
BRIDGWATER B.C.*	323
CHARD B.C.	324
GLASTONBURY B.C.*	324
TAUNTON B.C.*	324
WELLS CITY C.*	325
WESTON-SUPER-MARE B.C.*	325
YEOVIL B.C.	326
CLEVEDON U.D.C.*	326
CREWKERNE U.D.C.*	326
KEYNSHAM U.D.C.	327
BATHAVON R.D.C.*	327

STAFFORDSHIRE

	PAGE
STAFFORDSHIRE C.C.*	328
BURTON-UPON-TRENT C.B.C.*	329
SMETHWICK C.B.C.*	329
STOKE-ON-TRENT CITY and C.B.C.*	330
WALSALL C.B.C.*	331
WEST BROMWICH C.B.C.*	331
WOLVERHAMPTON C.B.C.*	332
BILSTON B.C.*	333
LICHFIELD CITY C.*	333
NEWCASTLE-UNDER-LYME B.C.*	334
ROWLEY REGIS B.C.*	335
STAFFORD B.C.*	336
TAMWORTH B.C.	336
TIPTON B.C.*	336
WEDNESBURY B.C.*	337
ALDRIDGE U.D.C.	337
BRIERLEY HILL U.D.C.*	338
CANNOCK U.D.C.*	338
COSELEY U.D.C.*	339
DARLASTON U.D.C.*	340
KIDSGROVE U.D.C.*	340
LEEK U.D.C.	340
STONE U.D.C.	340
TETTENHALL U.D.C.*	340
UTTOXETER U.D.C.	341
WEDNESFIELD U.D.C.	341
WILLENHALL U.D.C.*	341
SEISDON R.D.C.*	342

CONTENTS

SUFFOLK

	PAGE
EAST SUFFOLK C.C.*	343
WEST SUFFOLK C.C.*	344
IPSWICH C.B.C.*	344
ALDEBURGH B.C.*	344
BECCLES B.C.	345
BURY ST EDMUNDS B.C.*	345
EYE B.C.*	346
LOWESTOFT B.C.*	346
SOUTHWOLD B.C.*	346
SUDBURY B.C.*	347
FELIXSTOWE U.D.C.*	348
HADLEIGH U.D.C.*	348
NEWMARKET U.D.C.*	349
GIPPING R.D.C.*	349

SURREY

	PAGE
SURREY C.C.*	350
CROYDON C.B.C.*	350
BARNES B.C.*	351
BEDDINGTON AND WALLINGTON B.C.*	352
EPSOM AND EWELL B.C.*	353
GODALMING B.C.*	353
GUILDFORD B.C.*	354
KINGSTON-UPON-THAMES B.C.*	354
MALDEN AND COOMBE B.C.*	355
MITCHAM B.C.*	356
REIGATE B.C.*	356
RICHMOND B.C.*	357
SURBITON B.C.*	358
SUTTON AND CHEAM B.C.*	358
WIMBLEDON B.C.*	359
BANSTEAD U.D.C.	360
CARSHALTON U.D.C.*	360
DORKING U.D.C.	361
EGHAM U.D.C.*	361
ESHER U.D.C.*	361
FARNHAM U.D.C.*	361
LEATHERHEAD U.D.C.*	362
MERTON AND MORDEN U.D.C.*	363
WALTON AND WEYBRIDGE U.D.C.*	363
WOKING U.D.C.*	364

SUSSEX

	PAGE
EAST SUSSEX C.C.*	365
WEST SUSSEX C.C.*	365
BRIGHTON C.B.C.*	365
EASTBOURNE C.B.C.*	366
HASTINGS C.B.C.*	366
ARUNDEL B.C.*	366
BEXHILL B.C.*	367
CHICHESTER CITY C.*	368
HOVE B.C.*	368
LEWES B.C.*	369
RYE B.C.	369
WORTHING B.C.*	369
BOGNOR REGIS U.D.C.*	369
EAST GRINSTEAD U.D.C.	370
HORSHAM U.D.C.*	370
LITTLEHAMPTON U.D.C.*	371
SEAFORD U.D.C.	371
SHOREHAM-BY-SEA U.D.C.*	371
CHICHESTER R.D.C.*	371
UCKFIELD R.D.C.*	372
CRAWLEY DEVELOPMENT CORPORATION*	373

WARWICKSHIRE

	PAGE
WARWICKSHIRE C.C.*	374
BIRMINGHAM CITY and C.B.C.*	375
COVENTRY CITY and C.B.C.*	376
LEAMINGTON B.C.*	376
NUNEATON B.C.*	377
RUGBY B.C.*	378
STRATFORD-UPON-AVON B.C.*	378
SUTTON COLDFIELD B.C.*	378
WARWICK B.C.*	379
BEDWORTH U.D.C.	380
KENILWORTH U.D.C.*	380
SOLIHULL U.D.C.*	380

WESTMORLAND

	PAGE
WESTMORLAND C.C.*	381
APPLEBY B.C.*	381
KENDAL B.C.*	382

WILTSHIRE

	PAGE
WILTSHIRE C.C.*	383
SALISBURY CITY C.*	383
CALNE B.C.*	384
CHIPPENHAM B.C.*	385
DEVIZES B.C.*	385
MALMESBURY B.C.*	386
MARLBOROUGH B.C.*	386
SWINDON B.C.*	387
WILTON B.C.	388
MELKSHAM U.D.C.*	388
TROWBRIDGE U.D.C.*	388
WARMINSTER U.D.C.*	389
WESTBURY U.D.C.*	389

WORCESTERSHIRE

	PAGE
WORCESTERSHIRE C.C.*	390
DUDLEY C.B.C.*	390
WORCESTER CITY and C.B.C.*	390
BEWDLEY B.C.*	391
DROITWICH B.C.*	391
EVESHAM B.C.*	392
HALESOWEN B.C.*	392
KIDDERMINSTER B.C.*	393
OLDBURY B.C.*	394
STOURBRIDGE B.C.*	394
MALVERN U.D.C.*	395
REDDITCH U.D.C.*	395
UPTON-ON-SEVERN R.D.C.*	396

YORKSHIRE

	PAGE
EAST RIDING C.C.*	397
NORTH RIDING C.C.*	397
WEST RIDING C.C.*	397
BARNSLEY C.B.C.*	399
BRADFORD CITY and C.B.C.*	399
DEWSBURY C.B.C.*	400
DONCASTER C.B.C.*	401
HALIFAX C.B.C.*	402
HUDDERSFIELD C.B.C.*	403
KINGSTON-UPON-HULL CITY and C.B.C.*	403
LEEDS CITY and C.B.C.*	404
MIDDLESBROUGH C.B.C.*	404
ROTHERHAM C.B.C.*	405
SHEFFIELD CITY and C.B.C.*	406
WAKEFIELD CITY and C.B.C.*	407
YORK CITY and C.B.C.*	408
BATLEY B.C.*	408
BEVERLEY B.C.*	408
BRIDLINGTON B.C.*	409
BRIGHOUSE B.C.*	409
GOOLE B.C.*	409
HARROGATE B.C.*	410
HEDON B.C.	410
KEIGHLEY B.C.*	411
MORLEY B.C.*	412
OSSETT B.C.	412
PONTEFRACT B.C.*	412
PUDSEY B.C.*	412
REDCAR B.C.*	413
RICHMOND B.C.*	414
RIPON CITY C.*	414
SCARBOROUGH B.C.*	414
THORNABY-ON-TEES B.C.*	415
TODMORDEN B.C.*	415
BAILDON U.D.C.*	416
BINGLEY U.D.C.	416
CASTLEFORD U.D.C.*	417
ELLAND U.D.C.	417
FILEY U.D.C.*	417
HALTEMPRICE U.D.C.*	418
HEMSWORTH U.D.C.*	419
HORBURY U.D.C.*	419
HORSFORTH U.D.C.	419
KIRKBURTON U.D.C.	419
KNARESBOROUGH U.D.C.	419
KNOTTINGLEY U.D.C.*	419
MIRFIELD U.D.C.	419
OTLEY U.D.C.*	420
QUEENSBURY AND SHELF U.D.C.	420
SALTBURN AND MARSKE-BY-THE-SEA U.D.C.*	420
SELBY U.D.C.*	421
SKIPTON U.D.C.*	421
SPENBOROUGH U.D.C.*	422
WHITBY U.D.C.*	422
WOMBWELL U.D.C.	423
DONCASTER R.D.C.*	423
KIVETON PARK R.D.C.*	423
WETHERBY R.D.C.*	424

APPENDIX—AN APLPHABETICAL LIST OF MOTTOES OF LOCAL AUTHORITIES 425

INDEX—A. PERSONS AND FAMILIES 431

B. PLACES AND SUBJECTS 437

PART I

CHAPTER I

SOURCES OF CIVIC HERALDRY

THE use of armorial bearings by corporations is not new. Even in the Middle Ages, when heraldry was mainly a personal and family matter, certain cities and towns such as London, Norwich, Shrewsbury, and Kingston-upon-Hull, placed in their seals heraldic shields, which are still their civic arms, borne by prescriptive right. In the sixteenth and seventeenth centuries the heralds, in the course of their Visitations, recorded and sanctioned many such arms adopted by corporations, and in some cases formally granted arms where none had been used before. By 1700, 90 English cities and towns had acquired armorial bearings. To-day, some 500 local authorities in England and Wales bear arms by right (excluding those using some device of local adoption which has not been recognized or granted by the Kings-of-Arms), and of these arms about three-quarters have been granted during the last hundred years. Civic heraldry is thus largely of modern growth, though it is firmly rooted in antiquity and tradition. In the steady progress towards popular government, local authority has passed from the feudal families and the squirearchy to democratic bodies—the county, borough, and district councils—and it is natural and fitting that these bodies should bear not only the public duties which the 'nobility and gentry' performed (not unworthily in their day), but also the appropriate dignities, including the right to use tokens of honour and authority.

The origins of civic heraldry are found in the symbolic devices on official and corporate seals. Among English boroughs, the use of such seals began during the latter part of the twelfth century, and became general during the fourteenth and fifteenth centuries.

The designs on the majority of early town seals fall into four categories: royal and seignorial emblems; religious emblems, especially the image or symbol of the town's patron saint; castles, representative of and sometimes faithfully illustrating the stronghold by which the town had grown in prosperity; and ships, denoting maritime interests.

As towns rose to importance and became increasingly conscious of their individuality and corporate spirit, they began to imitate the state of the seignorial class, and one sign of this was the adoption of armorial bearings.

In some cases, this was simply achieved by placing on a shield the design on the town seal and giving it colours. The arms of Reading and of Bedford were produced in this way. Another example is provided by the arms of Great Torrington, which reproduce not only the fleur-de-lis and wavy bars in the seal, but also the decorative cusps of the inner rim which in the arms become an engrailed border.

In some cases the design on the seal had to be slightly modified to conform with heraldic custom. For example, on the seal of Lydd, bearing a ship and a church, there hung from a hook in the border a quartered shield charged with four lions rampant, and in the arms this became a canton charged with a cross between four lions.

Some towns found that the emblems in their seals were too elaborate or pictorial to be reproduced as armorial bearings, yet in their arms they carried out the same theme as on their seals. An early seal of Lynn bore the figure of St Margaret standing under a canopy with her cross thrust into the jaws of a dragon writhing at her feet. The arms bear three dragons' heads each transfixed by a cross. The seal of London bore the figure of St Paul, sword in hand; in the arms he is represented by the sword alone. On the seal of Canterbury was a representation of the martyrdom of St Thomas; the arms incorporate Becket's personal coat, three Cornish choughs.

Since the influence of seals on early civic heraldry was so strong, the themes which have been mentioned as dominant in ancient seals, namely royal and seignorial emblems, religious emblems, castles, and ships, are also dominant in early civic arms. Of the ninety coats of arms of cities and boroughs recorded, confirmed, or granted by the heralds before the year 1700, twenty-seven are composed mainly of royal or seignorial emblems; eighteen bear religious emblems, mostly the symbols of national or local patron saints; eighteen have castles as their principal feature; and seventeen bear ships, fish, or other tokens of maritime or riverside interests. Of the remainder, three are rebuses, two refer to forests, one to the woollen industry, and four are unclassifiable.

It is not possible similarly to classify arms granted to local authorities since 1700, because modern civic arms are generally more complicated than those of the earlier period, and contain a blend of two or more themes, which makes it impossible to assign a coat to a particular class. But the following generalizations show how the character of civic arms has changed.

Firstly, the day of the casual assumption of emblems from the Royal Arms is past, and their use is now carefully controlled. Parts of the contemporary royal insignia have been specially granted to a few authorities, but generally when counties and towns wish to mark royal associations emblems of an historic character are used; for example, a crown of some ancient pattern instead of the present Royal Crown.

References to seignorial and local families, ancient and modern, are still common in civic arms.

Emblems of a religious character still occur, occasionally denoting the patron saint of the ancient parish church, but more frequently relating to former religious houses, the parishes into which the town is divided, or the see in which it lies or to which the manor belonged. While the religious element is still present in civic heraldry, its historic rather than its devotional aspect is now more apparent.

Arms giving prominence to emblems of industry are common, especially in north-country towns. Symbols of the sea, shipbuilding, and seaside resorts are frequent in the arms of coastal counties and towns.

Rebuses occur occasionally, and castles are prominent in only a few modern coats.

This brief comparative survey of ancient and modern corporate arms shows how the character of civic heraldry has changed with changing times. Those who view it purely from the aesthetic or antiquarian point of view may regret the introduction of such emblems as the locomotive engine in the arms of Swindon, or the corps of miners, glass-blowers, smiths, fishermen, and other industrious but unpicturesque figures who have been called from their work to uphold the arms of their cities. But this element in modern civic heraldry proves that it is a living art, capable of expressing the present-day character of our towns and cities as vividly as the castles and ships of the medieval towns represented their main interests.

In the following chapters the chief features of civic heraldry are dealt with in greater detail, and arms of similar character are brought together for comparison. Before closing this general survey it will be well to distinguish between authorized armorial bearings and devices adopted by local authorities without official grant or sanction; and also to describe the various parts which make up a complete achievement of arms.

It has been shown that early town arms came into existence by local assumption; these acquired official status when they were placed on record by the heralds during their Visitations in the sixteenth and seventeenth centuries. Nowadays, arms can only be acquired by a grant by Letters Patent, or (in rare instances) by Royal Warrant.

Armorial bearings are granted by the Kings-of-Arms under the authority of the Earl Marshal (the Duke of Norfolk), to whom 'the determining and ordering of all matters touching Arms' has been delegated by the Crown. They therefore derive ultimately from the Sovereign, who is 'the fount of honour,' and while arms are not 'honours' in quite the sense that a peerage or a knighthood is an honour, they are certainly 'tokens of honour.'

There is no obligation on a local authority to obtain arms. If it requires some device for use on its seal, letter-heading, etc., but does not wish to petition for arms, it may assume some non-heraldic emblem or design. Such a device, while it may serve all necessary purposes, will not have the status of 'tokens of honour' derived from the Crown. In no circumstances should a device of local assumption be placed on a shield or crest-wreath, or otherwise be given the semblance of armorial bearings. Unfortunately, there are still some local authorities who disregard this rule. In using heraldic forms for the display of their insignia, they are creating not a true coat of arms but a piece of bogus heraldry; and although in England there are no longer penalties (as there are in Scotland) for the use of false heraldry, a sense of propriety should deter one responsible administrative body from transgressing the rules made by another.

Some authorities which do not possess arms of their own display those of an institution or family with which they are historically connected. For example, Durham C.C. uses the arms of the see; Brackley has on its seal the arms of the third Earl of Bridgewater who in the seventeenth century held the manor and presented the seal; and Eton U.D.C. uses those of Eton College.

Even provided the local authority has obtained the consent of the family or institution concerned, such permission does not entitle the authority to regard the arms as its own. They remain those of the family or institution to which they were first granted, for no bearer of arms has power to confer his arms on another person or body; and the authority which displays such arms, though it may have the sanction of the true owners to do so, still remains without arms of its own.

If the authority wishes to acquire the right to such arms, it can only do so by application to the Heralds' College, when, if possible, they will be granted with some mark of difference. Where the original institution or family still exists, considerable differences may have to be made.

As this book is intended not only for those who are already versed in heraldry but also for those who have no prior knowledge of the subject, it is necessary to supply a few definitions.

Armorial bearings may comprise several component parts:

ARMS

This word, though often loosely applied to the whole heraldic achievement, including crest, supporters, and accessories, strictly means only the combination of emblems displayed on the shield. Arms are an essential part of armorial bearings; crests and supporters are only granted as accompaniments to arms. Many ancient towns which derived their heraldry from their seals have only arms, and a number of authorities which have obtained grants in recent years have been content with arms unaccompanied by crest or supporters.

The shape of the shield on which the arms are displayed is a matter of artistic taste, but generally speaking it should be as simple as possible. A shield of fanciful shape is not only false to tradition but also tends to distract attention from the emblems placed upon it. Generally it will be found that the 'heater' shaped shield (with a straight top and curving sides, like the bottom of a flat-iron) is the most appropriate and graceful form. But the emblems must not be cramped or distorted to suit the shape of the shield: the shield form must be adapted to suit the emblems upon it, and it may therefore be necessary in some cases to adopt a straight-sided shield with an obtuse angle at the base.

CREST, HELMET, AND MANTLING

The crest represents the ornament which a knight wore on his helmet at tournaments and on ceremonial occasions (but rarely in battle), and it is therefore generally displayed upon a helmet placed above the shield. The helmet appropriate to a local authority is that of an esquire, being of steel, which may be adorned by gold or silver, set in profile and with the vizor closed. The only purpose of the helmet in heraldic display is to support a crest, and where there is no crest a helmet should not be used. The helmet is not essential, even where there is a crest, and I have generally omitted it from the illustrations in this book.

The knight's crest was modelled in wood or leather; this fact should be borne in mind when a local authority is discussing with the heralds what its crest is to be. Things which are incapable of being modelled—for example, clouds and water—should be avoided, or should be represented as painted on a fan-shaped top to the helmet.

The crest is set upon a crest-wreath on the top of the helmet. The crest-wreath represents the twisted scarf or ribbon by which the modelled crest was bound to the helm. Convention decrees that six twists be visible, and these are tinctured according to the 'colours' appropriate to the arms. The 'colours' generally are the first metal and the first colour mentioned in the official blazon or description of the arms. (In the descriptions given in this book I have specified the colours of crest-wreaths instead of leaving them to be deduced from the arms.)

The crest-wreath must be used as the basis for the crest even when the helmet is not shown; but a crest-wreath is sometimes omitted when the crest issues from a mural crown, coronet, or circlet.

When a helmet is used (but not otherwise), an ornamental cloak, known as the mantling or lambrequin, is shown falling from the crest-wreath over the back of the helmet.

This is supposed to represent the cloth worn by the knight to protect him from the heat of the sun. It is said that the scalloped form usually given to the mantling originated in the tatters to which it was torn in battle; but this is fanciful, and there are no real grounds for believing that the mantling owes its decorative form to anything but artistic treatment. The mantling, like the crest-wreath, is of the 'colours,' the outside being colour and the inside metal.

Some heralds take the view that it is inappropriate for corporations to have crests, because a crest implies a helmet (even though the latter may not be used in heraldic display), and a corporation has no head on which to put a helmet. I do not concur with this opinion: it might equally be argued that a corporation should not bear arms because it has no arm on which to carry a shield, or neck around which to hang it. The outcome of this theory would be that corporate heraldry should consist only of badges. Moreover, the crest serves a very useful purpose in preserving the dignity of corporate heraldry: it provides a place for the display of some of the emblems which the corporation wish to be introduced but which, if placed on the shield, would result in overcrowding.

SUPPORTERS

Any county, metropolitan borough, or municipal corporation may obtain supporters to maintain and guard its arms. Supporters can be borne with or without crests. They consist generally of beasts, birds, or monsters, sometimes of human beings, and in rare instances of fish.

Some animal supporters present the heraldic artist with a difficult problem, for the reason that animals in a state of nature rarely ramp, and it is difficult to give them a natural appearance on their hind legs. Some beasts, notably the lion, have, during many generations in the heraldic circus, learned their tricks so thoroughly that an armorial type has been evolved, capable of adopting any attitude with apparent ease. But the elephant of Oxford, and the camel of Inverness, are awkward beasts. Either they must be credited with an unnatural capacity for balancing themselves on their hind legs, or they must lean heavily upon the shield, becoming the supported rather than the supporters.

Since the supporters themselves need support they are frequently drawn standing on a grassy mound, or in the case of fish, sea-horses, and other maritime creatures, wavy lines indicating water. Sometimes supporters are placed upon pediments like table-tops, or scroll work of the 'gas-bracket' type, but these tend to be too heavy and elaborate and to distract the eye from the armorial bearings; while to stand them on the ribbon bearing the motto, obviously incapable of carrying their weight, gives an impression of instability.

MOTTO

The sanction of the College of Arms is not necessary for the adoption of a motto, though where a motto is adopted at the time the arms are devised it is generally shown on the drawing of the arms on the Letters Patent.

There are no rules regarding mottoes; they may be in any language, and express any sentiment; but the College of Arms would decline to include in their official drawing of the achievement a motto to which they had good grounds for objecting. They would not, for instance, recognize the adoption by a local authority of the royal motto, or that of an order of chivalry.

A motto may be used by more than one family or corporation, and there are, in fact, instances of several local authorities having the same motto.

Some authorities have more than one motto, but as a rule only one of the mottoes is used in any representation of the arms. Cardiff, however, and some Scottish authorities, place a motto above the crest as well as one below the shield.

In drawing the scroll bearing the motto, the artist must take care that any decorative twists he may introduce are so arranged that the inscription is on one side of the scroll throughout.

Badge

Some authorities, in addition to their arms, have obtained badges by grant from the Kings-of-Arms; others use badges which have been locally assumed. A badge should never be placed upon a shield or crest-wreath, or otherwise be given the appearance of arms or crest.

Standard

A few local authorities have been granted standards, e.g. the Port of London Authority, Hertford, and Nottingham. A standard bears the arms of the authority in an oblong compartment nearest the staff, and badges and motto on the tapering part.

Banner

Any authority possessing arms may display them on an heraldic banner. This is a rectangular flag bearing the arms, but *not* the crest, supporters, or motto. The shield-form is omitted, and the emblems forming the arms are spread out over the whole area of the flag (as the Royal Arms are displayed on the flag known as the 'Royal Standard').

A banner of the county or town arms may be flown over public buildings on all local occasions, and in conjunction with the Union Jack on national occasions.

In these chapters I may sometimes refer to the arms of this and that county or town, but it should be noted that strictly the arms are not granted and do not appertain to the community as a whole, but to the council constituting the local government authority. The armorial bearings should be used only by the council for their official purposes, e.g. on the common seal, letter-heading, badges of office, maces, the decoration of the council house, and flags flying over public buildings, etc. A local authority is not entitled to communicate its arms, granted to denote its identity, to any other body or organization. It may permit its arms to be displayed where it will, e.g. in a local school, but the arms remain those of the authority, and the school (or other organization) displaying them has no right to regard the arms as its own. If it wants arms of its own, it must apply to the Kings-of-Arms for a grant. The point is of importance, since the idea sometimes prevails that the arms of a local authority may be used by various organizations in the locality. In Scotland it is permissible for a local authority to empower tradesmen to display its arms with the words 'By appointment,' or 'Purveyors to . . .' In England it is generally regarded as inadvisable for a council to consent to the use of its armorial bearings, or any part thereof, by a person or firm for business purposes.

It is permissible for a mayor who possesses personal arms to impale them with the Corporation arms during his mayoralty; his shield is divided vertically, the Corporation arms being placed on the dexter (or right-hand side as you stand behind the shield), and the personal arms on the sinister. The chief use of this facility is to inscribe a piece of plate or other article as a memento of a man's mayoralty.

Local authorities which have sought to prevent the unauthorized use of their arms have met the difficulty that the powers formerly exercised by the Earl Marshal to prevent the improper use of armorial bearings have fallen into desuetude. However, the Kingston-upon-Hull Corporation has given a lead to other authorities by obtaining the following clause in the Kingston-upon-Hull Corporation Act, 1952:

If any person without the consent of the Corporation uses in connection with any trade business calling or profession the armorial ensigns of the City (or armorial ensigns so closely resembling the same as to be calculated to deceive) in such a manner as to be calculated to lead to the belief that he is duly authorised so to use the armorial ensigns of the City he may at the suit of the Corporation be restrained by injunction from continuing to use the same; Provided that nothing in this section shall be construed as affecting the right (if any) of the proprietor of a trade mark registered under the Trade Marks Act, 1938 and containing such armorial ensigns to continue to use such trade mark.

In the foregoing notes I have made certain observations on the artistic representation of armorial bearings. In this respect I am conscious that this book must teach by precept rather than by example, for my drawings are in the nature of simple diagrams to illustrate and supplement the verbal descriptions of civic heraldry—descriptions which, in some cases, necessarily lack exactitude because I have to some extent modified heraldic language for the sake of those who are not familiar with it. I have omitted the hatching lines and dots sometimes used to denote colours and metals; they are not only unnecessary, but frequently detract from the grace of heraldic emblems. In short, my illustrations represent civic heraldry reduced to its simplest forms. Artistically some of them are inferior to the excellent designs used by authorities which have employed expert heraldic artists to draw their arms; but not all authorities have done this, and to some my drawings may suggest that their arms would gain in beauty and dignity by the elimination of florid shields and other elaborate and meaningless embellishments which distract attention from what really matters—the emblems themselves. Here it may be noted that the painting of armorial bearings incorporated in the documentary grant of arms is not intended to be a pattern to be copied exactly in all other representations. Within the limits of heraldic accuracy an artist may use discretion in such matters as the shape of the shield and the arrangement of the mantling.

CHAPTER II

ROYAL AND KINDRED EMBLEMS

LOYALTY to the Crown, pride in associations therewith, is a characteristic of English local authorities which finds expression in the incorporation of royal emblems in their insignia.

A distinction must be drawn between parts of the contemporary Royal Arms and badges, and emblems which, though historically associated with royalty, are not strictly part of the royal heraldry of to-day. To the former class belong the gold lion passant guardant—the 'lion of England'—and the ostrich feathers of the Heir Apparent; such emblems are nowadays only granted by Royal Warrant. The latter class includes ancient crowns of various types, the fleur-de-lis from the old Royal Arms, the cross and doves of Edward the Confessor, and royal badges which are no longer in use.

In the Middle Ages there seems to have been little control over the use of royal emblems by civic authorities; many towns embodied lions and fleurs-de-lis in their insignia, and in due course obtained the heralds' sanction. This casual assumption of charges from the Royal Arms is no longer permissible, and some authorities which have adopted devices including a portion of the regalia, such as the crown, have been corrected.

The following letter from the Home Office expresses the official view of the matter:

I am directed by the Secretary of State to say that the Royal Crown and the Royal Arms are personal to His Majesty and except in the case of civic maces cannot be used without His special permission. From time to time the position has had to be pointed out to local authorities who have been using these emblems without permission, but no general instruction has been issued. It has been customary for many centuries for civic maces to bear the Royal Arms, the right to do so being held to follow from the grant of a charter of incorporation.

CROWNS

The *Royal* or *Imperial Crown*, with alternate crosses paty and fleurs-de-lis on the jewelled rim, and two pearl-studded arches surmounted by a ball and cross, forms part of the crest of Eye, not, however, as the Royal Crown of England but, as the wording of the grant shows, the Imperial Crown of the Sun, with the eye of Jehovah set in a star above it.

Princes' coronets, composed of crosses paty and fleurs-de-lis, without arches, appear in the arms of Boston and Evesham, and (surmounting ostrich feathers) in those of Norfolk C.C.

The *Ducal coronet* when a charge on a shield or part of a crest differs from the coronet of a duke in that it shows only three strawberry leaves. The coronets in the arms of Hull (Kingston-upon-Hull) are technically ducal coronets, but probably were originally intended for kingly crowns in allusion to a 'King's town.'

Ancient crowns have spikes set on the circlet, five being visible. Seven such crowns, denoting the Saxon Heptarchy, occur in the arms of Ilford.

The *Saxon crown*, consisting of a plain circlet with four elevated balls (three visible), is found in the arms of Middlesex C.C. and the crest of Brentford-and-Chiswick, with reference to the old Kingdom of the Middle Saxons; and also in the arms of Doncaster, Taunton, and other authorities. Bognor Regis displays Saxon crowns in token both of the ancient kingdom of the South Saxons and of the fact that the town earned the suffix to its name when King George V convalesced there after his illness in 1929.

Surrey C.C. has in its arms a representation of the crown of King Edgar, and Egham has King John's crown above Magna Carta in allusion to the sealing of the charter at Runnymede.

In the shield of Wigan is a crown of fleurs-de-lis, approximating to the type worn by Plantagenet kings.

(The three crowns attributed as arms to the East Anglian Kingdom, and borne by several authorities in the eastern counties, are dealt with later in this chapter; and mural and naval crowns or coronets are described in Chapter VI.)

Lions

The lion is the most favoured royal emblem in English civic heraldry. Since Richard I's reign the Royal Arms of England have been: Gules, three gold lions passant guardant; i.e. on three legs, the right forepaw raised, and the head turned so as to present the full face. A lion in this attitude was anciently termed a lion *leopardé*, or a leopard, and the arms of England are still sometimes quoted as leopards.

Richard I's brother John, before ascending the throne, bore two lions passant (but not guardant), and there is reason to believe that two lions were used as a device by their father, Henry II. Consequently two gold lions have been attributed to the earlier Norman kings, and Berkshire C.C. bears them with reference to the early history of the county. John's two lions appear with other emblems in the arms of Droitwich.

Several ancient towns placed the Royal Arms of England on their seals and, when it occurred to them to adopt arms of their own, took the royal lions as the basis and made some change of tincture, or some addition to the bearings, to create insignia at once similar to, and distinct from, the Royal Arms. New Romney, for instance, simply changed the field of the Royal Arms to blue, and to this day bears, azure, three gold lions passant guardant. Maldon bears the same impaling a ship. Hereford retained the red field of the Royal Arms but made the lions silver, and in the seventeenth century was granted a blue border charged with silver saltires of St Andrew in allusion to the siege of the town by the Scots during the Civil War. But some towns failed to secure sanction for arms based upon those of England; Faversham, which merely made the lions' nether-halves silver, and Appleby, which crowned the lions—in token, it is said, of the town's services against the Scots—have never obtained authority for their arms.

In some town arms the Royal Arms are dimidiated with another coat; that is to say, they have been cut down the middle, and the half bearing the lions' heads and forequarters has been joined to the complementary half of the other coat.

In the case of the Cinque Ports, the coat with which the Royal Arms were dimidiated consisted of three gold ships' hulls on blue, and the resulting arms are: Parted palewise gules and azure, three gold lions passant guardant halved and joined to three gold ships' sterns. These are the arms of the Corporation. Of the individual Ports, Sandwich bears these arms but with the ships silver;[1] Hastings eliminates the middle ship and completes the middle lion; and Dover surrounds its shield, bearing St Martin, with a red border charged with gold lions. A shield bearing the arms of the Cinque Ports forms a pendant to the collar of one of the sea-lions supporting the shield of Kent C.C.

Of the 'limbs' and other towns associated with the Cinque Ports, Deal displays the arms of Sandwich, of which it was a member; and Ramsgate, Margate, and Bexhill has each a 'lion-hull' in its arms. Ipswich has the three half-ships impaled with a lion rampant. Great Yarmouth, whose herring fisheries were formerly controlled by the Cinque Ports, dimidiates the Royal Arms of England with an ancient coat consisting of three silver herrings on blue, with the result that the lions appear to end in fish-tails.

Other instances of the dimidiation of the Royal Arms in civic heraldry are provided by Chester, which halves them with the wheatsheaves of the Earldom of Chester; and Stamford, which combines them with the Warenne chequers.

A single lion of England, with other emblems, occurs in the arms of several ancient towns; it is borne on a red chief by Canterbury, Chichester, Maidstone, and Rochester; it is associated with the cross of the national patron, St George, in the arms of York, and the London C.C.; and in conjunction with a castle in the arms of Guildford, Northampton, Norwich, Stafford, and Winchester.

The banner of Edward II, bearing the three lions of England, is upheld by one of the sea-lion supporters of the arms of the Port of London Authority.

Lions' or leopards' faces in English civic insignia are probably all derived from the royal beast, though in the case of Shrewsbury (and hence of the Salop C.C.) there is a counter-theory that the lions' faces came from the arms of the De La Poles. (See also Stratford-on-Avon, Shaftesbury, and Woolwich.)

The lion is also popular as a supporter. As such he must always have some differencing mark or colour to distinguish him from the dexter supporter of the Royal Arms. Among local authorities only Southampton has gold supporting lions unadorned, and they differ from the royal supporter in that they are uncrowned and not guardant; moreover they are customarily perched on the stern ends of two ships flanking the shield. The following shows how other authorities difference their supporting lions from the royal lion and from one another:

Aldershot. Red lions guardant with gold collars and vaire shields hanging therefrom.

Doncaster. Seated gold lions, each with a white rose of York in its mouth.

Gloucester. Red lions, each with a sword in the right forepaw.

Leicester. Red lions reguardant (i.e. looking backwards), each with a gold ducal coronet about the neck, and hanging therefrom an ermine cinquefoil.

Manchester. A gold lion guardant with a red mural crown on its head and a red rose of Lancaster on the shoulder.

Plymouth. Two gold lions reguardant with blue naval crowns about their necks and hanging therefrom red medallions each charged with a silver boar's head.

---

[1] Sandwich, Massachusetts, has based its arms on those of its English namesake, removing the lions and bearing three complete ships' hulls of silver on blue.

Staffordshire C.C. A red lion reguardant crowned with a gold ducal coronet.
Wigan. Two gold lions, each bearing a branch of mountain ash (the wiggin tree).

There are many other instances of counties and towns bearing lions as national emblems. These are not all true 'lions of England' (this description being applicable only when they are so termed in the grant or confirmation of arms), but they may be regarded as the offspring of the royal lion. One must not assume that every lion found in civic arms has a royal or national significance; the lion, in various tinctures and attitudes and combined with various emblems, appears in the arms of a large number of private families, and it is from such arms that Barking, Redcar, Thornaby-on-Tees, Wednesbury, and some other local authorities derive their lions. (See Chapter III.)

Lions and Fleurs-de-Lis

The three lions alone formed the arms of English kings from Richard I to Edward III. In 1340, in token of his claim to the throne of France, Edward gathered the French fleurs-de-lis, set them on his shield, and thereafter bore: Quarterly, 1 and 4, France Ancient: Azure, strewn with gold fleurs-de-lis; 2 and 3, England: Gules, three gold lions passant guardant in pale. An instance of these arms is found in the device of Dorchester, based on an ancient seal.

Henry IV, following the example of the French king, reduced the number of fleurs-de-lis in the French quarters to three, and the coat known as 'France Modern and England quarterly' remained the Royal Arms of English monarchs until the end of Elizabeth I's reign. This coat is used without authority by Walsall and is incorporated in the insignia of Berwick, Bridgnorth, and Windsor. From it is derived the combination of the lion and fleurs-de-lis in the arms of Lancaster (whence those of Lancaster, Massachusetts), Newark, Bridport, Sudbury, and other towns.

The fleur-de-lis thus became an emblem of English royalty, and so found its way into the seals of Godmanchester and Tamworth, and the arms of Great Torrington. Wakefield claims that its fleur-de-lis originally commemorated its assistance to Queen Henrietta Maria during the Civil War. In Wareham's unauthorized device three fleurs-de-lis appear upside down; this is probably due to the error of an artist or seal-engraver, but there is a local tradition that Queen Elizabeth I ordered their reversal in token of her displeasure that the town failed to ring its bells when she passed through.

Like the lion, the fleur-de-lis has passed into general heraldic usage, and must not be credited with royal significance whenever it appears in civic heraldry. In Blackpool's and some other arms it stands for a private family. In those of St Marylebone, Kensington, and perhaps Lincoln, it represents the Virgin Mary.

The contemporary Royal Arms are displayed in a banner upheld by one of the sea-lions which support the arms of the Port of London Authority.

Royal Badges and Persons

Several badges anciently used by English monarchs have found their way into civic seals and arms. One of the oldest is the star and crescent, which seems originally to have been the sun and moon. This appeared on the first Great Seal of Richard I and perhaps alluded to his vocation as a crusader, the moon being an emblem of the Byzantine Empire. Portsmouth, which obtained a charter from Richard I, took the star and crescent as the device for its seal, and now bears them as arms. A star and crescent appear in some representations of the arms of Dartmouth, whence the crusading host sailed; and are found in the crest of Nottingham and the seals of Ashburton, Barnard Castle, Malmesbury, and other towns.

Planta genista, the broom plant whence the Plantagenets derived their name, is found in the insignia of Derby; and what is generally described as 'three ears of wheat on one stalk' in the seal of Malmesbury may be in fact broom-cods. The broom in the arms of Bromley and Gillingham is not the royal broom, but alludes in the former case to the name of the borough, and in the latter to the district of Brompton.

The golden tree stump, a badge of Edward III allusive to the Manor of Woodstock, is borne by the Borough of Woodstock. The hart in the arms of Derby may have been derived from that of Richard II, and Chesterfield's pomegranate device may have sprung from the punning pomegranate of Granada which Henry VIII included among his badges when he married Catherine of Aragon.

Monmouth has as supporters the lion and antelope of Henry V, a native of the town, and those of Sutton Coldfield are the greyhound and dragon of Henry VIII from whom the town received its charter. In each case mural crowns are added to difference the beasts from the old royal supporters.

An emblem for which royal associations are claimed, though it is not a royal badge, is the pear of Worcester; this is said to have been introduced into the City arms to commemorate the transplanting of a pear-tree to the centre of the city on the occasion of a visit by Queen Elizabeth I. Worcestershire C.C., following the lead of the county town, has obtained arms which include a pear-tree, and the pear, having thus been accepted as the symbol of the County, has been included in the arms of Stourbridge.

Not only the emblems but the figures of several royal persons appear in civic insignia. St Edmund, King of the East Angles, forms the crest of Southwold. The head of Edward the Martyr appears in the seal of Reading; the crest of Wigan includes the head and shoulders of a king, 'a conventional likeness to an early English monarch,' modelled on a portrait of Edward III but in particular symbolizing Henry I. The king in the arms of Dartmouth is Edward III, whose queen, Philippa, is portrayed on the seal of Queenborough. Wallingford's seal bears a king fully armed on horseback, either Henry VI or Edward IV. Hemel Hempstead uses as a device a portrait of Henry VIII.

ROSES

Of frequent occurrence in civic heraldry is the rose. Henry III was the first English monarch to use this flower as a badge; his rose was of gold, and he derived it from his wife, Eleanor of Provence. The golden rose continued as a badge of the first three Edwards, the Black Prince, and Richard II. It is found in the arms of Carlisle, Guildford, and Wimbledon.

Henry III's son, Edmund, Earl of Lancaster, inherited the rose, but changed its tincture to red to distinguish his flower from that of the king. His descendants, the Earls and Dukes of Lancaster, made the red rose their most prominent badge; in modern times it has become the particular emblem of Lancashire and appears in the arms of the Lancashire C.C. and many towns in the county.

The red rose was thus an emblem of the House of Lancaster long before the Wars of the Roses; similarly the white rose of the House of York. This was originally a Mortimer badge, and as Richard Plantagenet claimed the throne by virtue of his Mortimer descent, the white rose was doubly appropriate as an emblem to oppose to the red rose of the Lancastrian Henry VI. Like its ancient rival, the white rose has now become a county emblem and occurs in the arms of the three County Councils in Yorkshire and several towns in the county. Morecambe-and-Heysham, situated in Lancashire but populated largely from the West Riding of Yorkshire, combines the roses of Lancaster and York in its arms; and Todmorden and Audenshaw denote their geographical situation near the Lancashire-Yorkshire border by bearing red and white roses.

Northamptonshire, having historic associations with both the Houses of York and Lancaster, has white and red roses in the arms of the County Council, together with the Yorkist badges of a falcon and fetterlock.

When, after the Wars of the Roses, the Houses of York and Lancaster were united in the Tudor dynasty, their roses were combined to form the Tudor double rose—generally a red rose with a white centre, but sometimes vice versa—and henceforward not only the Tudor rose but the red and white single roses were used as royal emblems.

Tudor roses appear in the heraldry of Derbyshire C.C., Cardiff, Fulham, Lowestoft, and Oxford; and in conjunction with the Beaufort portcullis (a favourite Tudor badge) in the arms of Richmond (Surrey) and Westminster. Red and white roses occur in the arms of Southampton, and Cambridge has two white roses. The red and white double rose in the arms of Bewdley is not strictly a Tudor rose, but is an instance of that temporary union of the roses effected by Edward IV when he married the Lancastrian Elizabeth Woodville.

OSTRICH FEATHERS

The ostrich feather, nowadays associated with the Heir Apparent, was introduced into English royal heraldry by Edward III, who probably derived it from his wife, Philippa of Hainault. From Edward III's insignia the crowned ostrich feathers, with the motto *Ich Dien*, in the arms of Norfolk C.C. have been taken. There is no truth in the tradition that the feathers were adopted by the Black Prince from King John of Bohemia, killed at Crécy; nevertheless it was the Black Prince who made them famous. Probably because they were his mother's device, he set them in his 'shield for peace' (his 'shield for war' being his father's Royal Arms, duly differenced); and although the plume of ostrich feathers remained a badge of the monarch throughout Tudor and Stuart times it is now peculiarly the badge of the Heir Apparent, and in civic heraldry frequently indicates some association with a Prince of Wales.

The ostrich feathers are part of the crests of Caernarvonshire C.C., Flint C.C., and Cardiff; they occur in the arms of Calne, Carmarthen, and Evesham and in the seal of Llandovery; and they are sometimes used as an accessory by Coventry which also uses as a motto the words *Camera Principis* in allusion (it is said) to the time when the Black Prince, as Lord of the Manor of Cheylesmore, was closely associated with the City. The feathers are also found in the insignia of several authorities in Cornwall and Cheshire, the heir to the throne being born Duke of Cornwall and usually created Earl of Chester. In the arms of Barnes, the ostrich feathers stand for the Duke of Windsor, who is a native of the Borough.

Ostrich feathers, variously tinctured, were used as badges by several descendants of Edward III, and the ermine feather in the arms of the Leicestershire C.C. alludes to John of Gaunt.

THE BEZANTS OF CORNWALL

Though not of regal origin, the golden roundels or 'bezants' in the arms of Cornwall have royal associations because they now form part of the heraldry of the Duke of Cornwall. They originated in the arms of King John's second son, Richard, Earl of Cornwall and Count of Poictou: Silver, a lion rampant gules with a gold crown, within a border sable charged with bezants. Associated with Cornwall since the thirteenth century, the bezants occur in the heraldry of both the Duchy and the County Council. The red lion appears in the arms of the Devon C.C. and the crest of Exeter, and its head forms the crest of Launceston. Farther afield, Evesham, Great Berkhamstead, and Lambeth have black borders charged with bezants, denoting associations with the Princes of Wales and Dukes of Cornwall.

THE CHESTER WHEATSHEAVES

The arms of the Earldom of Chester are: Azure, three gold wheatsheaves. Cheshire C.C., Chester, and several other towns in the county include the wheatsheaves in their insignia; and outside Cheshire they are found in the heraldry of Evesham, Salford, Warrington, and Spalding U.D.C.

Chester and Salford have each a wolf as a supporter, and Stalybridge has one in its crest, in allusion to Hugh Lupus, created Earl of Chester in 1071.

SCOTTISH ROYAL EMBLEMS

A few English authorities have Scottish emblems in their arms. In allusion to the fact that in the twelfth century the Earldom of Cambridge was held by David I, King of Scotland, Cambridgeshire C.C. bears the tressure of fleurs-de-lis from the Scottish Royal Arms, and Huntingdonshire C.C. has for crest a red lion rampant with a flory collar. The red lion crest and supporters of Tottenham B.C. denote that the manor was anciently held by members of the Scottish royal house. Luton has incorporated the Scottish thistle in its arms in reference to the straw plaiters who followed James I and VI into England and started the industry for which the town became famous; and Cheshunt bears a united rose and thistle in allusion to James's residence at Theobalds.

ANCIENT KINGDOMS

Many local authorities bear arms based upon or incorporating emblems from the arms ascribed to the pre-Conquest Kingdoms of the English, and the insignia associated with the Roman and Romano-British rulers. Although these are not strictly part of the royal heraldry, it is convenient to consider them in this chapter.

The Roman eagle perched on a piece of Hadrian's Wall appears in the arms of Wallsend, which was Segedunum. The eagle in the arms of Wimbledon also alludes

ROYAL AND KINDRED EMBLEMS

to the Roman period, with particular reference to the camp and well associated (somewhat dubiously) with the name of Caesar. Wimbledon's eagle is two-headed, a form which is generally regarded as standing for the Holy Roman Empire rather than for Ancient Rome. Walton-and-Weybridge has an eagle in allusion to Caesar's attempt to cross the Thames there. North of the Tweed, Perth and Perthshire have supporting eagles in allusion to the Roman period of their history. These arms are all of modern invention, and it is not to be supposed that the Roman eagle has had an unbroken career in the insignia of this land since it entered it as the standard of the conquering legions. But the eagle's colleague, the dragon, the standard of the cohort, has been in practically continuous use since the Romans brought it to Britain. When Rome withdrew her troops the dragon remained as the symbol of authority and unity among the Romanized Britons, and became their standard in the wars against the invading Angles and Saxons. From this emblem the war-leader took the name Pendragon, which is particularly associated with the semi-mythical King Arthur. To this day the red dragon remains the national emblem of the remnant of the ancient British people, the Welsh, and as such appears in the heraldry of many Welsh authorities.

Carmarthenshire displays the dragon supporting a Welsh harp, Flintshire with one of the Prince of Wales's feathers, and Cardiff with a leek, while Colwyn Bay's dragon bears a Saxon's head. The shield of Caernarvonshire C.C. is supported by sea-dragons.

Lions are also found in the heraldry of Welsh authorities, being derived from the arms of the Principality: Quarterly gold and gules, four lions passant guardant counterchanged. One or more lions from this source occur in the arms of Caernarvonshire, Wrexham, and Colwyn Bay.

The English lion and the Welsh dragon support the arms of Monmouthshire and Pembrokeshire C.C.s, these counties having a heritage from both races.

The West Saxons adopted a dragon as their standard, perhaps in token of their conquest of the Britons, and the Wessex dragon appears in the heraldry of Dorset, Somerset, and Wiltshire C.C.s.

The leader of the invaders who settled in Kent bore a horse (perhaps that of Odin) on his standard, and was accordingly called by his followers 'hengst' or 'horsa,' both meaning 'horse.' Hence arose the legend of the brothers Hengist and Horsa. A white horse rampant on red has been attributed as arms to the Kentish Kingdom, and is used by Kent C.C. The white horse appears in the arms of several Kentish towns.

To the former Kingdoms of the East Saxons and the Middle Saxons the medieval heralds assigned for arms three seaxes (or 'notched swords') on red, in allusion to what they believed to have been the typical weapon from which the Saxons derived their name. These occur in the arms of Essex and Middlesex C.C.s and of many towns in these counties.

The arms attributed by the medieval heralds to the former Kingdom of the South Saxons were: Azure, six gold martlets. The martlet is an heraldic generalization for various kinds of birds and in this case appears to represent the swallow, *l'hirondelle* being suggested by the name of Arundel, the honour which comprised a large part of Sussex. As in the case of Middlesex, the arms attributed to the ancient kingdom have become the basis of those granted to the modern County Councils, other charges being

B

added for difference. Bexhill, Brighton, and Hove appropriately and artistically employ the swallows of the county to form a border to town emblems.

Northumberland C.C. uses arms based on those ascribed to the Kingdom of Bernicia; Durham C.C. those attributed to St Oswald, first Christian King of Northumbria, reputed founder of the See; and Oswestry, which derived its name from Oswald, who fell there in battle, uses a variation of his arms.

To the East Anglian Kingdom the heralds attributed as arms: Azure, three gold crowns. These with the crowns pierced by arrows in allusion to the martyrdom of St Edmund, last King of the East Angles, are borne by Bury St Edmunds, and one such crown appears in the arms of Southwold. The Isle of Ely C.C. incorporates in its arms three crowns in allusion to St Etheldreda, a lady of the East Anglian royal house, who founded the monastery which became Ely Cathedral. The crowns in the arms of Colchester were also probably adopted in reference to the East Anglian realm.

A cross flory is regarded as the emblem appropriate to the kings of the English realm which in the tenth century emerged from the Heptarchy, and as such this emblem appears in the arms of Oldbury. For Edward the Confessor the heralds placed five gold doves (taken from one of his coins) about the cross, also gold, and set them on a blue shield, and these form part of the arms of Westminster and (with only four doves) of Eye. West Suffolk C.C. displays the arms of the Confessor, and Bournemouth, Cheltenham, Mansfield, and Woking U.D.C. have taken emblems therefrom for inclusion in their arms. Wanstead-and-Woodford combines in its shield emblems from the arms attributed to the Confessor and King Harold.

HASTINGS

CHAPTER III

FEUDAL AND FAMILY EMBLEMS

MANY modern civic arms include emblems from those of some person or family prominent in local affairs now or in the past, whether feudal magnates, lords of the manor, leading landowners, or industrial families. In many cases the family whose arms form the basis of the civic coat is that which anciently took its name from the town, or on being raised to the peerage has taken its title therefrom; and often the association between the town and the family has now been severed, so that the significance of the arms has become wholly historic. Sometimes the town's first mayor, or some townsman who has achieved fame, is honoured by the inclusion in the civic shield of tokens from his arms.

The sphere of influence of some of the great baronial families of the Middle Ages is traceable by the occurrence of their arms or badges in the heraldry of a number of local authorities in different parts of the country. Among such families the Warennes are remarkable. William de Warenne, a kinsman of the Conqueror, was by him created Earl of Surrey, and he and his successors were granted lands in Surrey, Sussex, Yorkshire, and Lincolnshire. The Warenne arms, gold and blue chequers, are accordingly found in the insignia of Beddington-and-Wallington, Lambeth, Reigate, Wandsworth, and Wimbledon; Lewes and Hove; Dewsbury and Halifax; and Grantham and Stamford.

The Clares, who held the Earldoms of Gloucester and Hertfordshire and the Lordship of Glamorgan, bore three red chevrons on gold, which are found in the heraldry of Glamorgan C.C., Gloucestershire C.C., Gloucester, Hertford, and Cowbridge. They also occur in the arms of Weymouth and Tonbridge.

The power of the De Lacys, Earls of Lincoln, in Lancashire and North Wales, is indicated by the presence of their purple lion (its colour sometimes altered) in the heraldry of Accrington, Burnley, Colne, Congleton, Haslingden, and Walton-le-Dale, and in the seals of Denbigh and the Denbighshire C.C. The lion supporter of Holborn refers to Lincoln's Inn, originally the London house of the De Lacys.

The lion 'proper' (i.e. naturally coloured) of the Ferrers, Earls of Derby, is found in the insignia of Lancashire C.C. and Macclesfield; the lion of De Braose in the heraldry of Cowbridge, Shoreham-by-Sea, Swansea, and Horsham; and the blue lion of Bruce in the arms of Middlesbrough and of Thornaby-on-Tees. Ludlow bears the white lion badge of the Mortimers, Earls of March, and the ermine lions of the Cecils are found in the heraldry of Barking, Hatfield, Hertford, Peterborough C.C., and Westminster.

The Staffords, Earls of Stafford and Dukes of Buckingham, have left several emblems to civic heraldry. The red chevron from their arms is found in the insignia of Lichfield, Newport (Mon.), and the Staffordshire C.C.; their badge, the Stafford knot, occurs in the arms of Stafford and Staffordshire, and in the crest of Stoke-on-Trent; another badge, the swan which the Staffords derived from the Bohuns, is found in the arms of Buckingham C.C., Buckingham, High Wycombe, and Slough; and the mantle in the shield of Brecknock is also held to be a badge of Edward Stafford, third Duke of Buckingham.

The following are among the towns whose arms are based on those of families which were anciently seated there, and derived their names therefrom: Ashton-under-Lyne (Assheton family), Birmingham (de Bermyngham family), Bootle, Brighouse, Chorley, Dukinfield, Fleetwood, Heywood, Hyde, Keighley, Middleton, Oldham (specially referring to Hugh Oldham, Bishop of Exeter), Pudsey, Radcliffe, Rochdale (the Rashdale family), Stalybridge (the Staveley family), Stockport, Sudbury (with particular reference to Simon of Sudbury, Archbishop of Canterbury), Thornaby-on-Tees. Several towns which have not obtained arms of their own have filled their need for armorial bearings by adopting those of the old local family bearing the town's name.

Another fruitful source of emblems in civic arms is the heraldry of peers connected by title with the town or county. The arms and crest of Abergavenny are composed of the arms and badges of Nevill, Marquess of Abergavenny. The arms of Bedfordshire C.C. are based on those of the Beauchamps, barons of Bedford, and include the scallop shells of the Russells, Dukes of Bedford (which also occur in the arms of Holborn and St Pancras). Burton-on-Trent bears the fleurs-de-lis of Bass, Baron Burton; Chatham the chequers of Pitt, Earl of Chatham; Dudley the lion's-head crest of the Earl of Dudley; Norfolk C.C. the arms of Ranulf de Guader, first Earl of Norfolk; Kensington the cross bottony of Rich, Baron Kensington; Leicester and the Leicestershire C.C. emblems from the arms of various holders of the Earldom of Leicester; Mansfield the stars of Murray, Earl of Mansfield; East Suffolk the arms of the former Earls and Dukes of Suffolk; Warwick, the Warwickshire C.C., and Rugby, emblems from the heraldry of the Beauchamps and Nevilles, Earls of Warwick, of which the bear and ragged staff (borne also by Walsall) are the most famous.

A full list of families commemorated by the inclusion of tokens from their armorial bearings in civic insignia will be found in the Index. The following are some which are represented in the heraldry of more than one local authority: Assheton (Ashton-under-Lyne, Audenshaw, Middleton, Stalybridge), Byron (Hucknall, Droylsden), Cavendish, and in particular the Dukes of Devonshire (Derbyshire C.C., Barrow-in-Furness, Buxton, Eastbourne, Keighley, Mansfield), Copley (Batley, Dewsbury); Courtenay (Lymington, Maidstone); Dukinfield (Dukinfield, Stalybridge); Howard (Glossop, Mansfield); Massey (Altrincham, Bowdon, Birkenhead); Montfichet (East Ham, West Ham, Leyton); Ramsden (Barrow-in-Furness, Huddersfield); Savile (Dewsbury, Leeds); Spencer, Le De Spenser (Islington, Loughborough, Wimbledon, Woking); and Stanley (Brackley, Chelsea).

In some cases the emblems selected from family arms refer less to the family as a whole than to some individual of national or local repute. Hugh Oldham and Simon of Sudbury have already been mentioned. The following are among others commemorated in civic arms: Edward Alleyn, founder of Dulwich College (Camberwell); Thomas Becket (Canterbury and others); Sir Nicholas Crisp and Edward Latymer, local benefactors (Hammersmith); Sir Francis Drake (Devon C.C. motto); Sir Charles

FEUDAL AND FAMILY EMBLEMS

Mark Palmer, Bt (Jarrow); Thomas of Rotherham, Archbishop of York (Rotherham); William Shakespeare (Warwickshire C.C. motto); William Tyndale (Dursley); Archbishop Whitgift (Croydon); William of Wykeham (Twickenham). Paddington, St Helens, Watford, and Worksop have honoured the first mayor by the inclusion of some emblem relating to him in the town arms.

GLOSSOP

CHAPTER IV

RELIGIOUS AND ECCLESIASTICAL EMBLEMS

THE religious motive was strong in medieval heraldry, especially so in that of towns, many of which were closely linked with some religious institution. The patron saint of the parish church was chosen by some towns as a figure for their seals and arms; others adopted insignia based upon that of an abbey or priory around which the town had grown up, or of an episcopal see with which it was connected. Some modern civic and county arms carry on this tradition, though nowadays references to local religious houses are of purely historical significance. In some arms the emblems of local parishes are combined; and in a few are to be found representations of ecclesiastical buildings.

EMBLEMS OF THE DEITY

In no English civic coat of arms is there any representation of the Deity or of Jesus Christ; but on the seal of Christchurch the figure of Christ appears, on that of Berwick-upon-Tweed there is a royal figure which may be intended for the Divine Majesty, and on the seal of Wenlock the Trinity is represented by God the Father supporting a Crucifix above which is the Holy Spirit in the form of a dove. In the arms of Southend-on-Sea the Trinity is symbolized by a trefoil.

The True Cross is seen in the arms of Colchester, in allusion to the legend of St Helena, daughter of King Coel, who is reputed to have found the Cross during a pilgrimage to the Holy Land.

The seal of Honiton bears a representation of the baptism of Christ, and the crest of Lambeth includes the Holy Lamb, in allusion to the name; the Agnus Dei in civic heraldry generally indicates some association with St John the Baptist (see page 23).

THE VIRGIN MARY

The Virgin with the Child in her arms forms the crest of St Marylebone; but while she also appears in the heraldry of several Scottish towns, she is usually represented in English civic arms by her emblems. Her lilies occur on the shields of Southend-on-Sea and Southwark, and in the fleur-de-lis form on those of Kensington, Lincoln, Nuneaton, and St Marylebone; the last-named borough also bears a rose, an emblem of the Virgin in allusion to the legend that when her tomb was opened it was found to be full of lilies and roses.

SAINTS

The following saints are represented, either in effigy or by their symbols, in the arms of English and Welsh authorities:

St Andrew, holding his saltire cross, forms the crest of Holborn, and one of the supporters of Maidenhead. He is represented by the saltire in the arms of Hove and Plymouth and the seal of Ashburton.

St Chad supports the arms of Lichfield.

St Clement, who is said to have been bound to an anchor and cast into the sea, is denoted by the anchor in the arms of Southend-on-Sea.

St Cuthbert is represented by the cross flory in the heraldry of Gateshead, Lytham St Annes, Sunderland, and Worksop.

St Dunstan is represented in the arms of Stepney by the fire-tongs with which he pulled the Devil by the nose.

St Edmund, last king of the East Angles, is represented by crowns pierced by arrows in the arms of Bury St Edmunds and of Southwold. He is dealt with more fully in the previous chapter.

St Edward the Confessor is dealt with in Chapter II.

St Elli is portrayed in the arms of Llanelly.

St Etheldreda, of the royal house of East Anglia, is commemorated in the arms of the Isle of Ely C.C. by the three crowns of the East Anglian Kingdom.

St George does not appear in person but is represented by his red cross in the arms of the City of London, London C.C., City of Durham, Gillingham, Lincoln, Rochester, and York, and in the unauthorized device of Aylesbury. The red crosses in the arms of Lambeth, Stepney, and Wandsworth refer to the fact that these boroughs are within the County of London. In the arms of Holborn and of Southwark, the red cross alludes to St George as the patron of local parishes.

St Giles, patron of cripples, is symbolized by a hind pierced by an arrow, commemorating that the Saint was maimed by an arrow in the knee when interposing himself to save from the huntsman a hind which took refuge in his cell. Camberwell and Holborn bear the hind in allusion to the dedication of local parishes to St Giles. In Scotland, the hind of St Giles supports the arms of Edinburgh, and the Saint himself is represented in those of Elgin.

St James, the fisherman, is represented by the dolphin supporter of Finsbury, and by scallop shells in the arms of Bromley and the crest of Clacton. He was the patron of pilgrims, who wore the scallop shell in his honour. Shells as the emblems of pilgrimage are found in the arms of Sittingbourne, and pilgrims with shells in their hats are the supporters of the shield of Reigate—both towns being on the Pilgrims' Way.

St John the Baptist is frequently denoted by the Holy Lamb because it was he who hailed Jesus as 'the Lamb of God' (John i. 29). Probably because the Lamb was his emblem, St John the Baptist became the patron of wool merchants. The parish church of Halifax, an ancient wool town, is dedicated to him, and the civic insignia include his head—the 'holy face' also alluding to the name of the town—and the Holy Lamb. The seal of Yeovil shows the Baptist carrying the Holy Lamb on his arm. The Lamb also appears in the arms of Preston (the parish church being dedicated to St John the Baptist) and Hendon. In the shield of Droylsden it refers to the local settlement of the Moravian Church.

St Laurence is represented in the arms of Southend-on-Sea by the grid-iron, the instrument of his martyrdom.

St Leonard is denoted by the pair of leg-irons in the arms of Hove.

St Luke's winged bull supports the arms of Finsbury and appears in those of Chelsea.

St Margaret holding a pearl (*margarita*) forms the crest of Lowestoft. In the arms of King's Lynn she is represented by her symbol, a dragon's head pierced by a cross, in allusion to the legend that she was devoured by a dragon which was rent open by the power of the cross she wore.

St Martin, dividing his cloak with the Beggar, is depicted in the arms of Dover.

St Michael the Archangel, with the dragon beneath his feet, appears on the seals of Alnwick, Basingstoke, Helston, and some other towns, generally in allusion to the dedication of the parish church. In the crest of Bishop's Stortford he is represented by a cross pommelled.

St Nicholas appears in the arms of Brentford-and-Chiswick.

St Oswald is dealt with in Chapter II.

St Pancras forms the crest of the borough which bears his name.

St Paul is represented by the sword, the instrument of his martyrdom, in the arms of the City of London. Crossed swords form the arms of the See of London, dedicated to St Paul, and appear in the heraldry of several towns historically connected with the See, including Braintree, Chelmsford, Ealing, Fulham, Hornsey, Paddington, and Willesden. As patron of London, St Paul is portrayed rising from the Keep of the Tower of London in the arms of the Port of London Authority.

St Peter's keys, emblematic of his celestial office, form part of the crest of Wolverhampton and are found in the arms of Peterborough C.C. and City.

St Peter and St Paul appear together in the arms of Wisbech, and the keys and sword of the two saints are combined in the arms of Dagenham, Fareham, and Mitcham.

St Thomas the Archbishop (Becket) is represented on the shield of Canterbury by the three beckets, or choughs, assigned to him as arms; these also appear in the heraldry of Croydon and the device of Deptford. Two choughs in the crest of Wimbledon stand for Thomas Cromwell, who derived them from Cardinal Wolsey, who in his turn had adopted them from Becket's arms. In Scotland, Becket himself in archiepiscopal robes supports the arms of Arbroath, the abbey there having been dedicated to him.

St Tydfil the Martyr appears in the arms of the town which bears her name, Merthyr Tydfil.

SEES AND RELIGIOUS HOUSES

Several towns bear in their arms emblems of the episcopal see with which they are historically connected. Mention has already been made of those which bear the swords of St Paul in allusion to the See of London.

The Province of Canterbury is denoted by the archiepiscopal cross and mitre in the arms of Lambeth, by the cross pall in those of Hayes-and-Harlington and Twickenham, and by the crosslets on the collar of Barnes's dexter supporter.

Durham C.C., having no arms of its own, bears those of the See, which are those attributed to its founder, St Oswald (Chapter II); and Lytham St Annes includes in its arms a cross and two lions from those of the See of Durham, which owned the Benedictine Priory at Lytham. The mitre of the Bishop of Durham, encircled by a coronet in token of palatinate jurisdiction, is found in the arms of Sunderland.

Bangor has produced civic insignia by adding a mace to the arms of the See. The

RELIGIOUS AND ECCLESIASTICAL EMBLEMS

Isle of Ely C.C. has embodied the three crowns of St Etheldreda, borne by the See of Ely, in its arms. Gloucester bears roundels derived from the See of Worcester, in which the city anciently lay. Bolton's crest, an elephant and castle, was taken from the arms of Coventry, the headquarters of the ancient Diocese of Mercia to which Bolton belonged. The mitre in the arms of Aldershot refers to the Bishops of Winchester, who formerly owned the land on which the town has arisen.

Abingdon and Reading provide instances of ancient civic arms referring to local houses of religion. Abingdon Abbey bore for arms a cross flory and four martlets, black on white; these are quartered by Kensington, the Abbey having held the manor; the borough of Abingdon based its arms on those of the Abbey, changing the martlets to crosslets paty and altering the tinctures. Reading's arms, consisting of five maidens' heads, were developed from an ancient seal containing *inter alia* the head of Edward, King of the English (975–8), in expiation of whose murder his stepmother founded the nunnery which is now St Mary's Church, Reading.

A remarkable instance of unintentional corruption of the arms of a religious house is provided by Dunstable, whose unauthorized arms, an ale-warmer within an engrailed border, are traceable to those of the local priory which consist of a pile with a horseshoe interlaced by a ring.

Other towns whose heraldry contains references to religious houses include Barking, Barnsley, Bermondsey, Dartford, Heston-and-Isleworth, Ilford, Jarrow, Leyton, Nuneaton, Southend-on-Sea, Watford, Worksop, and Wrexham.

Ecclesiastical buildings occur in the insignia of Eccles, Hackney, and Lydd. The arms of Lydd are particularly interesting because they contain a representation of the Church of All Saints, and being based on a thirteenth-century seal they probably preserve the appearance of the church as it was at that date.

The crest of Chingford consists of the tower of the town's ancient church, and Paignton has in its arms the Coverdale Tower of the episcopal palace.

Three neighbouring Metropolitan Boroughs show in their arms the sphere of the great religious orders of knighthood, the Hospitallers and Templars. Islington bears a gold cross potent (from the arms of the crusaders' Kingdom of Jerusalem) in reference to the Knights of the Hospital of St John of Jerusalem, and Finsbury represents the same Order by a white cross. Hackney denotes both the Hospitallers and the Templars by a parti-coloured white and red Maltese cross on a black and white field. A Maltese cross also figures in the shield of Penzance in allusion to a local chapel of the Knights of St John.

CHAPTER V

CASTLES, GATES, AND BRIDGES

THE debt which many English towns owed to the royal or baronial stronghold beside which they sprang up and grew in size and prosperity is reflected by the popularity of the castle in civic heraldry. The neighbouring castle was not only the town's protector (if occasionally its oppressor); it was often the best customer for the town's produce. It stood for authority, security, and prosperity, and it was natural that the townsfolk, when they attained to corporate status, should represent the most prominent feature of the town on their seal. As so many civic arms are adaptations of old seals, castles and towers are of frequent occurrence in municipal heraldry. Some towns of modern incorporation have followed the tradition of older boroughs by including castles in their arms.

The illustrations in this book show a variety of castles on civic shields. A common type consists of two towers flanking a gateway, with sometimes a third tower rising above the port (Bridport, Guildford, Wigan). Another style frequently used is a single tower with three turrets, known as 'a castle triple-towered' (Morpeth, Worcester). The arms of Exeter contain a triangular castle (though the shape is but vaguely indicated); those of Pontefract and Stafford represent quadrangular castles of two different types; and the castle in the arms of Devizes is hexagonal. Castles rising in three tiers are found on the shields of Bedford and Launceston.

These variations in style may be largely due to the work of old seal engravers. It is probable that the engraver's design was, in some cases, influenced by the appearance of the local castle; on some seals (e.g. Rochester) he attempted a faithful representation of it.

Accurate representations of existing castles are found in the arms of the Port of London Authority, which displays the Keep of the Tower of London, and the crest of Merioneth C.C., which includes Harlech Castle.

One or more castles of various types and tinctures form the only charges in the arms of Barnstaple, Clitheroe, Devizes, Exeter, Launceston, Newcastle-upon-Tyne, Pontefract, and Worcester (ancient).

Castles are combined with one or more royal lions in the arms of Bridport, Guildford, Newcastle-under-Lyme, Northampton, Norwich, Stafford, Swansea, and Winchester; with the feathers of the Prince of Wales in the arms of Calne; with a crown in the arms of Wigan; with the arms of feudal families in those of Bedford and of Morpeth; and with other emblems in those of Farnham, Gravesend, Marlborough, Swindon, Totnes, etc.

In conjunction with ships, castles appear in the arms or seals of several ports, including Bristol, Cardigan, Flint, and Scarborough. The heraldry of the Isle of Wight C.C. and Stockton-on-Tees combine castles with anchors.

CASTLES, GATES, AND BRIDGES

Castles form the crest of Cambridgeshire C.C., Nottingham, Newbury, and Tonbridge. A kindred crest is the Martello tower of Bexhill.

Castellated gateways, which are scarcely distinguishable from some forms of castle, are borne by Doncaster, Finsbury (in allusion to the gates of the City of London), Reigate (a punning device), and Torquay. The arms of Richmond (Surrey) contain a representation of the gatehouse of the old Palace of Richmond.

A portcullis, representing the local castle, appears on the seal of Wallingford. The portcullis in the crest of Gateshead refers to the first syllable of the name, that of Harwich denotes the port, and those in the arms of Richmond (Surrey) and Westminster are Tudor badges.

Several towns which owe their situation and growth partly to the bridging of a river bear bridges in their arms or seals. Cambridge has a bridge with towers on its shield and a castle-like bridge as a crest. Bideford, Chelmsford, Cowbridge, Maidenhead, Tonbridge, Stourbridge, and Bridgwater also have bridges in their arms, and bridges appear in the devices of Hebden Bridge, Lampeter, and West Bridgford. Poplar's seal contains a shield bearing a bridge between bows, for Bow Bridge.

In the arms of Rotherham a bridge stands not only for the town's own ancient bridge, but also for old Southwark Bridge, which was built by Rotherham ironmasters, and for the Bailey bridge, invented by a Rotherham man.

CAMBRIDGE

CHAPTER VI

THE SEA, RIVERS, AND SPRINGS

Most English coast towns, and many which are situated on the bank of some important river, make reference in their insignia to the element with which they are closely associated, whether as ports, fishing centres, or health resorts. The frequency of ships on early civic seals, and particularly on the seals and arms of the Cinque Ports and dependent towns, has been noticed in Chapter II. Of the principal English ports at the present day, Bristol, Liverpool, Manchester, Middlesbrough, Southampton, and South Shields have ships (in some cases with other marine emblems) in their heraldry, while Cardiff and Newcastle have sea-horses, and Sunderland has a sextant. Many lesser ports and seaside towns similarly proclaim their interests; but in some cases—for example, Hedon and Lydd—the ship in the town's insignia has a merely historic significance, the sea having receded and the ancient port being now a mile or two inland.

Ships of all kinds, from the Norse galley to the early steamer, are found in civic heraldry. Anchors, lighthouses, fish, seamen, and mythical creatures of the deep assist to express the maritime interests of English towns.

The Sea

The conventional heraldic method of representing water is by 'barry wavy,' generally silver and blue, and this appears in the arms of Cornwall C.C., Bridport, Lyme Regis, Lytham St Annes, Poole, Swansea, Worthing, and other seaside towns. Blackpool has barry wavy black and gold, the black alluding to the name and the gold to the sands. When waves of the sea are represented naturally they are so specified in the blazon (official description) of the arms; the shield of Bexhill provides an instance.

Ships

In only a few instances can the ships displayed in civic arms be assigned to any exact period of nautical history. The crests of Fulham and Wandsworth include Danish ships in allusion to the ninth-century inroads via the River Thames, and the arms of Lindsey C.C., East Suffolk C.C., and Sidmouth contain Viking ships. The crest of Hove consists of a sixteenth-century French galley ashore on a shingle beach. But frequently the blazon merely specifies an 'ancient ship' and leaves it to the artist to select the most appropriate type. When the Corporation possesses an old seal of naval character the type of ship illustrated on the seal may fittingly be chosen for the arms. Many such seals bear a single-masted ship, sometimes with towers at prow and stern and a crow's nest above the yard, sometimes with a pennon at the mast-head and banners over the towers. Single-masted ships of ancient type appear in the crests of Greenwich and the Port of London Authority, the arms of Jarrow, Llanelly, Maldon, Southport,

Harwich, and Stepney, and in the insignia of Beaumaris, Folkestone, Hythe, Lymington, and other towns. The 'ancient ship' in the arms of the Devon C.C. is generally represented as having only one mast with pennons at prow and stern, but as the accompanying motto, *Auxilio Divino*, is that of Sir Francis Drake, possibly a ship of the Elizabethan period is intended.

Exmouth's arms contain ten ancient ships—the tale of the town's contribution to Edward III's fleet in 1346. The Elizabethan ship forming the crest of Bideford has on its sail a clarion from the Grenville arms, showing that it represents the *Revenge* in which Sir Richard Grenville, with 'men of Bideford in Devon,' fought his last fight. The crest of Penzance shows a sailing ship sinking by the stern with her guns firing; this is held to be a pirate vessel, and one of the 'pirates of Penzance' is a supporter of the arms.

Old three-masted ships occur in the arms of Bermondsey, Blyth, Bristol, Chatham, Tenterden (with armorial sails), Truro, Wallasey, and Weymouth, in the crest of Ipswich, the accessories of Southampton, and the device of Aldeburgh; and three-masted ships of more modern type are borne by Eccles, Middlesbrough, Redcar, Torquay, West Ham, and Manchester—the last, it seems, having been prophetic of the Ship Canal, for the arms were devised before its construction.

Barrow-in-Furness provides an instance of an early steamship with sails, and Seaham has a cargo steamer in its arms.

Morecambe-and-Heysham, Ryde, and Weston-super-Mare display sailing yachts. South Shields, where the first lifeboat was built, has a lifeboat in its insignia.

Ships' masts occur in the crests of Kent C.C., Margate, and Southend-on-Sea.

Naval crowns, composed of the sterns and sails of ships set alternately on a circlet, are found in the heraldry of Chatham, Plymouth, Ramsgate, and Southport.

Anchors

Several towns denote associations with the sea by bearing anchors, e.g. Birkenhead, Gillingham, Greenwich, Stepney, Stockton-on-Tees, Thornaby-on-Tees, and West Hartlepool. An instance of special interest is Bewdley, whose anchor tells that the town, though far inland, has a maritime history, being connected with the sea by the River Severn.

Anchors sometimes have other than seafaring significance; that in the arms of Southend refers to St Clement; that of Walthamstow to the Monoux family; and those of Brierley Hill and Dudley to the iron industry.

Fisheries and Health Resorts

The fish best known to civic heraldry is the dolphin, the king of fishes and esteemed for his friendliness towards mankind. Dolphins appear in the arms of Brighton, Poole, and Ramsgate, the crest of Wallasey, and the devices of Deptford and Ilfracombe. As a supporter of the arms of Finsbury the dolphin is the emblem of St James.

Great Yarmouth honours the herring to which it owes its prosperity, bearing three of these fish on its shield in conjunction with the royal lions. Kingston-on-Thames and Bournemouth display salmon. Erith has three pike, or luces, not in allusion to fisheries, but to the Lucy family which bore these punning emblems.

Fishermen support the arms of Cornwall C.C., Cleethorpes, Southend-on-Sea, and Truro.

The amenities and healthful character of seaside towns are indicated by such emblems as the sun in the arms of Bexhill, Lowestoft, and Weston-super-Mare; the martlets (representing sand-martins) and blue and gold colour scheme of Bournemouth's arms; the figure of Hygieia which forms the crest of Worthing; the serpent, symbol of healing, in the crest of Southend; and by such mottoes as *Pulchritudo et Salubritas* (Bournemouth) and *Beauty surrounds, Health abounds* (Morecambe-and-Heysham).

OTHER MARINE EMBLEMS

Neptune with his crown, trident, and sea-green cloak, accompanied by a triton blowing a conch, supports the arms of Liverpool. His trident occurs in the crests of Chatham and Wallasey.

Mermaids are the supporters of Boston, where there is a tradition that they were crowned to commemorate the town's association with Anne Boleyn and Princess Mary, Duchess of Suffolk. Poole also has a mermaid as a crest.

Sea-horses occur in the crests of Eastbourne and Margate, and support the arms of Cardiff, Ipswich, and Newcastle-upon-Tyne. One inland town, Cambridge, has sea-horses as supporters, recalling that the River Cam once brought sea-going craft to the town. Heraldic sea-lions (i.e. lions with fish-tails) are the supporters of the Port of London Authority and Kent C.C.

Lighthouses form the crests of Bootle, Eccles, and Ramsgate.

RIVERS

Wavy 'ordinaries' (fesses, bends, chiefs, pales, etc.), or a field barry wavy, generally silver and blue, are common ways of representing rivers. Darwen, Haslingden, Maidstone, and Todmorden have each a blue wavy fess, Cambridgeshire a gold wavy bend, and Watford a blue wavy pale on another of silver. Blackburn, as befits its name, has a black wavy fess, and Burnley's wavy chief is also black.

Bromley indicates the name of its river, the Ravensbourne, by placing three flying ravens on its silver wavy fess. Similarly, the sheaves in the arms of Sheffield refer to the River Sheaf, and Keighley tells its riverside situation by means of the doubly significant motto, *By Worth*.

The River Thames and its tributaries are represented by barry wavy silver and blue, or blue wavy bars, in the arms of the London C.C., Brentford-and-Chiswick, Finsbury, Fulham, Hackney, Holborn, and St Marylebone; by Battersea's blue and silver shield; by swans in the arms of Richmond and of Twickenham; and by Oxford's supporting beaver—a beast whose heraldic colours befit his element, being green in the body and blue and silver in the tail. The arms of Newark-on-Trent are supported by an otter and a beaver. Probably Exeter's silver and blue pegasi are also river emblems.

Other riverside authorities which embody barry wavy in their arms or crests include Beverley, Burton-upon-Trent, Doncaster, the Isle of Ely C.C. (in allusion to the Fens), Jarrow, Keighley, and Nuneaton.

Two oars, one light and the other dark blue, in the arms of Barnes refer to the University Boat Race.

THE SEA, RIVERS, AND SPRINGS

Fords

Several towns which derive their names from a ford bear a reference thereto in their arms; for instance, Ilford has barry wavy silver and blue, and Chelmsford blue wavy bars, in the base of the shield. Oxford and Hertford, and the counties of which they are the centres, have punning insignia, the former consisting of an ox fording a stream, the latter of a hart in a ford.

Springs and Wells

The heraldic fountain—a roundel barry wavy silver and blue—is frequently used in civic heraldry to denote springs or wells. Buxton has eight such fountains corresponding to the number of its thermal springs, set about a Rod of Aesculapius, the symbol of health. Cheltenham has in its crest a fountain, and perched thereon a pigeon, recalling that it was the concourse of birds which led to the discovery of the saline springs for which the place is famous. Croydon, Harrogate, and Tunbridge Wells also display fountains.

Actual representations of wells occur in the insignia of Camberwell (Motto, *All's Well*), Finsbury (in allusion to Clerkenwell), and Wells.

The arms of Bath, containing silver wavy bars on blue in the upper part of the shield, and a masoned wall in the lower part, represent the Roman baths.

Southampton

CHAPTER VII

FOREST AND MOORLAND

EMBLEMS of the woodland appear in the arms of some authorities whose boundaries embrace or march with remnants of ancient forests, and sometimes commemorate forests which have long since disappeared. The commonest emblems are deer and trees.

The deer's head in the arms of Windsor, based on a fifteenth-century seal, and the stag and oak-tree forming the crest of Berkshire, represent the forest land where the Norman kings were wont to hunt. Malden-and-Coombe has a stag in reference to Richmond Park.

Ilford bears the Fairlop Oak in Hainault Forest, and its arms are supported by a forester. The extensive forests which anciently covered a large area north of London are recalled by trees in the heraldry of Hornsey, Southgate, and Stoke Newington, and Finchley's ragged chevron and stag.

Among authorities near London which remember their rural past and strive to preserve their amenities, Beckenham has the beautiful emblem of a chestnut-tree in bloom, Southall displays two thorn-trees in allusion to Elthorn Hundred, and Surbiton has an elm for Elmbridge Hundred. Heather in the crest of Bexley represents Bexley Heath, while purple in Lewisham's shield stands for Hither (heather) Green.

Surrey's oaks and the beeches of Buckinghamshire are represented in the arms of the County Councils.

Sherwood is indicated by oak-trees in the arms of Nottinghamshire and the crest of Mansfield; by the ragged cross and staves, and the royal stags in the heraldry of Nottingham; and by the supporting forester of Worksop. For Robin Hood we have to turn to the seal of Huntingdon which bears a huntsman who, despite his anachronistic costume of peaked cap, breeches, and top-boots, is claimed to be the famous outlaw on whom tradition has conferred the title of Earl of Huntingdon.

The arms of Rawtenstall, commemorating the Forest of Rossendale, contain a squirrel, a wolf, and a red hand cut off at the wrist—an allusion to the penalty for killing the king's deer. The arms and crest of Bacup also contain a squirrel and a stag in reference to Rossendale.

Bolton 'le Moors' or 'super Moras' has for crest an elephant (referring to Coventry and the Diocese of Mercia) standing on a rocky moor. The motto, *Supera Moras*, has a double meaning; it indicates the town's situation and enjoins the townsfolk to 'overcome delays.'

In the arms of Cumberland C.C., Parnassus flowers represent the marshy uplands of the county.

CHAPTER VIII

INDUSTRY

Civic arms containing emblems denoting local industries are mostly modern but there are a few ancient examples. Woolpacks appear on the fourteenth-century seals of Boston and Lincoln; the arms of Droitwich, containing moulds for salt-making, date from the fifteenth century; and those of Leeds, including a golden fleece in reference to the woollen industry, were recorded in 1662. Therefore, those who object to industrial emblems in so many modern coats cannot claim that they represent a departure from heraldic tradition. On artistic grounds there may be reason to condemn such charges as the Nasmyth steam-hammer (Eccles) or the blast furnace (Redcar); but actual representations of machinery and plant are unusual, industry being generally represented by symbols such as the fleece, the cotton flower, the shuttle, and the pick —objects which have a dignity of their own, and are not incongruous when set beside older heraldic forms.

The misfortune of much civic heraldry of industrial character is not that the charges are unsuitable to armorial display, but that the arms, having been designed during a period of poor heraldic taste, are too often ill arranged and overcrowded.

Industry is personified by the smith who, accompanied by a woman representing Art, supports the shield of Birmingham. A common symbol of industry is the bee, which occurs in many civic devices, especially those of towns whose names begin with a B—Bacup, Barrow-in-Furness, Blackburn, Burnley, Bury. A terrestrial globe covered with bees forms the crest of Manchester and suggests world-wide business. In the device of South Shields, Commerce is represented by a woman bearing Mercury's Rod, which also appears in the crest of Rotherham.

The particular industries most widely represented in English civic heraldry are agriculture, textiles, mining, metals, and transport.

Agriculture

The commonest heraldic emblem of agriculture is the wheatsheaf (or garb), which is found in the arms of many rural counties and market towns. In the case of Luton the wheatsheaf refers not only to agriculture but also to the straw-plaiting industry, while in Harpenden's arms it is a token of the agricultural research work carried on at Rothamsted. In Cheshire (as has been noted in Chapter II) the wheatsheaves are primarily a county emblem derived from the arms of the Earldom of Chester.

Fruit-growing is represented by apples in the arms of Bexley, and the cherry-tree crest of Sittingbourne. Worcestershire's pear-tree, while referring to local produce, is primarily associated with Queen Elizabeth I (see Chapter II).

Mitcham's arms and crest contain lavender, for which the place was famous. Slough displays a white pink, Uxbridge chrysanthemums, and Spalding tulips, in reference to flower nurseries, while Exmouth has in its crest two *Magnoliae grandiflorae Exmouthiensis*.

The heads of cattle are found in the insignia of Lindsey C.C., Darlington, and St Ives (Hunts). Local breeds of cattle and sheep are represented in the heraldry of Herefordshire (a Hereford bull's face), Oxfordshire (Oxford Down rams), Westmorland (a Herdwick ram's head), and Derby (a Derby ram). A shepherd's crook occurs in the arms of Cumberland C.C.

Textiles

The oldest emblem of the woollen industry is the woolpack, which is found in the heraldry of Boston and Guildford, and (among more modern coats) the arms of Godalming, Pudsey, Rawtenstall, Rochdale, and Wolverhampton.

Another common emblem of wool is the fleece, which is a charge in the arms of Bacup, Bury, Leeds, and Nelson, and in the insignia of other authorities. Rams or rams' heads are displayed by Bradford (which also has an Angora goat), Boston, Godalming, and Leominster.

Woolhooks and teazles are found in the arms of Kendal; and those of Newbury also contain teazles.

Among Lancashire towns, sprigs of the cotton plant are borne by Burnley, Bury, Darwen, Middleton, Nelson, Rawtenstall, and Rochdale, while Farnworth has cotton cops. In Yorkshire, cotton is borne by Huddersfield and Morley. Bales of cotton are found in the heraldry of Bacup and Salford, and hanks in that of Ilkeston and Mansfield.

Shuttles, representing textile weaving, are charges in the heraldry of Accrington, Barnsley, Blackburn, Bolton, Bury, Darwen, Haslingden, Morley, Pudsey, Salford, and Todmorden. Nelson uses reedhooks to symbolize weaving.

Other charges connected with textiles are the calico-printing rollers in the arms of Accrington and the silkworm moth in those of Middleton. A piece of Maltese lace occurs in the arms of Ilkeston.

Mining

Miners are portrayed in the heraldry of Cornwall C.C., Barnsley, Truro, and Tynemouth, but are more often represented by their tools. Picks, spades, and lamps are borne by Barnsley, Blyth, Haslingden, Hyde, Ilkeston, Morley, and other towns.

In the arms of Burnley and Nuneaton coal is represented by charges described in heraldry as 'lozenges sable,' but in popular and more significant terms, 'black diamonds.' Black roundels in the arms of Heywood and Morley, and black fields in those of Wallsend and Wednesbury, also stand for coal.

The Davy lamp is found in the heraldry of Blackwell, Ilkeston, and Ystradgynlais.

Metals

Metal workers are represented by Thor and Vulcan, who support the arms of Sheffield. The astronomical symbol of Mars as typifying iron is borne by Ilkeston, Staffordshire C.C., Wednesbury, and Wrexham. Another emblem of iron is the mill-rind (the metal clamp at the centre of a mill-wheel) which is borne by Rochdale, Salford, and West Bromwich. The last has also a gold millrind standing for brass.

The horseshoe and nails in the ancient arms of Gloucester, and the anvils of Bury,

INDUSTRY

Dartford, and Halesowen, also indicate metal works. Wallsend bears golden drops to represent copper, and Llanelly's badge includes a piece of tinplate.

The furnaces of the Black Country are indicated by the beacons of Wolverhampton and Brierley Hill, Wednesbury's flaming tower, and, more symbolically, by Dudley's salamander. A blast furnace is the crest of Scunthorpe.

Transport and Communications

Ermine in the arms of Cheshunt, Kesteven C.C., and Glanford Brigg R.D.C. represent the ancient highway called Ermine Street, while Friern Barnet has a white pale on green for the Great North Road with its grass verges.

Motor transport is represented by a cog-wheel in the arms of Acton, and a motor wheel in those of Leyland. Redditch has in its crest a swift, the fastest of British birds, standing on a cog-wheel, alluding to both motor-car and aeroplane accessory manufacture.

As a token that London's omnibuses are made in the borough, Southall has as a supporter a griffin, the emblem of the former London Passenger Transport Board, while the motto, 'For all,' put into Latin, is another reference to the omnibus.

Railways are represented by Stephenson's 'Locomotion No. 1' in the device of Darlington, and a more modern locomotive engine in the arms of Swindon, which also has a winged wheel in its shield. Surbiton's crest includes a railway bridge, and Feltham refers in its arms to its marshalling yards.

The first flight of a heavier-than-air machine is commemorated by a falcon in the arms of Crayford. Wings, representing flight and local air-ports, occur in the arms of Heston, Hayes-and-Harlington, and Farnborough—the last denoting thereby that it is the birthplace of the Royal Air Force. Feltham has a winged sword for the London Air-port, and Hendon a winged air-screw, while to Beddington-and-Wallington belongs the distinction of being the first authority to include an aeroplane as a charge in its arms.

Ancient and modern methods of transport are illustrated in Crewe's pictorial device, including a canal boat, stage coach, pack-horse, pillion, and railway.

Other Industries

Among other industries represented in the insignia of English authorities are the following:

Boots and shoes. Kettering: a hide.

Brushes. Kingswood: a boar's head.

Chain Cables. Halesowen and Stourbridge: a chain.

Chemicals. Widnes: an alembic. Dartford: golden roundels representing tabloids.

China. Lowestoft: a Lowestoft china plate.

Electrical Industry. Rugby: a thunderbolt.

Glass. Barnsley: a glassblower. Knottingley: an ancient bottle.

Gloves. Ilkeston: two left-hand gloves.

Hats. Hyde: a flake and a hatter's bow. Denton: a beaver.

Leather and Skin Dressing. Stourbridge: a fleece. Northamptonshire C.C.: a bull.

36 CIVIC HERALDRY

Locks. Willenhall and Wolverhampton: padlocks.

Needles and fishing tackle. Redditch: a needle and a salmon-fly.

Paper. Bury: papyrus plant. Dartford: a fool's cap. Farnworth: hornets. Sittingbourne: a scroll of parchment.

Pottery. Stoke-on-Trent: the Portland vase, and a potter of ancient Egypt.

Rope. Crewkerne: flax.

PUBLIC WORKS AND ADMINISTRATION

The arms of the Institution of Municipal Engineers represent various undertakings of local authorities. The field is barry wavy silver and green, for water and land, and bears a black pale indicating a highway and bridges. Transport is denoted by a winged wheel, public lighting and education by a torch, and municipal building construction by a mural crown. (See dedication page.)

Water supply is the theme of the arms of the Metropolitan Water Board, which contain the hand of God showering down rain on a green field, the shield being supported by Aquarius and Hygieia.

Blackpool bears a thunderbolt in allusion to its pioneer work in using electricity for lighting and traction. The motto of Shoreditch, *More light, more power,* besides having a moral significance refers to the municipal electric undertaking. Torches represent electricity and gas in the arms of Barking and of East Ham.

Emblems of local government and administration include the mural crown, which is common in civic heraldry (see London C.C., Birmingham, Carlisle, Manchester, etc.), the crown vallary composed of palisades (Chorley and Dukinfield), and the mace (Bangor and Somerset C.C.). Croydon, and Beddington-and-Wallington U.D.C., have embattled fesses, and Keighley an embattled border, suggesting town walls.

Themis, the classical personification of civic rule, supports the arms of Workington.

ILKESTON

CHAPTER IX

REBUSES

THE rebus, or heraldic pun, is found in a number of civic arms and crests and is employed by many local authorities which have not obtained arms. This practice accords with ancient custom, for among early seals rebuses are found on that of Hartlepool, a hart in a pool; of Appleby, an apple-tree (now borne in the arms of the Westmorland C.C.); of Berwick-on-Tweed, a bear standing against a tree which may be a wych-elm; and of Congleton, two conger-eels and a tun.

Most rebuses are obvious, but in a few cases, e.g. Wigan's mountain ash or wiggin tree and Dukinfield's raven or docken, the pun involves an unusual word.

The following are instances of civic arms and crests containing emblems allusive to the name of the authority, and in some cases bearing on the derivation of the name:

Accrington. An oak bough, bearing acorns, bent into the shape of an A.
Acton. An oak-tree.
Arundel. A swallow (*hirondelle*).
Barrow-in-Furness. A bee and an arrow.
Beverley. A beaver.
Bromley. Broom plant.
Buckinghamshire C.C. A buck.
Cowbridge. A cow on a bridge.
Dukinfield. A docken (raven).
Eccles. An ecclesiastical building.
Ely C.C., Isle of. An eel.
Enfield. An enfield (heraldic hybrid).
Eye. The eye of Jehovah, with the motto, *Oculus in coelum*.
Finchley. A finch.
Gateshead. A goat's head and gateway.
Hammersmith. Hammers.
Haslingden. Hazel.
Herne Bay. A heron.
Hertford and the Hertfordshire C.C. A hart in a ford.
Huntingdon C.C. A hunting horn.
Lambeth. A Holy Lamb.
Lindsey C.C. (Lincs). Links of a chain. Motto: *Service links all*.
Liverpool. A liver (cormorant) with laver (seaweed) in its beak.
Maidenhead. A maiden's head.

Oldham. Owls (from the arms of the Oldham family. The pun depends for its effect on the local pronunciation of the name).

Oxford. An ox fording a stream.

Ruislip-Northwood. Rye slips and a hurst of trees below the pole star.

Sale. Sallow twigs.

Sheffield. Sheaves, alluding both to the city and the River Sheaf.

Wigan. The wiggin tree (mountain ash).

Allied to the rebus is the rare practice of incorporating in the arms the initial letter of the town's name. Instances are provided by Bermondsey, Bridlington, Horsham, and Rochester. An R or a K is sometimes added to the arms of Kingston-upon-Thames. The unauthorized device of Colne includes a C. The fess dancetty of two points in the arms of Melksham forms the letter M, and Workington has two piles forming the letter W.

OXFORD

CHAPTER X

HISTORY, TRADITION, AND LEARNING

NEARLY every civic coat of arms is to some extent an historical document, though most of them refer to purely local history. There are, however, some in which allusion is made to national events which occurred in the locality; for example, the sealing of Magna Carta at Runnymede is commemorated in the arms of Egham by a representation of the charter with King John's crown.

Some battles have record—Brunanburgh in the arms of Axminster, Neville's Cross in those of Spennymoor, and two engagements of the Civil War in Newbury's arms; while the border struggles between England and Scotland are recalled by Appleby's salamander, betokening a town which, as its motto tells, was destroyed 'neither by the sword nor by fire.' A modern instance is the flame contained by a chain in the arms of Leatherhead, referring to the local Civil Defence Services during the Second World War.

Towns which look back to prehistory include Maidstone, with an iguanodon supporting its shield, and Weston-super-Mare with an ancient Briton, while Farnham has a stone axe in its crest. Antiquities represented in civic insignia include Whiteleaf Cross (Buckinghamshire C.C.), the Queen Eleanor memorial cross (Northampton R.D.C.), and Hadrian's Wall (Wallsend). (References to the Roman occupation and the Saxon kingdoms are dealt with in Chapter II.)

Some arms and devices commemorate ancient local customs and traditions. Rutland's horseshoe recalls the custom whereby every nobleman on his first entry to the town of Oakham was required to give a shoe from his horse or money in lieu thereof. Marlborough's arms contain greyhounds, a bull, and capons in allusion to the presentation due from a newly admitted burgess to the Mayor and Aldermen. The boars' heads of Grimsby are said to refer to the right of the Mayor and Corporation to hunt the boar in Bradley Woods. The arms of Bradford, Ripon, and Wallasey commemorate service by 'cornage' and horn-blowing ceremonies. The seal of Bethnal Green illustrates the ancient legend of the daughter of the 'seely blind beggar' who turned out to be Henry de Montfort, son of the famous Simon.

One of the 'pirates of Penzance' supports the arms of the borough, while the 'Lincolnshire poacher' is a supporter of the Lindsey C.C. shield. Banbury's crest is 'a fine lady upon a white horse.'

The heraldry of Harrow and Rugby contains emblems from the arms of their famous schools, and John Lyon, the founder of Harrow School, is commemorated by a lion in the arms of Wembley, his birthplace. Eton U.D.C. uses the arms of the College. Schools are represented by books in the shields of Acton, Leatherhead, and Cheltenham, the last having the motto: *Salubritas et Eruditio*. Spalding has a book in reference to the Spalding Gentlemen's Society, claimed to be the second oldest learned society in the country, while the book in Edmonton's arms stands for associations with Lamb and

Keats. The only instance of a particular book in English civic arms, except for the Bible and the Gospels, is in the shield of Jarrow, which contains a volume inscribed *Beda Historia Ecclesiastica* in commemoration of the Venerable Bede and his work.

Twickenham's arms contain a lamp to recall the borough's connection with the arts, literature, and science through many distinguished townsmen, and Harrow has a quill pen for literary associations and a clarion alluding to Handel's residence in the district.

Some towns bear in their arms emblems from the heraldry of Oxford or Cambridge colleges which own land in their areas. Thus Cleethorpes denotes its connection with Sidney Sussex College, Cambridge; Hornchurch with New College, Oxford; and Malden-and-Coombe with Merton College, Oxford. The supporters and motto of Holborn refer to Lincoln's and Gray's Inns.

The discovery of Uranus by Sir William Herschel is commemorated by its astronomical sign in the arms of Slough.

MARLBOROUGH

CHAPTER XI

MOTTOES

MOTTOES of local authorities, though diverse in wording, may be grouped under a few headings according to their themes. Many are of a religious character, many extol industry and labour, and other considerable groups are those which express the ideas of progress, unity, loyalty and fidelity, amenity and health. Some refer to the town's situation, some embody its name, and a few allude to national defence.

Most civic mottoes are in Latin; English is often used, especially in mottoes adopted in recent years; and a few authorities in Wales have Welsh mottoes. Examples of the several classes of mottoes are given below.

RELIGIOUS. *Domine dirige nos* (City of London); *Deus noster refugium et virtus* (Dewsbury); *Heaven's light our guide* (Portsmouth, in allusion to the star and crescent, or sun and moon, in the arms). Some mottoes are extracts from the Bible, especially the Psalms, and are sometimes contracted, e.g. *Nisi Dominus frustra* (Chelsea) for, 'Except the Lord keep the city, the watchman waketh but in vain' (Psalm cxxvii. 1). An interesting example of the religious motto is that of Newark: *Deo fretus erumpe*; this is the Latin version of the mayor's brave words when the town was besieged by the Parliamentary forces, 'Trust God, and sally.'

INDUSTRY. *Labor omnia vincit* (Ashton-under-Lyne, Bradford, Ilkeston; in English it is the motto of Erith U.D.C.); *Floreat Industria* (Batley, Darlington); *Floret qui laborat* (Mossley, Rawtenstall); *Industry and prudence conquer* (Accrington); specific industries are occasionally referred to, e.g. in *Mare et ferro*, Redcar alludes to its character as a seaside resort and a centre of the steel industry; and *Sal est vita* expresses the interest of Northwich in salt.

PROGRESS. *Forward* (Birmingham); *Onward* (Fleetwood, Hyde); *Progress* (Blackpool); *Erimus* (Middlesbrough). Leicestershire C.C.'s *For'ard, For'ard* expresses the idea of progress in the language of a hunting county.

UNITY. *Non sibi sed toti* (Hampstead); *United to serve* (Southwark); *Many minds, one heart* (Chelmsford); *One and All* (Cornwall C.C.); *Undeb sydd nerth*, 'Union is Strength' (Pembrokeshire C.C.).

LOYALTY AND FIDELITY. *Pro Rege et Lege* (Leeds); *Civitas in bello, in pace, fidelis* (Worcester). The motto of Bridgnorth, *Fidelitas urbis salus Regis*, alludes to the support given to the Royalist cause during the Civil War. That of Bedfordshire C.C., *Constant be*, is from John Bunyan's hymn, 'Who would true valour see.'

AMENITY AND HEALTH. *Salus populi suprema lex* (Lewisham, Lytham St Annes, and others—a quotation from Cicero); *Amoenitas salubritas urbanitas* (Ryde); *Sol et salubritas* (Bexhill).

SITUATION. *Inter sylvas et flumina habitans* (Morpeth); *Jewel of the Thames* (Maidenhead); *Situ exoritur Seguduni* (Wallsend, Roman Segedunum); *Supera Moras* (Bolton 'le Moors'); *By Worth* (Keighley, on the River Worth). The last two have a double meaning.

NAME. *Floreat Actona*; *Floreat Hova*, and several similar mottoes; *Oculus in coelum* (Eye, which has the eye of Jehovah in its crest); *Mon Mam Cymru*, 'Mona Mother of Wales' (Anglesey C.C.); *Reddite Deo* (Redditch); *Spe nemo ruet* (Spennymoor). In the case of Chichester R.D.C., the name is hidden in the motto, *Adhuc hic hesterna*.

DEFENCE. *With Fort and Fleet for Home and England* (Gillingham); *Pugna pro Patria* (Aldershot); *Clamant nostra tela in Regis querela* (Woolwich).

Some mottoes allude to charges in the arms, e.g. *Y Ddraig Goch ddyry gychwyn*, 'The Red Dragon will lead' (Cardiff); *The knot unites* (Staffordshire C.C.). Some are those of local families. Devon C.C. uses the motto of Sir Francis Drake, and Warwickshire C.C. that of Shakespeare.

An alphabetical list of civic mottoes recorded in this book is given in the Appendix.

STANDARD OF HERTFORD

PART II

A DESCRIPTION OF THE ARMORIAL BEARINGS OF LOCAL AUTHORITIES IN ENGLAND AND WALES

IN THE following pages local authorities are grouped in their geographical counties, which are arranged alphabetically. In each geographical county, the arms of the administrative county (or counties) are given first, followed by those of county boroughs, other cities and boroughs, urban and rural districts, and other authorities (e.g. new town development corporations).

All armorial bearings officially granted to such authorities, or on record at the College of Arms, before 31st December 1952 are described and illustrated. In the case of unauthorized devices, only a representative selection is given, and these are not all illustrated.

In order that the record may be understood by those who are not familiar with the language of heraldry, technical terms have to a large extent been eliminated. Where they occur a reference to the illustration should show their meaning. Students of heraldry will find that this modification of heraldic language may sometimes render the description of arms less explicit, but where heraldic details are omitted the drawings will supply them.

The descriptions of arms always begin with the 'field' or surface of the shield. This may be of one 'tincture' (metal, colour, or fur), e.g. *argent* or *azure*; or it may be *parted*, i.e. divided, *palewise* (vertically), *fesswise* (horizontally), etc., into two or more tinctures. After the field, the objects that lie on it are described. The traditional words for the tinctures are generally retained, but sometimes for clarity the English equivalent is used. The traditional words (*argent*, *azure*, *gules*, etc.) are placed after the object which they describe. Where the English equivalents (gold, silver, etc.) are used, they are usually placed before the object.

The following are the heraldic names of the tinctures with their English equivalents:

METALS:
  Argent—silver, or white.
  Or—gold.

COLOURS:
  Azure—blue.
  Gules—red.
  Purpure—purple.
  Sable—black.
  Vert—green.

FURS:
  Ermine—a white fur with black tufts.
    Black tufts on gold are here described as *gold ermined sable*.

Vaire—a fur represented by cup-shaped pieces alternately blue and white. Where other tinctures occur, the term *vairy* is used and the tinctures stated, e.g. *vairy gold and gules.*

Proper means that the object so described is represented in its natural or ordinary colours.

Where the ground is particoloured, and the object thereon is similarly parted but with the tinctures reversed, the object is described as *counter-changed.* Thus, *Quarterly argent and gules, a cross counter-changed,* means that the shield is divided into silver and red quarters, and the cross is similarly divided but coloured red where it lies on the silver, and silver where it lies on the red.

Dexter means right and *sinister* left, from the point of view of the man bearing the shield. Consequently dexter and sinister are respectively left and right to the person looking at armorial bearings, this being applicable to the supporters as well as the emblems on the shield.

Anglesey C.C.

ANGLESEY

ANGLESEY County Council

The seal of the Anglesey C.C. displays the arms of the family of Owen of Bodowen, Anglesey, and Orielton, Pembrokeshire: Gules, a gold chevron between three gold lions rampant. Beneath the shield is the motto, *Mon Mam Cymru*.

These are the arms attributed to Awfa ap Cynddelw (or Hova son of Kundhelw), one of the Fifteen Peers of North Wales in the twelfth century; from whom descended Owen ap Merick (*temp.* Henry VII), ancestor of the present family.

The motto preserves the old Welsh name of Anglesey, '*Mon*' (possibly meaning 'separate'), better known in its latinized form 'Mona.' The motto is so ancient as to be quoted by Giraldus Cambrensis in the record of his *Itinerary through Wales*, made in 1188:

This island is incomparably more fertile in corn than any other part of Wales, from whence arose the British proverb, *Mon Mam Cymbry*, Mona mother of Wales; and when the crops have been defective in all other parts of the country, this island, from the richness of its soil and abundant produce, has been able to supply all Wales.

The motto is comparable with the *Ave Mater Angliae* of Canterbury.

BEAUMARIS Borough Council

The Corporation seal contains a one-masted ship with sails furled, on one side of it the Royal Arms of England (three lions passant guardant), and on the other a castle with four towers; above the yard-arm is a small castle.

The Royal Arms are those of Edward I, who built Beaumaris Castle as part of his plan to keep the Welsh under control. The combination of ship and castle in the seal recalls that the Castle was built on low-lying ground, its fosse communicating with the sea, so that vessels could come under its walls.

BEDFORDSHIRE C.C.

BEDFORDSHIRE

BEDFORDSHIRE County Council

ARMS: Quarterly gold and gules, a fess wavy barry wavy of four pieces argent and azure, and over all a pale sable charged with three silver scallop shells.

CREST: On a wreath gold and gules, a swan's head and neck proper issuing from a wreath of oak or.

SUPPORTERS: Dexter, a lion gules; and sinister, a gold bull.

MOTTO: *Constant be.*

These were granted in 1951.

The quarterly field is from the arms of the Bedfordshire Beauchamps who, as Constables of Bedford Castle, chiefly directed the affairs of the County for two centuries following the Norman Conquest. The scallop shells are from the arms of the Russell family, and commemorate their services to the State and the County, while the supporting lion is derived from the dexter supporter of the Russell Dukes of Bedford. The bull refers to agriculture, and the wavy fess and swan to the River Ouse and the ford from which Bedford derives its name. The motto is taken from the hymn, 'Who would true valour see,' by the famous Bedfordshire man, John Bunyan.

BEDFORD Borough Council

ARMS: Argent, an eagle displayed sable, looking towards the sinister, with a gold crown on its head, and on its breast a gold castle of three tiers.

These were recorded by the heralds in 1566.

BEDFORDSHIRE

The castle is clearly intended to represent the old stronghold of the Beauchamps, and Mr Gale Pedrick, in *Borough Seals*, states: 'the eagle is derived from the bearings of the Beauchamps, the ancient Barons of Bedford, namely, argent, an eagle sable, beak and claws or.'

But the arms of the Beauchamps of Bedford (which form the basis of the arms of the Bedfordshire C.C.) were gold and red quarters with a black bend. It seems that the designer of the fifteenth-century seal on which the arms of Bedford were based may have incorporated the eagle of another family of Beauchamps.

BEDFORD

Arms of the Priory

Device used by the Borough

DUNSTABLE

DUNSTABLE Borough Council

Dunstable provides a complex heraldic problem. Fox-Davies, in the *Book of Public Arms*, quotes the arms of the town (used without authority) as: 'Argent, an ale-warmer ... within a bordure engrailed sable.' These are the arms in actual use, and they might suggest a tendency on the part of the town to conviviality but for the fact that they are in reality a corruption of arms of a very different character, those of Dunstable Priory. These are quoted by Burke, in the *General Armory*, as: 'Argent, on a pile sable a horseshoe interlaced to a staple affixed to the centre of the pile, or.' Another form of these arms, quoted in *Notitia Monastica*, is: 'Sable, a pile in point argent, a horseshoe conjoined, or, and interlaced with an annulet of the second, pendent.'

The Corporation, having no arms of its own, incorporated those of the Priory in its seal. In the course of time corruption crept in, perhaps through the lack of skill or the ignorance of some seal engraver; the pile became longer and narrower, the horseshoe and ring degenerated into a meaningless twist projecting from the side of the pile, until finally the emblems assumed the shape of an ale-warmer.

LUTON

LEIGHTON BUZZARD

LUTON Borough Council

ARMS: Quarterly gules and azure, on a silver cross a bee; in the first quarter a wheatsheaf, in the second a beehive, in the third a rose with stalk and leaves, and in the fourth a thistle, all proper.

CREST: On a wreath argent and gules, a grassy mound, and thereon a forearm bendwise in a sleeve azure with a white cuff, the hand holding seven gold ears of wheat.

MOTTO: *Scientiae et labori detur*—'Due to knowledge and labour.'

These were granted in 1876.

The bee is the emblem of industry, and the hive represents in particular the straw-plaiting industry for which Luton has become famous, thanks to the excellent supply of wheaten straw, represented by the wheatsheaf. This industry was started locally by a colony of straw plaiters who followed James I from Scotland, and settled under the protection of Sir Robert Napier of Luton Hoo. The arms of Napier contain a rose, and I am inclined to think that the rose in the Luton arms bears reference to the patron of the straw plaiters, while the thistle denotes the country whence they came. An alternative theory is that the rose was incorporated as a national emblem, and the thistle was taken to indicate the connection of the Borough for a long period with the Marquess of Bute, who formerly owned the Manor of Luton Hoo.

The ears of wheat in the crest carry on the motive of the wheatsheaf; they probably allude also to John Whethamsteade, Abbot of St Albans, who in the fifteenth century rebuilt the chancel of St Mary's Church, Luton, where his arms, three bunches of ears of wheat, may still be seen.

LEIGHTON BUZZARD Urban District Council

Use is made of the arms and crest of the family of Bossard: Gules, on a gold saltire a star azure, and on a gold chief an eagle displayed sable with a gold crown on its head.

CREST: A crowned eagle as in the arms.

Berkshire C.C.

BERKSHIRE

BERKSHIRE County Council

ARMS: Azure, two gold lions passant guardant in pale within a border embattled ermine.

CREST: On a wreath gold and azure, upon a mount vert a stag at gaze argent in front of an oak-tree bearing acorns proper.

These were granted in 1947.

Berkshire is a Royal County, and the two lions are derived from the arms attributed to the Norman kings. The embattled border, of royal ermine, refers to the castles in the County, notably Windsor Castle. The crest is based on an old County emblem allusive to the forest lands which gave royal sport to the Saxon and Norman kings. William I, who 'loved the tall deer as if he were their father,' had an eye for good hunting country when he chose Windsor for his residence and began its famous Castle.

READING

ABINGDON

READING County Borough Council

ARMS: Azure, a maiden's head and neck full-face and cut off at the shoulders proper, wearing a royal crown of gold with its cap gules, and about the neck a gold necklace with pendant; between four similar maidens' heads without crowns and necklaces.

These are recorded at the College of Arms, having been confirmed to the Corporation in 1566. In the fourteenth-century seal on which the arms were based the heads were those of men, the middle one wearing a Saxon crown. It has been suggested that this represented Edward, King of the English (975–8), who was assassinated at the instigation of his stepmother Ælfthryth, jealous that her own son did not occupy the throne. In expiation of the murder, Ælfthryth founded a nunnery (now St Mary's Church) at Reading.

A document illustrating the arms as confirmed in 1566 shows the central maiden's head placed between the letters RE, which may have been a reference to Queen Elizabeth I.

ABINGDON Borough Council

ARMS: Vert, a gold cross flory between four silver crosses formy.

These were recorded by the heralds in 1556.

The arms may have been based on those of the Abbey: Silver, a cross flory and four martlets, all sable; which seem to have been suggested by the arms attributed to Edward the Confessor. In replacing the martlets by crosses the creators of the Abingdon arms produced a coat generally resembling that of the crusaders' Kingdom of Jerusalem: Silver, a gold cross potent between four gold crosslets; to which has been attributed the significance that the central cross stands for Christ, and the other crosses for the four Evangelists. It is possible that the townsmen of Abingdon intended their arms to have a similar meaning.

BERKSHIRE

MAIDENHEAD

MAIDENHEAD Borough Council

ARMS: Azure, three pales wavy argent issuing from a bridge of three arches in chief or.

CREST: On a wreath argent and azure, a maiden's head full-face proper, with a molet azure on the top of the head, and on the neck a saltire gules with its limbs cut short.

SUPPORTERS: Dexter, St Andrew, and sinister, St Mary Magdalen, both proper.

MOTTO: *Jewel of the Thames.*

These were granted in 1947.

The present bridge over the Thames at Maidenhead was built in 1772–7, but the river has been bridged at this point for nearly seven centuries, and this link in the ancient highway between London and the west has been an important factor in the growth of the town.

NEWBURY Borough Council

ARMS: Gules, on a fess argent a bar wavy azure; in chief a teazle flower between two wheatsheaves, and in base two swords crossed saltirewise, points upwards, all gold.

CREST: On a wreath gold and azure, a castle of three domed towers gules, with a pennon argent charged with a bar wavy azure flying from the central tower, and a flag azure on each of the other towers.

MOTTO: *Floruit floreat*—'May it flourish as it has flourished.'

These were granted in 1948.

The wavy bars in the arms and crest refer to the River Kennet. The teazle stands for cloth manufacture, an important industry of Newbury in the sixteenth century, and the wheatsheaves represent agriculture. The castle alludes to the Norman stronghold, and the swords to the two battles near Newbury during the Civil War.

NEWBURY

NEW WINDSOR

NEW WINDSOR Borough Council

ARMS: Parted fesswise argent and vert, over all a silver stag's face with antlers sable, and between the antlers a shield bearing the arms of France Modern and England quarterly; in base a castle wall with three towers argent, in the central tower a gateway vert with a gold portcullis.

These were recorded at the College of Arms in 1566.

The castle is, of course, a reference to Windsor's famous fortress, and the stag's head recalls that the town's environs formed a happy hunting ground for the Norman kings.

New Windsor is a Royal Borough.

WALLINGFORD Borough Council

The Corporation uses as a device a portcullis, presumably in allusion to the ancient castle which, having been held for Charles I, was destroyed during the Commonwealth.

WOKINGHAM Borough Council

The Corporation seal bears a sprig of oak with an acorn; this appears to be an allusion partly to the name, which, since the middle of the sixteenth century, has been spelt 'Oakingham' alternatively with 'Wokingham,' and partly to the fact that the town was anciently situated in the Forest of Windsor.

BRACKNELL DEVELOPMENT CORPORATION

BRACKNELL *Development Corporation*

ARMS: Vert, three gold rings interlaced palewise within an orle of eight gold roundels.

CREST: On a wreath gold and vert, a stag's head torn off at the neck proper, charged on the neck with three gold rings, one above the other two and interlaced.

MOTTO: *Home, Industry, Leisure.*

These were granted in 1951.

The three linked rings, placed on the green of the countryside, represent the inseparable components of a new town, namely: home, industry, and leisure. The stag's head indicates that the area now occupied by Bracknell was formerly covered by Windsor Forest.

BRECONSHIRE C.C.

BRECKNOCK

BRECONSHIRE

BRECONSHIRE County Council

Having no arms of its own, the Breconshire C.C. uses those attributed to the Celtic chieftain Brychan, under whose leadership the Goidels reoccupied the Usk valley on the withdrawal of the Romans. From Brychan was derived the name Brycheiniog, now Brecknock.

The arms are quarterly; the first and fourth quarters sable with a gold fess with cotises between two swords proper with gold hilts, the upper sword point upwards and the lower one point downwards (for Anlach, Brychan's father); the second and third quarters gold with three rere-mice (bats) azure, their beaks and legs gules (for Marchell, his mother).

The motto is *Undeb Hedd Llwyddiant*—'Unity, Peace, Prosperity.'

BRECKNOCK Borough Council

ARMS: Argent, a red robe with ermine lining, and gold tasselled strings interlaced.

These are attributed to Brecknock by Guillim in his *Display of Heraldrie* (second edition, 1632).

I am indebted to Miss G. E. F. Morgan, M.A., ex-Mayor of Brecknock, for the following note:

We have a very beautifully illuminated Charter granted to the Borough of Brecknock in 1556 by King Philip and Queen Mary, and in that it is stated that they granted the Borough a coat of arms, *Luna, a mantle of state Mars, doubled ermine, bushed Sol, garnished with strings fastened fretwise, pendent and tasselled of the same*, which arms we continue to use to this day. We have no crest, crests not having been granted to towns until 1561.

Until the grant of Philip and Mary, Brecon had used the seal of Edward Stafford, Duke of Buckingham, who was Lord of Brecknock and the owner of large possessions here. My theory is this: Edward Stafford was a great friend and supporter of Katherine of Aragon,

Mary's mother, and his downfall was principally due to his devotion to her. One of his many badges, which still adorn Thornbury Castle, was a blue mantle, one of the devices of Edward III, and this was used by the Duke. Mary had stayed as a girl at Thornbury, so would have been familiar with it in its association with him, and I think she may have chosen it for the Borough which had belonged to him, changing it to the royal scarlet, being her gift.

The Duke of Buckingham's livery, it is said, was red and black. The livery of our mace-bearers, etc., is still red and black—a case of unconscious continuity.

Ystradgynlais

YSTRADGYNLAIS *Rural District Council*

ARMS: Parted fesswise gold and azure; in chief a Davy lamp sable, the glass proper, between two horological balance-wheels also sable; and in base a battlemented gateway with two towers argent on a mount vert, and perched on the battlements a nightingale proper.

CREST: On a wreath gold and azure a dragon rampant gules supporting with the left foreclaw and the right hindclaw a pick proper, its head downwards.

MOTTO: *Amser yw'n golud*—'Time is our wealth.'

These were granted in 1951.

The Davy lamp and pick denote mining, the District's main industry, while the balance-wheels allude to recently established clock and watch factories. The castle is that of Craig-y-Nos, the former home of Madam Patti, the famous singer, to whom the nightingale refers. The mount alludes to agriculture.

BUCKINGHAMSHIRE

One of the badges of the Staffords, Earls and Dukes of Buckingham, was a swan which they derived from the Bohuns by the marriage of Edmund, Earl of Stafford (d. 1403), with Anne, daughter of Thomas of Woodstock, Duke of Gloucester and Earl of Buckingham, and Eleanor, co-heiress of the Bohun Earls of Hereford and Northampton. (Eleanor's sister, Mary, married Henry IV who, with his son Henry V, also used the swan of Bohun as a badge.) The Bohuns had derived the swan from the Mandevilles, who may have adopted it in token of their descent from Adam FitzSwanne.

The swan of the ducal house of Buckingham became a charge in the arms of the towns of Buckingham and High Wycombe, and was adopted as the sinister supporter when Buckinghamshire C.C. obtained arms in 1948. It has thus become the general emblem of the County, and as such occurs in the arms of Slough and the crest of Newport Pagnell.

BUCKINGHAMSHIRE C.C.

BUCKINGHAMSHIRE County Council

ARMS: Parted palewise gules and sable, a swan rousing proper with a gold ducal coronet about its neck, and affixed thereto a gold chain turned over the back; on a gold chief a roundel vert charged with a white cross on a pyramidal base.

CREST: A beech-tree with its roots on a mount proper with a gold Saxon crown about the trunk.

SUPPORTERS: Dexter, a buck, and sinister, a swan, both proper.

MOTTO: *Vestigia nulla retrorsum*—'No backward step.'

These were granted in 1948.

BUCKINGHAMSHIRE

The swan of the Stafford Earls and Dukes of Buckingham stands on their livery colours of red and black. The swan forming the sinister supporter differs from the one in the arms in being free—that is, it has no collar and chain—and is thus an emblem of the River Thames.

The roundel bears a representation of Whiteleaf Cross, a prehistoric feature of the County, and a conspicuous landmark. It has been conjectured that it celebrates some ancient Christian victory over the pagans. The beech-tree stands for the famous beech woods of the Chiltern Hills, and the Saxon crown about its trunk refers to the fact that the Saxons were the first settlers in the greater part of the County. The buck is allusive to the name, and also refers to the park lands of North Buckinghamshire.

The motto, appropriate to a progressive local authority, is that of the Buckinghamshire patriot, John Hampden, and of the present Earl of Buckinghamshire.

 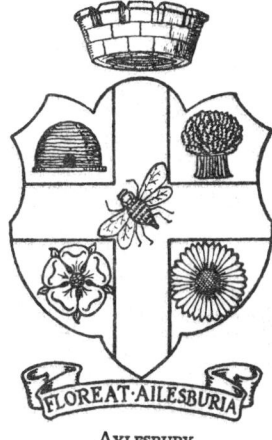 

BUCKINGHAM   AYLESBURY   HIGH WYCOMBE

AYLESBURY Borough Council

The Corporation has not obtained arms, but has assumed a device invented in 1923 by a local jeweller, and consisting of: Azure, a silver cross charged at the centre with a bee; in the first quarter a golden beehive, in the second a golden wheatsheaf, in the third a red rose, and in the fourth a golden sunflower. Above the shield is a mural coronet.

MOTTO: *Floreat Ailesburia.*

The cross is from the arms of the family De Ailesbury, and the other emblems stand for industry, agriculture, and fertility. The designer seems to have had before him a copy of the arms of Luton.

BUCKINGHAM Borough Council

ARMS: Parted palewise sable and gules, a swan argent with wings outspread, about its neck a gold ducal coronet.

The swan of the Stafford Dukes of Buckingham stands on their livery colours as in the shield of Buckinghamshire C.C.

CIVIC HERALDRY

HIGH WYCOMBE (or Chepping Wycombe) Borough Council

ARMS: Sable, on a green mount a swan argent with a gold ducal coronet about its neck, and attached thereto a gold chain.

MOTTO: *Industria ditat*—'Industry enriches.'

These are recorded at the College of Arms. See the note under the County heading for the significance of the swan.

SLOUGH

SLOUGH Borough Council

ARMS: Parted chevronwise argent and gules, in chief two roses gules with seeds and sepals proper, and in base a swan holding in its beak a white pink with stalk and leaves also proper; on a chief azure the astronomical sign of Uranus irradiated, between two brick-axes, all gold.

SUPPORTERS: Dexter, Mercury in a white tunic and a mantle azure, holding in the right hand a caduceus proper; and sinister, Vulcan, also in a white tunic and holding in the right hand a pair of pincers proper.

MOTTO: *Fiducia et vi*—'By confidence and strength.'

These were granted in 1938.

The swan is the County emblem and the flowers represent the horticultural interests of the Borough. The supporters symbolize trade and industry, and the brick-axes refer particularly to brick-making. The sign of Uranus is from the arms of the family of Herschel of Slough, and relates to the discovery of the planet by Sir William Herschel.

BUCKINGHAMSHIRE

ETON

NEWPORT PAGNELL

ETON Urban District Council

The U.D.C. exhibits the arms of Eton College: Sable, three silver lilies; the chief parted palewise azure and gules, with a fleur-de-lis and a lion of England, both gold.

MOTTO: *Floreat Etona.*

The lilies are emblematic of the Virgin Mary, to whom the College is dedicated. The emblems in the chief denote that the College is a royal foundation.

NEWPORT PAGNELL Urban District Council

ARMS: Gold, two lions passant in pale and in base two bars wavy, all azure, within a bordure gyronny of eight pieces gules and sable.

CREST: On a wreath or and azure, a swan with wings spread issuing from the battlements of a tower and supporting a staff, all proper; and flying from the staff a banner parted palewise gules and sable charged with a sword point upwards surmounted of two keys crossed saltirewise, all gold.

MOTTO: *Praecepta non homines*—'Principles, not men.'

These were granted in 1951.

The blue lions are from the arms of the Paganel family (from which the town derived its name) and their descendants, the Somerys; while the two blue wavy bars represent the rivers Ouse and Ouzel. The red and black of the border, and also of the banner in the crest, are the County colours, and with the swan were derived from the insignia of the Dukes of Buckingham (see above). The battlements refer to the ancient castle of the Paganels, and the keys of St Peter and sword of St Paul allude to the dedication of the parish church.

Caernarvonshire C.C.

CAERNARVONSHIRE

CAERNARVONSHIRE County Council

ARMS: Quarterly gold and gules; between four lions passant guardant counter-changed, a fess vert charged with three eagles displayed or.

CREST: On a wreath gold and vert, a gold castle with two towers standing on a mount vert, and issuing from the castle a plume of three ostrich feathers argent.

SUPPORTERS: Two sea-dragons, their heads, forelegs, and wings gules and their tails proper.

MOTTO: *Cadernid Gwynedd*—'The strength of Gwynedd.'

These were granted in 1949.

The shield combines the arms of two great native Princes of Wales—the lions of Llewelyn the Last (which form the arms of the Principality of Wales), and the eagles of Owen Gwynedd. The eagles have long been associated with the County, and according to Michael Drayton they appeared on the banner borne by the men of Caernarvonshire at Agincourt.

The castle stands for the great strongholds in the County—Caernarvon, Conway, and Criccieth—and the feathers of the Heir Apparent are a token of the traditional link between the Princes of Wales and the County. The supporting sea-dragons allude to the maritime situation of Caernarvonshire, and the rocky base on which they rest refers to its coast and mountains.

The motto, derived from the eleventh-century *Mabinogion*, refers to the rugged fastnesses of Caernarvonshire.

CAERNARVONSHIRE

BANGOR City Council

The Corporation has adapted the arms of the See of Bangor and uses: Gules, a gold bend sprinkled with black drops and surmounted by a bend wavy azure on which is a gold civic mace; on either side of the bend is a silver spur-rowel.

CREST: A crouching griffin.

The arms of the See seem to have been based on those borne by Bishop Skevyngton who (c. 1532) added the tower and nave to Bangor Cathedral.

BANGOR

CAERNARVON Borough Council

Use is made of a shield bearing the arms of England with a label of five points, and above the shield an eagle—a combination of the insignia of the English Princes of Wales and Owen Gwynedd, native Prince of North Wales (see Caernarvonshire C.C.).

CONWAY Borough Council

The seal bears a castle with three domed towers, water flowing at its base. Conway Castle was built by Edward I as part of his scheme of fortresses to secure his conquest of North Wales.

PWLLHELI Borough Council

The seal bears an elephant with a castle on its back. This is very ancient, and the reason for its adoption is unknown.

LLANDUDNO Urban District Council

The seal contains three shields, each supported by an eagle from the arms of Gwynedd and the Caernarvonshire C.C. The first shield bears the Royal Arms of England with the label of the King's eldest son, being the arms of the first English Prince of Wales. The second bears the arms of the Welsh Princes of Wales, now attributed to the Principality: Quarterly gold and gules, four lions passant guardant counter-changed. The third, which is flanked by two Welsh dragons, bears a representation of the Church of St Tudno.

CAMBRIDGESHIRE C.C.　　　　　　　　ISLE OF ELY C.C.

CAMBRIDGESHIRE

CAMBRIDGESHIRE County Council

ARMS: Azure, a bend wavy and a double-tressure set with fleurs-de-lis, their heads pointing alternately inwards and outwards, all gold.

CREST: On a wreath gold and azure, a castle with an open helmet above the port, proper.

SUPPORTERS: Two great bustards proper.

MOTTO: *Per undas, per agros.*

These were granted in 1914.

The wavy bend stands for the River Cam, formerly a channel of trade and a source of prosperity, wherefore it is tinctured gold; it also represents the Cambridgeshire fenlands, the last English home of the great bustard (now extinct in this country) which supports the shield and represents the wild life of the shire. The motto, 'By water and land,' is an allusion to the river, the fens, and the agriculture which is the County's main industry. In this fenland William I encountered the sturdy opposition of Hereward the Wake and his followers, and the castle forming the crest is that which the Conqueror built at Cambridge as his headquarters against 'the last of the English.'

The double-tressure of fleurs-de-lis is from the Royal Arms of Scotland, its presence in the arms of this English County being due to the fact that in the twelfth century the Earldom of Cambridge (united with that of Huntingdon) was held by David I, King of Scotland, husband of Earl Waltheof's daughter Matilda.

The helmet is a sign of a knight bachelor in token of Sir H. G. Fordham, Chairman of the County Council when the arms were granted.

CAMBRIDGESHIRE

ISLE OF ELY County Council

ARMS: Argent, three bars wavy azure, a pile gules charged with three open crowns of gold.

CREST: On a wreath argent and azure, a human arm, the wrist charged with the Wake knot, the hand grasping a gold trident entwined by an eel proper.

These were granted in 1931.

Here again are allusions to the fen country and Hereward the Wake. Genealogy does not support the tradition that Hereward was the ancestor of the family named Wake, but he has been credited with their knot.

The eel refers to the supposed derivation of the name from 'eel isle,' stated by Bede to be due to 'the great plenty of eels taken in those marshes.'

The three gold crowns on red are from the arms of the See of Ely (which were used by the County Council before they obtained arms of their own) and refer particularly to St Etheldreda, the foundress of the religious house which has become the Cathedral. Etheldreda was a lady of the royal house of East Anglia to which, long after its extinction, the heralds assigned for arms three gold crowns on blue (see Chapter II).

When it approved the arms the County Council had before it the suggestion that the motto should be *Per aquam ad astra*—'Through water to the stars,' but a councillor pointed out that this motto, placed on Wisbech bridge, might be an incentive to suicide, and it was decided to do without a motto.

CAMBRIDGE

CAMBRIDGE City Council

ARMS: Gules, a gold arched bridge with three towers, above it a fleur-de-lis or between two roses argent, and in base barry wavy silver and azure, and thereon three ships sable, each with one mast and the sail furled.

CREST: On a wreath or and gules, a grassy mound, and thereon a silver bridge.

SUPPORTERS: Two sea-horses, their bodies gules and their tails proper, with gold fins.

These were granted in 1575.

Cambridge owes its name and early development to the bridge at the farthest navigable part of the Granta or Cante, now Cam. In past days it derived much prosperity from river-borne traffic from the coast; hence the ships and sea-horses—unusual emblems for an inland town. The fleur-de-lis and roses are royal and national emblems.

The crest, though described as a bridge in the record, is more like a castle, and perhaps the intention was to represent a fortified bridge in allusion to the fact that Cambridge Castle stood on the hill just above the point at which the bridge spanned the river.

The arms reproduce certain features of a fifteenth-century seal bearing a bridge over a stream and above the bridge two angels supporting a shield of the then Royal Arms (France and England quarterly).

WISBECH Borough Council

ARMS: Azure, representations of St Peter and St Paul, standing within a double canopy, all gold.

CREST: On a wreath or and azure, a gold sixteenth-century ship with three masts and on each a square sail azure, the centre one charged with two gold crossed keys and each of the others with a gold castle.

These were granted in 1929.

The figures of St Peter and St Paul, to whom the parish church is dedicated, appeared on the Corporation seal. The crossed keys in the crest refer to St Peter. The ship recalls the town's former note as a port. The castles refer to the ancient stronghold built, it is said, by William I, and converted in the fifteenth century into a palace for the Bishops of Ely.

WISBECH

CARDIGANSHIRE C.C.

ABERYSTWYTH

CARDIGANSHIRE

CARDIGANSHIRE County Council

ARMS: Quarterly, the palewise division indented; the first quarter sable with a lion rampant reguardant or; the second, barry wavy of six pieces argent and azure with a herring erect head upwards proper; the third, azure with a gold wheatsheaf banded gules; the fourth, sable with a silver chevron between three white roses with gold seeds and sepals.

Above the shield is a gold mural crown.

MOTTO: *Golud gwlad rhyddid*—'The wealth of the land is freedom.'

These were granted in 1937.

The arms in the first quarter are associated with St David and represent religion. The second and third quarters stand for fisheries and agriculture. The fourth quarter represents literature, the chevron and roses being from the arms of Dafydd ap Gwilym, the fourteenth-century Welsh poet, who was a Cardiganshire man.

ABERYSTWYTH Borough Council

The Corporation has no arms, but the seal contains a lion rampant reguardant. This emblem has been used on the seal (though not continuously) since 1810. It was probably derived from the arms of the local family of Pryse of Gogerddan which formerly owned much of the land within and adjoining the Borough, and has long been closely associated with the town. Their arms are: Gold, a lion rampant reguardant sable.

CARDIGAN Borough Council

The Corporation has not obtained arms, but uses a shield parted palewise, on one side a castle and on the other a ship in full sail. These emblems, appropriate to an old fortified port, are derived from the Corporation seal, which bears the legend: *Anchora spei Cereticae est in te Domine*—'The anchor of hope of the people of Cardigan is in Thee, O Lord.'

LAMPETER Borough Council

The seal bears a bridge. The old name of the place was 'Llanbedr-pont-Stephan,' commemorating St Pedr, a sixth-century missionary, and one Stephen, who built a bridge over the Teifi.

Carmarthenshire C.C.

Carmarthen

CARMARTHENSHIRE

CARMARTHENSHIRE County Council

Arms: Quarterly indented gold and gules, in the first and fourth quarters a dragon rampant gules and in the second and third a lion rampant or.

Crest: On a wreath gold and gules, a dragon passant gules supporting with the right foreclaw a golden harp, and about the dragon's neck a collar flory counter-flory or.

Motto: *Rhyddid gwerin ffyniant gwlad*—'The freedom of the people is the prosperity of the country.'

These were granted in 1935.

The arms combine the Welsh dragon and the lion of Rhys ap Tewdwr Mawr, King of South Wales in the eleventh century, whose descendants still form a notable county family. The harp symbolizes Welsh music and poetry, of which the County is an important centre.

CARMARTHEN Borough Council

Arms: Gules, a silver castle with three towers between two ostrich feathers erect argent, on each of the outer towers a Cornish chough proper facing inwards, and in base a gold lion passant reguardant.

Crest: On a wreath argent and gules, a fisherman carrying a coracle proper.

Motto: *Rhyddid hedd a llwyddiant*—'Freedom, peace, and prosperity.'

These were granted in 1936.

CIVIC HERALDRY

The arms were based on a seal in previous use. The feathers are from the insignia of the Princes of Wales, and the lion may have been derived from the arms ascribed to Cadell, Prince of South Wales in the last part of the ninth century. The crest represents the salmon and sewin fishing industry, in connection with which the coracle is still in use.

KIDWELLY Borough Council

The seal bears a shield charged with a cat. This may be due to a mistaken derivation of the name Kidwelly from the tribe of Cadwell or Cathwell.

LLANDOVERY Borough Council

The seal bears the Prince of Wales's feathers.

LLANELLY Borough Council

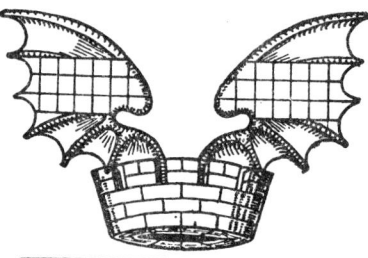

LLANELLY

ARMS: Parted chevronwise argent and gules, in chief two ancient galleys sable and in base the figure of St Elli, silver.

CREST: Rising from a mural crown proper, two dragon's wings gules each charged with a fess chequered gold and azure.

MOTTO: *Ymlaen Llanelli.*

BADGE: In front of two miner's pickaxes saltirewise, a Stepney motor wheel, and therein a wooden box containing a sheet of tinplate, all proper.

These were granted in 1913.

The town derives its name from the Church of St Elli, a grand-daughter of Brychan (see Breconshire). She is reputed to have been martyred by the heathen Saxons. The ships stand for the port. The wings are those of the Welsh dragon, and the chequers on them are from the arms of the Stepney family, Lady Stafford Howard, heiress of the late Sir Arthur Stepney and first Mayoress of the Borough, having presented the arms and badge to the Corporation, with other gifts. The badge sums up the industries on which Llanelly's prosperity is based.

AMMANFORD Urban District Council

ARMS: Parted fesswise dancetty gold and sable, in chief a cross sable, its limbs cut short.

CREST: On a wreath gold and sable, a demi-boar gules with gold tusks rising from a wreath of oak leaves sable.

MOTTO: *Hanfod tref trefn*—'The essential of a good town is orderliness.'

These were granted in 1952.

CARMARTHENSHIRE

AMMANFORD

CARMARTHEN R.D.C.

CARMARTHEN Rural District Council

ARMS: Vert, a pale argent between two gold wheatsheaves, and on the pale two palets sable enclosing a five-pointed star between four six-pointed stars all gules; a chief parted palewise embattled gold and gules and thereon two lions passant guardant counter-changed.

CREST: On a wreath argent and gules a gold mural crown, and hanging from the central battlement an escutcheon bendwise gold charged with three piles azure.

MOTTO: *Oni heuir ni fedir*—'Without sowing one cannot reap.'

These were granted in 1951.

The lions are from the arms of Wales. The green field and wheatsheaves refer to agriculture, and the black palets to coal. The points of the stars total 29, corresponding with the number of parishes in the District. One of these is Laugharne, which has a fine castle, represented by the mural crown, on which is the shield of Guy de Brian, a former lord of Laugharne.

CHESHIRE

The arms associated with the ancient Earldom of Chester are: Azure, three gold wheatsheaves (or, in heraldic language, *garbs*.) These were borne by Ranulph de Blondeville (d. 1232). Arms consisting of the lions of England dimidiated with the garbs of the earldom were granted to the City of Chester in 1580. When Cheshire C.C. obtained armorial bearings in 1938 the arms of the earldom were taken as the basis, and the wheatsheaf thus became the general emblem of the County. One or more wheatsheaves occur in the heraldry of many authorities in Cheshire.

CHESHIRE C.C.

CHESHIRE County Council

ARMS: Azure, a gold sword erect, point upwards, between three gold wheatsheaves.

CREST: On a mural crown gules, a gold lion statant guardant between two silver ostrich feathers.

SUPPORTERS: Two gold lions, each supporting between the forelegs a silver ostrich feather.

MOTTO: *Jure et dignitate gladii*—'By the right and dignity of the sword.'

These were granted in 1938.

To the arms of the ancient Earldom of Chester has been added a sword—fitting emblem of the County Palatinate which the earl 'held as freely by his sword as the King of England held by his crown.' To this the motto refers.

The lions and ostrich feathers recall that since 1254 the Earldom of Chester has generally been held by the Heirs Apparent of the English throne. Since 1399 the earls have usually been Princes of Wales.

CHESTER

CHESTER City and County Borough Council

ARMS: Gules, three gold lions passant guardant in pale, dimidiated with azure, three gold wheatsheaves.

CREST: On a wreath gold, gules, and azure, a sheathed sword erect, point upwards, tied with a belt, all gold. (The mantling, not shown above, is gules and azure lined with silver.)

SUPPORTERS: A gold lion with a silver ducal coronet about its neck; and a wolf argent with a similar coronet of gold.

MOTTO: *Antiqui colant Antiquum Dierum*—'Let men of the ancient virtues worship the Ancient of Days.'

The arms were confirmed, and the crest and supporters granted, in 1580.

The shield contains the Royal Arms of England joined with those of the old Earls of Chester by 'dimidiation'; rather more than half the lions is shown, and one wheatsheaf and a half. The sword is stated in the grant to be 'the emblem of Majesty and Justice.' The supporting lion is a royal emblem, and the wolf denotes Hugh Lupus, first Earl of Chester, who was so created in 1071. The wheatsheaves are also found in the arms used by the Cheshire C.C. and a number of towns in Cheshire and Lancashire.

The crest is usually placed on a closed helm set *affronté*.

BIRKENHEAD

STOCKPORT

BIRKENHEAD County Borough Council

ARMS: Quarterly gold and silver, on a cross gules a crozier or and two crescents argent; in the first quarter a lion passant gules, in the second an oak-tree growing on a mount proper, in the third a star azure, and in the fourth two lions passant in pale gules.

CREST: On a wreath or and gules, a lion statant azure on a rock in front of a gold crozier, supporting a gold anchor with the right forepaw.

MOTTO: *Ubi fides ibi lux et robur*—'Where there is faith there is light and strength.' (The word *robur* refers to the oak-tree in the arms.)

These were granted in 1878.

The lion in the first quarter and in the crest is from the arms of the family of Massey; Hamon de Massey having, in 1150, founded the Benedictine Monastery to which the croziers refer. The tree stands for Tranmere, the star (or perhaps starfish) for Bebington, and the two lions for Oxton. The crescents possibly represent the family of Laird, which did much for the development of the town.

STOCKPORT County Borough Council

ARMS: On a field azure strewn with cross-crosslets or, three gold lozenges, within a gold border charged with three wheatsheaves and three double-headed eagles alternately azure.

CREST: In a gold mural crown, a mount vert and thereon a castle with two towers proper.

CHESHIRE

Motto: *Animo et fide*—'By faith and courage.'

These were granted in 1932.

The arms in the centre of the shield are those of the ancient family of Stockport, formerly Lords of the Manor, and the wheatsheaves stand for the Earldom of Chester and the County. The crest represents the medieval castle which has long since disappeared. The eagles refer to the old local family D'Eton.

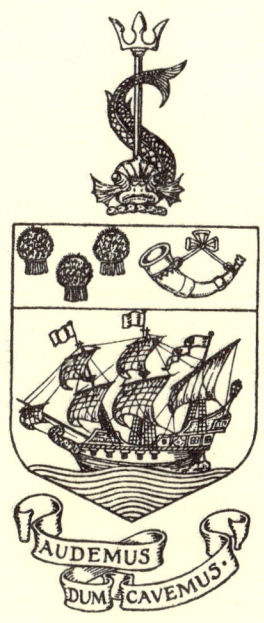

WALLASEY

WALLASEY County Borough Council

Arms: Gold, a three-masted ship in full sail on the sea proper; on a chief azure, three gold wheatsheaves and a bugle-horn proper with gold strings and ornaments.

Crest: On a wreath gold and azure, a gold trident entwined by a dolphin, head downwards, proper.

Motto: *Audemus dum cavemus*—'We dare though we are wary.'

These were granted in 1910.

The ship and crest represent Wallasey's maritime interests. The wheatsheaves are from the arms of the Earldom of Chester, and the horn is the 'Wirral Horn' in the possession of the family of Stanley, late of Hooton. I am indebted to the Town Clerk for the following note on the horn:

The entire Hundred of Wirral was formed into a forest by Randle Meschines, third Earl of Chester. The Master Forestership thereof was granted to Alan Sylvester in fee with the Manors of Storeton and Puddington to hold by cornage, or in the words of the Quo Warranto, 'Cum quodam cornu nomine tituli ballivae praedictae.' The Master Forestership subsequently passed through the families of Storeton and Banville to the Stanleys of Stanley in Staffordshire.

ALTRINCHAM

ALTRINCHAM *Borough Council*

ARMS: Azure, two gold wheatsheaves and in base a gold cog-wheel.

CREST: On a wreath or and azure, a gold lion passant guardant supporting with the right forepaw a staff gules with truck or, thereon a banner azure charged with a gold cornucopia with fruit proper.

SUPPORTERS: Dexter, a unicorn ermine with gold horn, mane, and hoofs, about its neck a collar gules and pendent therefrom by a chain gules a shield barry of six pieces argent and azure; and sinister, a gold lion with a collar gules and pendent therefrom by a chain gules a shield quarterly gules and or with a silver lion passant in the first quarter.

MOTTO: *Altrincham en avant*—'Altrincham leads the way.'

These were granted in 1937.

The wheatsheaves and cog-wheel refer to the agricultural and engineering industries, while the former are also County emblems. The lion in the crest supports a banner symbolic of plenty, recalling the town's former motto, *Pax et abundantia*.

The supporters stand for two great families of past and present importance in Altrincham's history. The unicorn is from the heraldry of the Earl of Stamford, whose arms (for the family of Grey) hang from the collar. The lion, with the arms of Massey on its pendent shield, represents the old Barons of Dunham Massey, one of whom, Hamon de Massey, granted the town a charter in 1290.

BEBINGTON

CONGLETON

BEBINGTON Borough Council

ARMS: Parted chevronwise azure and gold, in chief a saltire argent with its limbs cut short between two wheatsheaves or, and in base an ancient galley sable, its sail furled and flags gules flying to the dexter.

CREST: On a wreath gold and azure, a representation of Bromborough Market Cross proper in front of the rising sun or.

MOTTO: *Civitatis fortuna cives*—'The fortune of the state depends on the citizens.'

These were granted in 1934 to the former Urban District.

The wheatsheaves are County emblems and the ship is appropriate to a town with a frontage to the River Mersey and the Manchester Ship Canal. Prominent among its industries are those of Lever Brothers Limited at Port Sunlight, to which reference is made in the crest. The saltire is the emblem of St Andrew in allusion to the parish church.

CONGLETON Borough Council

The Corporation has not obtained a grant of arms, but has adopted the following: Sable, a chevron between three tuns argent.

CREST: A tun floating in water between two gold conger eels rising from the water, and on the tun a lion statant guardant gules.

MOTTO: *Sit Tibi sancta cohors comitum*—'To Thee be the band of comrades dedicated.'

The crest is taken from the device on a fifteenth-century seal. The congers and tun form a rebus on the name, and the lion probably represents Henry de Lacy, Earl of Lincoln, who granted the burgesses a charter early in the fourteenth century.

Apparently the shield was invented to suit the crest; but unfortunately it is identical with the arms of the Vintners Company, so that if Congleton seeks to place its heraldry on an official footing there will, presumably, have to be a considerable change in the arms.

CREWE Borough Council

The Corporation has no arms, but makes use of a quartered shield containing devices of a pictorial character representing ancient methods of transport; namely, a canal boat, a stage coach, a pack-horse, and a pillion. Above the shield is a railway locomotive expressing the modern form of transport which constitutes Crewe's importance. The motto is, *Never behind.*

DUKINFIELD

DUKINFIELD Borough Council

ARMS: Quarterly azure and argent, a pointed cross voided (i.e. in outline) quarterly silver and sable; in the first quarter a gold raven and in the fourth a gold wheatsheaf.

CREST: Rising from a gold crown palisado, a forearm in a sleeve azure with a cuff argent, the hand grasping a shield azure charged with the sun or; on either side of the forearm a silver ostrich feather.

MOTTO: *Integrity*.

These were granted in 1900.

The arms and crest are based upon those of the Dukinfield family, whose pointed cross also appears in the arms of Stalybridge. The raven, being known locally as a 'docken,' is a rebus. The feathers and wheatsheaf are from the heraldry of the Princes of Wales, Earls of Chester. The crown vallary, composed of palisades set on a rim, is an alternative to the mural crown as a civic emblem.

CHESHIRE

HYDE

MACCLESFIELD

HYDE Borough Council

ARMS: Azure, a silver chevron nebuly between three gold lozenges; on a chief argent a flake surmounted by a hatter's bow between a cog-wheel and two miner's picks saltirewise with a safety-lamp hanging from them, all proper.

CREST: On a wreath argent and azure, a pack of blue cotton prints with gold bands and marked with gold mascles, and thereon a sprig of the cotton-tree crossed by a shuttle proper.

MOTTO: *Onward.*

These were granted in 1882.

The lower part of the shield contains the arms of the local manorial family of Hyde, differenced by a change of tincture and the nebuly treatment of the chevron. The other emblems stand for the appropriate industries; the mascles (empty lozenges) on the crest are probably intended for the design on the printed cotton goods.

MACCLESFIELD Borough Council

The Corporation uses a device consisting of a lion rampant guardant bearing a wheat-sheaf; with the motto: *Nec virtus nec copia desunt*—'Neither virtue nor plenty are lacking.'

This appears to be the lion of the Ferrers Earls of Derby bearing a wheatsheaf from the arms of the Earldom of Chester (see Cheshire C.C.).

SALE

SALE Borough Council

ARMS: Azure, a silver pile between two gold wheatsheaves, and on the pile three lozenges sable.

CREST: On a wreath argent and azure the battlements of a tower argent, and thereon a moorcock proper.

SUPPORTERS: Dexter, a silver unicorn with gold horn and hoofs and azure mane; and sinister, a badger proper; each supporter with a collar of sallow twigs proper about its neck.

MOTTO: *Salus et felicitas*—'Health and happiness.'

The arms and crest were granted to the Sale U.D.C. in 1920 and the supporters to the Borough in 1945 to commemorate the tenth anniversary of its incorporation.

The wheatsheaves are County emblems, and the lozenges are from the arms of Massey of Sale. The crest refers to the district of Sale Moor. The unicorn, suggested by the unicorn's head crest of Carrington, represents the Ashton-on-Mersey district of Sale, and the badger, or brock, is a punning allusion to Brooklands. The sallow twigs, and the first word of the motto, refer to the name of the Borough.

STALYBRIDGE   BOWDON

STALYBRIDGE Borough Council

ARMS: Silver, a chevron engrailed gules between in the chief two crosses pointed and voided sable and in base a pierced molet (or spur-rowel) sable; flanches azure, each charged with a silver cinquefoil.

CREST: On a wreath argent and gules, a wolf argent standing in front of a gold wheatsheaf.

MOTTO: *Absque labore nihil*—'Nothing without labour.'

These were granted in 1857.

The town derives its name from the family of Staveley who anciently held the manor, and their arms: Silver, a chevron engrailed gules, form the basis of those of the town. The pointed crosses denote the family of Dukinfield (see Dukinfield) and the spur-rowel that of Assheton (see Ashton-under-Lyne). The wolf and wheatsheaf represent the Earldom of Chester (see City of Chester and Cheshire C.C.).

BOWDON Urban District Council

ARMS: Parted per chevron arched gold and vert, in chief two yew-trees proper and in base a wheatsheaf or; on a chief gules a lion passant argent.

CREST: On a wreath gold and vert, a demi-unicorn ermine with gold horn, mane, and hoofs, and with a collar vert about its neck, holding a bow strung proper.

MOTTO: *Beau don.*

These were granted in 1945.

D

The arched chevronwise division of the shield represents the rounded hill from which Bowdon derives its name. The yews refer to the wooded parts of the district, and represent the trees from which the famous bowmen of Cheshire obtained their bows, one of which is seen in the crest. The wheatsheaf is the Cheshire emblem and also stands for agriculture. As in the arms of Altrincham, the unicorn is from the heraldry of the Earl of Stamford and the lion from that of the Masseys. The motto, besides being a play on the name, alludes to the 'splendid gift' of the arms to the U.D.C. by its then Chairman, and also to the gift of Denzell House as a cultural centre, and to the opening of Dunham Park to the public by the Earl of Stamford.

BREDBURY AND ROMILEY *Urban District Council*

The seal of the Council displays the arms and crest of the Arderne family who for three centuries owned the greater part of Bredbury, viz. Gules, three gold cross-crosslets pointed at the foot and a chief or. Crest: In a crest-coronet, a panache of ostrich feathers gules turned down or.

Hazel Grove and Bramhall

Cheadle and Gatley

Nantwich

CHEADLE AND GATLEY *Urban District Council*

The Urban District embodies the former villages of Cheadle Bulkeley and Cheadle Moseley; and the parish of Etchells-in-Stockport; and the device which, lacking authorized arms, the Council has assumed represents the union of these districts. It consists of a shield parted chevronwise and the chief palewise. The first compartment contains the arms of the family of Bulkeley: Silver, a chevron and three bulls' heads sable (alluding to the name). The second contains those of the family of Moseley: Quarterly, 1 and 4, Sable, a silver chevron and three silver millpicks, 2 and 3, Gold, a fess and three eagles sable. The base of the shield, which represents Etchells-in-Stockport, contains three mascles (empty lozenges); I have not been able to ascertain their origin or colours, but it is possible that they were suggested by the arms of the family of Stockport (see Stockport), in which case they should be gold on blue.

CHESHIRE

HALE Urban District Council

The seal, adopted in 1900, bears a representation of the old Tithe Barn which formerly stood at Hale Barns, together with a wheatsheaf; and in the foreground a shield bearing the arms of the Earl of Stamford, Lord of the Manor: Barry of six pieces silver and azure; and below it his motto: *A ma puissance*—'According to my power.'

HAZEL GROVE AND BRAMHALL Urban District Council

The U.D.C. has not obtained arms, but has adopted a device consisting of a shield charged with a cross, in the first quarter a lion rampant, from the arms of the family of Bramhall; in the second and third quarters a sprig of hazel allusive to the name; and in the fourth a wheatsheaf from the arms of the Earldom of Chester (see Cheshire).

KNUTSFORD Urban District Council

The seal contains a representation of King Knut fording a stream.

NANTWICH Urban District Council

The U.D.C. uses the arms attributed to Malbank, or Malbanus, Barons of Nantwich (Wicus Malbanus) in the eleventh century: Quarterly gold and gules, a bendlet sable.

NORTHWICH Urban District Council

The seal of the U.D.C. bears the arms of the Earldom of Chester (see Chester) surrounded by a ribbon bearing the motto, *Sal est vita*, supported by a lion and a sea-wolf (presumably a variation of the Chester supporters) and ensigned by an earl's coronet, above which is placed as crest a steamship. The motto, 'Salt is life,' refers to the local salt industry.

SANDBACH Urban District Council

The Council uses the arms of the family of Sandbach: Azure, a gold fess between three gold wheatsheaves. These are a differenced form of the arms of the Earls of Chester.

WILMSLOW Urban District Council

ARMS: Argent, a bend between two bendlets wavy all azure, and on the bend three gold wheatsheaves.

CREST: On a wreath argent and azure, an antique crown of gold with a wreath of cotton round its base, and issuing from the crown a bear's head sable with a muzzle gules, on its neck a silver star.

MOTTO: *Nobis habitatio felix*—'A happy dwelling place for us.'

These were granted in 1951.

The arms are based on those of the old local family of Fitton—argent, on a bend azure

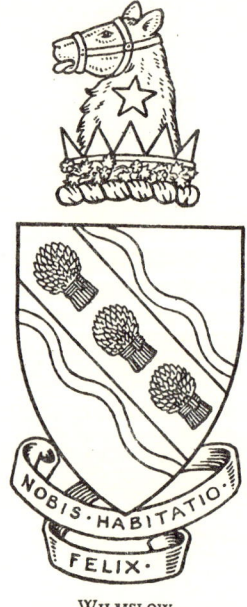

Wilmslow

Congleton R.D.C.

three gold wheatsheaves (derived from those of the Earldom of Chester)—to which are added the blue wavy bendlets alluding to the Rivers Bollin and Dean. In the crest, the bear's head of the Breretons is charged with a silver star from the Handforth arms, with reference to the families which held the manor of Handforth. The crown is from the insignia of the Greg family, who operated some of the earliest cotton mills at Styal.

CONGLETON Rural District Council

ARMS: Azure, a chevron argent between two gold wheatsheaves in chief and a crystal of rock salt proper in base, and on the chevron seven drops azure.

CREST: On a wreath argent and azure a silver wolf's head cut off at the neck, with a collar azure and hanging therefrom by a gold ring a shield argent charged with three bends wavy azure and a canton ermine.

MOTTO: *Rura mihi placent*—'Things of the countryside please me' (from Horace).

These were granted in 1951.

The wheatsheaves represent both the County and agriculture, and the crystal refers to the salt and chemical industries. The drops on the chevron allude to the River Dane. The wolf's head is the crest of the Wilbraham family, and the shield on it bears the Wilbraham arms, the blue wavy bends incidentally being a reminder of the water supply of the district initiated by a member of the family.

CORNWALL

Cornwall C.C.

CORNWALL

CORNWALL County Council

ARMS: Sable, fifteen golden roundels in rows of five, four, three, two, and one, within a bordure barry wavy of eight pieces argent and azure.

CREST: On a wreath argent and azure, a Cornish chough proper resting the right claw on a gold ducal coronet.

SUPPORTERS: Dexter, a fisherman holding a net over his right shoulder; and sinister, a miner resting his left hand on a sledge-hammer, both proper.

MOTTO: *One and All.*

These were granted in 1939.

The golden roundels (or bezants) are from the arms of the Duchy of Cornwall, to which the coronet also refers. The border is appropriate to a County which is almost surrounded by sea, and the supporters indicate its principal industries.

As emblems of Cornwall, the bezants originated in the arms of King John's second son, Richard, Earl of Cornwall and Count of Poictou. It has been conjectured that they represented peas (*poix*) in punning allusion to Poictou. However derived, the bezants have been associated with Cornwall for centuries, and occur in the arms of some Cornish families and towns, and also of other places connected with the Duchy, for example Lambeth.

TRURO

LAUNCESTON

TRURO City Council

ARMS: Gules, a gold three-masted ship of ancient type under sail on the sea, in which two fish are swimming proper.

SUPPORTERS: Dexter, a miner with a candle in his hat and a pick in his hand; and sinister, a fisherman holding a coil of rope, all proper.

MOTTO: *Exaltum cornu in Deo*—'The horn is exalted in God.'

The arms were recorded by the heralds in 1573; the supporters were granted in 1877, when Truro became a City. The emblems refer to the main industries of fishing and tin-mining.

BODMIN Borough Council

The seal bears the figure of a king enthroned.

FALMOUTH Borough Council

The seal bears a two-headed eagle with wings outspread, with a tower on each wing and a rock on the body. The eagle is from the arms of the family of Killigrew, which held the Manor of Arwenack of which the hamlets of Smithick and Pennycomequick formed part. The place received a charter of incorporation, together with the name Falmouth, in 1661. The towers stand for Pendennis Castle and St Mawes Castle, built in Tudor times to safeguard the harbour, and the rock represents the Black Rock.

CORNWALL

FOWEY Borough Council

The seal bears a shield with a ship on the sea.

HELSTON Borough Council

The seal bears the figure of St Michael (the town's patron) destroying the dragon. The Archangel stands between two domed octagonal towers with battlemented walls adjoining them. On his left arm he bears a shield charged with the three lions of England, in allusion to the fact that the place was anciently part of the royal domain and was constituted a free borough by King John.

LAUNCESTON Borough Council

ARMS: Gules, a gold castle of three tiers within a border azure charged with eight gold domed towers.

CREST: In a gold ducal coronet, a lion's head gules between two ostrich feathers argent.

BADGE: A gold castle.

The arms and crest were granted in 1573, and the badge in 1907.

Launceston Castle was the seat of the Plantagenet Earls of Cornwall, who are denoted by the lion's head. The ostrich feathers refer to the Duke of Cornwall (see Chapter II).

LISKEARD Borough Council

The seal bears a fleur-de-lis with two birds perched on it, facing one another, flanked by two feathers, and above the fleur-de-lis two rings. The feathers are from the insignia associated with the Heir Apparent, and the rings may be intended for golden roundels from the arms of the Duchy of Cornwall.

LOSTWITHIEL Borough Council

The seal bears a shield charged with a castle rising from water between two thistles; in the water are two fish. Lostwithiel grew up under the shadow of the neighbouring castle of Restormel.

PENRYN Borough Council

The seal bears a shield charged with a Saracen's head.

PENZANCE Borough Council

ARMS: Argent, a Paschal Lamb proper and in base a Maltese cross azure; a chief embattled azure and thereon to the dexter two gold keys crossed in saltire with wards upwards, in the centre a silver roundel charged with a dagger point downwards gules, and to the sinister a saltire argent with its limbs cut short.

CREST: Within a gold mural crown, an ancient ship with three masts under full sail, sinking by the stern, and with guns firing, all proper.

SUPPORTERS: Dexter, a pirate holding in his right hand a cutlass; and sinister, a fisherman with a net over his left arm, all proper.

PENZANCE

Motto: *Quod improbum terret probo prodest* (see below).

These were granted in 1934.

The Paschal Lamb, or *agnus Dei*, standing for Penzance and Gulval, was derived from the 'hot mark' on smelted tin used by the family of Bolitho which for many years had smelting works in Gulval parish. St Peter's keys, St Paul's sword, and St Andrew's saltire represent the parishes of Newlyn, Paul, and Mousehole, while the Maltese cross stands for Heamoor and Madron because the Knights of St John of Malta had a chapel there.

The vessel in the crest is intended for a pirate ship sinking into the crown of St Anthony, who erected a chapel on the site of the present St Anthony Gardens. This, with the pirate and the fisherman, refers to the town's maritime associations. The granting of a pirate as a supporter raises an interesting question of principle: should a lawless and disreputable character, however romantic in retrospect, be included in the tokens of honour granted to an authority whose business it is to maintain law and order? There needs to be some justification for such a departure, and Penzance produces it in the motto under the arms. This is extracted from the town's charter of 1614, which prescribes that Penzance shall be 'a vill of peace and quietness, *to the dread and terror of the bad and to the reward of the good*, and that our peace and other acts of justice and good government there may be the better kept and executed.'

Perhaps we must presume this heraldic pirate of Penzance to be a reformed character; in any case, we have W. S. Gilbert's authority that he and his fellows were 'all noblemen who have gone wrong.'

St Ives (Cornwall)

Saltash

ST IVES Borough Council

The Corporation has no arms, but uses as a device a shield overspread by ivy, allusive to the name.

SALTASH Borough Council

The Corporation has not obtained arms, but uses on its seal those of the ancient Earls of Cornwall, Lords of Saltash, namely: Silver, a lion rampant gules with a gold crown, within a border sable charged with eight gold roundels. The shield is ensigned by a prince's coronet and flanked by two ostrich feathers, emblems associated with the Heir Apparent (see Chapter II); in the base is water.

BUDE-STRATTON Urban District Council

ARMS: Argent, two bars wavy azure within a border sable charged with golden roundels; a chief gules charged with a silver cross formy between two gold clarions.

CREST: On a wreath argent and azure, in front of a golden sun a falcon standing on a gloved hand, the fingers to the sinister, all proper.

These were granted in 1947.

Within a border representing the County in which the District lies (see Cornwall C.C.) are two waves denoting its coastal situation, and also referring to the probable derivation of Bude from a British river name. The silver field alludes to the family of Blanchminster, and the clarions are from the arms of the Grenville family. The cross formy is selected from the shield of Sir John Berkeley, who was created Baron Berkeley of Stratton for his part in the battle of Stamford Hill in 1643. The falcon is the crest of the Acland family who in 1939 presented their cliff lands to the public, while the sun stands for the District's reputation as a health and holiday resort.

BUDE-STRATTON   NEWQUAY

NEWQUAY Urban District Council

ARMS: Gold, a saltire azure charged with four silver herrings facing one another.

CREST: On a wreath gold and azure, a block of granite with a ring and thereon a bollard with a Cornish chough perched on it, all proper.

MOTTO: *Ro an mor*—'Gift of the sea.'

These were granted in 1951.

The herrings represent the fishing industry, the granite block stands for local stone, the bollard alludes to the harbour, and the Cornish chough is the County emblem.

The motto is in the old Cornish language.

ST AUSTELL Urban District Council

The Council has not obtained arms, but uses: Silver, a saltire raguly gules. In Burke's *General Armory* these are given as the arms of Austell, sheriff of Cornwall *temp.* Edward III and Henry VI.

CUMBERLAND C.C.

CUMBERLAND

CUMBERLAND County Council

ARMS: Parted fesswise wavy vert and barry wavy of six pieces argent and azure, in chief three Parnassus flowers proper.

CREST: Issuing from a gold mural crown, a wreath consisting of oak, with acorns, on the dexter side, and ash on the sinister side, and in front of it a pick and shepherd's crook crossed saltirewise, and perched upon the crown a curlew, all proper.

SUPPORTERS: Dexter, a representation of the Dacre bull at Naworth, gules with gold horns and hoofs, with a gold collar about its neck and therefrom a gold chain turned over its back; and sinister, a roebuck gules with gold antlers and hoofs.

MOTTO: *Perfero*—'I carry through.'

These were granted in 1951.

The arms represent the natural features of the County, the flowers referring to the grass of Parnassus which grows on the marshy uplands, while the base of the shield stands for the rivers, lakes, and seaboard. The pick and crook allude to mining and sheep-rearing, and the curlew is a bird common in the uplands of the County. The bull of the ancient Cumberland family of Dacre is an historic emblem associated particularly with the old Border warfare, and the roebuck is traditional to the County. The supporters are shown standing on a masoned base representing Hadrian's Wall.

Carlisle

CARLISLE City and County Borough Council

ARMS: Gold, a cross formy gules and four red roses; on the cross a gold rose with seeds and sepals proper. Above the shield is placed a gold mural crown in the form of a castle, its gateway azure and its lining gules.

SUPPORTERS: Two wyverns gules, the wings strewn with golden roses, their sepals proper.

MOTTO: *Be just and fear not.*

The arms were registered at the College of Arms in 1924, but were in use for many years before that date.

The fact that Sir William de Carlyell, of Cumberland, in the reign of Edward II, bore a red cross patonce on gold may have given rise to the old device on which the present arms are based. Possibly the red roses refer to Carlisle's Lancastrian sympathies during the Wars of the Roses. The golden rose is an old royal badge; and the red wyverns, like the red dragons of Appleby, recall the British Kingdom of Cumbria (see Chapter II).

WHITEHAVEN Borough Council

The Corporation has no arms but makes use of those of Lowther, Earl of Lonsdale: Gold, six annulets sable; with his crest: a silver dragon. The Corporation differences the arms by adding a silver border, and places beneath them the motto, *Consilio absit discordia*—'Let discord be absent from counsel.'

WORKINGTON

WORKINGTON Borough Council

ARMS: Sable, two piles or, scattered with billets azure, and in the base a gold wheatsheaf.

CREST: On a wreath or and sable, a gold mural crown and issuing therefrom a silver unicorn's head holding in its mouth an anchor sable.

SUPPORTERS: Dexter, Vulcan with hammer and anvil all proper; and sinister, Themis, wearing a blue robe and having in her right hand a cornucopia and in her left hand a pair of scales, all proper.

MOTTO: *Levavi oculos meos in montes*—'I lifted up mine eyes unto the hills.'

These were granted in 1950.

The black field is for coal, the wheatsheaf for agriculture, and the blue billets for steel. The piles, forming the initial letter W, are gold for the prosperity derived from these industries. The crest is that of the Curwen family, to which has been added an anchor denoting Workington's maritime associations. Vulcan is the god of metal workers, and Themis is the classical personification of civic rule.

KESWICK Urban District Council

The seal bears a view of mountains with the motto: *Montes unde auxilium meum*—'The hills whence cometh my help' (from Psalm cxxi).

PENRITH

PENRITH *Urban District Council*

ARMS: Parted chevronwise azure and gules; issuing from the point of the chevron rays of the sun between two sheaves of corn all gold; in base a castle with three towers or.

CREST: On a wreath gold and azure, a silver saltire edged with azure encircled by an ancient crown of gold.

MOTTO: *Fide et fortitudine*—'By faith and fortitude.'

These were granted in 1952.

The shield represents Penrith Castle, anciently a royal residence, on the hill of red sandstone from which the name Penrith (red hill) is thought to be derived; while the flames represent the beacon pike at the top of Beacon Hill. The sheaves stand for agriculture. The saltire of St Andrew alludes both to the dedication of the parish church and to the fact that the district was once included in the Scottish Kingdom of Strathclyde, and the crown is that of the English Kings.

DENBIGHSHIRE

COLWYN BAY WREXHAM WREXHAM R.D.C.

DENBIGHSHIRE

DENBIGHSHIRE County Council

The seal of the Denbighshire C.C. contains a lion rampant, the same emblem which appears on a shield (with other devices) on the seal of Denbigh. The motto is, *Duw a Digon*—'With God, enough.' In each case the lion seems to be that of Henry de Lacy, Earl of Lincoln, who built Denbigh Castle as part of Edward I's scheme of fortresses to keep the newly won principality in subjection.

COLWYN BAY Borough Council

ARMS: Argent, on a mount vert an oak-tree proper with gold acorns, and on a chief parted palewise or and gules a lion passant guardant counter-changed.

CREST: On a wreath argent and vert, a demi-dragon gules holding between its claws a man's head in profile, cut off at the neck, argent.

MOTTO: *Iechyd, harddwch, heddwch*—'Health, beauty, and tranquillity.'

These were granted in 1934, when Colwyn Bay became a borough.

The oak-tree is from the device formerly used by the Urban District Council. The lion is derived from the arms of the Principality of Wales, which are those of Prince Llewelyn, with whom the district has historic associations. The Welsh dragon, on a wreath of the Tudor livery colours, bears a Saxon's head from the arms of Ednyfed Fychan, who displayed three heads in his shield in token of his victories against the English army under Ranulph, Earl of Chester. It is perhaps well for Colwyn Bay that heraldry is not now taken too seriously, or the townsfolk might find their crest discouraging to the English invaders whom they now wish to attract.

(For notes on the arms of Wales and the Welsh dragon, see Chapter II.)

DENBIGH Borough Council

The seal bears a castle rising in three tiers; in the gateway is a lion's face with a fleur-de-lis issuing from the mouth; on a mount in front of the castle lies a greyhound; on one side of the castle is a shield bearing the Royal Arms of France and England quarterly, and on the other is a shield bearing a lion rampant—probably that of Henry de Lacy, Earl of Lincoln, builder of the castle in Edward I's reign (see Denbighshire); above each shield is a plume of ostrich feathers within a coronet, the badge of the Princes of Wales.

RUTHIN Borough Council

The seal bears a castle, presumably representing the *rhudd ddin*, or red castle, from which the town derived its name.

WREXHAM Borough Council

ARMS: Ermine, two gold croziers saltirewise; the chief dancetty and parted palewise gules and gold, and thereon two lions passant guardant counter-changed.

CREST: On a wreath argent and gules, a dragon gules standing on a mount vert and supporting a gold shield charged with the astronomical symbol for Mars, sable.

MOTTO: *Fear God, honour the King.*

These were granted in 1857.

I am informed by the Borough Librarian that

one crozier represents Wrexham Abbot, which part formerly belonged to Valle Crucis Abbey. The other signifies the grazing land around Wrexham. Sir Leonard Rowland told me that his father, Thomas Rowland, who was Mayor in 1868, had much to do with this design, and that the wool sales which were then one of the principal industries of this place were represented by the other shepherd's crook.

The lions are from the arms of Wales, and the dragon is the Welsh national emblem (see Chapter II). The symbol for Mars indicates that Wrexham is a mining centre.

WREXHAM Rural District Council

ARMS: Vert, two gold croziers crossed saltirewise, between a bull's face proper in chief and another in base, and to dexter and sinister a gold lozenge charged with another sable.

CREST: On a wreath gold and vert, an oak-tree proper with gold acorns and in front of it a dragon passant gules resting its right foreclaw on an escutcheon gules masoned argent.

MOTTO: *Suum cuique tribuere*—'To assign to each his own.'

These were granted in 1948.

The croziers, which also appear in the arms of the Borough of Wrexham, refer to Valle Crucis Abbey and to grazing land in the district. The bulls' heads represent stock raising, and the black and gold lozenges symbolize coal mining and mineral wealth. In the crest, the Welsh dragon stands in front of a tree alluding to forestry, and supports a shield bearing an heraldic representation of a brick wall referring to building.

DERBYSHIRE

Derbyshire C.C.

DERBYSHIRE

DERBYSHIRE County Council

ARMS: Or, a rose gules surmounted by another argent, each with seeds and sepals proper; on a chief sable three silver stags' faces with antlers.

MOTTO: *Bene consulendo*—'By good counsel.'

These arms were granted in 1937.

The Tudor rose has been an emblem of the County for many years, having appeared on an unofficial device which preceded the grant of arms. The stags' heads are from the arms of the Duke of Devonshire.

Derby

DERBY County Borough Council

ARMS: Argent, on a mount vert within park palings, a stag lodged between two oak-trees, all proper.

CREST: On a wreath argent and vert, a ram passant proper with a gold collar, between two sprigs of broom also proper.

SUPPORTERS: Two stags, each charged on the shoulder with a sprig of broom proper.

MOTTO: *Industria, virtus et fortitudo*—'Diligence, courage, and strength.'

These were granted in 1939.

The stag lodged (i.e. at rest) amid palings, locally known as 'the buck in the park,' has been a badge of the Corporation from time immemorial, and may have been derived from Richard II's badge of a white hart. It has now been given the status of arms, with the addition of supporting stags and the crest of a Derby ram. The broom (*planta genista*) represents the Plantagenet kings from whom Derby received its early charters.

BUXTON Borough Council

ARMS: Vert, a gold serpent entwining a gold rod, encircled by eight heraldic fountains (i.e. roundels barry wavy argent and azure).

CREST: On a wreath or and vert, a buck at gaze proper, standing upon a rock.

MOTTO: *Benedicite fontes Domino*—'O all ye springs, bless ye the Lord.'

These were granted in 1917.

The fountains stand for Buxton's eight thermal springs, and the Rod of Aesculapius indicates their healing properties.

The buck is both allusive to the name and commemorative of the Dukes of Devonshire, to whom the town owes much of its development.

BUXTON

CHESTERFIELD Borough Council

The seal bears a pomegranate-tree decoratively treated. This emblem was in use by Chesterfield in the reign of Elizabeth I, and may have been derived from the pomegranate of Granada which Henry VIII had adopted as a badge on his marriage with Katherine of Aragon; he combined it with the Tudor rose. It has, however, been claimed that the pomegranate as the device of Chesterfield was in use long before Tudor times. In the seventeenth century it was discarded in favour of arms: Gules, on a gold fess a lozenge azure; but the pomegranate was restored to the Corporation seal in 1893.

DERBYSHIRE

CHESTERFIELD

ILKESTON

GLOSSOP

GLOSSOP Borough Council

ARMS: Silver, a red rose with seeds and sepals proper between three cross-crosslets pointed at the foot gules, and above the rose a mural crown gules.

MOTTO: *Virtus Veritas Libertas*—'Virtue, Truth, and Freedom.'

These were granted in 1919.

The rose is that of the Duchy of Lancaster, within which Glossop lies, though geographically in Derbyshire. The crosslets are from the arms of the Howard family.

ILKESTON Borough Council

ARMS: Silver, a saltire sable; above and below it a cotton hank, and on either side a left-hand glove, all proper; and on the saltire the astronomical symbol for Mars, gold; on a chief azure a piece of Maltese lace argent.

CREST: On a wreath argent and sable, a bear's head holding in the mouth a miner's safety-lamp proper, and charged on the neck with the astronomical symbol for Mars, sable.

MOTTO: *Labor omnia vincit*—'Labour overcomes all things.'

These were granted in 1887.

The emblems refer to local industries, the symbol for Mars standing for iron.

BELPER Urban District Council

The seal bears the arms of France Ancient and England quarterly, with a label. These are presumably the arms of John of Gaunt, Duke of Lancaster, who is said to have had a residence at Belper; the label should therefore be ermine.

LONG EATON Urban District Council

The seal bears a hart lodged in a field ringed by palings, derived from the County insignia.

MATLOCK Urban District Council

The Manor of Matlock was successively held by Edward the Confessor and the Norman kings, the Ferrers Earls of Derby, and the Earls and Dukes of Lancaster. The last ducal holder was King Charles I, in whose reign the manor was sold to the City of London. The seal of the Council summarizes this history. On a ground of vaire, from the Ferrers arms, are set the cross patonce and five doves of the Confessor, surmounted by a horseshoe (also from the Ferrers insignia), and a headsman's axe in token of Charles I. Above is a coronet and thereon a lion bi-corporate (i.e. having two bodies with one head between them) holding a shield bearing the arms of the City of London.

NEW MILLS Urban District Council

The device consists of a hart within park palings, from the County insignia.

SWADLINCOTE Urban District Council

ARMS: Quarterly ermine and gules, a cross quarterly counter-changed between in the first and fourth quarters a Tudor rose with seeds and sepals proper, and in the second and third quarters a fleur-de-lis argent, the whole within a bordure vairy ermine and gules.

CREST: On a wreath argent and gules, issuing from flames proper rising from a mount sable, a forearm proper holding in the hand a gold billet fesswise.

MOTTO: *E terra divitiae*—'From the earth, riches.'

These were granted in 1947.

WIRKSWORTH Urban District Council

The seal is parted palewise and bears on the dexter side a crown with a rose above it, and on the sinister side a group of miner's tools.

BLACKWELL Rural District Council

ARMS: Argent, a spade and pickaxe crossed saltirewise, hafts upwards, proper, within an orle of roundels sable; on a chief sable, three silver stags' faces with antlers.

CREST: On a wreath argent and sable, a left arm bent at the elbow, the hand holding a Davy safety-lamp, all proper.

MOTTO: *Lux et humanitas.*

These were granted in 1942.

The arms and crest combine emblems of the coal-mining industry with the stags' heads from the arms of the Duke of Devonshire, Lord of the Manor of Hardwick, which are also borne by the Derbyshire C.C.

Blackwell R.D.C.

Swadlincote

Shardlow R.D.C.

SHARDLOW *Rural District Council*

ARMS: Vert, a gold chevron between in chief two gold wheatsheaves and in base a roundel barry wavy argent and azure, and on the chevron four annulets sable.

CREST: On a wreath gold and vert, a tower azure rising from a circlet of eight gold roundels (five visible).

MOTTO: *Quanti est sapere*—'How great it is to be wise.'

These were granted in 1952.

The wheatsheaves stand for agriculture; the chevron (suggesting a roof) for housing; and the annulets for the iron pipe industry. The roundel, or heraldic fountain, represents water supply and public services. The tower is from the crest of the Earl of Harrington, and the golden roundels represent the wealth which the local industries produce.

Devon C.C.

DEVONSHIRE

DEVON County Council

ARMS: Argent, a lion rampant gules with a golden crown; a chief wavy parted fesswise azure and barry wavy silver and azure, and thereon an ancient ship, also silver.

MOTTO: *Auxilio Divino*—'By Divine aid.'

These arms were granted in 1926.

The lion is that of Richard Plantagenet, Earl of Cornwall (younger brother of Henry III), and his son, Edmund, Earl of Cornwall. Its presence in these arms, and as the crest of Exeter, is a reminder that the influence and possessions of the ancient Earls of Cornwall were wider than the territory from which they took their title. The crowned lion denoted their royal descent.

The ship represents Devon's seafaring tradition, and is perhaps intended for the *Golden Hind*, in which Sir Francis Drake sailed round the world; for the motto is that of Drake, who bore it in conjunction with the crest of a ship on a globe around which it is being drawn by a cable held by the hand of God issuing from a cloud. The ship in the Devon arms is generally represented as having only one mast and sail, with a pennon at the mast-head, and a flag at poop and stern; but as the details are not laid down in the official description of the arms, I have felt at liberty to illustrate it as a three-masted ship rigged as Drake's may have been.

EXETER

EXETER City and County Borough Council

ARMS: Parted palewise gules and sable, a gold triangular castle with three towers.

CREST: On a wreath or and sable, a demi-lion rampant gules wearing a gold crown and carrying a golden orb with a band azure.

SUPPORTERS: Two silver winged horses, their wings charged with three bars wavy azure and their manes and hoofs gold.

MOTTO: *Semper fidelis*—'Ever faithful.'

BADGE: In front of two gold swords crossed saltirewise, their points upwards, a red Tudor hat with gold embroidery.

The arms were confirmed, and the crest and supporters granted in 1564; the badge was granted in 1907.

The lion is that of Richard, Earl of Cornwall (see Devon C.C.), who was elected King of the Romans, in token of which the lion bears the orb. Richard was granted by Henry III the City and Castle of Exeter as an appendage to the Earldom of Cornwall. The castle in the arms is that called Rougemont, and possibly the red of the field is an allusion to its name. The significance of the supporters is obscure, but the wavy blue bars on their wings suggest that they are intended to refer to the River Exe.

PLYMOUTH

PLYMOUTH City and County Borough Council

ARMS: Argent, a saltire vert between four towers sable.

CREST: In a naval crown azure a gold lion's paw holding an anchor gules.

SUPPORTERS: Two gold lions reguardant, each with a naval crown azure about its neck, and hanging therefrom by a red ribbon a medallion gules charged with a silver boar's head.

MOTTO: *Turris fortissima est nomen Jehovae*—'The name of Jehovah is the strongest tower' (from the Proverbs of Solomon).

The arms are on record at the Heralds' College. The crest and supporters were granted in 1931, before which date two gold lions were used, without authority, to support the shield.

The saltire is that of St Andrew, to whom the mother church of Plymouth is dedicated. The towers represent the fortifications, and the naval crowns and anchor the associations of the City with the senior Service. The anchor is taken from the crest of neighbouring Devonport, and the boars' heads are from the arms of the Mount Edgcumbe family, who held the Manor of East Stonehouse. The heraldry of Plymouth thus includes emblems of the 'Three Towns.' The supporters are national symbols.

BARNSTAPLE Borough Council

ARMS: Gules, a silver castle.

These are recorded at the College of Arms

Barnstaple Castle was built by Juhell of Totnes in the reign of William the Conqueror. The town is said to have been fortified by earthworks as early as the time of Athelstan.

BARNSTAPLE

BIDEFORD

DARTMOUTH

BIDEFORD Borough Council

ARMS: Silver, over water in the base a stone bridge of three arches proper masoned with gold, and passing through the middle arch an ancient ship, the mast rising behind the bridge, also proper; and on a chief gules three gold clarions.

CREST: An Elizabethan ship in full sail proper, the centre sail charged with a gold clarion.

MOTTO: *Pro Rege ac Fide audax*—'Bold for King and Faith.'

These were granted in 1936.

The arms are based on an old seal, dated 1577, the central feature being a portion of the important bridge of twenty-four arches which spans the Torridge and links the two parts of the town. The clarions (or heraldic organs) are from the arms of Sir Richard Grenville, a native of Bideford, whose last fight in the *Revenge*, and the part played therein by 'men of Bideford in Devon,' was nobly sung by Lord Tennyson. This is recalled by the crest, standing for Bideford's seafaring traditions, and also by the motto.

DARTMOUTH Borough Council

ARMS: Gules, in the base barry wavy argent and azure, and thereon a gold ship's hull in which is a king, crowned, robed, and holding a sceptre, between two lions guardant seated on the bow and the stern, their breasts towards the king, all gold.

These are recorded at the College of Arms. They are based on an ancient seal of the Corporation.

The king is believed to be Edward III, who granted the town a charter. The arms bear a general resemblance to his gold noble, in which he was represented as 'Lord of the Sea'; and they serve as a reminder that Dartmouth furnished ships for his French wars.

On the seal, and in some representations of the arms, a crescent and star are placed on either side of the king's head. These were originally crusading emblems (see Chapter II), and are held to refer to the fact that Richard I's host sailed from Dartmouth for the Holy Land; but this may be a chance allusion, for these emblems passed into general usage and are found in the arms of many towns which have no crusading associations.

GREAT TORRINGTON *Borough Council*

ARMS: Silver, in the base two bars wavy azure, and over all a fleur-de-lis within a border engrailed sable.

These arms, based on the device on a fifteenth-century seal of the Corporation, were recorded by the heralds in 1564. The wavy bars refer to the River Torridge. The fleur-de-lis was probably derived from the Royal Arms. The engrailing of the border is traceable to decorative work on the seal.

HONITON *Borough Council*

The seal bears a hand above two half-length human figures, one robed and the other unclad; below is a spray of honeysuckle. The figures probably represent the baptism of Christ, and may have been placed in the seal in allusion to St John the Baptist, patron of wool merchants, who formerly flourished at Honiton. The honeysuckle is a play on the name of the town.

OKEHAMPTON *Borough Council*

The Corporation has not obtained arms, but use is made of the following: Checky gold and azure, two silver bars; with the crest of a castle with three towers.

SOUTH MOLTON *Borough Council*

The Corporation uses a device consisting of a crown, a fleece (in allusion to the woollen industry), and a mitre, with the motto: *Fiat iustitia*—'Let justice be done.'

TIVERTON *Borough Council*

The Corporation has no arms. The seal bears a representation of St Peter's Church and the remnant of the Castle which neighbours it. Below is a line of houses with a bridge over water at each end, representing the town's main features. In the base of the shield is a woolpack, standing for the ancient woollen industry.

DEVONSHIRE

GREAT TORRINGTON   TORQUAY   TOTNES

TORQUAY Borough Council

ARMS: Ermine, three bends azure, and thereon a three-masted ship in full sail proper with flags gules; on a chief wavy gules two wings argent and between them a silver pale charged with a castellated gateway on a mound proper.

CREST: On a wreath argent and azure, a rock, and thereon a gull proper supporting an anchor sable with a gold cable.

MOTTO: *Salus et Felicitas*—'Health and Happiness.'

These were granted in 1893.

TOTNES Borough Council

ARMS: Sable, a silver castle with a round central tower between two silver keys.

These were recorded by the heralds in 1560. The castle was founded by one Juhell, a Breton, shortly after the Conquest.

ASHBURTON Urban District Council

The fourteenth-century seal bears a representation of the chapel of the Chantry of St Lawrence, founded in 1314 by Bishop Stapleton of Exeter. On one side is a teazle, alluding to the woollen industry, and on the other is a cross of St Andrew in reference to the dedication of the parish church. Above are the sun and the moon, which are stated by Mr Gale Pedrick (*Borough Seals*) to be 'old Phoenician emblems' and 'are held to indicate the Stannary rights'; but in view of the frequency of these symbols in civic seals, they probably have the same significance in that of Ashburton as in so many others, and are tokens of royalty (see Chapter II).

AXMINSTER Urban District Council

ARMS: Parted saltirewise gules and azure, an orb between two battle-axes erect, their blades inwards, and in base a shuttle, all gold.

CREST: On a wreath or and gules, a mount vert and thereon a minster proper.

MOTTO: *Steadfast and faithful.*

These were granted in 1945.

The field and orb are from the arms attributed to King Athelstan, and the battle-axes allude to the Battle of Brunanburgh in 938, after which Athelstan endowed the Church at Axminster with lands so that prayers might be offered up for the souls of his earls who had been slain. The axes are also a play on the name. The shuttle refers to the carpets which take their name from the town where they were formerly made; and the crest symbolizes the ancient minster round which the town grew up.

AXMINSTER   EXMOUTH

EXMOUTH Urban District Council

ARMS: Silver, two anchors crossed saltirewise gules between four fish naiant azure, and on a chief azure ten ancient ships in full sail argent, placed in two rows of five.

CREST: Rising from a silver mural crown, two *Magnoliae grandiflorae Exmouthiensis* proper, and between them a gold tower with a flagstaff and thereon a white flag charged with a red cross, flying to the sinister.

MOTTO: *Mare ditat flores decorant*—'The sea enriches and the flowers adorn.'

MANTLING: Azure and argent.

These were granted in 1947.

DEVONSHIRE

I am indebted to the Clerk to the Council for the following note:

The anchors are naval emblems, and indicate the town's association with the Royal Navy, while the fish denote the town's connection with the fishing industry. Ten ancient ships in full sail are depicted on a chief azure to commemorate the fact that in 1346 ten ships and 193 seamen were contributed from Exmouth to the fleet which, under Edward III, set out for the siege of Calais. As to the crest, out of a mural crown rises a tower or fort, which commemorates the fact that in 1646 a fort at the mouth of the Exe was defended from 7th February to 15th March, when on account of naval pressure the defenders had to surrender to Colonel Shapcote with 13 pieces of iron ordnance, 72 muskets, and 12 barrels of powder. From the flag-pole of the fort flies the banner of St George. On each side of the tower is depicted the flower and leaves of the magnolia; this commemorates the fact that Sir John Colleton, Bart (who died in 1754, is buried at Withycombe Raleigh School Burial Ground, and was the owner of Rill Manor), grew this beautiful flower at Exmouth for the first time in England, and called it *Magnolia grandiflora Exmouthiensis*.

ILFRACOMBE

NEWTON ABBOT

ILFRACOMBE *Urban District Council*

The U.D.C. has adopted a device consisting of a quartered shield; the first quarter black, a silver fess between three silver battle-axes erect, with red hafts, for the family of Wrey; the second silver with six single-masted ships, representing the six ships which Ilfracombe provided for Edward III's French wars; the third silver, a red engrailed cross between four black water budgets, for the family of Bourchier; and the fourth silver, three blue wavy bars and an oar lying in bend sinister, from the seal of the old Local Board of Health. The shield is flanked by two dolphins, head downwards, and beneath is the motto: *Ilfracombe potens salubritate*—'Ilfracombe strong for health.' The Wrey and Bourchier quarters represent the Bourchier-Wrey family, formerly Lords of the Manor.

NEWTON ABBOT *Urban District Council*

The device consists of two shields placed side by side, one blue with a gold mitre flanked by two gold croziers, a silver fleece with a red band in chief, and a silver tower in base; the other red with three silver tuns.

PAIGNTON

SIDMOUTH

PAIGNTON Urban District Council

ARMS: Barry wavy of six pieces argent and azure, a representation of the Coverdale Tower or.

CREST: On a wreath argent and azure, a dolphin swimming proper in front of a gold mitre.

MOTTO: *Semper acceptus*—'Ever welcome.'

These were granted in 1947.

Against a background representing the sea is the tower of the episcopal palace built by Osbertus, first Norman Bishop of Exeter, and last occupied by Bishop Miles Coverdale, the translator of the Bible into English. The mitre alludes to the fact that the Manor of Paignton belonged to the See of Exeter, and the dolphin is symbolic of the merchant venturers of Devon.

SIDMOUTH Urban District Council

ARMS: Gules, on water barry wavy argent and azure a gold dragon-ship, sail set and oars in action; on a chief argent a cross gules with its limbs cut short between two fleurs-de-lis azure.

CREST: On a wreath or and gules, a demi-lion gules issuing from water barry wavy argent and azure, holding in the forepaws a sun or.

These were granted in 1949.

DEVONSHIRE

The dragon-ship, telling of Sidmouth's long seafaring history, is on a red ground representing the red cliffs of Devon rising from the sea. In the crest the red lion of Devon is accompanied by tokens of sea and sunshine. The cross of St George and fleurs-de-lis are from the arms of Edward, Duke of Kent, who had a house at Sidmouth where his daughter, Queen Victoria, spent part of her childhood. The fleurs-de-lis also stand for the floral beauties of the town's gardens and pleasure grounds.

TAVISTOCK Urban District Council

Arms are not recorded at the Heralds' College but the following are used: Parted palewise gules and azure, a golden fleece, and in chief a lion passant guardant and a fleur-de-lis, both gold. In the *General Armory*, Burke quotes in chief a lion between two fleurs-de-lis. The fleece refers to the ancient woollen industry; the lion and fleur-de-lis are royal emblems.

TAVISTOCK

TEIGNMOUTH

TEIGNMOUTH Urban District Council

The device embodies a shield charged with a saltire between four fleurs-de-lis, their heads pointing towards the centre. In the *Book of Public Arms*, Fox-Davies quotes the following unofficial arms: 'Argent, a saltire engrailed gules between four fleurs-de-lis, each pointing outwards (either azure or gules).'

West Teignmouth was held as a mesne borough by the Dean and Chapter of Exeter, and the device was probably suggested by the arms used by the officers of the See; the Chancellor bears a saltire between four cross-crosslets, the Treasurer an engrailed saltire between four leopards' faces, and the Precentor a saltire charged with a fleur-de-lis.

Dorset C.C.

DORSET

DORSET County Council

ARMS: Argent, three lions passant guardant in pale and in base a fleur-de-lis all gules. Above the shield is placed a gold mural crown with towers.

SUPPORTERS: Two gold dragons with wings spread, each with a Saxon crown gules about its neck.

MOTTO: *Who's afear'd?*

These were granted in 1950.

Before the arms were obtained, the seal of the County Council displayed three lions passant guardant not set upon a shield. These were probably derived from the old seal of Dorchester which bore the royal arms of England.

The dragons recall the Saxon kingdom of Wessex.

BLANDFORD FORUM Borough Council

The seal contains the Royal Arms of England with a label, placed between two ostrich feathers and the letters 'D L.' The label is omitted in some representations. The letters are said to stand for the Duchy of Lancaster, to which the Manor of Blandford formerly appertained.

DORSET

BLANDFORD FORUM   BRIDPORT

BRIDPORT *Borough Council*

ARMS: Gules, a silver castle with two towers rising from water (represented by barry wavy argent and azure); over each tower a gold fleur-de-lis, and between them a gold lion passant guardant crowned; and in the portway of the castle three spinning cogs.

These are based on a seal recorded at the College of Arms.

DORCHESTER

DORCHESTER *Borough Council*

The Corporation uses as a device that which appears on a fourteenth-century seal, namely a castle with three towers, and in front of it the Royal Arms as they were used from 1340 until about 1405, namely France Ancient and England quarterly; the quarters of France containing an indefinite number of fleurs-de-lis instead of only three as in the 'Modern' form.

Lyme Regis

Poole

Shaftesbury

LYME REGIS Borough Council

Arms are not officially recorded, but the following are used: Argent, two bars wavy azure, on a chief gules a lion passant guardant or. I am informed that these date from the seventeenth century. The lion refers to the second part of the name, which the town acquired when, in the fourteenth century, one of its three manors passed into the possession of the Crown. The wavy bars indicate the town's seaboard position.

POOLE Borough Council

ARMS: Barry wavy of eight pieces sable and gold, a silver dolphin embowed, its tongue gules; and on a chief wavy argent three escallop shells sable.

CREST: On a wreath sable and gold, a mermaid supporting with her right hand an anchor with cable but no beam, all proper, and holding in her left hand a roundel sable.

MOTTO: *Ad morem villae de Poole*—'According to the custom of the Town of Poole.'

The arms, recorded at the Heralds' College, were confirmed in 1948, when the crest, formerly used without authority, was granted.

SHAFTESBURY Borough Council

Arms are not officially recorded, but the following have been used since at latest 1570: Quarterly argent and azure, a cross counter-changed; in the first and fourth quarters a fleur-de-lis azure, and in the second and third a gold lion's face.

The charges and their arrangement suggest that they were derived from the Royal Arms of the Tudors, one of the two manors into which the place was anciently divided having been held by the Crown.

WAREHAM

WEYMOUTH AND MELCOMBE REGIS

WAREHAM Borough Council

The Corporation has not obtained arms, but the Borough has been credited with the following: Gules, a crescent with a star between the horns, between three fleurs-de-lis upside down, all gold.

These seem to have originated in a seal bearing royal emblems. (The fleur-de-lis and star and crescent are dealt with in Chapter II.) There is a tradition in the town that the fleurs-de-lis were reversed by order of Queen Elizabeth I as a mark of her displeasure that the Mayor failed to have bells rung when she passed through Wareham: a pretty story, but the probability is that the reversal of the fleurs-de-lis was due merely to the whim of a seal engraver.

WEYMOUTH AND MELCOMBE REGIS Borough Council

ARMS: Azure, on waves of the sea a gold three-masted ship with sails furled; on the foremast a square banner parted palewise gules and vert and charged with three gold lions of England; on the mizzen, a square banner quarterly, the first and fourth quarters silver with a purple lion rampant, and the second and third gules with a gold tower with three turrets; on the side of the ship is a shield parted fesswise gold and gules, in chief three chevrons gules and in base three gold lions of England.

These were granted in 1592.

The arms on the banners are (with slight variations of colour) those of Edward I, from whom Melcombe Regis received its first Charter, and his queen, Eleanor of Castile, who held the manor. (The lion and castle are allusive to Leon and Castile.) The chevrons on the shield are those of Gilbert de Clare, Earl of Gloucester, who held the Manor of Weymouth in the thirteenth century.

Durham C.C.

Durham City

DURHAM

DURHAM County Council

For more than seven centuries, closing in 1836, the County of Durham lay under the palatinate jurisdiction of the Bishops of Durham, and it is therefore natural to find the County making use of the arms of the See: Azure, a gold cross and four gold lions. These arms appear on the seal of the Durham C.C.

The See appears to have derived them from the traditional arms of its reputed founder, the Saint-King Oswald (605–42). Oswald was one of those historic personages for whom arms were devised centuries after their death. In assigning him a cross, the medieval heralds clearly intended to mark his work for the spread of Christianity in Northumbria. They probably added the lions to denote Deira, the southern part of the Northumbrian kingdom, to which they had attributed a lion perhaps out of compliment to the great family of Percy.

These arms may be compared with those of Oswestry (Shropshire) which also commemorate King Oswald.

DURHAM City Council

Arms: Sable, a cross argent charged with another cross gules.

These are recorded at the College of Arms.

Durham owes its origin to the monks who, late in the tenth century, founded the Church to contain the shrine of St Cuthbert. It is natural, therefore, that the arms of the City should be of a religious character. The habit of the Benedictine monks who were installed in the present Cathedral (begun in 1093) consisted of a white cassock and a black cloak, and this may have suggested the tinctures of the City arms, the red cross being added as the emblem of the national patron.

DURHAM

DARLINGTON County Borough Council

The Corporation has not obtained arms, but has adopted a silver shield with a red chevron charged with three woolpacks; above the chevron is a representation of 'Locomotion No. 1,' the first locomotive that ran on a public railway, which is preserved at Darlington Station; below the chevron is the head of a shorthorn. The crest is a hand grasping a pickaxe, and the motto is *Floreat Industria*.

GATESHEAD County Borough Council

ARMS: Silver, in the base water, and therefrom rising a gateway tower sable between two crosses of St Cuthbert azure.

CREST: On a wreath silver and azure, a goat's head torn off at the neck, argent with gold horns, and about the neck a ribbon from which hangs a portcullis sable.

These were granted in 1932.

The Corporation formerly used an unauthorized device consisting of an embattled gate on a silver shield, with a goat's head for crest, and the motto, *Caput inter nubila condit* —'The head is set amongst the clouds' (Virgil, *Aeneid* iv. 177, and x. 767).

The arms preserve the features of the former device and comprise a double play on the name. The goat's head refers to the old derivation of the name Gateshead, rendered by the Venerable Bede as *ad caput capreae*, while the gateway tower indicates its modern interpretation. The portcullis is an heraldic difference, probably chosen as an allusion to the first syllable of the name. The water indicates the town's situation on the River Tyne, and the crosses denote that it was anciently part of the Palatine of Durham and therefore under the patronage of St Cuthbert.

GATESHEAD

SOUTH SHIELDS County Borough Council

The Corporation has not obtained arms, but has adopted a device consisting of a shield showing a lifeboat, manned, and in the chief the words 'Always Ready.' This is supported by a sailor, shown holding sometimes a telescope and sometimes a sextant; and a woman in a white robe and gold mural crown holding a caduceus, the staff of Mercury, god of commerce. From behind the shield appear two Union Jacks, and above them is a black anchor with a cable. Below the shield is the date 1850, and the motto, *Courage, Humanity, Commerce*.

Following the wreck of the *Adventure*, of Newcastle, in 1789, a meeting was held at South Shields, as a result of which a prize was offered for the best model of a lifeboat. The prize was awarded, and the order given, to Henry Greathead of South Shields, who thus became the pioneer of lifeboat building.

SUNDERLAND

SUNDERLAND *County Borough Council*

ARMS: Argent, a sextant sable, and on a chief azure two silver keys saltirewise, wards upwards and outwards, between two silver mitres each with a gold ducal coronet about its rim.

CREST: On a wreath argent and azure, an ancient ship sable, the sail azure charged with the cross of St Cuthbert silver, and flags flying, each argent charged with a cross gules.

SUPPORTERS: Two silver lions, the dexter supporting an anchor and the sinister a pickaxe, both gold.

MOTTO: *Nil desperandum auspice Deo*—'With God as our leader there is no cause for despair.'

These were granted in 1949. The sextant and motto formed part of an earlier device of the Corporation.

The emblems on the chief refer to the early ecclesiastical history of the Borough, which was divided into Monkwearmouth and Bishopwearmouth. The former is represented by the keys of St Peter, the patron of the church attached to the monastery founded by Benedict Biscop in 674. Bishopwearmouth is represented by the mitres, which are encircled by coronets—a distinction enjoyed only by the Bishops of Durham as former Palatinate lords.

The ancient ship is coloured black in allusion to the coal traffic of the district, and the crosses on the sail and flags are respectively those of St Cuthbert, patron saint of the County of Durham, and St George of England.

The supporting lions are from the arms of the See of Durham (see Durham C.C.), and the anchor and pick are tokens of Sunderland's principal industries, coloured gold for the prosperity they bring.

DURHAM

West Hartlepool

Jarrow

WEST HARTLEPOOL County Borough Council

The Corporation has adopted a device consisting of a blue shield with a silver fess charged with a running hart between two anchors; above the fess is a bird (perhaps a gull), and below a ship under steam and sail, all in proper colours. The crest is a rampant hart rising out of water, supporting an anchor; and the motto is, *E mare ex industria*—'From the sea and from industry.'

The hart, of course, refers to the name; a hart in a pool is the device on a thirteenth-century seal of Hartlepool.

The other emblems are appropriate to a port.

HARTLEPOOL Borough Council

The device on the seal, which dates from the thirteenth century, is a hart standing in a pool with a deerhound springing on to its haunches.

JARROW Borough Council

ARMS: Parted saltirewise azure and barry wavy of six pieces argent and azure; in chief a silver cross flory; in base an open book, bound in gold, bearing the words *Beda Historia*

Ecclesiastica in black letters on white pages; and in fess two gold one-masted ships, their sails furled and flags flying, their prows pointing towards the centre of the shield.

CREST: Rising from a gold antique crown a demi-dragon azure, wings vert, holding between its claws a gold crescent.

MOTTO: *Labore et Scientia*—'By labour and science.'

These were granted in 1930.

The cross stands for the monastery founded in 681 by Benedict Biscop and endowed with lands by King Egfrid. Here the Venerable Bede wrote his famous book, represented in the shield; he was buried in the monastery, but his body was removed to Durham by Edward the Confessor. The ships refer to the port and shipbuilding. The crest is based upon that of Sir Charles Mark Palmer, Bart, through whose great industrial enterprises Jarrow rose from a mere village to its present importance.

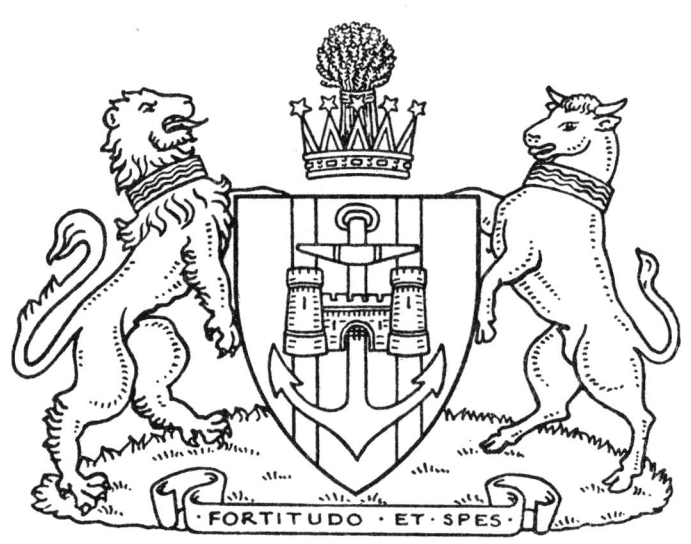

STOCKTON-ON-TEES

STOCKTON-ON-TEES Borough Council

ARMS: Gules, two gold pales surmounted by a gold anchor, and over all a castle proper, the portcullis raised.

CREST: Within a celestial crown gules, a wheatsheaf or.

SUPPORTERS: Dexter, a gold lion, and sinister, a gold bull, each with a collar barry wavy argent and azure.

MOTTO: *Fortitudo et spes*—'Endurance and hope.'

These were granted in 1951.

DURHAM

The following note is issued by the Corporation:

The castle is taken from the town badge which has been used by the Corporation for many years past, and is, no doubt, Stockton Castle, which existed until 1671, and a reminder of the close connection which was established with the succession of Prince Bishops of Durham up to that time. The anchor is also from the town badge, and can be taken to indicate the fact that the town is a port. The two gold parallel lines are indicative of the town's association with the Stockton and Darlington Railway, the world's first passenger railway.

The wheatsheaf is symbolic of the town's ancient markets and its long tradition as a centre for the sale of agricultural produce. The lion stands for England, and the bull represents the stock side of agriculture and the town's weekly cattle market. The collars of silver and blue on each of the supporters represent water—the River Tees, on the banks of which the town stands.

The celestial crown denotes that the land on which Stockton is built formerly belonged to the Church.

BARNARD CASTLE Urban District Council

The seal bears a cross between a crescent and a star.

BILLINGHAM Urban District Council

ARMS: Argent, three bars gules and three fleurs-de-lis azure; a canton gules charged with a silver lion passant.

CREST: On a wreath argent and gules, an ancient ship of three masts or, the mainsail azure with a gold cross, and the foresail and mizzen sail argent with a fleur-de-lis azure.

MOTTO: *Faith.*

These were granted in 1951.

In the shield the arms of the Billingham and Bellasis families are combined. The ship represents the district's close associations with the River Tees and shipping, and the cross on the mainsail is that of St Cuthbert, in whose name the parish church is dedicated.

BISHOP AUCKLAND Urban District Council

The Council uses a device consisting of a bishop's mitre between sprigs of oak, with a sword on one side, a crozier on the other, and a tree below; with the motto, *Tempori parendum*—'We must move with the times.'

FELLING Urban District Council

The device is the stump of an oak-tree in flames, the crest of the local family of Brandling.

HEBBURN Urban District Council

The device is an eagle's head, from the crest of the family of Ellison of Hebburn.

HOUGHTON-LE-SPRING Urban District Council

The device is a hog in front of a tree.

*E

BILLINGHAM   SEAHAM

SEAHAM Urban District Council

ARMS: Parted chevronwise and the chief palewise, the dexter side vert, the sinister sable, and the base azure; in chief a wheatsheaf and a miner's lamp both gold, and in base on water barry wavy argent and azure a cargo steamer bow-on proper.

CREST: On a wreath gold and azure, a pick and spade sable placed saltirewise with hafts downwards and tied with a ribbon.

MOTTO: *By courage and faith.*

These were granted in 1951.

The emblems refer to coal-mining, shipping, and agriculture.

SHILDON Urban District Council

The device consists of three shields between two picks and a hammer representing mining and engineering. One shield is red and bears a representation of Timothy Hackworth's locomotive, 'Royal George,' built at Shildon in 1827. The second is gold with a cross-crosslet gules, for the family of Byerley of Middridge Grange. The third is argent with three water-budgets sable, for the family of Lilburn of East Thickley.

SPENNYMOOR Urban District Council

ARMS: Quarterly gules and sable, a cross or charged with ten drops gules, in the first and fourth quarters a lion rampant argent and in the second and third a gold fleur-de-lis.

CREST: Standing on the battlements of a mural crown sable, a salamander reguardant also sable amid flames proper holding with the right foreclaw a sword erect, the blade proper and the pommel and hilt gold.

DURHAM

SPENNYMOOR

WASHINGTON

SUNDERLAND R.D.C.

MOTTO: *Spe nemo ruet*—'With hope, no one shall fail.'

These were granted in 1952.

The cross is from the arms of the Durham C.C., the blood-red drops recalling the border warfare and the battle of Neville's Cross. The lions and fleurs-de-lis refer to the families of Attwood and Coulson, pioneers in the development of the local steel industry, to which the sword alludes. The black mural crown is emblematic of a coal town. The salamander refers to the Shafto family. The motto plays on the name of the District.

WASHINGTON Urban District Council

Use is made of the arms of the family of Washington: Argent, two bars and in chief three molets, all gules. George Washington came of the family which bore these arms. The theory that they suggested the form of the flag of the United States of America is well known.

SUNDERLAND Rural District Council

ARMS: Azure, a gold cross; in the first and fourth quarters two silver lions passant guardant, and in the second and third a cross patonce or.

CREST: On a wreath gold and azure, a gold lion rampant supporting with the left forepaw a quadrant sable.

MOTTO: *Vincit amor patriae*—'Love of country prevails.'

These were granted in 1952.

The cross and lions are from the arms of the Diocese of Durham, also used by the County, and the sextant is from the arms of Sunderland County Borough.

ESSEX

The three seaxes, or notched swords, attributed by the medieval heralds to the ancient kingdoms of the East and Middle Saxons are found in the arms of both Essex and Middlesex C.C.s. Several local authorities in Essex have one or more seaxes in their insignia in reference to the County.

Essex C.C.

ESSEX *County Council*

ARMS: Gules, three seaxes barwise, with silver blades and gold pommels and hilts, their points to the sinister and cutting edges upwards.

These were granted in 1932, but were in use before that date.

East Ham

West Ham

ESSEX

EAST HAM County Borough Council

Having no arms, the Borough uses a design prepared in 1896 by its then Surveyor. This consists of a shield parted palewise; on the dexter side is a three-masted sailing ship on the sea, and above it a red chief charged with three torches; the sinister side is ermine with a gold crozier. Above the shield is a rising sun, and below it the motto, *Progressio cum populo*—'Progress with the people.'

The official explanation states that the device is intended

to represent the contrast between the Hame of Norman times, when East Ham belonged to one lord, and the rapidly growing commercial centre of to-day. The original owners—the Norman family of Montfichet—are represented by the crozier which occupies one half of the shield, William de Montfichet being the founder of the Abbey of Stratford Langthorne, in the twelfth century. The torches on the shield represent the gas-making industry at Beckton, and the ship in full sail represents the Docks from whence cargoes go to all parts of the world. The rising sun is typical of the ascending of East Ham, which within a few years developed with such marvellous rapidity.

The crozier and sun also occur in the arms of West Ham.

SOUTHEND-ON-SEA

SOUTHEND-ON-SEA County Borough Council

ARMS: Azure, a silver pile between a gold anchor, a gold grid-iron, and in base a gold trefoil; on the pile a spray of lilies growing from a pot proper.

CREST: In a mural crown gules, a ship's mast flying the banner of St George proper.

SUPPORTERS: Dexter, a medieval fisherman trailing a net; and sinister, a Cluniac monk with a red book in one hand and a staff in the other, both proper.

MOTTO: *Per Mare per Ecclesiam.*

These were granted in 1915.

The motto, acknowledging Southend's debt to Church and sea, sums up the whole achievement. The anchor is the emblem of St Clement, patron saint of Leigh, in allusion to the legend that he was bound to an anchor and cast into the sea; the grid-iron stands for St Lawrence, patron saint of Eastwood, being the instrument of his martyrdom; the trefoil is a symbol of the Holy Trinity, the dedication of the parish of Southchurch; and the lilies are from the old seal of St Mary's Priory, Prittlewell. The mother parish is that of Prittlewell, its 'south end' being an offspring which has far outgrown the parent village. At Prittlewell was the Cluniac foundation represented by the monk.

The ship's mast, with a crow's nest like that of an ancient galley, refers to Leigh's former reputation as a port, and the Borough's general connection with shipping; the fisherman denotes the long-standing industry of the place.

WEST HAM County Borough Council

ARMS: Parted fesswise gules and gold, in the chief a ship under sail proper, and two crossed hammers of gold; and in the base three chevrons gules; over all a pale ermine with a gold crozier.

CREST: On a wreath or and gules, the rising sun in front of a sword and a crozier saltirewise, the sword-blade proper and the hilt and crozier gold.

MOTTO: *Deo confidimus*—'We trust in God.'

These were granted in 1887.

The Manor of West Ham was bestowed on Stratford-Langthorne Abbey (denoted by the croziers) by its founder, William de Montfichet, whose arms were three gold chevrons on red; these, with the tinctures reversed, occupy the base of the shield. The ship and hammers stand for the docks and industry. These arms are similar to the device adopted by East Ham.

BARKING Borough Council

ARMS: Sable, a pale ermine between two gold lions rampant facing one another; on the pale two abbess's croziers saltirewise, gold.

CREST: On a wreath argent and sable, a representation of the curfew tower at Barking proper.

SUPPORTERS: Two gold lions, each holding a flaming torch proper.

MOTTO: *Dei gratia sumus quod sumus*—'By the grace of God, we are what we are.'

These were granted in 1931, when Barking became a borough.

The croziers stand for the nunnery at Barking founded about 670 by Erkenwald, Bishop of London, destroyed by the Danes some two centuries later, and restored by King Edgar in 970. The motto is a variation of that of the nunnery.

ESSEX

BARKING

The lions stand for the Cecil and Monteagle families, and the torches held by the supporters represent the two chief local industries, namely gas and electricity.

The curfew tower was used as a device by the former Urban District Council.

CHELMSFORD Borough Council

ARMS: Silver, a bridge of three arches proper; above it two croziers crossed between two lions rampant; and in base two bars wavy, all azure.

CREST: On a wreath argent and azure, a golden crozier erect upon a rock, and in front of it two crossed swords proper with gold hilts entwined by a wreath of oak vert.

MOTTO: *Many minds, one heart.*

These were granted in 1889.

The River Chelmer, represented by the wavy bars, was bridged in the twelfth century by one of the Bishops of London, who held the Manor of Bishop's Hall. Chelmsford's second manor, that of Moulsham, was in the possession of Westminster Abbey. The ecclesiastical influences in the town's early history are denoted by the croziers, which proved to have a prophetic as well as a historic significance, for since the arms were devised Chelmsford has become the seat of a bishopric of its own. In the sixteenth century both manors passed into the hands of the Mildmay family, from whose arms the blue lions were taken.

CHELMSFORD

CHINGFORD

COLCHESTER

CHINGFORD Borough Council

ARMS: Vert, two bars wavy argent, over all a stag's face with antlers proper, and between the antlers a seax erect, the blade proper and the pommel and hilt gold, and the blade encircled by a gold mural crown.

CREST: On a wreath argent and vert, a representation of the tower of Chingford Old Church proper.

MOTTO: *All things for the glory of God.*

These were granted in 1938.

Chingford contains within its boundaries many acres of forest land, and marches with Epping Forest on the north and east.

COLCHESTER Borough Council

ARMS: Gules, two silver ragged staves joined in the form of a cross, its arms and foot pierced by Passion Nails; and three golden crowns, the bottom one encircling the foot of the cross.

These arms, which appear on a fifteenth-century seal, are recorded at the College of Arms.

Colchester's eponymous hero is Coel, known in nursery rhyme as 'old King Cole'; he is stated by Geoffrey of Monmouth to have been the father of Helena, wife of the Emperor Constantius, though if Coel had any existence apart from legend he was probably identical with Cunobelin (Shakespeare's Cymbeline) who lived some three hundred years before Helena. However, Colchester regards Helena as a local princess, and commemorates her in its arms. Tradition tells that about A.D. 326, during a pilgrimage to Palestine, Helena discovered the True Cross together with the crosses of the two malefactors. Its identity was proved by its power to restore the sick to health. She encased the Cross in silver, and built a church in Jerusalem to enshrine it.

In some representations of the Colchester arms the nails are omitted, which is a pity because they emphasize the fact that the staves represent the Cross of Christ. The crowns are those of the Kingdom of the East Angles (see Chapter II). These arms may be compared with those of Nottingham.

DAGENHAM

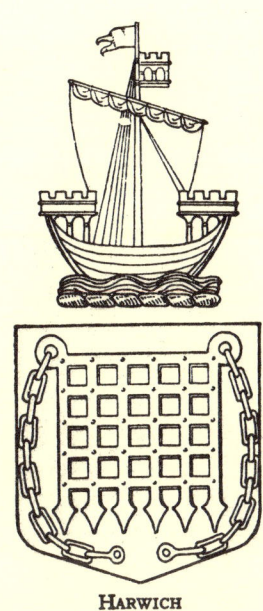

HARWICH

DAGENHAM Borough Council

ARMS: Parted saltirewise gules and barry wavy of eight pieces argent and azure; in chief a sword erect, point downwards, passing between two keys crossed saltirewise with their wards upwards, all gold; in base three gold lilies with stems and leaves, one erect and the others crossed saltirewise; and in fess two martlets gules.

CREST: On a wreath argent and gules, a gold rising sun charged with three cog-wheels gules, the cogs engaged.

MOTTO: *Judge us by our deeds.*

These were granted in 1936.

The barry wavy of silver and blue represents the River Thames, an important feature in the town's industrial life to which the cog-wheels refer. The keys and sword of St Peter and St Paul allude to the dedication of the old parish church, while the lilies of St Mary refer to the town's association with the ecclesiastical parish of Barking. The martlets are from the arms of the old local family of Valence, and the rising sun looks forward to a bright future for the Borough.

HARWICH Borough Council

ARMS: Gules, a gold portcullis with chains, the studs and spikes azure.

CREST: On a wreath gold and gules, waves of the sea proper, and thereon a gold one-masted ship with silver turrets at bow and stern and a silver tower affixed below the top of the mast, the sail furled argent and at the masthead a pennon gules.

MOTTO: *Omnia bona bonis*—'To the good all things are good.'

These were granted in 1943, but were in use unofficially before that date.

The emblems are appropriate to a port which was formerly a walled town.

ILFORD

ILFORD Borough Council

ARMS: Ermine, an uprooted oak-tree proper between seven ancient crowns of gold, and in the base of the shield two bars wavy azure.

CREST: On a wreath argent and azure, rising from a chaplet of oak a demi-buck proper, supporting a seax, blade upwards proper, the pommel and hilt gold.

SUPPORTERS: Dexter, a forester holding a bow, and sinister, an abbess holding a book, both proper.

MOTTO: *In Unity Progress*.

These were granted in 1926.

The following notes were prepared for the information of the Borough by the Hon. Phillip P. Cary, York Herald:

Upon a background of Royal ermine are arranged seven crowns representing the seven Kings of the Saxon heptarchy and in their midst an oak-tree in memory of the Fairlop Oak in Hainault Forest, perhaps one of Essex's most celebrated trees. Under this oak, from 1725 until the tree was blown down in 1820, an annual fair was held on the first Friday in July.

ESSEX

In the base of the shield is conventional water representing the 'ford' which forms part of the name of the Borough.

The Crest is composed of a demi-buck, symbolical of the Forest of Hainault which is so closely bound up with the history of Ilford, supporting a seax or scimitar, a weapon also found connected with Essex.

On the dexter side is a representation of a forester in further allusion to the Forest of Hainault. He is armed with his bow, quiver, and hunting-knife and carries a hunting-horn.

On the sinister side is a representation of a lady in the dress of an Abbess. This is in allusion to Adeliza, the sister of Payne Fitzjohn, who was appointed Abbess of Barking Abbey by King Stephen. Adeliza is connected with Ilford through the fact that she was the founder of Ilford Chapel and Hospital in about 1145. She died in about 1173, and was succeeded as Abbess by Mary, sister of Thomas à Becket.

The motto 'In Unity Progress' alludes to the rise of Ilford from a village to the status of a Borough and its determination to rise still higher—by Unity.

LEYTON   MALDON   ROMFORD

LEYTON Borough Council

ARMS: Gold, three chevrons gules; on a chief gules a gold lion passant.

CREST: On a wreath gold and gules, a lion rampant palewise gold and sable supporting a gold crozier.

MOTTO: *Ministrando dignitas*—'Dignity in service.'

These were granted in 1926.

I am indebted to the Town Clerk for the following note:

The design of the arms of the Borough was prepared from the arms of the owners of the ancient Manors of Leyton, Ruckholt, and Marks. The lion rampant in the crest is from the arms of Fraunceys; Sir Adam Fraunceys held the Manor of Ruckholt and died in 1417. The crozier is from the arms of the Abbey of Stratford. The lion passant in the arms is derived from the arms of Withipole; the Manor of Marks belonged to the Priory of St Helens and was granted in 1545 to Paul Withipole and his son. The chevronels are from the arms of Montfichet; Gilbert Montfichet gave to the Abbey and Convent of Stratford, which was founded by William Montfichet in 1134, the Church of Leyton, which gift was confirmed by the Charter of Henry II in 1182. The Manor of Leyton was given to the Abbot and Convent of Stratford in 1200.

Although the object in the crest is described as a crozier it is generally represented as a cross-staff such as is borne before an archbishop.

These arms are comparable with those of West Ham.

MALDON Borough Council

ARMS: Parted palewise, the dexter side azure with three gold lions passant guardant, and the sinister silver with a ship sable, the sail furled, on the mainmast a pennon gules, and on a mast above the tower at the stern a banner azure charged with three gold lions passant guardant; each mast topped by a gold fleur-de-lis.

These are on record at the College of Arms. In another version, the banner at the stern of the ship, instead of bearing the arms which appear on the dexter side of the shield, contains the cross of St George.

The lions are clearly derived from the Royal Arms, the town having been originally *terra regis*.

ROMFORD Borough Council

ARMS: Azure, a fess wavy barry wavy of four pieces argent and azure; in chief an eagle displayed and in base a Saxon crown, both or; and on the fess a gold ring set with a gem.

CREST: On a wreath or and azure, a gold castellated gateway with three towers, masoned sable and with windows azure; the middle tower having a dome azure topped by a red cross, and each of the outer towers having a steeple azure; and in front of the gateway two seaxes proper, pommels and hilts gold, crossed saltirewise.

MOTTO: *Serve with gladness.*

These were granted in 1938.

The eagle stands for the Roman settlement of Durolitum, which sprang up at the crossing of the river now called the Rom, which is represented by the fess. The Saxon crown refers to Romford's association with the pre-Conquest kings of the English through the royal palace at Havering-atte-Bower.

There is a tradition that Edward the Confessor, at the consecration of St John's Church at the place later called Havering, gave a ring as alms to an old pilgrim. The pilgrim was St John himself, who later sent the ring back to the King with the word that he should 'dispose of his goods, for within six months he shall be in the joy of Heaven with me, when he shall have his reward for his chastity and good living.'

To this legend the ring in the arms refers.

The gateway in the crest has occurred in the seals of the Liberty of Havering, the Romford U.D.C., and the Corporation. It is believed to be a representation of the gatehouse of Havering Palace. The seaxes are from the County insignia.

ESSEX

SAFFRON WALDEN Borough Council

The seal bears a castle and three saffron flowers. Saffron was cultivated at Walden from the reign of Edward III until the eighteenth century.

WALTHAMSTOW

WALTHAMSTOW Borough Council

ARMS: Silver, a maunch gules; on a chief azure a flying seamew between two anchors, all silver.

CREST: On a gold mural crown a dove azure, its beak and legs gules and wings gold, holding in its beak a sprig of oak with acorns proper.

SUPPORTERS: Dexter, a stag, and sinister, a piebald talbot, each with a wreath of oak round its neck, all proper.

MOTTO: *Fellowship is life.*

These were granted in 1929.

The following explanation is supplied by the Corporation:

The maunch, or sleeve ... was the insignia of the Toni family, and as a representative of this family was the first Norman lord of these parts this piece of heraldry reminds us of Walthamstow in Norman days.

The chief of the shield bears the familiar arms of George Monoux, further emphasized in the bird with the oak twig in its beak which forms the crest.... These remind us not only of Walthamstow in Tudor times, but of a very worthy citizen whose benefactions are well known throughout the town.... The ground colour of the Monoux device appears in blue, not red as is usual. This change in colour has been made in compliment to the Maynard family, whose supporters, the stag and talbot, appear on either side of our arms, and these features are introduced to memorialize a family connected with Walthamstow since the seventeenth century, particularly Henry Maynard, whose bequests to the Church, the School, and the poor were generous and noteworthy.

The legend, 'Fellowship is life,' comes from the pen of a celebrated citizen, William Morris, whose place in art, craftmanship, and letters is already well recognized, and will be much enhanced with the passage of time.

WANSTEAD AND WOODFORD

WANSTEAD AND WOODFORD Borough Council

ARMS: Azure, a cross flory argent between in the first and fourth quarters a leopard's face and in the second and third a martlet, all gold.

CREST: On a wreath argent and azure, a hurst of trees proper, and in front of the boles three roundels barry wavy argent and azure.

SUPPORTERS: Two herons proper each with a gold Saxon crown about its neck.

MOTTO: *Consilio et animo*—'By wisdom and courage.'

These were granted in 1937.

The cross refers to the ecclesiastical overlords of the Manors of Wanstead and Woodford, namely the Abbeys of Westminster and Waltham Holy Cross. The leopards' faces and martlets (representing doves) are from the arms attributed to King Harold and Edward the Confessor, who endowed the Abbeys with these manors. The Saxon crowns also allude to these kings.

Herons formerly abounded in the Essex marshes, and were therefore adopted as emblems by the Wanstead U.D.C. The trees represent the ancient forest from which Woodford takes its name, and the roundels (heraldic fountains) refer to the springs and streams of the district.

BRAINTREE AND BOCKING   BRENTWOOD   CHIGWELL

BRAINTREE AND BOCKING Urban District Council

ARMS: Gules, a gold cross quarter-pierced (i.e. the centre square is 'voided' to show the field), charged with two lions rampant azure on the vertical and two fleurs-de-lis vert on the horizontal limb.

CREST: On a wreath or and gules, two silver swords saltirewise encircled by a gold mural crown, and in front of them three molets (or spur-rowels) gules.

MOTTO: *Hold to the truth.*

These were granted in 1927.

I am indebted to the Clerk of the Urban District Council for the following note:

The two crossed swords on the crest are taken from the official arms of the See of London and commemorate the fact that the Bishops of London were for several centuries Lords of the Manor of Braintree. The two blue lions were taken from the arms of William de la Santa Maria, Bishop of London in the reign of King John, his personal arms being a lion rampant azure on a golden field. This Bishop obtained from King John a Charter for the holding of a market and fairs at Braintree, and this charge was added to the Braintree arms to commemorate this fact, which had the effect of changing Braintree from a country village to a market town. The green fleurs-de-lis on the golden field are taken from the arms of the Courtauld family, who were the first to establish an important manufacture in Braintree, and who have been great benefactors to the town. The three red spur-rowels in the crest are also taken from the Courtauld arms. The mural crown was added as it is commonly used in municipal arms. The red field is of no special signification. The motto is, in its French form, *Tiens à la Vérité*, also the Courtauld motto.

BRENTWOOD Urban District Council

ARMS: Parted fesswise rayonny argent and gules; in chief a chough proper between two pilgrims' staves erect sable, and in base three gold Saxon crowns.

CREST: On a wreath argent and gules, a gold demi-stag rising from the battlements of a tower azure.

MOTTO: *Ardens fide.*

These were granted in 1951.

The division of the shield represents flames with reference to the 'burnt wood,' the origin of the name. To this the motto also refers, the full significance attributed to it being 'burning with faith in God, our fellow men, and our future.' The crowns stand for the Abbey of St Osyth which held lands in Brentwood before the dissolution; while the chough is from the arms of St Thomas Becket, and, with the staves, alludes to the pilgrimages to Canterbury which passed this way. The stag is a reminder of the deer formerly seen in local parklands.

CHIGWELL Urban District Council

ARMS: Gold, a stag at rest proper; on a chief gules three silver axe-heads bendwise sinister with blades downwards.

CREST: On a wreath gold and gules, rising from a wreath of oak vert a right forearm in a sleeve vert, the hand proper holding a riband gules from which hangs a gold bugle-horn.

MOTTO: *Non progredi est regredi*—'Not to go forward is to go backward.'

These were granted in 1951.

The stag refers to Epping Forest, and the bugle-horn was the symbol of the Master Keeper, from whose office the lordship of the manor developed. The axe-heads were the symbols of the Verderers, whose court was held at Chigwell.

CLACTON Urban District Council

ARMS: Parted chevronwise, the upper part azure strewn with cross-crosslets and among them two cinquefoils all argent, and the lower part gules with two gold swords crossed saltirewise.

CREST: On a wreath argent and azure, a lymphad (ancient galley) gules with a gold anchor at the bow, the sail proper charged with a gold scallop shell, at the mast-head a pennant azure, and at the stem and stern a flag azure charged with a gold scallop shell.

MOTTO: *Lux, Salubritas, Felicitas*—'Light, health, happiness.'

These were granted in 1938, but before that date the Council used a somewhat similar device of local adoption.

The crosslets and cinquefoils are from the arms of the Darcy family, formerly Lords of the Manor of Clacton, while the swords stand for the See of London to which Clacton belonged from the Norman Conquest until 1545. The ship is appropriate to a seaside resort, and the scallop shells, emblems of pilgrimage, refer to the dedication of the local church to St James, and also to the seashore where present-day pilgrims seek the benefits referred to in the motto.

Clacton

Hornchurch

HORNCHURCH *Urban District Council*

ARMS: Argent, a saltire gules between three red roses with seeds and sepals proper, and in base a heart also gules; and on the chevron a gold martlet.

CREST: On a wreath argent and gules, a bull's head full-face couped at the neck or, in front of a church gable proper.

MOTTO: *A good name endureth.*

These were granted in 1948.

The roses are from the arms of William of Wykeham, founder of New College, Oxford, which owns property in the district. The heart, from the heraldry of Bernard of Savoy, recalls the association of the Counts of Savoy with the hospice founded at Hornchurch by Henry II. The martlet denotes Edward the Confessor's historical links with the district. The crest, derived from a bull's head in stone with copper horns which is built into the gable-end of the parish church, refers to the ancient name, 'Hornedechirche.' The motto comes from Ecclesiasticus xli. 13.

RAYLEIGH *Urban District Council*

The seal bears a shield with a red fess charged with a seax (for Essex); in the chief, rising from the top of the fess, are rays of the sun, presumably alluding to the name; and in the base is a representation of Rayleigh Mount—an earthwork, and the remains of Rayleigh Castle.

CIVIC HERALDRY

WALTHAM HOLY CROSS Urban District Council

The device consists of a cartouche bearing a Calvary cross on three steps between two kneeling angels. Above the cartouche is a lion's face, and below is the legend, *In hoc signo vinces*—' In this sign thou shalt conquer.'

The reference is to the portion of the True Cross which the famous abbey at Waltham was built to contain. The lion's face is presumably from the arms attributed to King Harold, who owned Waltham and extended the original church.

BASILDON   HARLOW

BASILDON Development Corporation

ARMS: Parted chevronwise, the party line embattled, gules and gold; in chief a roundel barry wavy argent and azure between two silver molets, and in base an oak-tree proper on a mount vert.

CREST: On a wreath gold and gules a wyvern sable pierced by a sword bendwise or.

MOTTO: *Art, Industry, Contentment.*

These were granted in 1950.

The predominant colours, red and gold, are from the arms of the families of De Vere, Moyer, and Petre, which held land at Basildon, Pitsea, and Nevendon at various periods. The molets are also from the arms of De Vere. The embattled line represents the boundary of a town, the tree on a mount denotes the woodlands, and the roundel barry wavy (or heraldic fountain) signifies the lost River Lyge, and also refers to the family of Montchensy. The wyvern was suggested by a carving in Laindon Church, and the sword is that of St Paul to represent the long association of the district with the See of London.

HARLOW Development Corporation

ARMS: Argent, a cross engrailed sable charged with a fleur-de-lis or; on a chief azure three ancient crowns of gold, each pierced by two arrows crossed saltirewise, points downwards, sable.

CREST: On a wreath argent and sable, a demi-griffin sable holding in the right claw by the blade a seax proper with gold pommel and hilt, and charged on the shoulder with a spur-rowel argent.

MOTTO: *Members one of another.*

These were granted in 1948.

The arms are based on those of religious houses which formerly held the land where the new town is being developed. The arrow-pierced crowns stand for the famous Abbey at Bury St Edmunds, the cross represents Waltham Abbey, and the fleur-de-lis refers to the Premonstratensians at Beeleigh. The griffin is from the arms of Latton Priory, and the seax refers to the County.

FLINTSHIRE C.C.

FLINTSHIRE

FLINTSHIRE County Council

ARMS: Argent, a cross engrailed, each limb terminating in the head of a fleur-de-lis sable, between four Cornish choughs proper; and on the cross a silver mascle between four silver roundels.

CREST: On a wreath argent and sable, a demi-dragon gules supporting an ostrich feather argent.

MOTTO: *Gorau Tarian Cyfiawnder*—'The best shield is justice.'

These were granted in 1938.

The arms are based on those of Edwyn, Lord of Tegaingle, Founder of the XII Noble Tribe of North Wales and Powys. The crest shows the Welsh dragon supporting one of the Prince of Wales's feathers.

FLINT Borough Council

The seal bears a castle on a rock and a three-masted ship on the sea.

PRESTATYN Urban District Council

The device consists of the Welsh dragon without forelegs, standing against a tree trunk which is entwined by a scroll bearing the motto, *Y ddraig goch ddyry gychwyn*— 'The red dragon shall lead.'

GLAMORGAN

GLAMORGAN C.C.

GLAMORGAN

GLAMORGAN County Council

ARMS: Or, three chevrons gules between three Tudor roses barbed and seeded proper.

CREST: On a wreath or and gules, a demi-dragon gules, its wings raised, issuing from flames and supporting a staff bearing a banner gules charged with a gold clarion.

SUPPORTERS: Dexter, a miner; sinister, a steelworker, all proper.

MOTTO: *A ddioddefws a orfu*—'He that endureth overcometh.'

These were granted in 1950.

The chevrons are from the arms of the De Clare Lords of Glamorgan (1217–1317). They also refer to Iestyn ap Gwrgan, last native King of Glamorgan (c. 1030–80), to whom are attributed three silver chevrons on red. The roses are symbolic of the creation of the shire by Henry VIII. The arms thus represent the historical sequence of Welsh kingdom, Norman county, and Tudor shire.

The Welsh dragon rising from flames stands for the revival of Glamorgan after a long period of depression. The clarion on the banner is from the arms of the De Granvilles who held sway in the Neath district.

The supporters indicate coal and steel, the two main industries of the county, and the motto is that of Iestyn ap Gwrgan.

CARDIFF

MERTHYR TYDFIL

CARDIFF City and County Borough Council

ARMS: Argent, on a mount vert a dragon rampant gules supporting a banner gules charged with three silver chevrons; and growing from the mount a leek proper.

CREST: Rising from a mural crown proper three ostrich feathers argent, and in front of them a Tudor rose.

SUPPORTERS: Dexter, a Welsh goat; and sinister, a sea-horse, both proper.

MOTTOES: *Deffro mae'n Ddydd*—'Awake! It is day'; and *Y Ddraig Goch ddyry gychwyn*—'The Red Dragon shall lead.'

The arms were granted in 1906 and the supporters in 1907.

The origin and associations of the British Dragon are dealt with in Chapter II. The banner bears the arms of Iestyn ap Gwrgan (see Glamorgan C.C.); it also links the arms with those used by Cardiff before it obtained its grant, namely the three red chevrons on gold of the Clare Lords of Glamorgan.

The traditional origin of the leek as a Welsh emblem is the battle of Poictiers where (to quote Fluellen in Shakespeare's *Henry V*) 'the Welshmen did good service in a garden where leeks did grow, wearing leeks in their Monmouth caps.' An alternative theory is that the true Welsh emblem is not the vegetable leek, but 'St Peter's Leek'—the daffodil.

Cardiff's goat represents the mountains of Glamorgan, and the sea-horse stands for the highway whereby their mineral wealth is distributed to the world. The ostrich feathers, famous as a badge of the Heir Apparent, are dealt with in Chapter II. The Tudor rose is taken from an old Corporation seal.

GLAMORGAN

MERTHYR TYDFIL County Borough Council

ARMS: Azure, the figure of St Tydfil between in chief two crosses paty pointed at the foot, all gold.

MOTTO: *Nid cadarn ond brodyrdde*—'No strength but in fellowship.'

These were granted in 1908.

St Tydfil the Martyr (Merthyr), a daughter of Brychan (see Breconshire C.C.), was put to death by the Saxons. Of the same family, and also a martyr, was St Elli, portrayed in the arms of Llanelly.

SWANSEA

SWANSEA County Borough Council

ARMS: Azure, in the base three bars wavy argent, and rising therefrom a gold castle; in the chief an escutcheon gules charged with a gold lion passant guardant.

CREST: On a wreath argent and azure, an osprey with a fish in its beak proper.

SUPPORTERS: Dexter, a lion; and sinister, a dragon, both gules, and each with a gold mural crown about its neck.

MOTTO: *Floreat Swansea.*

These were granted in 1922.

The original device of Swansea seems to have been the osprey, now used as a crest. Prior to the granting of the present arms the Corporation used insignia said to have been bestowed on it in 1306 by William de Braose, Lord of Gower, who is recorded as having issued the following instructions to his herald:

The arms of my Borough of Swansea shall be a Castle with two towers and a portcullis; on each tower erect a banner charged with my Lion rampant; and to prove that it is a town of some standing place its ancient arms, the Osprey and Fish, on a shield in the chief.

The modern arms preserve the main features of the old ones. The castle is that which Henry de Beaumont erected in 1099, around which the town grew up. In 1203 this castle passed, with the lordship of Gower, to the De Braose family (see Chapter III) which is commemorated by the lion. The dragon is both the Welsh national emblem and a supporter of the arms of the present Lord Swansea.

BARRY

BARRY Borough Council

ARMS: Or, three bars gemel gules, in chief two fleurs-de-lis azure and in base a dragon passant gules.

CREST: On a wreath or and gules, an ancient ship sable on waves of the sea, the sail argent and strewn with lozenges sable, and the pennon gules.

SUPPORTERS: Two silver unicorns with gold horns, hoofs, manes, and tufts, each with a gold chain about its neck and pendent therefrom a shield, that on the dexter supporter being argent charged with three bars gemel gules, and that on the sinister being the arms of the Borough, as above.

MOTTO: *Cadernid, cyfiawnder, cynnydd*—'Stability, justice, progress.'

These were granted in 1939.

The bars gemel (or pairs of barrulets) are from the arms of the family De Barri. The fleurs-de-lis are from the heraldry of Lord Davies of Llandinam. Below is the Welsh dragon. The ship, with 'black diamonds' on its sail, alludes to Barry's export of coal. The supporters are those of the Earl of Plymouth, suitably differenced.

Cowbridge

Port Talbot

COWBRIDGE Borough Council

ARMS: Parted chevronwise gules and argent, the chief strewn with silver cross-crosslets and among them two lions rampant argent, and in base a cow passant on a bridge over water all proper.

CREST: On a wreath argent and gules, a cow proper holding in its mouth a gold ear of wheat and supporting a gold shield charged with three chevrons invected gules.

MOTTO: *Awn Rhagom.*

These were granted in 1888.

The lions amid crosslets commemorate the medieval family De Braose, and the chevrons are those of the Clares, anciently Lords of Glamorgan (see Chapter III). The cow on the bridge forms an obvious rebus; Cowbridge is a translation of the old Welsh name, *Pont-y-fon.*

NEATH Borough Council

The seal bears a tower with two turrets and other buildings, probably representing the castle built here in the twelfth century by the Lords of Glamorgan.

PORT TALBOT Borough Council

The Corporation has not obtained arms, but makes use of the following: Parted palewise, the dexter quartered: (1) and (4) two chevrons between three trefoils (apparently for De Cardonell); (2) and (3) a two-headed eagle; impaling, three organ rests (for Granville).

BRIDGEND

BRIDGEND Urban District Council

ARMS: Vert, a salmon proper leaping towards the dexter; on a chief sable a gold bridge of two arches.

CREST: On a wreath gold and vert, a raven between two wheatsheaves all proper.

MOTTO: *A vo penn bit pont*—'He who will be chief, let him be a bridge.'

These were granted in 1951.

The green field suggests pasture land; the salmon refers to the name of the River Ogwr; and the bridge stands for Bridgend. The raven alludes to Lord Dunraven, and the wheatsheaves are for agriculture.

PENARTH Urban District Council

The Council uses as a device a shield bearing a ship on the sea, and on a chief a dragon passant. The crest is a bear's head, and the shield is supported by two bears.

MOTTO: *Cynchori er llesiant*—'Consulting for betterment.'

The crest and supporters seem to have been adopted under a misapprehension that the name was derived from the words *pen*, a head, and *arth*, a bear.

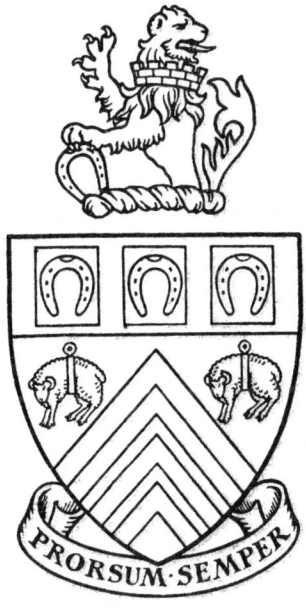

GLOUCESTERSHIRE C.C.

GLOUCESTERSHIRE

GLOUCESTERSHIRE County Council

ARMS: Parted chevronwise gules and or, in chief two gold fleeces and in base three chevrons gules; on a chief or, a billet azure between two billets vert, and on every billet a gold horseshoe.

CREST: On a wreath or and gules, a demi-lion rampant reguardant gules, with a gold mural crown about its neck and its left forepaw resting on a gold horseshoe.

MOTTO: *Prorsum semper*—'Ever forward.'

These were granted in 1935.

The chevrons are from the arms of the Clare Earls of Gloucester. The first horseshoe is derived from the old arms of the City of Gloucester, while the crest is based on that granted to the City in 1652. The second horseshoe is from the arms of the Allen family (whose motto has also been adopted by the County Council), and the third is from the arms of the Cripps family. The fleeces represent the woollen industry.

BRISTOL

BRISTOL *City and County Borough Council*

ARMS: Gules, on the sinister side a silver castle with two domed towers, on each a banner charged with the cross of St George, standing on a cliff proper, and in dexter base barry wavy argent and azure, and issuing therefrom a gold ship sailing from a port in the tower of the castle, masts and rigging sable and on each mast a gold round-top, a sail spread on the foremast and a sail furled on the mainmast, both argent.

CREST: On a wreath argent and gules, two bent arms rising from clouds, the forearms crossed, the dexter hand grasping a snake and the other holding a pair of scales; the arms and snake proper and the scales gold.

SUPPORTERS: Two sitting unicorns or, their horns, hoofs, and manes sable.

MOTTO: *Virtute et industria*—'By virtue and industry.'

These are on record at the College of Arms.

The arms clearly express the City's ancient character of a fortified port. They are traceable to the design on the fourteenth-century seal of the Mayoralty showing the prow of a ship issuing from the portway of a castle. On another seal of the same century is a single-masted ship sailing towards a tower on which is a watchman beckoning to the steersman in the ship. This seal bears the inscription:

SECRETI CLAVIS SV̄ PORT' NAVITA NAVIS
PORTĀ CVSTODIT PORT' VIGIL INDICE-PDIT

Mr Gale Pedrick (*Borough Seals*) gives the following translation: 'I am the key of the secret port. The pilot steers the helm of the ship. The warden points out the port with his forefinger.'

'The position of the castle was such that it commanded the entrance to the ancient town,' states Mr Pedrick. 'It had a secret port through which vessels of considerable build passed easily right into its area, the Avon being thus made to communicate with the ditch, and the archway towards which the ship is being guided is considered to represent this secret harbour.'

Although the interesting detail of the warden pointing the way into the harbour is omitted from the arms, they clearly refer to Bristol's secret port.

The snake in the crest is said to represent Wisdom, and the scales Justice. A similar crest is used by Bristol, Rhode Island.

GLOUCESTER

GLOUCESTER City and County Borough Council

ARMS: Or, three chevrons between ten roundels, all gules.

CREST: Issuing from a gold mural crown a demi-lion rampant guardant gules, holding in the right paw a broadsword and in the left a trowel, both proper.

SUPPORTERS: Two lions rampant gules, each holding erect in the right forepaw a broadsword proper.

MOTTO: *Fides invicta triumphat*—'Unconquered faith triumphs.'

The arms were recorded in 1623, and the crest and supporters were granted in 1652, during the Commonwealth; all grants made during that period were at the Restoration declared void, but the Corporation continued to use the armorial bearings. The position was regularized in 1945 when the crest and supporters were granted and confirmed.

The red chevrons are from the arms of the Clares, Earls of Gloucester (see Chapter III), and the roundels are from the arms of the See of Worcester, with which the See of Gloucester was formerly united.

An earlier coat of arms, granted in 1538, is green with a gold pale charged with a sword in a blue scabbard studded with gold roundels, the hilt and pommel red, and upon its point a purple cap of maintenance with an ermine lining; on either side of the pale is a silver horseshoe and three nails with their points towards the shoe; the chief is parted palewise gold and purple (or red) and charged with a silver boar's head (sometimes quoted as having a red 'quine apple' in the mouth) between a red rose and a white rose, each halved with a golden sun, its rays streaming towards the boar's head.

The sword is that carried before the Mayor by authority of the charter granted by Richard III in 1483; the horseshoes and nails stand for Gloucester's ancient trade in wrought iron, to which perhaps the trowel in the later crest also refers; the roses, suns, and boar's head are royal badges (see Chapter II), the last being particularly associated with Richard III who, before his accession to the throne, was Duke of Gloucester.

These arms were based upon a still earlier coat, adopted about 1483 for use on the seal of the then newly appointed Mayor, and consisting of a shield strewn with horseshoe nails with a sword of state bendwise between six horseshoes.

CHELTENHAM

CIRENCESTER

CHELTENHAM Borough Council

ARMS: Gold, a chevron engrailed gules between two pigeons and an uprooted oak-tree proper; on a chief azure a silver cross flory between two open books proper with gold binding and clasps.

CREST: On a wreath or and gules a mount vert, and thereon a roundel barry wavy silver and blue between two sprays of oak, and perched on the roundel a pigeon, all proper.

MOTTO: *Salubritas et Eruditio*—'Health and Learning.'

These were granted in 1887.

GLOUCESTERSHIRE

The following explanation is issued by the Corporation:

The crest embodies and denotes the legend of the discovery of the Mineral Waters, to which Cheltenham owed its rise as an Inland Watering Place, and to which attention was drawn by flocks of pigeons resorting to a saline spring which rose to the surface.

The cross in the arms is that of Edward the Confessor, to whom the Manor of Cheltenham at one time belonged. The Manor is consequently 'Terra Regis,' and of 'Ancient Demesne.'

The open books and the 'Eruditio' in the motto are emblematic of the educational advantages Cheltenham possesses and is so famed for, in the Ancient Foundation of Pate's Grammar School.

The oak-trees and sprays are symbolic of the avenues of trees in the public promenades and streets, for which Cheltenham is also celebrated.

The word 'Salubritas' in the motto is indicative of the high repute in which Cheltenham is held as a health resort.

TEWKESBURY Borough Council

The seal bears a castle.

CIRENCESTER Urban District Council

Arms are not officially recorded, but the town has been credited with the following: Silver, a phoenix in flames proper. This may have been derived from a device of Queen Elizabeth I, who adopted the phoenix, it is said, to signalize her recovery from smallpox.

KINGSWOOD Urban District Council

ARMS: Parted chevronwise vert and gold; in chief two stags' faces and antlers, each crowned with a gold coronet composed of four fleurs-de-lis, and in base a boar's head torn off at the neck sable; all within a bordure ermine.

CREST: On a wreath vert and gold, a demi-lion rampant gules with a gold chain about its neck, holding a torch sable with flames proper.

MOTTO: *Face the dawn.*

These were granted in 1945.

Kingswood, anciently a royal forest (as its name tells), is represented by the crowned stags' heads, while the boar's head stands for Hanham, in the Swineshead Hundred. The ermine border indicates the enclosure of these districts as the king's land.

The boar's head is black, to represent the coal of the district, while its bristly character betokens the local brush-making industry. The black torch also alludes to coal.

The chevronwise division of the shield symbolizes Kingswood Hill and Hanham Mount. The lion in the crest is from the arms of Gloucestershire C.C. The chain stands for engineering and other heavy industries, while the torch, besides its industrial significance, represents enlightenment in religion, education, and local government.

KINGSWOOD

DURSLEY R.D.C.

DURSLEY Rural District Council

ARMS: Gules, a Paschal Lamb proper within an orle of silver crosses formy; on a chief vert an open book proper garnished with gold and bearing the words *Holy Bible* in letters sable, between two gold cartwheels each having eight spokes.

CREST: In a gold crown vallary a mound of sand and standing thereon a white-fronted goose with wings closed proper.

MOTTO: *God with us.*

These were granted in 1952.

The Paschal Lamb, an emblem of the wool trade, recalls the former importance of Dursley as a centre of the Gloucestershire wool industry. The crosslets are from the arms of the Berkeleys, Viscounts Dursley.

On a green chief, standing for the rural area, is a Bible representing its translator, William Tyndale, who was born in this district, and to whose work the motto also alludes. Of the wheels, one stands for the Lister Engineering Company, and the other for Sir Isaac Pitman, who began teaching his shorthand system at Wotton-under-Edge, taking his basic symbols from the curves and radial lines of an eight-spoked wheel.

The crest represents the Severn Wildfowl Trust, the goose standing within the protective circle of a vallary crown.

The cost of the grant of arms was met by the staff of the Council to mark the Festival of Britain.

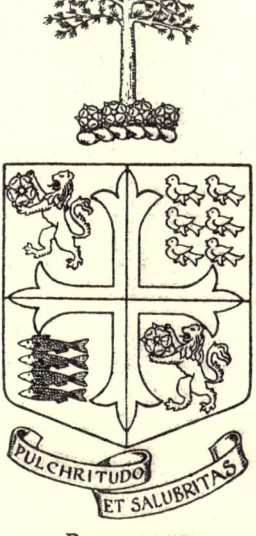
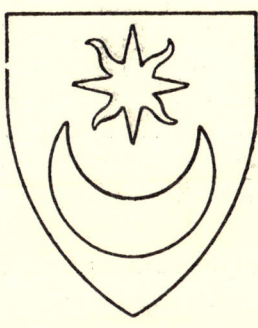

Hampshire C.C.   Bournemouth   Portsmouth

HAMPSHIRE

HAMPSHIRE County Council

The County Council of Southampton, having no arms, uses a device consisting of a red rose with a royal crown above it, between two sprays of laurel, and above the crown a cap of maintenance.

The present form of the device is the oldest of several versions. In one of the others the rose and crown are placed between oak and laurel sprays, the rose is of Tudor type, and there is no cap.

According to tradition, the red rose was granted to the County by John of Gaunt, Duke of Lancaster. Roses appear, with other emblems, on the fourteenth-century staple seal and the present arms of Southampton.

The cap of maintenance is of the conical pattern borne at the state opening of Parliament, not the heraldic chapeau. It was possibly included in the County insignia in allusion to the fact that the Marquesses of Winchester are hereditary bearers of the royal cap of maintenance.

BOURNEMOUTH County Borough Council

ARMS: Quarterly or and azure, a cross flory counter-changed; in the first and fourth quarters a lion rampant holding a rose, both azure; in the second, six gold martlets; in the third, four gold salmon.

*F

CREST: On a wreath or and azure, a green mount, and thereon a pine-tree proper with four gold roses at the base of the trunk.

MOTTO: *Pulchritudo et Salubritas*—'Beauty and Health.'

These were granted in 1891.

An explanation issued by the Corporation states that 'the whole district in the midst of which Bournemouth stands was originally a Royal Demesne of King Edward the Confessor. As this is the first existing item of authentic history relative to the place, it was felt that the arms of that monarch would properly form the field or basis of the corporate shield.' Hence the tinctures gold and blue, the cross flory, and the martlets. (For a note on the arms of the Confessor, see Chapter II.) The martlets are also locally regarded as sand-martins, representing Bournemouth's sand cliffs, while the colours and the fish suggest sky, sands, and sea.

The lion is that of England, coloured blue to distinguish it from the royal lion, and made rampant 'as indicating the constant calls to arms necessary in all that coast during the Middle Ages.' The pine-tree stands for the salubrity of Bournemouth's climate, and the use of the rose, 'the queen of flowers, emphasizes the motto: "For Beauty and Salubrity."'

PORTSMOUTH City and County Borough Council

ARMS: Azure, a star of eight rays above a crescent, both gold.

MOTTO: *Heaven's light our guide.*

The arms are recorded at the College of Arms. The origin and significance of the star and crescent as a royal badge are dealt with in Chapter II. Portsmouth received its first Charter from Richard I, from whose Great Seal these emblems were probably taken to serve on the seal and in the arms of the City. The motto is the same as that of the Order of the Star of India.

SOUTHAMPTON County Borough Council

ARMS: Parted fesswise argent and gules, three roses counterchanged.

CREST: On a green mount a gold tower in two tiers, from which rises the figure of Justice wearing a gold crown and a purple gown and holding in the right hand a silver sword with gold pommel and hilt and in the left a pair of scales sable with gold pans.

The shield rests on a mount in the midst of waves of the sea on which are two ships with sails furled and pennons of St George flying from the mast-heads; on the ships' sterns stand the SUPPORTERS: Two gold lions. This manner of placing the supporters is unparalleled in English municipal heraldry; the result is a very fine achievement of arms.

The arms, granted in 1575, embody the white and red roses of York and Lancaster which the Tudors united. Roses appear, with other emblems, on a fourteenth-century staple seal of Southampton. There is a tradition that the use of the red rose of Lancaster was granted to the County by John of Gaunt (see Hampshire C.C.).

HAMPSHIRE

Southampton

WINCHESTER City Council

ARMS: Gules, five silver castles, the middle one supported by two gold lions passant guardant.

These are recorded at the College of Arms. The lions are appropriate to the City which anciently vied with London for the position of capital of the Kingdom.

Winchester

Aldershot

ALDERSHOT Borough Council

ARMS: Quarterly gules and vaire, in the first a gold mitre and in the fourth two crossed swords proper, pommels and hilts or.

CREST: In a gold mural crown, a hind's head proper charged on the neck with a spur-rowel sable.

SUPPORTERS: Two lions guardant gules, each with a gold collar from which hangs a shield vaire.

156 CIVIC HERALDRY

Motto: *Pugna pro Patria*—'Fight for the country.'

These were granted in 1923.

Aldershot, as part of the Hundred of Crondall, anciently belonged to the Bishops of Winchester; hence the mitre in the first quarter.

In 1599 the Manor of Aldershot passed to the Tichborne family, from whose arms the vaire in the shield, the hind's head, the supporting lions, and the motto were taken.

By a coincidence the Tichborne motto is specially appropriate to the town which contains the headquarters of the largest military command in the British Empire—a fact to which the crossed swords also refer.

Before these arms were granted, Aldershot used an unofficial punning device consisting of a blue shield containing an alder-tree, and on a red chief three piles of shot.

ANDOVER

ANDOVER *Borough Council*

Arms: Argent, in front of an oak-tree proper growing from a mount vert, a lion statant guardant gules.

Crest: On a wreath argent and vert, a gold stag resting the right forehoof on a lozenge argent charged with a fleur-de-lis azure.

Supporters: Dexter, a lion guardant gules; sinister, an eagle azure, its wings spread and raised.

Motto: *Constantia basis virtutum*—'Steadfastness is the foundation of the virtues.'

These were granted in 1949.

HAMPSHIRE

A lion standing against an oak-tree was the device on a former seal of the Borough dating from at latest 1648. This is supposed to have been adopted because there was a royal hunting-lodge, at the place now called Woodhouse. The deer alludes to the forest and surrounding Andover, and the fleur-de-lis is for St Mary, the patron saint.

The supporting lion, besides being the national emblem, is from the insignia of the Earl of Suffolk and Berkshire, who is also Viscount Andover. The eagle indicates that Andover has been an important centre for the Royal Air Force.

The motto is that of Robert, Earl of Essex, who as High Steward of the Borough secured for it the charter granted by Queen Elizabeth I.

BASINGSTOKE Borough Council

The seal displays the Archangel Michael, to whom the parish church is dedicated.

CHRISTCHURCH Borough Council

The seal bears the image of Christ enthroned.

EASTLEIGH

FAREHAM

EASTLEIGH Borough Council

ARMS: Or, a bend checky sable and argent, in chief a mitre sable, in base a lily with stalk and leaves proper, and on the bend three roses gules, their seeds and sepals proper.

CREST: On a wreath gold and sable, in front of a rising sun a gold winged wheel.

MOTTO: *Salus populi suprema lex*—'The welfare of the people is the highest law.'

These were granted in 1934.

The chequered bend on a gold field signifies that the holder of the Manor of Eastleigh was Chamberlain of the King's Exchequer. The roses are emblems of Hampshire; the mitre refers to Bishopstoke; and the lily is for St Mary, patron of Bishopstoke and South Stoneham.

The crest consists of the winged wheel of transport, machinery, and industry against the rising sun of progress.

GOSPORT Borough Council

The Corporation uses as a device the Norman ship in which Henry of Blois landed at Gosport; with the motto, 'God's port our haven.'

LYMINGTON Borough Council

The Corporation seal, which dates from the fifteenth century, bears a one-masted ship with the sail furled, and hanging from the rigging a shield charged with three roundels and a label, the arms of the Courtenays, anciently Lords of the Manor: Gold, three roundels gules, and a label of three points azure.

ROMSEY Borough Council

The seal bears a portcullis.

FAREHAM Urban District Council

ARMS: Sable, issuing from water barry wavy silver and azure in the base, an ancient ship of gold, the sail furled, the flags argent charged with the cross of St George; on a chief argent two roses gules with seeds and sepals proper, and between them a pale gules charged with two keys bendwise, the upper silver and the lower gold, with a sword thrust between them in bend sinister, its blade silver and its pommel and hilt gold.

MOTTO: *Prest a faire*—'Ready to act.'

These arms were granted in 1947.

The black field represents Fareham's industrial background. A century ago it possessed a variety of industries, including ironworks which supplied the plates for our early ironclads.

The ship indicates the former importance of Fareham and Titchfield as ports. Before the days of the ironclads Fareham Creek was an anchorage for the Royal Navy.

The roses are from the insignia of Hampshire. The sword of St Paul and the keys of St Peter relate to the dedication of the parish church, and are also derived from the arms of the See of Winchester, the Bishops having been Lords of the Manor.

FARNBOROUGH Urban District Council

ARMS: Parted fesswise dancetty azure and gules, in chief two gold wings conjoined, and in base a gold fir-tree couped.

HAMPSHIRE

FARNBOROUGH

PETERSFIELD

CREST: On a wreath or and azure two fern-leaves saltirewise vert, and in front of them a cross between two roses all gold.

MOTTO: *Fides et justitia*—'Faith and justice.'

These were granted in 1934.

The dancetty treatment of the fesswise partition, forming three points, refers to three tumuli in the district and suggests its antiquities. The wings allude to the Royal Air Force, of which Farnborough was the birthplace; and the fir-tree stands for the pines with which the neighbourhood is richly wooded. The fern-leaves refer to the place-name, derived from Ferneberga. The cross symbolizes the religious life of the town, and the roses stand for the County.

HAVANT AND WATERLOO Urban District Council

The device is a rose.

PETERSFIELD Urban District Council

Arms are not officially recorded, but Burke gives: Argent, a rose gules with sepals vert, and thereon a silver escutcheon charged with an annulet between four roundels all sable.

Herefordshire C.C.

HEREFORDSHIRE

HEREFORDSHIRE County Council

ARMS: Gules, a fess wavy argent charged with a bar wavy azure; in chief a lion passant guardant argent and in base a Herefordshire bull's face proper.

CREST: On a wreath argent and gules, a demi-lion rampant guardant gules holding in the left paw a golden fleece.

SUPPORTERS: Dexter, a lion guardant or, with a wreath of hops proper about its neck; sinister, a talbot argent with a gold collar charged with three cider apples proper.

MOTTO: *Pulchra terra Dei donum*—'This fair land is the gift of God.'

These were granted in 1946.

The red field is from the arms of the City of Hereford and also represents the red earth of the County. The fess stands for the River Wye, and the lions are from the arms of the capital City. The crest is taken from the device of Leominster, the fleece referring to the woollen industry. The sinister supporter refers to the family of Talbot, Marcher Lords of Shrewsbury, and is also from the heraldry of Viscount Hereford. The other emblems indicate the produce of the County.

HEREFORD City Council

ARMS: Gules, three lions passant guardant argent within a bordure azure charged with ten silver saltires.

CREST: On a wreath argent and gules, a silver lion, as in the arms, holding erect a sword proper with a golden hilt.

HEREFORD

SUPPORTERS: Two silver lions rampant guardant, each with a collar azure charged with three gold buckles.

MOTTO: *Invictae fidelitatis praemium*—'The reward of faithfulness unconquered.'

Hereford bore on an early seal the Royal Arms of Richard I, from whom it received its first charter. It appears to have tinctured the lions silver for the purpose of creating a distinctive (but unauthorized) coat of arms. In 1645, as a Royalist centre, it was besieged by the Scots under Leslie, Earl of Leven, and in token of its loyalty the City received a grant of arms which not only recognized the arms which it had been using, but added emblems commemorative of the siege. The lions surrounded by saltires, or St Andrew's Crosses, represent the Royalist forces hemmed in by the insurgent Scots, and the buckles on the collars of the supporting lions are from the arms of the Earl of Leven.

The terms of the grant, dated 1645, printed in full in Fox-Davies's *Book of Public Arms*, set forth that,

ther hath not any City since this unnaturall Rebellion Exprest greater fidelity & Courage then ye City of herefford in Continuing there alleaganc & resisting ye many attempts of ye rebells but ye greatness of there loyallty Courages & undaunted resolution did then most eminently appeare when being straitly beseiged for ye space of 5 weeks by a powerfull army of Rebellious Scotts & having noe hopes of releife they Joyning with garison & doeing ye duty of souldiers then defended themselves & repelled ther fury & assaults with such singular constansy & resolution & with soe great distinction of ye beseidges that they are therby become ye wonder of ther Neighboring garisons & may be an Example to all other Citties & therfore doe justly deserve such caracters of honor as may be certified to posterity.

LEOMINSTER Borough Council

The device consists of a lion rampant holding a horned lamb in its left forepaw. This has been displayed on a shield, the lion being red and the lamb proper on a gold ground.

The lion was probably adopted in allusion to the first part of the name (which, however, has nothing to do with lions, but appears to be derived from the British place-name, Llan-lieni). The lamb refers to the woollen industry for which Leominster was famed from the thirteenth to the eighteenth century.

LEOMINSTER

Hertfordshire C.C.

HERTFORDSHIRE

HERTFORDSHIRE County Council

ARMS: Barry wavy of eight pieces azure and argent, thereon a gold escutcheon charged with a hart lodged proper.

Above the shield is placed a gold mural crown.

SUPPORTERS: Two harts proper, each with a gold chain about its neck and pendent therefrom a shield azure charged with a gold saltire.

MOTTO: *Trust and fear not.*

These were granted in 1925.

The arms are based on those of the Borough of Hertford, and are allusive to the name, the blue and white wavy bars standing for the ford.

The shields hanging from the necks of the harts bear the arms of St Albans.

The motto is that of Sir Charles Nall-Cain, who bore the cost of the grant to commemorate his year as High Sheriff.

HEMEL HEMPSTEAD Borough Council

The Corporation uses as a device a shield bearing the head and shoulders of a man in Tudor costume, representing Henry VIII. This has been in use since the sixteenth century, and was probably adopted in token of the fact that Hemel Hempstead received its first charter from Henry VIII.

See also Hemel Hempstead Development Corporation (below).

Hertford

HERTFORD Borough Council

ARMS: Argent, a hart proper lodged on water barry wavy azure and argent.

SUPPORTERS: Two lions ermine each with a collar gules about its neck and pendent therefrom by a chain gules a gold shield charged with three chevrons gules.

MOTTO: *Pride in our past, faith in our future.*

BADGE: Within a chaplet of red roses a hart's face and antlers proper, between the antlers a gold shield charged with three chevrons gules.

STANDARD: In the portion adjoining the staff are the arms of the town, and the tapering part is white and bears the badge three times repeated together with the legend *Pro Hertfordae Honore* in letters of gold on blue bands; the fringe of the standard is white and blue.

The arms, which are recorded at the Heralds' College, are based upon a seal bearing a hart standing in water, in the background a tree and a castle with three domed towers, and between the hart's antlers a crosslet pointed at the foot. The badge and standard were granted in 1925. The arms on the shield which forms part of the badge are those of the family De Clare, by whom the Earldom of Hertford was held in the twelfth century.

The grant of supporters was obtained in 1937 to commemorate the coronation of King George VI. The lions are those of the Marquess of Salisbury differenced by shields bearing the Clare arms. The Cecil Lords Salisbury have, with one exception, held the office of High Steward of the Borough since 1605.

HERTFORDSHIRE

HERTFORD STANDARD

ST ALBANS City Council

ARMS: Azure, a saltire or.

These are recorded at the College of Arms. They are the arms ascribed by the medieval heralds to the Kingdom of Mercia, and appear to have been adopted by St Albans in consequence of the foundation, in 793, of the monastery to the memory of St Alban by Offa, King of Mercia.

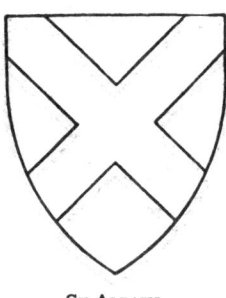

ST ALBANS

WATFORD

WATFORD Borough Council

ARMS: Gules, on a pale wavy argent another azure, and thereon a silver fasces; on either side of the pale a gold scallop shell; on a gold chief two harts statant gules, and between them a roundel azure charged with a gold saltire.

MOTTO: *Audentior*—'Bolder.'

These were granted in 1922.

The Town Clerk informs me that

the fasces refers to the Roman occupation as there is said to have been a Roman station at Watford. The pallet wavy azure and pale wavy argent are intended to represent the River Colne and its banks. The escallops are taken from the arms of Lord Clarendon, the first Mayor of Watford; the harts represent Hertfordshire and the saltire is from the arms of St Albans, the greater part of Watford having at one time belonged to the Abbey of St Albans.

BALDOCK BERKHAMSTED BISHOP'S STORTFORD

BALDOCK Urban District Council

ARMS: Or, a cross gules, in the first and fourth quarters three chevrons gules, and on the cross a gold barley sheaf; on a chief sable a gold hart's head torn off at the neck between two Madonna lilies proper.

CREST: On a wreath gold and gules, the head of a Roman centurion's standard of S.P.Q.R. with thunderbolt, laurel wreath, and eagle all or.

MOTTO: *Sic vos non vobis.*

These were granted in 1951.

The red cross alludes to the Knights Templar, and the black chief is from their banner. The chevrons are from the arms of Richard 'Strongbow,' Earl of Pembroke. The barley sheaf alludes to the malt industry, the hart's head to the County, and the lilies to St Mary's Church. The crest refers to the Roman settlement at Baldock.

BERKHAMSTED Urban District Council

ARMS: Or, a castle azure with three domed towers, over each of the outer towers a banner argent charged with a cross gules, all within a bordure sable charged with gold roundels.

These are recorded as the arms of the former Borough of Great Berkhamsted. The border indicates that the castle appertains to the Duchy of Cornwall. It was the principal home in England of Edward, the Black Prince.

CHESHUNT

HARPENDEN

BISHOP'S STORTFORD Urban District Council

ARMS: Vert, a pale argent surmounted by a fess wavy argent charged with a bar wavy azure, the tinctures of the fess and bar counter-changed where they lie on the pale; and on the pale a mitre in chief and a wheatsheaf in base, both proper.

CREST: On a wreath argent and vert, a mount vert and thereon the battlements of a tower proper, and rising therefrom a cross pommelled gules.

MOTTO: *Pro Deo et populo*—'For God and the people.'

These were granted in 1952.

The emblems on the shield refer to the River Stort, the rural and agricultural area through which it flows, the ford from which the town takes its name, and the Bishops of London who formerly held the manor.

The battlements represent the castle, whose ruins form a ring on a mound in the town, and the cross is that of St Michael, in whose name the parish church is dedicated.

CHESHUNT Urban District Council

ARMS: Argent, a fess wavy azure surmounted by a pale ermine; on a chief azure a gold castle with three towers, between a conjoined rose and thistle with stalk and leaves, and an uprooted oak-tree bearing acorns, all proper.

CREST: On a wreath argent and azure, a falcon proper with gold bells resting its right claw on a cross formy or.

On a scroll below the shield is the name CESTREHUNT.

These were granted in 1945.

The pale and wavy fess represent Ermine Street crossing the River Lea. The united rose and thistle refers to King James I's residence at Theobalds. The castle is from the arms of Castile in allusion to Queen Eleanor, one of whose memorial crosses is at Waltham Cross. The tree represents Goff's Oak. The crest recalls Cheshunt's former fame for falconry, and the cross is from the arms of the Meux family, benefactors of the district.

EAST BARNET Urban District Council

The Council uses a device consisting of a shield parted palewise argent and gules with two roses counter-changed, between them two swords crossed saltirewise proper, and above the swords the Greek letter *omega*; a chief azure charged with a fleur-de-lis between two crosses flory, all gold. The swords and roses, with the *omega*, stand for the last battle of the Wars of the Roses, fought at Barnet. The emblems on the chief refer to St Mary's Church.

HARPENDEN Urban District Council

ARMS: Bendy of six pieces gules and argent, three gold wheatsheaves; on a chief azure a pale between two saltires all gold, and on the pale a fess dancetty sable.

CREST: On a wreath argent and gules, a mount vert within wattled palings proper, and on the mount a hart lodged proper.

MOTTO: *Fide et labore*—'By faith and industry.'

These were granted in 1949.

The fess dancetty is from the arms of the Wittewronges, Lords of the Manor, and the saltires represent the Diocese of St Albans. The three wheatsheaves are symbolic of the great contribution to the growth of wheat by the Rothamsted Laboratory at Harpenden. The crest alludes to the County.

HITCHIN Urban District Council

ARMS: Gules, a fess arched and embattled argent between a lion passant guardant and a barley sheaf both or; and on the fess a fleshing-knife proper.

CREST: On a wreath argent and gules, two shepherd's crooks crossed saltirewise and hanging therefrom a fleece, all proper.

MOTTO: *Et patribus et posteritati*—'For both ancestors and posterity.'

These were granted in 1936.

The lion is appropriate to a royal manor, and the other emblems indicate local industries.

HERTFORDSHIRE

HITCHIN

LETCHWORTH

ROYSTON

LETCHWORTH Urban District Council

ARMS: Argent, three chevrons gules; overlying the point of the top chevron a chief embattled azure charged with two white roses, their seeds and sepals proper.

CREST: On a wreath argent and gules an owl argent full-fronted between two branches of oak vert with gold acorns.

MOTTO: *Prudens futuri*—'Prudent for the future.'

These were granted in 1944.

The chevrons relate to the old families of Montfichet and Barrington, Lords of the Manor of Letchworth, and the roses allude to the garden city.

ROYSTON Urban District Council

ARMS: Silver, a fess gules and thereon another fess checky argent and sable; in chief two Tudor roses and in base a tripping hart proper; the whole surmounting an archiepiscopal staff also proper.

CREST: On a wreath silver and gules, a hooded crow perched on a representation of the Roys Stone all proper.

MOTTO: *A bonis ad meliora*—'From good things to better.'

These were granted in 1952.

The roses refer to Tudor associations, and the chequers, from the Stuart heraldry, to the connection of King James I with the town. The hart alludes to the County, and the archiepiscopal staff denotes Royston Priory. In the crest, the hooded crow, a bird found in the district, is perched on the 'Roys Stone,' a two-ton boulder which was originally at the base of the Roys Cross which stood for several centuries at the crossing of Ermine Street and the Icknield Way.

HATFIELD R.D.C.   HERTFORD R.D.C.

HATFIELD Rural District Council

ARMS: Barry of ten pieces argent and azure, a lion rampant ermine; on a chief gules three open crowns of gold; all within a gold border charged with eight Tudor roses.

CREST: On a wreath argent and azure, an oak-tree proper charged with a Tudor rose.

MOTTO: *Semper serio*—'Always in earnest.'

These were granted in 1945.

The arms summarize Hatfield's history. The monks of Ely set up a community here, and built the church and palace, originally the Bishop's residence. They are represented by the three crowns of St Etheldreda (cf. Isle of Ely C.C.).

Hatfield became a royal palace in the reign of Henry VIII and so continued throughout Tudor times; hence the roses, and the oak which represents the tree under which Queen Elizabeth I is said to have been sitting when she was told of her accession.

When James I came from Scotland he stayed at Theobalds, the seat of Sir Robert Cecil, first Earl of Salisbury, and so liked the place that he offered him the royal palace at Hatfield in exchange. This was effected, and Hatfield has since been the principal seat of this branch of the Cecil family. The barry field and the ermine lion are from the Cecil heraldry.

The motto is a combination of Queen Elizabeth I's *Semper eadem* and Lord Salisbury's *Sero sed serio*.

HERTFORDSHIRE

HERTFORD Rural District Council

ARMS: Azure, on a gold saltire a hart's face with antlers gules, all within a border barry wavy of eight argent and azure.

CREST: On a wreath argent and azure, a gold hart rearing on its hind legs, its head facing, in front of an oak-tree proper with gold acorns.

MOTTO: *Pro rure pro patria*—'For countryside and Country.'

These were granted in 1951.

They combine the saltire from the arms of the City and Diocese of St Albans with emblems of the County and token of the woods and waters of the countryside.

HEMEL HEMPSTEAD DEVELOPMENT CORPORATION

HEMEL HEMPSTEAD Development Corporation

ARMS: Vert, a Tudor rose, the outer petals white and the inner ones red, with seeds and sepals proper, within a surveyor's chain of silver.

CREST: On a wreath argent and vert, a hart proper lodged on a mount vert within a mural crown gules.

SUPPORTERS: Dexter, a greyhound, and sinister, a hart, each proper with a mural crown gules about its neck.

MOTTO: *Majora, uberiora, pulchriora*—'Greater, more fruitful, and more beautiful.'

These were granted in 1948.

The harts refer to the County. The double rose and the greyhound, Tudor emblems, allude to the period in which Hemel Hempstead's original charter was granted, and the surveyor's chain indicates development.

STEVENAGE DEVELOPMENT CORPORATION

STEVENAGE Development Corporation

ARMS: Gold, a four-barred gate sable and a chief indented of six points azure.

CREST: On a wreath gold and sable an oak-tree with its roots and bearing acorns all proper with a mural crown gules about the base of the trunk.

SUPPORTERS: Two harts proper each with a gold chain about its neck and hanging therefrom a gold escutcheon charged with an acorn proper.

MOTTO: *Consider thy purpose.*

These were granted in 1950.

The oak-tree and strong gate are symbolic of old and new Stevenage respectively, and the supporting harts stand for Hertfordshire. The indented chief represents the ancient monument of Six Hills and also refers to the family of Lytton of Knebworth.

Huntingdonshire C.C.

HUNTINGDONSHIRE

HUNTINGDONSHIRE County Council

ARMS: Barry wavy of twelve argent and azure, a lozenge vert, its points touching the edges of the shield, charged with a fess embattled between in chief three wheatsheaves and in base a cornucopia all gold.

CREST: On a wreath argent and azure, a lion rampant gules with a gold collar of fleurs-de-lis lying alternate ways, supporting a staff proper and thereon a banner vert charged with a gold hunting-horn with gold strings.

MOTTO: *Labore omnia florent*—'All things prosper by industry.'

These were granted in 1937.

I am indebted to the Clerk of the Council for the following explanatory note by the Earl of Sandwich:

The lozenge on the shield represents the natural geographical shape of the County; the colour green, its grazing nature. This shape lent itself into division into two triangles, the upper with corn sheaves representing the highlands, the lower with a cornucopia signifying the plenty of the fen districts. The battlemented bar stands for Huntingdon, the fortress commanding the passing of the River Ouse, a fact of great importance in early history. The blue and white barry wavy lines on the shield indicate the River Ouse and water-courses of the fen area.

In early history the County was a fief of the Scottish Crown, so it was thought proper to show this. The red lion rampant is the emblem of Scotland [and the fleurs-de-lis forming its collar are from the Royal Arms of Scotland; cf. the arms of Cambridgeshire C.C.]. The banner with the hunting horn is a play on the name of the County, and signifies the forest of the uplands and hunting from early times (including that of James I, who at one time considered the purchase of Hinchingbrooke for a hunting box) down to the present day.

GODMANCHESTER Borough Council

The seal bears a fleur-de-lis.

HUNTINGDON Borough Council

The seal bears a device consisting of a hunting scene, in allusion, of course, to the name. In the centre is a tree with a bird perched on a lower branch; on one side is a stag chased by two hounds, and on the other is a huntsman winding a horn and carrying a bow.

The huntsman is represented in a peaked cap, belted coat, breeches, and top-boots—a costume much at variance with the local tradition that he is Robin Hood. The identification of Robin as an Earl of Huntingdon is a late addition to the lore that clusters round the famous outlaw, and is probably based upon a jocular description of any huntsman as the Earl of Huntingdon.

ST IVES Borough Council

The Corporation has not obtained arms, but has adopted the following: Argent, four bulls' heads gules.

MOTTO: *Sudore non sopore*—'By toil, not by sleep.'

The Town Clerk has supplied the following note:

This Borough is not an ancient borough, but was incorporated in 1874. It was at that time, I think, the smallest town in the country which had been granted incorporation, and the grant was made almost entirely in consequence of the importance of the market, which at one time was supposed to be the second largest market in the country. The Borough arms were accordingly selected on that account, the four bulls' heads being intended to be significant of the importance of the town as a market. The bulls' heads are coloured red on a white shield on a blue setting.

St Ives

Isle of Wight C.C.

ISLE OF WIGHT

ISLE OF WIGHT County Council

Arms: Azure, a silver castle with three towers between three gold anchors.

Crest: On a wreath argent and azure, a gold mural crown charged with three anchors azure.

Supporters: Dexter, a horse, and sinister, a sea-horse, both argent.

Motto: *All this beauty is of God.*

These were granted in 1938.

The blue field and the anchors represent the sea, and the castle is that of Carisbrooke, once the capital of the island. The supporters allude to farming and seafaring interests.

NEWPORT Borough Council

The seal, which dates from the thirteenth century, bears a ship with one mast and the sail spread.

CIVIC HERALDRY

RYDE

RYDE Borough Council

ARMS: Argent, a schooner yacht in full sail on the sea proper, within a border azure charged with eight gold stars.

CREST: On a wreath argent and azure, a rock, and thereon a sea-horse proper, charged on the body with two gold stars.

MOTTO: *Amoenitas salubritas urbanitas.*

These were granted in 1869.

The significance of the stars (technically 'estoiles') is unknown, but it is possible that they were suggested by the estoile in the arms of Portsmouth, which faces Ryde across Spithead; or they may represent starfish, emblems of the seaside.

VENTNOR Urban District Council

The seal bears the figure of Hygieia.

KENT C.C.

KENT

KENT County Council

ARMS: Gules a horse rampant argent.

CREST: Rising from a mural crown, three masts rigged with courses set and topsails furled, all proper; at each mast-head a white pennon charged with a red cross.

SUPPORTERS: Two gold heraldic sea-lions, each with a collar gules with pendent shield, the dexter bearing the arms of the See of Canterbury and the sinister those of the Cinque Ports.

MOTTO: *Invicta*—'Unconquered.'

These were granted in 1933.

The arms are those attributed to the ancient kingdom of Kent; they have for long been associated with the modern County, and have now been confirmed to the County Council. The horse was the steed of Odin. It was displayed on the standard of the Saxon chieftain who first invaded Kent; he was accordingly called 'the Horse'—*hengst* in the tongue of some of his followers, and *horsa* in that of others. Hence arose the fable of the brothers Hengist and Horsa.

The other emblems refer to the maritime situation and interests of the county, and to its ecclesiastical associations.

CANTERBURY

CANTERBURY City and County Borough Council

ARMS: Argent, three Cornish choughs sable with beaks and legs gules; on a chief gules a gold lion of England.

MOTTO: *Ave Mater Angliae*—'Hail, Mother of England.'

These arms are on record at the Heralds' College.

Canterbury was anciently part of the royal domain. The choughs are from the arms of Thomas Becket, and their combination with the royal lion is a reminder of the fatal quarrel between Henry II and the Archbishop, and of the ultimate reconciliation between Church and State. The murder of Becket is depicted on the fourteenth-century seal.

BECKENHAM Borough Council

ARMS: Vert, two bars wavy argent, between in chief two uprooted chestnut-trees in full bloom proper, and in base a horse rampant argent.

CREST: On a wreath argent and vert, a gold demi-lion guardant supporting a pastoral staff of silver enfiled by a mitre proper.

SUPPORTERS: Dexter, a gentleman, and sinister, a lady, each in the costume of the early sixteenth century, proper.

MOTTO: *Non nobis solum*—'Not for ourselves alone.'

The arms and crest were granted in 1931 to the Beckenham Urban District Council, and the supporters were granted in 1935 when Beckenham became a borough.

The following explanation was supplied by the Clerk to the U.D.C.:

The general colour scheme of the shield is green. That is suggestive of the Beckenham we have known of old—a township with a rural setting—and of a characteristic we are doing our best to preserve.

The two chestnut-trees in bloom are in keeping with that idea, and are indicative of the beauty of the flowering trees and shrubs in many parts of our town during spring and summer, and of our parks and well-wooded gardens.

The wavy white lines are the heraldic symbol of the River Beck which (though actually only a stream) has given the town its name.

Below we have the famous white horse of Kent, linking us up with one of the most famous counties of England.

BECKENHAM

For a crest, reference has been made to the ancient and modern ownership of large areas of Beckenham. The lion is the lion of the Cator family; and the ecclesiastical symbols in its grasp are representative of Odo, Bishop of Bayeux. He was half-brother to William the Conqueror, who presented the land and manors of Beckenham to the Bishop.

BEXLEY Borough Council

ARMS: Parted fesswise vert and or, a fess wavy barry wavy of four pieces argent and azure; in the chief an eagle displayed between two apples with leaves and stalks all gold, and in the base an uprooted oak-tree proper.

CREST: A gold coronet of four fleurs-de-lis and therein a mound of heather proper with a horse argent rearing upon it.

MOTTO: *Non nobis sed communitati*—'Not for ourselves but for the community.'

These were granted in 1937.

The green and gold field suggests old Bexley's rural setting of grass and cornland, and the oak-tree stands for the woods which abounded before the town grew, and survive in many beautifully wooded parks. The becks (which may have given rise to the place-name) are indicated by the fess, and the former heath-land of Bexley Heath is recalled by the heather, on which stands the Kentish white horse. The apples represent the famous fruit-growing areas of East Wickham, Welling, and Bexleyheath.

The crown was included in token that the arms were granted in King George VI's coronation year. It may also be taken as one of the crowns in the arms of Oxford University, which still owns land at Bexley bequeathed by Sir William Camden to found the Camden Professorship. The eagle is from the arms of Lord Bexley.

BEXLEY BROMLEY CHATHAM

BROMLEY Borough Council

ARMS: Quarterly gules and azure on a fess wavy argent three flying ravens proper; in the first quarter two silver branches of broom saltirewise, in the second the sun or, in the third a gold scallop shell, and in the fourth a horse rampant argent.

CREST: On a wreath argent and gules, two bars wavy azure and argent, and thereon a gold scallop shell between two branches of broom proper.

MOTTO: *Dum cresco spero*—'While I grow I hope.'

These were granted in 1904.

The broom, ravens, and sun are allusive to the name of the Borough, the River Ravensbourne, and the Manor of Sundridge. The scallop shell is from the arms of the See of Rochester, which held the Manor from the reign of Ethelbert; the See bears it in allusion to St James, patron of pilgrims. The horse is that of Kent.

CHATHAM Borough Council

ARMS: Argent, a fess checky gules and gold, in chief two ancient ships with three masts, the sails set, proper, the pennants gules, and in base a sword proper with a gold pommel and hilt, and a trident crossed saltirewise and entwined by a wreath of laurel proper.

CREST: Rising from a gold naval crown a trident adorned with a wreath of laurel proper.

MOTTO: *Loyal and true.*

These were granted in 1891.

The chequered fess is from the arms of Pitt, Earl of Chatham; the Borough has changed the tinctures both for difference and to denote the town's military associations. The sword, trident, and laurel wreath refer to the Royal Marines, and the ships and naval crown to the senior Service.

In American civic heraldry, the arms of the Pitt family form the basis of those of Pittsburgh, Pennsylvania; and Pittsfield, Massachusetts.

DARTFORD

DARTFORD Borough Council

ARMS: Gules, on a fess argent a barrulet wavy azure, in the chief a jester's head cut off at the neck, and wearing a fool's cap, all gold, between two gold roundels each charged with an ear of wheat proper, and in the base an anvil or.

SUPPORTERS: Dexter, a hermit holding a staff in his right hand; and sinister, a prioress holding a pastoral staff in her left hand, all proper.

MOTTO: *Tenax et fidelis*—'Steadfast and faithful.'

These were granted in 1933 on the incorporation of Dartford as a borough.
The official explanation states:

The waters of the Darent ... are aptly rendered in heraldic convention by means of the stretch of silver traversed by a winding band of blue which reaches across the shield. Other charges mark some of the great industries for which the borough is famous. Paper-making is represented in the playful spirit, which is traditional in heraldry, by the Fool's Cap. It is of interest in this connection to note that the emblem is found as a water-mark in paper as early as the reign of King Charles II. On either side are golden roundels, which are as near as heraldry permits to get to the familiar tabloids of our chemical factories. These are charged with ears of wheat, symbolizing another of the staple industries of the borough. The golden anvil at the base of the shield is emblematical of the great engineering and metal-working interests.

In the supporters ... we are carried back to the ancient history and traditions of Dartford.

On the one side stands the hermit, who serves to typify those recluses who, by their holy lives and untiring devotion to the cause of humanity, set a noble example for all time. It may, moreover, be recalled that it was through their exertions that funds were obtained for erecting the first bridge over the Darent. The earliest hermit of whom there is any record, John Sodeman by name, under the title of 'Hermit of the Chapel of the Blessed Virgin and Martyr, St Katherine of Dertford, for reformation of the poor,' obtained Letters of Indulgence from the Bishop of the Diocese on the 1st of June 1438. The prioress... takes us back to an even earlier date, since it was in 1355 that the Augustinian nunnery was established by King Edward III.

DEAL

DOVER

DEAL *Borough Council*

Having no arms of its own, the Corporation uses those of Sandwich (*q.v.*) with two towers for crest. Within the organization of the Cinque Ports, Deal was attached to Sandwich, which is recorded at the Heralds' College as bearing the arms of the Cinque Ports with a slight variation of tincture.

DOVER *Borough Council*

ARMS: Argent, St Martin on horseback, with his sword in his hand, in the act of dividing his cloak with a beggar, all proper, within a border gules charged with gold lions of England.

These arms, recorded at the Heralds' College, are based on a fourteenth-century seal of the Corporation.

St Martin of Tours became the Patron of Dover by the dedication of a collegiate church founded in 696 and reconstituted as a Benedictine Priory in the twelfth century. The sequel to the charitable act commemorated in the arms was a vision in which St Martin saw Christ wearing the half of the cloak which the saint had given to the beggar.

The accompanying drawing of the arms is based upon the design on the seal.

KENT

Erith

Faversham

Gillingham

ERITH Borough Council

ARMS: Argent, a fleur-de-lis sable between three luces (pike) erect, heads upwards, gules, and on a canton gules a horse rampant argent.

CREST: On a wreath argent and sable, a running stag gules in front of a gold wheatsheaf.

MOTTO: *Labour overcomes all things.*

These were granted in 1906.

The luces are from the arms of the family De Luci, anciently Lords of the Manor of Lesnes. Henry de Luci founded Lesnes Abbey in 1178, and the Abbey arms also incorporated the luces. The wheatsheaf is from the crest of the family of Wheatley, Lords of the Manor of Erith until 1875. The horse represents Kent.

FAVERSHAM Borough Council

A thirteenth-century seal of the Barons of Faversham—from a very early date a limb of the Cinque Ports—bears the three lions of England on a shield. The arms of the town are claimed to be: Gules, three lions passant guardant, parted palewise gold and silver. These are not recorded at the College of Arms; they are clearly a variation of the Royal Arms. Presumably the tincturing of the lions' hindquarters silver was carried out to produce a distinctive coat of arms for the town, but the actual effect is that Faversham is using, without authority, the arms of the great Irish family of O'Brien. The reverse of the seal bears a ship with a banner on which are the three chevrons of Clare.

FOLKESTONE Borough Council

A member of the Cinque Port of Dover, Folkestone bears on its seal an ancient ship with the legend, *Sigill Baronum Folkestanie*.

GILLINGHAM Borough Council

ARMS: Argent, a cross gules; in the first quarter an ancient harp, in the second an antique ship on the sea, in the third a tower on a rock rising out of the sea, and in the fourth a sprig of broom, all proper.

CREST: On a wreath argent and gules, two crossed swords, one sheathed, in front of an anchor with cable, all proper.

MOTTO: *With Fort and Fleet for Home and England.*

These were granted in 1904.

The cross of St George, and the fort and ship in the arms, symbolize the idea summed up in the motto. The broom alludes to the district of Brompton. The crossed swords recall the battle, in 1016, between Edmund Ironside and Canute.

GRAVESEND

LYDD

GRAVESEND Borough Council

ARMS: Argent, a tower gules charged with a gold bull's head, breathing flames, in a gold coronet; a border azure charged with five fleurs-de-lis alternating with five buckles, all or.

MOTTO: *Decus et tutamen*—'An honour and a protection.'

The bull's head is from an old seal. The border of fleurs-de-lis and buckles was granted in 1635 to commemorate the Duke of Lennox's connection with the town.

HYTHE Borough Council

The Corporation has no arms. The seal bears a ship on the sea, with one mast, and two men on the yard-arm. Hythe is one of the Cinque Ports.

LYDD Borough Council

ARMS: Azure, rising from water in the base, a silver church with tower and spire, and behind it a gold ship, its stern half showing on the sinister side of the shield, the sail furled; on the stern of the ship a man blowing a horn; a canton argent charged with a cross and four lions rampant all gules.

These arms are recorded at the Heralds' College. They are a development of a thirteenth-century seal, on which the accompanying illustration is based. Burke and Fox-Davies both describe the building as a castle, but there is no doubt that it in fact represents the Church of All Saints, and the seal is the more valuable because it preserves the appearance of the church as it stood at an early date. Lydd, at one time associated with the Cinque Port of Romney, now lies nearly three miles from the sea, and the ship in its arms has therefore only an historic and rather melancholy significance. What is a canton in the arms is, in the seal, a shield hanging from a hook; the cross is very thin, and may be intended only as lines dividing the shield into quarters. The lions were probably derived from the Royal Arms.

MAIDSTONE

MAIDSTONE Borough Council

ARMS: Or, a fess wavy azure between three roundels gules, and on a chief gules a gold lion passant guardant.

CREST: Out of a gold mural crown, a horse's head argent with a chaplet of hops proper about its neck.

SUPPORTERS: Dexter, an iguanodon proper, and sinister, a gold lion, each with a collar gules and hanging therefrom by a gold chain a scroll of parchment proper, that on the

*G

iguanodon inscribed with the date 1549, and that on the lion with the date 1949 in black characters.

Motto: *Agriculture and Commerce.*

The arms on a seal, without tinctures, were recorded at the Heralds' Visitation of Kent in 1619. They were confirmed, with tinctures, in 1949, the crest and supporters being granted at the same time as part of the celebration of the 400th anniversary of Maidstone's first charter of incorporation.

The wavy fess represents the River Medway, and the red roundels are from the arms of Archbishop Courtenay who, at the close of the fourteenth century, built All Saints' Church. Above is a lion of England, which gave rise to the choice of a lion as the sinister supporter. The iguanodon stands for the town's prehistoric background, a complete skeleton of this creature having been found within the Borough. The horse's head is from the County insignia, and its collar of hops refers to the produce for which the district is famous.

MARGATE

NEW ROMNEY

MARGATE Borough Council

Arms: Parted palewise gules and azure, a silver chevron between in chief a demi-lion passant guardant joined with the stern end of a ship's hull or, and in base a horse rampant argent.

Crest: On a wreath argent and gules, a sea-horse supporting a ship's mast proper.

Motto: *Porta maris portus salutis*—'A gate of the sea and a haven of health.'

These were granted in 1858.

Anciently a non-corporate limb of Dover, Margate bears the lion-hull of the Cinque Ports. The white horse is that of Kent.

NEW ROMNEY Borough Council

ARMS: Azure, three lions passant guardant or.

These are recorded at the College of Arms.

One of the original Cinque Ports, Romney appears to have combined the Royal Arms with those of the Ports by placing the lions of England on blue, the tincture of the field of the Cinque Ports arms.

QUEENBOROUGH Borough Council

The seal bears a castle from the battlements of which rises the figure of a queen, who is obviously intended for Queen Philippa after whom Edward III named the town. Edward built Queenborough Castle about 1361.

RAMSGATE

RAMSGATE Borough Council

ARMS: Quarterly gules and azure, a cross composed of two narrow palets and two barrulets interlaced argent; in the first quarter a horse rampant argent; in the second a silver demi-lion joined to the stern end of a gold ship's hull; in the third a dolphin proper; and in the fourth an ancient ship of gold.

CREST: Within a gold naval crown, a lighthouse upon a pierhead proper.

SUPPORTERS: Dexter, a lifeboatman, and sinister, a coastguard holding a telescope in his left hand, all proper.

MOTTO: *Salus naufragis salus aegris*—'Safety to the shipwrecked, health to the sick.'

The arms and crest were granted in 1884 and the supporters in 1935.

The white horse stands for Kent. The lion joined to a ship's hull is from the arms of the Cinque Ports (see Chapter II), Ramsgate being a member of Sandwich. The other emblems are all appropriate to a watering place and seaport.

The supporters were adopted as marking Ramsgate's association with the sea through the Royal Harbour since 1760.

ROCHESTER City Council

ARMS: Or, on a cross gules a gold letter r, and on a chief gules a lion of England or.

These are recorded at the Heralds' College.

The lion recalls that Rochester was originally a royal borough. The arms are remarkable for the inclusion of a letter of the alphabet, the initial of the name.

SANDWICH Borough Council

ARMS: Parted palewise gules and azure, three gold lions of England halved and joined to the stern ends of three silver ships' hulls.

These are recorded at the College of Arms.

As one of the original Cinque Ports, Sandwich bears the arms of the Ports (see Chapter II), changing the tincture of the ships' hulls from gold to silver.

ROCHESTER

TENTERDEN

SANDWICH

TENTERDEN Borough Council

ARMS: Gules, on the sea a three-masted ship of gold, the foresail furled; the mainsail parted palewise gules and azure and charged with three gold lions passant guardant halved and joined to the stern ends of three silver ships' hulls; and the mizzen sail silver and charged with a bend sable between four lions' heads gules, torn off at the neck, with three gold stars on the bend.

These are recorded at the College of Arms.

KENT

The arms on the mainsail are those of the Cinque Ports (but with the ships' hulls tinctured silver), Tenterden being a member of the Port of Rye. A ship bearing these arms on its sail and a banner of St George at the stern stands on the fifteenth-century seal of Tenterden. On the reverse of the same seal, beneath a figure of St Mildred, the Patron of the town, is a shield bearing the arms which appear on the mizzen of the ship in the town arms. These are the arms of the Pillesden or Pitlesden family, one of whom was the first Bailiff of Tenterden.

ASHFORD   TUNBRIDGE WELLS   CRAYFORD

TUNBRIDGE WELLS Borough Council

ARMS: Gules, sprinkled with silver drops, and in base two heraldic fountains (i.e. roundels barry wavy argent and azure); a gold pile charged with a lion rampant gules.

CREST: On a wreath gold and gules, a well proper, and therefrom rising a lion rampant gules holding in the forepaws an heraldic fountain.

MOTTO: *Do well, doubt not.*

These were granted in 1889.

The allusions in arms, crest, and motto to the medicinal springs to which the town owes its name are obvious. The lions recall that Tunbridge Wells is officially styled 'Royal.'

ASHFORD Urban District Council

The device, used in lieu of arms, consists of a red shield with a silver fess between in chief a white horse rampant, and in base a locomotive engine of early type in proper colours; and three black rings on the fess. The horse is that of Kent, and the engine indicates the town's importance as a railway centre. The rings are from the arms of the family of Fogge, a member of which in the fifteenth century built the church; they have sometimes been taken to represent the ends of barrels, in allusion to the hop industry.

HERNE BAY   SITTINGBOURNE AND MILTON   TONBRIDGE

CRAYFORD *Urban District Council*

ARMS: Azure, a horse rearing argent, and on a chief argent two bars wavy azure and thereon a falcon facing with wings outspread gules.

MOTTO: *Fortiter et recte*—'Boldly and justly.'

The arms were granted in 1945.

The horse stands for Kent, and the wavy bars for the Rivers Thames and Cray. The falcon is an allusion to the first heavier-than-air flying machine, which was invented by Sir Hiram Maxim and flown on rails in a field in Crayford. Sir Hiram was a partner in the firm of Vickers, Son & Maxim, now Vickers-Armstrong Ltd, who have the largest factory in Crayford.

HERNE BAY *Urban District Council*

ARMS: Barry wavy of six pieces argent and azure, on a chief azure a gold heron between two silver crosses formy, the lower limbs pointed.

CREST: On a wreath argent and azure a lymphad (or ancient galley) gules, the sail argent and charged with a bull statant sable, its horns and hoofs gules, and from the masthead a pennant flying per fess argent and azure.

MOTTO: *Ne cede malis*—'Yield not to adversity.'

These were granted in 1948.

The references to the sea are evident. The heron, allusive to the name, was the device of the Council before the arms were obtained. The crosses, ecclesiastical emblems of Christ Church, denote the cathedral church of the Diocese and the parish church of Herne Bay. The lymphad recalls the Roman occupation of the fort of Regulbium, now Reculver, and the ox is from the arms of Sir Henry Oxenden, one of the chief landowners in the district when Herne Bay was developed in the eighteen-thirties.

SEVENOAKS Urban District Council

The device consists of seven acorns.

SHEERNESS Urban District Council

The device consists of an ancient ship with one mast and the sail furled, on the sea, between on one side a tower with a flag, and on the other a rose; above the ship is a naval crown, and below is a prancing horse.

SITTINGBOURNE AND MILTON Urban District Council

ARMS: Or, a lion rampant towards the sinister gules and a wyvern rampant towards the dexter vert, supporting between them a scroll of parchment erect proper; on a chief azure a Saxon crown between two scallop shells, all gold.

CREST: On a wreath or and gules, a cherry-tree bearing fruit, growing on a mound, all proper.

MOTTO: *Known by their fruits.*

These were granted in 1949.

The wyvern, associated with the manor of Milton, was formerly used as a device by the Milton Regis U.D.C., and by the present Council before arms were obtained. The lion was introduced to represent Sittingbourne, with particular reference to the ancient Red Lion Inn, an important place on the Dover road, especially in the coaching days. Here King Henry V is reputed to have been entertained on his return from the Agincourt campaign; and this way, a few years later, his body was brought from France for interment in Westminster Abbey. The place is also associated with visits by Henry VII, Henry VIII, and James I.

The scroll refers to the town's paper-making industry. The Saxon crown indicates that Milton was a royal manor before the Conquest. The scallops stand for both the Milton fisheries and for the pilgrims who passed this way bound for Canterbury or the Continent. The crest points to the fact that Sittingbourne is the centre of the cherry-growing area of the country; it is said that cherries were first planted in England at Teynham, near Sittingbourne, by Henry VIII.

TONBRIDGE Urban District Council

ARMS: Argent, five palets wavy azure and a chief gold, over all a masoned bridge of five arches proper, and superimposed on the palets in the base of the shield an ancient ship with sail set and oars in action sable, flags gules.

CREST: On a wreath argent and azure, a masoned portway proper, on each of its two towers a conical roof azure, the dexter tower charged with a roundel gules with a lion passant guardant or, and the sinister tower charged with a roundel gold with three chevrons gules.

MOTTO: *Salus populi suprema lex*—'The welfare of the people is the highest law.'

These were granted in 1935.

The official explanation is as follows:

The bridge of five arches indicates the five waterways that once crossed Tonbridge High Street. Three of these have now been covered or filled in. The ship implies the importance to Tonbridge of the making navigable of the river for one hundred years before the coming of the railway. The two towers represent Tonbridge Castle. The lion passant guardant on the dexter tower is allowed because the Great Seal of England was kept for some time in Tonbridge Castle during one of the visits to France of Edward I.

The chevrons are from the arms of the family of Clare, ancient Lords of Tonbridge.

DARTFORD Rural District Council

ARMS: Parted fesswise vert and gules, a fess argent; in chief a wheatsheaf between two millrinds, all gold, and in base an ancient galley with sail set and oars in action proper on water barry wavy argent and azure; and on the fess a bar wavy azure.

CREST: On a wreath argent and vert, a roundel vert charged with a white horse rampant.

MOTTO: *We serve.*

These were granted in 1950.

The wheatsheaves refer to agriculture, and the millrinds (iron clamps at the centre of millstones) represent agricultural engineering. The fess indicates the River Darent, and the ancient galley alludes to the Roman occupation of the district. The crest incorporates the County emblem, while the green roundel, or *pomeis*, suggests an apple in allusion to fruit growing.

DARTFORD R.D.C.

LANCASHIRE

LANCASHIRE

The red rose, originally a badge of the Earls and Dukes of Lancaster, and the device of the Lancastrian faction in the Wars of the Roses (see Chapter II), has become the County emblem. It is found in the arms of the Lancashire C.C. and in the insignia of many authorities in the County. A modern development is what has been termed 'a coronet of Lancaster,' consisting of a rim set with red roses forming part of a crest.

LANCASHIRE C.C.

LANCASHIRE County Council

ARMS: Gules, three gold piles, the middle one reversed, each charged with a red rose, seeds and sepals proper.

CREST: On a wreath or and gules, a lion passant guardant proper, charged on the body with a mascle gules, its right forepaw resting on a shield bearing the above arms.

SUPPORTERS: Two lions rampant proper, each with a vaire collar from which hangs a shield of the arms.

MOTTO: *In concilio consilium*—' In council is wisdom.'

These were granted in 1903.

The red roses of Lancashire are the principal features of the arms. The lions are derived from the heraldry of the Ferrers, Earls of Derby, who held the land between Ribble and Mersey in the thirteenth century before the Earldom (later the Duchy) of Lancaster was created.

BARROW-IN-FURNESS

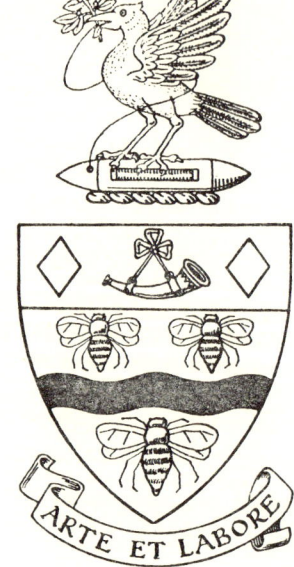
BLACKBURN

BARROW-IN-FURNESS County Borough Council

ARMS: Gules, on a gold bend an arrow pointing upwards towards a bee, both proper; above the bend, a gold serpent twined in a knot, and below the bend a gold tripping stag; the chief argent with a paddle-wheel steamship under steam and sail, on water, proper.

CREST: On a wreath or and gules, the battlements of a tower, and thereon a ram's head proper, with gold horns and wearing a gold collar.

MOTTO: *Semper sursum*—'Ever upwards.'

These were granted in 1867.

The bee is an emblem of industry and, with the arrow, forms a rebus on the name. The serpent is the crest of the Duke of Devonshire, the stag that of the Duke of Buccleugh, and the ram's head is from the arms of Sir James Ramsden, first Mayor of Barrow —three men to whom the town largely owed its development during the nineteenth century, and after whom three docks are named. The type of ship dates Barrow's rise to prominence as a shipbuilding centre.

BLACKBURN County Borough Council

ARMS: Argent, a fess wavy sable between three bees proper; a chief vert charged with a silver bugle between two gold lozenges.

CREST: On a wreath argent and sable, a white dove with wings outspread, standing on a gold shuttle; in its beak an olive branch and the thread of the shuttle both proper.

MOTTO: *Arte et labore*—'By skill and toil.'

These arms were granted in 1852.

LANCASHIRE

The following explanation has been issued by the Corporation:

The three bees volant, the bee being an emblem of skill, perseverance, and industry, are characteristic of the merchants, etc., who have been the means of raising the town to its present eminence. B is also the initial of the name of the town. The shield being white is emblematical of the production of the town, namely calico. The fess wavy sable represents the Black Brook (Blakewater) on the banks of which the town is built. The chief vert has allusion to the ancient history of the town in the time of Edward the Confessor when it was one of the royal forests. The bugle horn is the arms of the first Mayor of Blackburn (W. H. Hornby, Esq.), and is also an emblem of strength, and the lozenges represent the arms of the Lord of the Manor (Joseph Feilden, Esq.), and are also the heraldic emblems of spinning. The shuttle is the emblem of weaving which has contributed to the prosperity of the town, whilst the dove taking wing with an olive branch in her beak (the emblem of peace) united to the thread of the shuttle, represents the beneficial results emanating from the art of weaving.

BLACKPOOL   BOLTON   BOOTLE

BLACKPOOL County Borough Council

ARMS: Barry wavy of eight pieces sable and gold, thereon a flying seagull proper; on a chief argent a thunderbolt proper between a fleur-de-lis and a lion rampant both gules.

CREST: On a wreath or and sable, the battlements of a tower gold, and thereon the sails of a windmill proper, with a red rose of Lancaster at the centre.

MOTTO: *Progress.*

These were granted in 1899.

The black and gold wavy bars refer to the name, and depict the sea and sands; and the gull is an emblem of a seaside resort. A document issued by the Corporation explains:

The thunderbolt . . . is intended to allude to the enterprise of Blackpool as a pioneer in the adoption of electricity for lighting and traction purposes. The fleur-de-lis and the lion rampant . . . were distinguishing charges in the arms of the Banks and Cocker families respectively, and their inclusion in the arms of the Borough is meant to perpetuate the close association of those families with the early history of the town.

It has been suggested that the battlements of a tower are supposed to represent the idea of 'corporateness,' but in heraldry a tower is the emblem of grandeur and solidity. The sails of a windmill . . . refer to 'the Fylde,' a district in which Blackpool, being the only borough, occupies a very important and prominent position. 'Fylde' is an old word meaning 'field,' from which it will be inferred that the district is chiefly devoted to agriculture, for which it has long held a high reputation. The Fylde formerly contained many, and does still retain a few windmills for the grinding of corn; quaint, picturesque old landmarks which have for many years past formed a peculiar and distinguishing feature of this countryside. It may also be said that the windmill sails allude to the health-giving breezes for which Blackpool is so well known.

BOLTON *County Borough Council*

ARMS: Gules, two gold bendlets; above them an arrow, point upwards, a shuttle, and a mule spinning spindle, all upright and of gold, and below the bendlets a gold escutcheon charged with a red rose of Lancaster.

CREST: On a wreath or and gules, an elephant proper standing on a rocky moor, on its back a gold castle with a red rose above the portway, the trapping and surcingle parted palewise gules and vert and charged with a gold mitre.

MOTTO: *Supera Moras.*

These were granted in 1890.

An explanation issued by the Corporation states that the bendlets are intended to represent a soldier's shoulder belt, and that the arrow was adopted 'in memory of the famous archer soldiers of Bolton.' The latter emblem also alludes to the first syllable of the name. The shuttle stands for weaving, and the spindle commemorates the invention of the mule by Samuel Crompton, a native of Bolton. The red rose of Lancaster refers not only to the County but also to Edmund, Earl of Lancaster (son of Henry III), who enlarged the Honour of Lancaster so as to include Bolton, which was formerly in that of Chester.

The 'rocky moor' on which the elephant stands refers to the topographical situation which earned the town the name Bolton-le-Moors, or Bolton-super-Moras. This is alluded to in the motto, which may also be translated 'Overcome delays.'

The elephant is from the arms of the City of Coventry, and recalls that Bolton was anciently within the Diocese of Mercia (denoted by the mitre) of which Coventry was the seat.

Burnley   Bury

BOOTLE County Borough Council

ARMS: Argent, three fleurs-de-lis azure, and a chevron azure charged with three gold stags' faces; on a chief sable three mural crowns argent.

CREST: On a wreath argent and azure, a lighthouse on a rock proper.

MOTTO: *Respice aspice prospice*—'Look to the past, the present, and the future.'

These were granted in 1869.

The stags' faces are from the arms of the Earls of Derby, and the mural crowns from those of the family of Bootle. The lighthouse, an unusual and graceful crest, denotes the town's position at the mouth of the Mersey.

BURNLEY County Borough Council

ARMS: Gold, a chevron engrailed gules with two fusils above it and a lion rampant below, all sable; on a chief wavy sable a silver right hand between two gold bees.

CREST: On a wreath or and gules, a white stork with red beak and legs standing on a green mount and holding in its right claw a stone and in its beak a cotton flower proper.

MOTTO: *Pretiumque et causa laboris*—'Both the prize and the motive of labour.'

These were granted in 1862.

They were based upon the seal of the Burnley Improvement Commissioners, and I am indebted to the Town Clerk for a copy of a letter written in 1854 by the designer of the seal, who explains that the lion is that of the family De Lacy,

Lords of Blackburnshire for several generations down to the end of the thirteenth century. According to the learned Dugdale, in 1294 Henry de Lacy obtained a charter for a Market every Tuesday at his Manorhouse of Brunley in Lancashire, as also a Fair yearly. . . .

At once to acknowledge that we have not forgotten what Burnley was when these men were its Lords, to compare the present with the past, and to award due honour to both, we adopt the lion of the Lacys; but instead of allowing it to occupy the whole shield we place it 'in base,' and in chief two fusils to show the high and honourable position attained by science over mere valour. Fusils or spindles in heraldry . . . are here intended, of course, to symbolize the art of cotton spinning by which this town, in common with several others in Lancashire, has attained its wealth and position; the same colour is given to the fusils as to the lion to show that the dignity of the arts of peace is equal to that of the art of war. . . .

The chevron is an honourable charge; it is resembled to a pair of rafters such as are set on the highest part of a house, and betokens the achieving of some business of moment or the finishing of some chargeable or memorable work. It may here refer to the position which Burnley has attained, to the wealth it has acquired. . . .

The chevron is engrailed, the edges appearing as if pieces were struck out by a hailstorm. This represents a fierce encounter in battle, and may here signify the encounters which the men of this town have had with others in honourable competition in business. . . .

The wavy edge of the chief signifies the River Brun. The hand signifies power, equity, fidelity, and justice; open, it represents bounty and liberality, and is here intended to signify the extending of these qualities to the 'bees' by which the industrious classes, the people, are represented. Bees are also the symbol of concord, peace, economy, and people obedient to their rulers.

The crest is a slight departure from the original seal, which displayed a crane, the emblem of vigilance.

BURY County Borough Council

ARMS: Quarterly argent and azure, a cross composed of two narrow palets and two barrulets interlaced and counter-changed; in the first quarter an anvil sable; in the second a golden fleece; in the third two crossed shuttles; and in the fourth three culms of the papyrus plant growing on a mount proper.

CREST: On a wreath argent and azure, a green mount and thereon a bee between two cotton flowers proper.

MOTTO: *Vincit omnia industria*—'Industry overcomes all things.'

These were granted in 1877.

The emblems in the quarters represent the iron, wool, cotton, and paper-making industries.

LIVERPOOL City and County Borough Council

ARMS: Argent, a liver (cormorant) with a branch of laver (seaweed) in its beak, proper.

CREST: The liver with laver as in the arms, but with its wings spread.

SUPPORTERS: Dexter, Neptune in a sea-green mantle and with a wreath of laver about his loins, wearing a golden Eastern crown, and holding in his right hand a black trident and in his left a banner bearing the arms of Liverpool; and sinister, a Triton, similarly wreathed with laver, blowing a shell and holding with his right hand a banner displaying a ship under sail, all proper, the banner staves being gold.

MOTTO: *Deus nobis haec otia fecit*—'God hath granted us this ease.'

These were granted in 1797.

LANCASHIRE

LIVERPOOL

Proverbial for voracity, and used by Milton as a simile for Satan, the cormorant is not a popular heraldic emblem, and its use by Liverpool is due only to a desire to allude to the name. The liver and laver hint at two theories as to the derivation of the name, but the theory which finds wider acceptance traces Liverpool to the Norse *hlithar pollr*— 'the pool of the slopes.' The maritime significance of the supporters is obvious.

The motto is a quotation from Virgil's first *Eclogue*; the words, 'It is a god who has granted us this ease,' are spoken by a peasant who has successfully petitioned Caesar against the confiscation of his lands. 'Deus' refers to Augustus Caesar. In the Liverpool motto it may either refer to Neptune, signifying Liverpool's debt to the sea-god, or it may mean the Almighty. In the translation I have favoured the latter interpretation.

MANCHESTER City and County Borough Council

ARMS: Gules, three gold bendlets enhanced (i.e. raised above their normal position across the middle of the shield); on a chief argent a ship in full sail on the sea proper.

CREST: On a wreath or and gules, the terrestrial globe with seven bees upon it proper.

SUPPORTERS: Dexter, a silver heraldic antelope with gold horns, collar, and chain; and sinister, a gold lion guardant, wearing a mural crown gules; each supporter charged on the shoulder with a red rose.

MOTTO: *Concilio et labore*—'By counsel and by labour.'

These were granted in 1842.

MANCHESTER

The bendlets are from the arms of the family of Grelley, feudal lords of Manchester. The antelope, a Beaufort emblem, represents the Duchy of Lancaster, to which the roses likewise allude. The crest signifies world-wide industry.

'Was the chief a prophecy of the Ship Canal?' asked Mr Fox-Davies in his *Book of Public Arms*. It may well have been so, for although the canal was not opened until 1894 it was projected much earlier, and designs for it were prepared in 1840, two years before these arms were granted.

OLDHAM *County Borough Council*

ARMS: Sable, a gold chevron invected with plain gold cotises, between three owls argent; on a gold chief engrailed a red rose between two rings gules.

CREST: On a wreath or and sable, a rock, and thereon an owl argent; in front of the rock three red roses, their seeds and sepals proper.

MOTTO: *Sapere aude*—'Dare to be wise.'

These were granted in 1894.

They are based on the arms of the ancient family of Oldham, of which the most notable member was Hugh Oldham, Bishop of Exeter (d. 1519). The arms of the family are sable, a gold chevron between three owls argent, and on a gold chief three red roses. The owls suggest that the family, like the town, called itself 'Owdham,' and adopted the birds in allusion to its name. To the owls, the birds of wisdom, the motto refers. Unlike other Lancashire towns which bear red roses, Oldham has not derived them immediately from the insignia of the Duchy, but takes them from the arms of the Oldham family. It is, however, possible that the family set the red roses on their shield to denote their Lancastrian sympathies. Hugh Oldham's arms are also embodied in the shield of Corpus Christi College, Oxford, of which he was a benefactor.

Oldham

Preston

PRESTON *County Borough Council*

ARMS: Azure, a Holy Lamb couchant argent supporting a gold cross-staff with a white pennant, and about its head a gold nimbus; below it the letters 'PP' in gold.

These are recorded at the College of Arms.

The Holy Lamb is the emblem of St John the Baptist (see Chapter IV), to whom Preston's ancient Church of St Wilfrid was re-dedicated when it was rebuilt in the sixteenth century. The letters stand for the name of the town, but since Preston has a reputation for pride because, in the eighteenth century, it was a centre of fashionable society, its neighbours allege that the letters are short for 'Proud Preston.'

ROCHDALE *County Borough Council*

ARMS: Argent, a woolpack encircled by two branches of the cotton-tree in flower proper; a border sable charged with eight silver martlets.

CREST: On a wreath argent and sable, a silver fleece with a gold band above a millrind sable.

MOTTO: *Crede signo*—'Trust in this sign.'

These were granted in 1857.

The fleece, woolpack, cotton, and millrind stand for the wool, cotton, and iron industries. The martlets are from the arms of the Rashdale and Dearden families: silver, a black escutcheon surrounded by black martlets. The Deardens came into possession of the Manor of Rochdale in 1823. The motto is based upon that of Lord Byron of Rochdale, *Crede Byron*.

ROCHDALE

ST HELENS

ST HELENS County Borough Council

ARMS: Argent, two bars azure and over them a cross sable; in the first and fourth quarters a saltire gules, and in the second and third a griffin rampant sable.

CREST: On a wreath argent and azure, a lion statant guardant proper with two fleurs-de-lis gules on the body, resting the right forepaw on an ingot of silver.

MOTTO: *Ex terra lucem*—'Light out of the earth.'

These were granted in 1876.

They are made up of emblems from the heraldry of local families. The blue bars stand for Parr, the black cross and one fleur-de-lis for Eccleston, the saltires for Gerard, the griffins for Bold, the lion for Walmsley, and the second fleur-de-lis for Sir David Gamble, first Mayor and a benefactor of the town.

SALFORD City and County Borough Council

ARMS: Azure, the field strewn with gold bees, and in the midst of them a gold shuttle between three gold wheatsheaves; on a chief or, a corded bale proper between two mill-rinds sable.

CREST: On a wreath or and azure, a silver demi-lion holding a lance proper from which flies a flag azure charged with a gold shuttle.

SUPPORTERS: Dexter, a gold wolf with a red chain about its neck from which hangs an escutcheon gules charged with a gold millrind; and sinister, a silver heraldic antelope with

LANCASHIRE

SALFORD

gold horns, tufts, and hoofs, with a similar chain and escutcheon, both gules, the latter charged with a white rose.

MOTTO: *Integrity and Industry*.

These were granted in 1844.

Salford was anciently part of the Earldom of Chester, to which the wolf and wheatsheaves refer (see Cheshire). It subsequently passed into the possession of the Earls of Lancaster, and became part of the Duchy, denoted by the antelope (which is also a supporter of Manchester).

The bees stand for industry, the shuttles and bale for cotton, and the millrinds for iron.

SOUTHPORT County Borough Council

ARMS: Argent, a fess dancetty sable, in the chief three cross-crosslets pointed at the foot sable, and in the base waves of the sea (represented by barry wavy of six pieces azure and argent) and thereon an ancient ship (or lymphad) proper with flags gules.

CREST: Within a gold naval crown a cross-crosslet as in the arms, entwined by a gold serpent.

MOTTO: *Salus populi*—'The welfare of the people.'

These were granted in 1923.

They were based on an unauthorized coat, formerly in use, which contained a lifeboat instead of the old ship, and differed in other particulars.

The original device was designed about seventy years ago by Dr Craven, a local councillor; and he appears to have based it upon the arms of his own family—silver, a fess dancetty between six cross-crosslets pointed at the foot, all gules. The crosslet entwined by a serpent bears a resemblance to the emblem known as Aaron's Rod, or the Rod of Aesculapius, and stands for healing.

SOUTHPORT

WARRINGTON

WARRINGTON County Borough Council

ARMS: Ermine, six lions rampant gules within a border azure charged with eight gold covered cups.

CREST: On a wreath argent and gules a rock, and thereon a silver unicorn rampant, its mane, horn, and hoofs gold, supporting a gold flagstaff from which flies a banner parted palewise argent and azure, and charged with a red rose and a gold wheatsheaf.

MOTTO: *Deus dat incrementum*—'God giveth the increase.'

These were granted in 1897.

The lions stand for Pain de Vilars (*temp.* Henry I), of whose barony Warrington was the head. The covered cups and unicorn are from the arms and crest of the Botelers, or Butlers, to whom the manor and barony passed. (This family bore cups in their arms in allusion to their name.) The red rose of Lancaster and the wheatsheaf of the Earldom of Chester on the banner denote that the Borough is on the borders of Lancashire and Cheshire.

WIGAN

WIGAN *County Borough Council*

ARMS: Gules, a silver castle with three towers, and above it a gold crown composed of fleurs-de-lis.

CREST: On a wreath argent and gules, the head and shoulders of a king in a red robe and a gold crown, and in front of him a gold lion couchant guardant.

SUPPORTERS: Two gold lions each holding a branch of mountain ash, or wiggin tree, proper.

MOTTO: *Ancient and Loyal.*

These were granted in 1922.

The following note is extracted from an article by Mr Arthur J. Hawkes, formerly Chief Librarian, printed in the *Corporation Year Book*:

Mr J. Paul Rylands describes this coat as 'perhaps the very best of all Lancashire town arms, for it might heraldically belong to the Middle Ages, and is indeed symbolical of antiquity and loyalty.' It is certainly a very privileged coat of arms, as few if any coats bear so many symbols of royal favour. . . . In Wigan's new grant there are (1) a King's head, crowned; (2) the royal 'leopard,' or 'lion couchant guardant'; (3) a medieval royal crown; and (4) the supporting lions.

The King's head in the crest . . . is intended to be a conventional likeness to an early English Monarch. It is actually modelled on the portrait of King Edward III, but from the point of view of the town it symbolizes especially King Henry I. On Wigan's earliest town seal— probably of twelfth century—there appears a towered or castellated gateway over the centre of which is depicted what seems to be the crowned head of Henry I. These devices, therefore, are taken as the chief symbols of the new bearings: the towered gateway becomes a Norman Castle, and the King's head becomes a crest, indicating Wigan as a town of consequence and royal patronage at the opening of the twelfth century.

The royal lion, again, marks another important period in Wigan history. Edward III by a charter of 1350 granted Wigan the right (with several other towns) to use a royal seal known as 'the King's Recognaisance Seal' on which was figured the King's head and the royal lion. The Somerset Herald expressed the opinion that as none of the other towns had made use of the

King's permission by adopting the figures in their arms Wigan could with propriety include them, and his view prevailed with the Chapter of Heralds.

The supporting lions give fine distinction to a highly dignified and privileged coat of arms. . . . The mountain ash, known in the northern dialects as the Wiggin or Wigan Tree, forms a 'rebus' or pun on the name of the town, and has the advantage of giving further symbolism to an already significant coat. The rebus has tradition behind it, for the Wiggin Tree is a conspicuous feature of several of the town's medieval seals.

The motto adopted, *Ancient and Loyal*, is in keeping with the arms. For a great many years Wigan has on all occasions, official and unofficial, invariably referred to itself as the 'Ancient and Loyal Borough,' but few are aware that authority for its use can be found in the Charter of Charles II—the governing Charter of the town down to the Municipal Corporations Act of 1835. In that Charter Wigan is designated by the King 'an ancient borough' and granted 'a special token of our favour' for its 'loyalty to us,' so that nothing could be more fitting than its adoption as the town's motto.

ACCRINGTON   ASHTON-UNDER-LYNE   BACUP

ACCRINGTON Borough Council

ARMS: Gules, on a fess argent a shuttle proper; in the base of the shield two printing cylinders and between them a piece of printed calico of parsley pattern, proper; on a chief parted palewise or and vert, a purple lion rampant and a gold running stag.

CREST: On a wreath argent and gules, a leafy branch of oak bent into the shape of an 'A,' in natural colours with gold acorns.

MOTTO: *Industry and prudence conquer.*

These were granted in 1879.

The shuttle stands for cotton spinning, and the cylinders and calico for the industry of printing that material. With this business the local family of Hargreaves, of Broad Oak, were closely connected, hence the stag from their arms.

The lion is that of the ancient family De Lacy, who held Accrington by grant of Henry II. The oak branch is trebly allusive to the name: it is bent into the shape of its initial letter; oak (Anglo-Saxon *ac*) expresses the first syllable; and the acorns recall the old form of the name, Akerenton.

ASHTON-UNDER-LYNE Borough Council

ARMS: Argent, a molet (or spur-rowel) sable, and in the dexter chief a crescent gules.

CREST: On a wreath argent and sable, the battlements of a tower proper, and thereon a griffin's head, torn off, gules, charged on the neck with a gold crescent.

MOTTO: *Labor omnia vincit*—'Labour overcomes all things.'

These were granted in 1926.

They are based on the arms of the old local family of Assheton, which the Corporation used before the grant was obtained. The Assheton spur-rowel, or 'molet pierced,' appears in the arms of Clitheroe, Stalybridge, and Middleton (*q.v.*).

BACUP Borough Council

ARMS: Azure, a gold fess charged with a fleece sable between two bees proper; above the fess a gold squirrel between two gold bales of cotton, and below it a block of stone, with lewis attached, proper.

CREST: On a wreath or and azure, a stag proper with a collar vaire, standing in front of a gold bale of cotton and resting its forefoot on a gold trefoil.

MOTTO: *Honor et industria*—'Honour and industry.'

These were granted in 1883.

The bees refer to industry in general, and stand for the initial letter of the name; and the bales of cotton, the fleece, and the block of stone represent particular local industries. The squirrel and stag are symbolical of the old Forest of Rossendale (cf. Rawtenstall).

CHORLEY Borough Council

ARMS: Gold, on a chevron gules three shields argent each charged with a bluebottle (or cornflower) with stem and leaves proper; on a chief gules a gold crown vallary.

MOTTO: *Beware.*

These were granted in 1882.

The arms are based on those of the family of Chorley of Chorley: Silver, a chevron gules between three bluebottles. These were used by the Local Improvement Commissioners before the incorporation of the town. The crown vallary, composed of palisades, is, like the more popular mural crown, a civic emblem.

CHORLEY

CLITHEROE

CLITHEROE Borough Council

ARMS: Azure, on a mount vert a gold castle with three domed towers, each with a pennon flying.

CREST: A lion's head argent torn off at the neck and rising from a coronet consisting of a gold rim set alternately with two gold crescents and two pierced molets sable.

SUPPORTERS: Two lions purpure, each with a gold chain about its neck and hanging therefrom a gold escutcheon charged with a red rose with seeds and sepals proper.

MOTTO: *Stabit saxum fluet amnis*—'The rock will remain and the river will flow.'

These, granted in February 1952, were the first civic arms to be assigned in the reign of Queen Elizabeth II.

The castle, representing the old fortress built on a limestone rock beside the River Ribble (to which the motto refers), has long been used as an emblem by Clitheroe. The Corporation acquired the castle from the Duke of Buccleugh, to whom the crescents in the coronet refer; while the molets (one visible in the illustration) are from the arms of the family of Assheton, Lords of the Honour of Clitheroe, and the lion's head represents General Monk who received the lordship from King Charles II.

The purple lions are from the arms of the De Lacy family, who built the castle and from whom Clitheroe received a charter. The roses are the County emblems.

LANCASHIRE

COLNE Borough Council

The Corporation has not obtained arms, but has assumed the following: Gules, on a gold fess a fig-leaf charged with the letter C, between two Roman coins; above the chevron a fleece and below it a sprig of cotton, both proper.

CREST: A lion rampant.

MOTTO: *We long endure.*

The following explanation is issued by the Corporation:

The fleece is typical of the woollen, and the cotton plant, at the foot, of the cotton trade.

On the centre fess is a fig-leaf between two Roman coins. The ancient Chapelry of Colne is historically described as being in shape like a fig-leaf, and as broad as it was long (six miles each way).

The coins are representative of the ancient Roman occupation of Colne (then Colunio), and the Roman C in the centre of the leaf is for the same purpose and stands for Colne or Colunio.

The rampant lion which forms the crest was the armorial insignia of the De Lacys, who were the ancient Lords of the Manor of Colne; it is therefore placed over all. The motto... appropriately indicates the ancientness of the place, which dates back to primitive British times.

CROSBY

CROSBY Borough Council

ARMS: Argent, a cross formy azure within an orle of billets sable.

CREST: On a wreath argent and azure a holly-wreath proper, and rising therefrom a demi-griffin sable holding erect a staff and thereon a banner azure charged with a pale argent between two gold stags' faces and antlers, and on the pale a representation of the Waterloo medal and ribbon proper.

SUPPORTERS: Two sea-horses azure with gold manes and fins, each charged on the shoulder with a gold anchor.

MOTTO: *Vis unita fortior*—'United strength is stronger.'

These were granted in 1937, when the Borough was formed by the incorporation of the Urban Districts of Great Crosby and Waterloo-with-Seaforth.

COLNE   ECCLES   DARWEN

DARWEN Borough Council

ARMS: Gold, a fess wavy with cotises wavy azure between three sprigs of the cotton-tree proper.

CREST: On a wreath or and azure, a miner, half-length, proper, holding over his shoulder a gold pick, and in front of him a gold shuttle.

MOTTO: *Absque labore nihil*—'Nothing without labour.'

These were granted in 1878.

The wavy fess stands for the River Darwen; the cotton, shuttle, and miner refer to local industries.

LANCASHIRE

ECCLES Borough Council

ARMS: Gold, on a mount vert an ecclesiastical building built of stone proper; on a chief azure two sprigs of the cotton-tree proper, and between them a silver pale charged with a Nasmyth steam-hammer sable.

CREST: On a wreath or and azure, a ship in full sail on the sea in front of a lighthouse on a rock, all proper.

MOTTO: *Labore omnia florent*—'All things flourish by labour.'

These were granted in 1893.

The ecclesiastical building is allusive to the name of the town. The steam-hammer commemorates James Nasmyth's chief invention (1839) and the cotton refers to local industry. The ship and lighthouse stand for the town's maritime associations, nowadays via the Manchester Ship Canal, and formerly via the River Irwell.

FARNWORTH

FARNWORTH Borough Council

ARMS: Azure, a chevron between three hornets, all gold, and on the chevron two cotton cops azure.

CREST: Out of a coronet composed of a gold rim set with four red roses, a gold stag's head and neck facing, between two branches of fern proper.

SUPPORTERS: Dexter, a stag, and sinister, a lion, each azure with a gold collar charged with three roses gules.

Motto: *Juste nec timide*—'Be just and fear not.'

These were granted in 1939 when Farnworth was incorporated as a Borough.

Mr H. Ellis Tomlinson, in *The Heraldry of Manchester*, states:

The shield is indicative of the Borough's industries, paper-making, and cotton spinning. 'Hornets are nature's paper-makers,' says a note issued by the Corporation, and these are certainly unique in civic heraldry. The stag's head is the crest of the Hulton family, and was formerly used by the Urban District Council. The branches of fern are a reference to the name of the Borough—'the settlement among the ferns.' The Hulton arms include a lion, and this gives the sinister supporter, while their stag's head crest provides the other. Although the blazon does not say so, the stag is shown without his head of antlers, as a symbol of the community's banding together, for the stag relinquishes his antlers when living in an organized herd.

FLEETWOOD   HASLINGDEN

FLEETWOOD Borough Council

ARMS: Parted saltirewise nebuly gold and azure, in the chief a red rose with seeds and sepals proper, in the base an ancient galley gules, and in fess two gold martlets.

MOTTO: *Onward.*

These were granted in 1933 when Fleetwood became a borough.

The red rose stands for Lancashire, the galley for the port, and the martlets for the Fleetwood family with particular reference to Sir Peter Hesketh Fleetwood, who laid out the town and gave it its name.

LANCASHIRE

HASLINGDEN Borough Council

ARMS: Quarterly gold and silver, on a fess wavy azure a gold shuttle with silver tips and thread; in the first quarter a purple lion rampant holding an ermine quatrefoil, in the second a red rose between six eagles displayed gules, in the third a cog-wheel sable, and in the fourth a pickaxe and spade saltirewise entwined by a chain, all proper.

CREST: On a wreath or and azure, a rocky mound, and thereon a moorcock holding in its beak a sprig of hazel, between two sprays of hazel, all proper.

MOTTO: *Nothing without labour.*

These were granted in 1892.

The lion is that of the De Lacy Earls of Lincoln (see Chapter III) who, in the twelfth and thirteenth centuries, held the Honour of Clitheroe, which included the Manor of Haslingden. The moorcock is the crest of the important local family of Holden, and the six eagles are from a coat of arms associated with the family (Silver, an escutcheon between six eagles, all gules), but not the arms generally attributed to them. In an article in the *Haslingden Observer* in August 1930, Mr W. H. Holden advanced the theory that the eagles were adopted by the Holdens as a secondary coat of arms to commemorate the fact that one Robert de Holdene, a follower of Thomas, Earl of Lancaster, was concerned in the slaying of Piers Gaveston, who bore six gold eagles on green.

The red rose is the County emblem. The hazel is, of course, allusive to the name, which is said to have been derived from the hazel-trees which formerly abounded. The rocky mound and the blue fess are topographical, and the other emblems stand for local industries.

HEYWOOD Borough Council

ARMS: Gold, five roundels between two bendlets engrailed and two mascles all sable.

CREST: On a wreath or and sable, an uprooted tree trunk with leaves sprouting therefrom, and thereon a falcon with wings outspread in the act of rising, all proper; the falcon charged on each wing with a roundel sable, and bearing in its beak a sprig of oak proper; in front of the trunk, three gold mascles interlaced.

MOTTO: *Alte volo*—'I fly high.'

These were granted in 1881.

They are based on the heraldry of the family of Heywood who bore: Silver, three roundels between two bendlets, all gules. Crest: A falcon rising from a tree trunk proper. Motto: *Alte volo*. In changing the colour of the roundels to sable, the heralds perhaps intended not only to distinguish the arms of the town from those of the family, but also to represent the iron and coal industries.

HEYWOOD

LANCASTER

LANCASTER City Council

ARMS: Parted fesswise azure and gules, in chief a fleur-de-lis and in base a lion passant guardant, both gold.

CREST: On a wreath or and azure, a lion passant guardant azure strewn with gold fleurs-de-lis.

SUPPORTERS: Two lions rampant guardant azure each strewn with gold fleurs-de-lis and wearing a gold collar from which hangs a silver shield charged with a red rose, seeds and sepals proper.

MOTTO: *Luck to Loyne.*

The arms were confirmed, and the crest and supporters granted, in 1907.

This achievement was clearly suggested by the arms and badge of Edmund, first Earl of Lancaster (son of Henry III), who bore the royal lions of England with a label of France (i.e. a blue label charged with gold fleurs-de-lis), and first among English princes used as a badge a red rose, derived from the golden rose which his mother, Eleanor of Provence, introduced into our royal heraldry (see Chapter II). 'Loyne' is a form of Lune, the river from which the town takes its name; the Latin form was 'Alauna,' derived from the Gaelic 'al-aon,' meaning 'white afon' (white river). Lancaster, Massachusetts, situated on the River Nashua, bears similar arms with the motto, *Ad Alaunam ad Nashuam.*

LANCASHIRE

LEIGH Borough Council

ARMS: Quarterly gules and argent, a cross counter-changed, in the first quarter a silver spearhead, in the second a star sable, in the third a shuttle sable, and in the fourth a sparrow-hawk proper.

CREST: On a wreath argent and gules, the battlements of a tower proper, and thereon a bear's paw gules holding erect a gold javelin.

MOTTO: *Aequo pede propera*—'Hasten steadily.'

These were granted in 1899.

The emblems in the shield are from the heraldry of local families. The spearhead represents the Urmestones of Westleigh, the star the Bradshaws, the shuttle the Shuttleworths, and the sparrow-hawk the Athertons (see Atherton U.D.C.). The bear's paw is from the crest of Lord Lilford.

LEIGH   LYTHAM ST ANNES   MIDDLETON

LYTHAM ST ANNES Borough Council

ARMS: Barry wavy of six pieces argent and azure, and thereon an ancient galley of gold, the sail sable with a silver bend charged with three stars gules; on a chief wavy azure a cross flory between two lions rampant all argent.

MOTTO: *Salus populi suprema lex*—'The welfare of the people is the highest law.'

These were granted in 1922.

The cross, which is that of St Cuthbert, and the lions were taken from the arms of the Dean and Chapter of Durham, the See having owned the Benedictine Priory founded at Lytham by Roger FitzRoger in the reign of Richard I.

The ship, against a background representing the sea, is from the device of the former St Annes-on-Sea U.D.C., and the arms on its sail are those of the family of Clifton of Lytham Hall.

MIDDLETON Borough Council

ARMS: Quarterly gules and argent, the palewise party line being nebuly; on a fess ermine three sprigs of the cotton-tree proper; in the first quarter a silver cross patonce, in the second a molet (or spur-rowel) sable, in the third a silkworm moth, and in the fourth a stork on a rock, both proper.

CREST: On a wreath argent and gules, a green mount, thereon a tower proper between two boars' heads, mouths upwards, sable; and hanging from the tower by a ribbon gules a gold escutcheon charged with a lion passant gules.

MOTTO: *Fortis in arduis*—'Strong in difficulties.'

These were granted in 1887.

The arms are partly made up of emblems from the arms of various families named Middleton. Red and gold quarters with a silver cross flory in the first quarter were the arms of Middleton of Middleton Hall, Lancashire. A blue boar's head erect is the crest of another family of the same name. A lion rampant on a tower was the crest of the Earl of Middleton (Scotland) whose motto was that adopted by the Borough.

The black spur-rowel is from the arms of the family of Assheton (see Ashton-under-Lyne). The cotton and the silkworm moth represent local industries, and the stork (as I am informed by the Town Clerk) 'represents the desire for the increase of the population.'

MORECAMBE AND HEYSHAM Borough Council

ARMS: Parted chevronwise or and azure, in the chief two united roses of Lancaster and York, with stalks and leaves proper, and in base a silver sailing yacht.

MOTTO: *Beauty surrounds, health abounds.*

These were granted in 1926.

The united roses were adopted in token of the fact that a large proportion of the population of this Lancashire town has migrated from Yorkshire. The yacht stands not only for the pleasure and health resort (referred to by the motto) but also for the old fishing industry.

MOSSLEY Borough Council

The Corporation has not obtained arms, but has assumed the following: Sable, a fess engrailed azure, and overlying it a silver pile charged with a sprig of the cotton-plant; the chief is divided into three compartments: silver with a red rose, azure with a gold wheatsheaf, and gules with a white rose. The shield is ensigned by a mural crown, and the motto is, *Floret qui laborat*—'He prospers who labours.'

The blue fess represents the River Tame, and the cotton stands for the staple industry of the town. The emblems in the chief refer to the fact that the town was formerly situated in the three counties of Lancashire, Cheshire, and Yorkshire.

Morecambe and Heysham   Mossley   Nelson

NELSON Borough Council

Arms: Azure, on a chevron argent two reed-hooks proper; in chief two sprigs of the cotton-tree, and in base a fleece, both or.

Crest: On a wreath argent and azure, a cock gules standing on a gold shuttle and holding in its beak a sprig of the cotton-tree proper.

Motto: *By industry and integrity.*

These were granted in 1891.

The references to the cotton and wool industries are obvious. The reed-hooks also are symbolic of textile weaving. The cock is derived from the arms of the Tunstall family, formerly considerable landowners in the locality and largely engaged in the cotton industry.

PRESTWICH Borough Council

Arms: Argent, a pile between two red roses with seeds and sepals proper; and on the pile two swans' heads torn off at the neck ermine and a fleur-de-lis argent.

Crest: On a wreath argent and gules, between two red roses as in the arms, a lozenge azure charged with a fleur-de-lis argent.

Supporters: Dexter, a wyvern or, and sinister, a lion argent, each looking backward and with a ribbon azure about its neck, and therefrom hanging a lozenge azure charged with a fleur-de-lis argent.

Motto: *Recte fac noli timere*—'Do right and fear not.'

* H

CIVIC HERALDRY

These were granted in 1939, when Prestwich was incorporated as a borough. Mr H. Ellis Tomlinson, in *The Heraldry of Manchester*, states:

The 'white field' of the arms refers, unconsciously perhaps, to the district of that name, and between the Lancaster roses is a pile carrying the heads of two of the swans from the arms of Baron Cawley of Prestwich, and also the fleur-de-lis which is often used as the symbol of St Mary and here indicates the Parish Church which bears her name.

The lozenges, resembling spindles in shape, represent the cotton industry. The supporters are the wyvern and lion of the Egertons, Earls of Wilton, duly differenced.

PRESTWICH

RADCLIFFE *Borough Council*

ARMS: Argent, two bendlets engrailed sable between a cross potent voided gules (i.e. in outline, the silver of the field showing within) and a red rose with seeds and sepals proper.

CREST: On a gold mural crown, a gold lion statant guardant resting the right forepaw on a pheon sable.

SUPPORTERS: Dexter, a bull argent with gold horns and hoofs charged on the shoulder with a fleur-de-lis sable, and with a gold mural crown about its neck and attached thereto a gold chain turned over the bull's back; and sinister, a lion sable charged on the shoulder with a fleur-de-lis argent and collared with a gold mural crown with a similar chain.

MOTTO: *Industria ditat*—'Industry enriches.'

These were granted in 1935, when Radcliffe became a borough.

The bendlets are from the arms of the family of Radcliffe, the cross from those of Pilkington, and the pheon from those of Egerton, Baron Grey de Radcliffe. The red rose is that of the County, and the lion and fleurs-de-lis are from the arms of the City of Lancaster, the black and white of the latter being symbolic of the coal and cotton industries. The supporters are those of the Radcliffe family, duly differenced.

RADCLIFFE

RAWTENSTALL Borough Council

ARMS: Or, on a fess gules a gold running wolf between two bales of wool proper; in chief a red left hand between two stags, tripping and at gaze proper; and in base two black cows grazing on a green mount.

CREST: On a wreath or and gules, a squirrel cracking a nut, sitting on a grassy mound from which grow two sprigs of the cotton-tree proper.

MOTTO: *Floret qui laborat*—'He prospers who labours.'

These were granted in 1891.

The squirrel, stags, and wolf are emblems of the Forest of Rossendale which once surrounded Rawtenstall. There is a tradition that before the deforestation, in the reign of Henry VII, the squirrel could leap from tree to tree. Wolves haunted the forest, and one part of the Borough formerly bore the name 'Wolfenden Booth.' The red hand, cut off at the wrist, recalls the penalty for killing the King's deer.

The cows represent agriculture; the Borough includes a former hamlet called Cowpe, anciently Cowup, said to have been a place in the uplands where cows used to graze.

The cotton and woolpacks stand for modern industries.

RAWTENSTALL

STRETFORD

STRETFORD Borough Council

ARMS: Argent, a fess gules charged with a gold lion passant; in chief a flail and a scythe saltirewise proper between two red roses with seeds and sepals proper; and in base upon waves of the sea a lymphad, or ancient galley, the sail furled and the oars in action, also proper.

CREST: A coronet composed of a gold rim on which are set eight red roses (of which five are visible in the illustration), and rising therefrom a forearm proper, the hand grasping a gold thunderbolt.

MANTLING: Gules and or.

MOTTO: *Service and Efficiency.*

These were granted in 1933.

The flail is from the crest of the local family of **Trafford**. This consisted of a thresher alluding to a picturesque but dubious legend of a Saxon ancestor who, pursued by Norman foes, disguised himself as a husbandman and busied himself among some threshers in a barn. The lion stands for John of Gaunt and the roses are, of course, Lancastrian. Stretford's long connection with the sea by means of the Rivers Mersey and Irwell is indicated by the lymphad, while the scythe represents its agricultural character in the past. The thunderbolt stands for the town's industrial development, in which electricity has played a principal part.

LANCASHIRE

SWINTON AND PENDLEBURY

SWINTON AND PENDLEBURY Borough Council

ARMS: Gules, a gold cockatrice, and on a chief parted palewise or and argent, a lion passant guardant gules between two red roses, their seeds and sepals proper.

CREST: On a coronet consisting of a gold rim set with six red roses (four visible), a boar's head torn off behind the ears argent with tusks azure.

SUPPORTERS: Two gold lions each grasping in the forepaw a pickaxe gules.

MOTTO: *Salus populi suprema lex*—' The welfare of the people is the highest law.'

These were granted in 1934 when Swinton and Pendlebury obtained Borough status.

The cockatrice is from the arms of Robert de Langley, who acquired Agecroft in Pendlebury in 1416. The chief alludes to the family of Worsley which held part of Swinton. The lions and roses refer to the Duchy and County, and the picks to local industries.

WIDNES Borough Council

ARMS: Quarterly argent and azure, a cross counter-changed; in the first and fourth quarters a red rose with seeds and sepals proper, and in the second and third a gold beehive with four gold bees.

CREST: On a wreath argent and azure, a furnace and thereon an alembic, both gold.

MOTTO: *Industria ditat*—' Industry enriches.'

These were granted in 1893.

The bees are emblems of industry, and the alembic refers to the particular form of industry for which Widnes is noted, namely alkali and soap manufacture.

CIVIC HERALDRY

ATHERTON

WIDNES

AUDENSHAW

ABRAM *Urban District Council*

The seal bears a tower with three turrets between two suns.

ASHTON-IN-MAKERFIELD *Urban District Council*

Use is made of the insignia of the baronetcy of Gerard, viz. Argent, a saltire gules, with the badge of a baronet.

CREST: A lion rampant.

MOTTO: *En Dieu est mon esperance*—'My hope is in God.'

ASPULL *Urban District Council*

The device consists of an ostrich.

ATHERTON *Urban District Council*

ARMS: Or, a bend gules between two lozenges sable, and on the bend a lion's foreleg, torn off, gold.

CREST: On a wreath gold and gules, a sparrow-hawk proper with wings spread, perched on a gold shuttle, resting the right claw on a millrind sable.

MOTTO: *Consilio et prudentia*—'By counsel and by wisdom.'

These were granted in 1951.

The three principal industries are represented in the arms—coal by the black lozenges, cotton by the shuttle, and engineering by the millrind. The lion's leg is from the arms of the family of Powys, and the sparrow-hawk is from the arms of the Atherton family, the second Powys Lord Lilford having married the heiress of the Athertons of Atherton Hall in 1797.

LANCASHIRE

AUDENSHAW Urban District Council

ARMS: Parted palewise argent and gules, a pickaxe erect and in base a pierced molet both counter-changed, the shaft of the pickaxe between two roses, that on the argent being red, and that on the gules white, each with seeds and sepals proper.

CREST: On a wreath argent and gules a mill-wheel proper between a white rose and a red rose, each with seeds and sepals proper.

MOTTO: *Festina lente*—'Hasten slowly.'

These were granted in 1950.

The parted field and red and white roses indicate the town's proximity to the Lancashire-Yorkshire boundary. The pick and mill-wheel refer to local industries, and the molet is from the arms of the Assheton family, Lords of the Manor.

BRIERFIELD Urban District Council

The U.D.C. has not obtained arms but has assumed the following: Gules, on a silver chevron two shuttles, in base a miner's pick and shovel saltirewise, and on a silver chief a spray of briar. In some representations the pick and shovel are replaced by a cock.

BRIERFIELD

CLAYTON-LE-MOORS Urban District Council

Use is made of the arms of the family of Clayton: Argent, a cross engrailed sable between four roundels gules.

CREST: A leopard's forepaw.

CROMPTON Urban District Council

The device consists of the achievement of arms of the Lancashire County Council with a spinning-wheel below it.

DENTON Urban District Council

ARMS: Parted palewise argent and sable, two bars parted palewise gules and argent, in chief three pierced cinquefoils ermine.

CREST: On a wreath argent and gules, a beaver proper charged with two gold molets of five points, one above the other.

MOTTO: *Persevere.*

These arms, granted in 1936, were based on a former unofficial device intended to represent the union of the townships of Denton and Haughton, and consisting of a combination of the arms of the two families of those names: Argent, two bars and in chief three cinquefoils, all gules (Denton); and, Barry of six pieces sable and argent (Haughton). The beaver, which also comes from the old device, is an emblem of the hat industry.

DENTON   DROYLSDEN   FAILSWORTH

DROYLSDEN Urban District Council

ARMS: Gold, three bendlets enhanced vert, and in base a lamb passant proper bearing a cross-staff flying a pennon argent charged with a cross formy gules.

MOTTO: *By concord and industry.*

These arms were granted in 1950.

The bendlets enhanced (i.e. raised above their normal position) are from the arms of the family of Byron, Lords of the Manor of Droylsden, who included the famous poet, Lord Byron. The Holy Lamb is the emblem of the Moravian Church, their settlement at Fairfield, Droylsden, in 1784, having been significant in the development of the town.

FAILSWORTH Urban District Council

ARMS: Parted palewise gules and argent, three bendlets enhanced parted palewise gold and gules; on a chief ermine a chapeau gules turned up ermine between two red roses with seeds, sepals, leaves, and stalks all proper.

CREST: On a wreath argent and gules a mount vert, and thereon a griffin rampant gules with three gold shafts of lightning issuing from its beak, and supporting a representation of the Failsworth Pole proper.

LANCASHIRE

Motto: *True worth never fails.*

These were granted in 1948.

The shield combines the arms of two former manorial families—the Grelleys, who bore three gold bendlets enhanced (i.e. raised above the normal position) on red, and the Byrons, who bore similar arms but with the bendlets red on white. The chapeau stands for the hat-making industry, and the roses refer to the County. In the crest, the griffin of the Chetham family (who succeeded the Byrons) supports the Pole set up as a token of loyalty to the Crown in 1793. The shafts of lightning represent the electrical industry. The motto plays on the name.

HAYDOCK Urban District Council

The device consists of a shield bearing an arm in armour, the hand grasping a staff on which is a pennon charged with a cross. Above the shield is a ram's head with a sprig in the mouth.

HINDLEY Urban District Council

The device consists of a hind, in allusion to the name, with the motto, *Prodesse*—'To serve.'

HORWICH Urban District Council

The U.D.C. has adopted a device consisting of a shield charged with a running deer, ensigned by a royal crown, and supported by two foresters with bows.

Motto: *Copia est labor*—'Labour brings plenty.'

HUYTON-WITH-ROBY Urban District Council

The device consists of an eagle hovering over a child in a cradle, apparently based on the crest of the Stanley family.

KIRKHAM Urban District Council

Arms: Azure, a flying dove, its right wing inverted, holding in its beak a branch of olive, all or; on a gold chief a red rose, seeds and sepals proper, between two choughs also proper.

Crest: A circlet set with four molets (three visible) gules, and rising therefrom a gold demi-lion supporting a pastoral staff gules, its head sable.

Motto: *Firma et stabilis*—'Safe and sure.'

These were granted in 1950.

The dove and olive branch is from the old Borough seal, and the rose and choughs are from the arms of Christ Church, Oxford, which received the Manor and Rectory of Kirkham from Henry VIII at the dissolution of the monasteries. The rose is also the County emblem. The molets are from the arms of the local family of Clifton. The lion is from the insignia of Shrewsbury Abbey, to which the lordship of St Michael, including Kirkham, was given by Count Roger of Poitou about 1093; while the pastoral staff represents the Abbey of Vale Royal to which Edward I granted the manor in 1280.

KIRKHAM LEYLAND LITTLE LEVER

LEYLAND Urban District Council

ARMS: Argent, a saltire azure between a water-budget gules in chief, a red rose with seeds and sepals proper in base, and two lions' faces sable in fess, and on the saltire a gold martlet.

CREST: Rising from a gold rim charged with drops vert, two branches of cotton plant in flower proper, and between them a right hand grasping a motor-wheel all proper, the wheel having two gold wings attached to the hubs.

MOTTO: *Semper proficimus*—'We progress continually.'

These were granted in 1950.

The shield combines the saltire of St Andrew, for the parish church, with emblems of local families—the water-budget for the Bussels, Barons of Penwortham, the lions' faces for the Farringtons, and the martlet for the Fleetwoods; while the saltire also refers to the Baldwin family. The red rose is the County emblem. The crest refers to the cotton and motor industries, the tyre of the wheel being also allusive to local rubber works. The green drops on the rim stand for the paint and varnish industry.

LITTLE LEVER Urban District Council

Having no arms, the U.D.C. uses those of the family of Lever: Argent, two bends sable, the under one engrailed. Crest: On a wreath argent and sable, a cock standing on a trumpet proper. Motto: *Mutare vel timere sperno*—'I scorn either to change or fear.' The crest, consisting of the bird and the instrument which bid one arise (*lever*), was probably adopted by the family in allusion to their name.

LANCASHIRE

POULTON-LE-FYLDE

PREESALL

THORNTON CLEVELEYS

POULTON-LE-FYLDE *Urban District Council*

ARMS: Azure, on water represented by barry wavy argent and azure, a gold lymphad (or ancient ship) with the sail furled, its flags argent and each charged with a cross gules; on a chief or, a red rose with seeds and sepals proper between two crosses formy gules.

CREST: On a wreath or and azure, a representation of Poulton-le-Fylde market-cross and stocks, all proper.

MOTTO: *Sub cruce floreamus*—'May we flourish beneath the Cross.'

These were granted in 1950.

The ship on water refers to the former port at Skippool ('ship pool') and to the name of Poulton ('the town by the pool'). Its sail is furled to show that the town's activity as a port is over. In the upper part of the shield is the red rose of the County and two crosses of St Chad, patron saint of the parish. The blue and gold of the crest-wreath (and the mantling when shown) are the colours of the Fleetwood family. The motto alludes to the crosses in the shield and the market-cross in the crest, and refers to the town's importance as both an ecclesiastical and commercial centre.

PREESALL *Urban District Council*

ARMS: Azure, a chevron between in chief two griffins' heads torn off, and in base a martlet, all gold, and on the chevron a red rose with seeds and sepals proper between two roundels barry wavy argent and azure.

CREST: On a wreath or and azure, an ancient galley of gold, sails furled, flying pennons of St George, and hanging from the mast-head by a knot azure a cross-bow gules.

Motto: *Prae salem notanda.*

These were granted in 1950.

The chevrons and griffins' heads are from the arms of the Elletsons of Parrox Hall, while the martlet is from the arms of the Fleetwoods of Hackinsall Hall. The rose refers to the County, and the fountains allude to the Fairy Well and the salt or brine workings. The ship indicates the maritime associations of the district, including its ancient fisheries and ferry. The knot stands for Knott End, and the cross-bow (or arbalest) is for Geoffrey l'Arbalestier, who received the Manor of Preesall and Hackinsall in 1190, and was the ancestor of local families.

The motto comprises a play on the name. It may be translated as either 'Famed for salt,' or 'The well-known place by the sea.'

RISHTON Urban District Council

The seal contains a shield charged with a lion passant and below it the word *Reviresco*—'I grow green again.' This is an adaptation of the arms and motto of the family of Rishton.

STANDISH-WITH-LANGTREE Urban District Council

The device consists of the crest of the family of Standish: an owl with a rat in its talons.

THORNTON CLEVELEYS Urban District Council

ARMS: Vert, a representation of the Thornton Marsh Mill proper; on a gold chief a barrulet wavy parted fesswise wavy azure and argent, and issuing therefrom the sun gules.

CREST: On a mount vert within a gold rim set with four red roses (three visible) with seeds and sepals proper, a wolf statant reguardant argent supporting with the right forepaw a flagstaff proper, thereon a banner azure charged with a silver saltire.

MOTTO: *Terra marique*—'On land and sea.'

These were granted in 1950.

I am indebted to Mr H. Ellis Tomlinson for the following note:

The shield and crest each represent the union of Thornton and Cleveleys. In the former, Thornton is represented by the old windmill, built 1794 and still standing, and said to be the finest of several in the Fylde area. It is placed on a green field to indicate the agriculture of Thornton. Cleveleys is represented by the blue and white sea, golden sands, and red sun for the famous sunsets observed there. The coronet of Lancaster contains the reguardant wolf crest of the Fleetwoods, former Lords of the Manor which included Thornton, supporting a banner of St Andrew, patron of the modern parish of Cleveleys. The motto indicates the district's dependence on the land and sea for its livelihood, combining an agricultural area and a seaside resort.

TYLDESLEY-WITH-SHAKERLEY Urban District Council

The U.D.C. displays the arms and crest of the family of Tyldesley: Silver, a chevron gules between three hillocks (or molehills) vert. Crest: A gold pelican in its piety, i.e. feeding its young with blood drawn from its own breast—a symbol of the Eucharist.

LANCASHIRE

In the minutes of the Council the objects in the shield are described as 'three hills, or bongs.' I am informed by the Clerk that 'the word "bongs" is a colloquialism for "banks," a reference to the physical configuration of the district, which is sometimes called "Tyldesley Banks" or "Bongs."' It is thought that the Tyldesley family, though the hills in their arms are officially called molehills, may have adopted these charges in allusion to the character of the district in which they lived and whence they took their name. 'The district is noted for the way it rises in several small hills, forming the commencement of the Lancashire hills, given special prominence by the way they overlook the great Cheshire plain, and also formerly for its "tilled leys" or rich grass lands.'

TYLDESLEY-WITH-SHAKERLEY   URMSTON   WALTON-LE-DALE

URMSTON *Urban District Council*

ARMS: Parted chevronwise, the chief azure and the base barry wavy argent and azure; a chevron ermine charged with a rose gules between two martlets or; in the dexter chief a griffin, in the sinister chief an uprooted oak-tree, both gold, and in the base a golden roundel charged with an anvil sable.

CREST: On a wreath argent and azure, a squirrel proper sitting and holding a gold balance.

MOTTO: *Salus populi suprema est lex*—'The welfare of the people is the highest law.'

These were granted in 1942.

The emblems are from the arms of the local families of Trafford (the griffin), Hyde and Ashawe (the chevron and martlets), and De Ornston (the squirrel). The oak-tree alludes to the preservation of the rural aspect of the district. Local industries are symbolized by the anvil, while the waves represent the River Mersey and the Ship Canal. The balance is the emblem of St Michael, the patron saint of the parish.

WALTON-LE-DALE Urban District Council

ARMS: Parted chevronwise argent and gules, a chevron counter-changed; two crosses patonce sable in chief, and a demi-pelican issuing from the base, wings spread and inverted, argent, piercing its breast with its beak, the wound gules.

CREST: Rising from a gold circlet charged with three drops of blood, a demi-lion purpure supporting a staff proper and thereon a banner sable charged with three bars argent.

MOTTO: *De bon cuer*—'With good heart.'

These were granted in 1952.

I am indebted to Mr H. Ellis Tomlinson for the following note:

The red parted chevron is adapted from that in the arms of the Waltons of Little Walton and the three chevronels in those of the Langtons of Walton. From an ancient seal and ring of the latter family, the pelican and motto are taken. The Banastre family held Walton and Lostock, and their black cross is shown twice for these portions of the modern District. The blood on the circlet is for the battle of Preston, fought at Walton in 1648, and for the defence of the Ribble against the Scots in 1715. The purple lion is that of the De Lacy family who held the manor in very early times, and the banner carries the arms of the De Hoghtons.

CHORLEY Rural District Council

ARMS: Argent, a pale sable between two cornflowers with stalks and leaves proper, and on the pale a silver standish between two cross-crosslets argent.

CREST: In a coronet consisting of a gold rim set with eight red roses with seeds and sepals proper, a mount vert and thereon a bull argent supporting a beacon sable with flames proper.

MOTTO: *Spectemur agendo*—'Let us be judged by our deeds.'

These were granted in 1952.

The cornflowers are from the arms of the family of Chorley, as in the shield of the Borough of Chorley. The pale represents trunk road A 6 which runs through the District, and the emblems on it stand for the local families of Standish and Charnock.

The crest consists of a coronet of Lancastrian roses ringing a mount and beacon representing Rivington Pike, the beacon supported by a white bull from the heraldry of the De Hoghtons, and also alluding to farming.

GARSTANG Rural District Council

ARMS: Parted fesswise gules and argent, a fess wavy barry wavy of four pieces argent and azure; in chief two gold croziers crossed saltirewise between two pierced cinquefoils ermine, and in base a red rose with seeds and sepals proper.

CREST: On a wreath argent and gules the battlements of a square tower proper and thereon a lion couchant resting the right forepaw on a gold wheatsheaf.

MOTTO: *Curandum omnium bonum*—'We must care for the good of all.'

These were granted in 1949.

The wavy fess stands for the River Wyre, the cinquefoils for the Hamilton family, and the croziers for Cockersand Abbey. The tower represents Greenhalgh Castle, and the lion the family De Lancaster.

Chorley R.D.C. Garstang R.D.C. Preston R.D.C.

PRESTON Rural District Council

ARMS: Parted saltirewise vert and gold, a fess wavy azure charged with another wavy argent; in chief an eagle displayed and in base a castle with three towers, both gold.

CREST: On a wreath or and vert, a silver dragon passant without wings, its head erect and its tail knotted, having a mural crown gules about its neck and grasping with the right forepaw a red rose with seeds, sepals, stalk, and leaves all proper.

MOTTO: *Unitate praestans*—'Excelling by unity.'

These were granted in 1948.

The shield represents pastoral and arable land crossed by the River Ribble, the eagle standing for the Roman settlement at Ribchester and the castle for the stronghold of the Barons of Penwortham. The dragon is from the crest of the Faringtons of Worden, and the rose is for the County. The motto contains a play on the name.

WHISTON Rural District Council

The Council has no arms, but has made use of those of Eton College (see Eton U.D.C.). There is no connection between the District and the College to account for this.

LEICESTERSHIRE C.C.

LEICESTERSHIRE

LEICESTERSHIRE County Council

ARMS: Quarterly argent and gules, the fesswise party line indented; in the first quarter a roundel gules charged with a cinquefoil ermine; in the second a silver double-tailed lion rampant; in the third an ostrich feather ermine; and in the fourth a sleeve sable.

CREST: On a wreath argent and gules, a running fox proper.

SUPPORTERS: Dexter, a black bull with a gold ducal coronet about its neck; and sinister, a Leicester ram proper.

MOTTO: *For'ard, For'ard.*

These were granted in 1930.

The first three quarters of the shield stand for former holders of the Earldom of Leicester. The first was Robert de Beaumont (*temp.* Henry I) whose great-grandson Robert, called FitzPernell after his mother, used a cinquefoil as the device on his seal, perhaps intending it to represent a pimpernel in punning allusion to his name. The cinquefoil has thus been taken to stand for the line of Beaumont Earls of Leicester, and as such appears in the arms of the City of Leicester.

At FitzPernell's death the Earldom of Leicester passed to his sister's husband, Simon de Montfort, whose arms, a silver double-tailed lion on red, occupy the second quarter of the County shield. Simon also held the Honour of Hinckley in Leicestershire, to which appertained arms consisting of a shield parted palewise indented silver and red; these are suggested by the fesswise indentation in the County arms.

After Simon's death, Henry III conferred the Earldom on his son Edmund, Earl of Lancaster, through whose grandson it ultimately passed to John of Gaunt, Duke of Lancaster, who is represented in the County arms by one of his badges, the ermine ostrich feather. When John of Gaunt's son ascended the throne as Henry IV, the Earldom of Leicester was merged in the crown.

Lord Robert Dudley, whom Queen Elizabeth I created Earl of Leicester in 1564, also bore in his arms a double-tailed lion, coloured green upon gold, so that he too is represented in the County arms.

The black sleeve, which also appears in the arms of Loughborough, is from the arms of Hastings, Barons Loughborough.

The great industries of the County—cattle-breeding, wool production, and, indirectly, hosiery manufacture—are represented by the supporters; while the crest and motto stand for the world-famous fox-hunting country.

The scroll bearing the motto is embellished with badges: a hazel leaf for Sir Arthur Hazlerigg, Bart, the Lord Lieutenant, and a red martlet (marten) for Lieut-Col R. E. Martin, C.M.G., Chairman of the County Council when the arms were granted.

LEICESTER

LEICESTER *City and County Borough Council*

ARMS: Gules, a cinquefoil ermine, pierced at the centre.

CREST: On a wreath argent and gules, a silver legless wyvern strewn with red wounds.

SUPPORTERS: Two lions reguardant gules, each with a gold ducal coronet about its neck, and hanging therefrom by a gold chain a pierced cinquefoil ermine.

MOTTO: *Semper eadem*—'Always the same.'

The arms and crest were recorded by the Heralds in 1619. The supporters were granted in 1926.

The cinquefoil was the device of Robert FitzPernell, Earl of Leicester (*d.* 1204), and was perhaps intended for a pimpernel in allusion to his surname (see Leicestershire C.C.). The wyvern was the crest of Thomas of Lancaster, second Lancastrian Earl of Leicester. It has sometimes been quoted as ermine. The motto is that of Queen Elizabeth I.

CIVIC HERALDRY

LOUGHBOROUGH

HINCKLEY

LOUGHBOROUGH Borough Council

ARMS: Gold, a bend between a sleeve in chief and a bull's head, torn off, in base, all sable; on the bend a fret between two scallop shells, all gold.

CREST: On a wreath or and sable, a gold lion rampant holding in the right forepaw a black sleeve, and resting the right hind foot on a fret sable.

MOTTO: *In veritate victoria*—'Victory is in truth.'

These were granted in 1889.

The following is the official explanation of the emblems:

The arms are based upon those of the Hastings family, who have been more closely and historically connected with the town than any other; two members of the family having taken the title of Baron from the town of Loughborough. Charges from the Arms of the families of Beaumont and Le De Spencer, formerly great landowners and Lords of the Manor of Loughborough, are incorporated. The Maunch (lady's sleeve) and Bull's Head erased are symbolical of the Hastings family; the Fret and Escallops in the bend for Le De Spencer (a Crusader); and the Crest of the Lion for Beaumont, with charges for Le De Spencer and Hastings. The colours are black and gold. The motto *In veritate victoria*, rendered 'Victory is in truth,' was the motto of the former barons of Loughborough.

HINCKLEY Urban District Council

ARMS: Parted palewise dancetty argent and gules; on a chief gold ermined sable a maunch (lady's sleeve) gules between two flames of fire proper.

CREST: On a wreath argent and gules a ram's head torn off at the neck sable with gold horns in front of five ostrich feathers argent.

MOTTO: *Angliae cor*—'The heart of England.'

These were granted in 1946.

The arms of the Honour of Hinckley, as borne by Simon de Montfort, Earl of Leicester, were: Parted palewise dancetty argent and gules. These were formerly used by the Urban District, and now form the basis of the arms. The lady's sleeve is the emblem of the Hastings family, who held the Manors of Barwell and Burbage in Norman times. The flame stands for the Flamvilles, who succeeded the Hastings family in the Manor of Burbage. The ostrich feathers are from the crest of the Grantmesnils, who held the Manor of Earl Shilton. The ram's head signifies the woollen industry on which Hinckley's hosiery manufactures were founded.

MARKET HARBOROUGH Urban District Council

The U.D.C. has in the past made use of the arms of the extinct Earldom of Harborough: Silver, a chevron and three roundels all gules. Crest: In a gold ducal coronet, a peacock's tail proper bound with a gold and red ribbon. Supporters: Two silver rams with gold horns and hoofs. Motto: *Hostis honori invidia*—'Envy is a foe to honour.' It is understood that a petition for arms for the Council is under consideration.

MELTON MOWBRAY Urban District Council

The device consists of a lion rampant, presumably from the arms of the Mowbray family.

LINCOLNSHIRE

HOLLAND County Council

The Council displays on its seal a quartered shield bearing in the first and fourth quarters the arms of the City of Lincoln, in the second those of the Borough of Boston, and in the third three gold wheatsheaves (placed one and two) on blue—a variation of the arms of the Earldom of Chester, here included to stand for Spalding U.D.C.

KESTEVEN C.C.

KESTEVEN County Council

ARMS: Vert, a pale ermine charged with an uprooted oak-tree proper.

CREST: On a wreath argent and vert, a heron with a pike in its beak proper.

SUPPORTERS: Dexter, a Roman soldier, and sinister, a Lincolnshire poacher (in the costume of the early nineteenth century), both proper.

MOTTO: *Perseverantia vincit*—'Perseverance succeeds.'

These were granted in 1950.

Across a shield of Lincoln green, referring to the County's verdant plains, runs an ermine pale alluding to Ermine Street. The oak-tree stands for the former wooded nature of the County, and the crest represents the Fens. The legionary recalls the Roman settlements in this part of Britain, and the other supporter was suggested by the well-known song, 'The Lincolnshire Poacher.'

LINCOLNSHIRE

HOLLAND C.C.   LINDSEY C.C.

LINDSEY County Council

ARMS: Barry wavy of six pieces argent and azure, thereon gold Viking ship with a silver sail; on a chief wavy azure bull's face and horns proper between two gold wheatsheaves.

CREST: On a wreath argent and azure a wreath of laurel, and rising therefrom two human arms bent at the elbows, the hands grasping a chain, all proper.

MOTTO: *Service links all.*

These were granted in 1935.

The Viking ship recalls the part of the Danish invasions in the history of Lincolnshire and, with the blue and white wavy bars, signifies the County's maritime interests. The sheaves of corn and the bull's head stand for agriculture, while the arms upholding a chain indicate other industries. The links of the chain are allusive to the name of the geographical county, and the word-play is carried on in the motto. The laurel wreath is from the arms of Alfred Lord Tennyson, who bore it as Poet Laureate.

GRIMSBY County Borough Council

ARMS: Silver, a chevron and three boars' heads cut off behind the ears, all sable.

These are on record at the Heralds' College.

A scallop shell is sometimes added as crest.

The boars' heads are said to commemorate the ancient right of the Mayor and Corporation to hunt the boar in Bradley Woods; an early Mayoral seal contains a representation of a boar hunt. The chevron may have been derived from the arms of the family named Grimsby, whose shield was parted chevronwise silver and black with two chevrons counter-changed.

GRIMSBY

LINCOLN

LINCOLN City and County Borough Council

ARMS: Silver, a cross gules charged with a gold fleur-de-lis.

These are recorded at the College of Arms.

The arms combine the cross of St George with a fleur-de-lis, which may be a royal or a religious emblem. As the Virgin Mary, to whom Lincoln Cathedral is dedicated, is portrayed on the ancient seals of the Corporation, I incline to the opinion that the fleur-de-lis in the arms refers to her. These arms occupy the chief of the shield of Lincoln, Massachusetts.

BOSTON

BOSTON Borough Council

ARMS: Sable, three gold crowns composed of crosses paty and fleurs-de-lis, palewise.

CREST: On a wreath or and sable, a woolpack proper charged with a ram couchant gold with horns sable.

SUPPORTERS: Two mermaids proper with gold hair and fins, and crowns azure.

MOTTO: *Per mare et per terram*—'By sea and land.'

These were confirmed in 1568.

The woolpack and ram allude to the fact that Boston was anciently a staple town for wool, and the mermaids recall its former importance as a commercial port. The Town Clerk informs me that there is a local tradition that the mermaids were crowned in order to signify the connection between the Borough and two women of note in the reign of Henry VIII, namely Anne Boleyn and Princess Mary, Duchess of Suffolk. The three crowns are said to represent the Dukes of Brittany, Richmond, and Suffolk. A woolpack occurs on a fourteenth-century seal.

CLEETHORPES

CLEETHORPES *Borough Council*

ARMS: Silver, a bend engrailed between two scallop shells all azure, and on the bend three gold owls.

CREST: On a wreath argent and azure, a silver pelican standing on a rock and wounding its breast with its beak, about its neck a silver strap with a gold buckle.

SUPPORTERS: Dexter, a Norseman holding in his right hand a shield; and sinister, a Cleethorpes fisherman holding in his left hand a net, all proper.

MOTTO: *Vigilantes*—'Watchful.'

These were granted in 1936, when Cleethorpes was incorporated as a borough.

The former U.D.C. used as a device: Silver, on a bend azure three gold owls; with a blue scallop shell above the shield. How this device came to be adopted is not known, but it has been suggested that the owls (to which the motto *Vigilantes* applied) were taken as symbolic of a community of watchful night-workers, the men of Cleethorpes in former times being vigilant with regard not only to fish, but also to wreckage. A more likely theory is that the owls were derived from the arms of the local family of Appleyard.

When the authorized arms were granted, the features of the former device were retained, the scallop being included in the shield, and the bend being engrailed so as to refer to Sidney Sussex College, Cambridge, the chief landowner in Cleethorpes; the College arms embody the engrailed bend of Radcliffe, Earl of Sussex. The pelican is from the arms of the Earl of Yarborough, Lord of the Manor, the strap about its neck being from the arms granted to the Pelham family to commemorate the capture of the French King at Poictiers by Sir John Pelham.

The supporters represent the town's past and present seafaring associations.

GRANTHAM

SCUNTHORPE

LOUTH

GRANTHAM *Borough Council*

ARMS: Checky or and azure within a border sable charged with silver trefoils.

These are recorded at the College of Arms.

The chequers are the arms of the Warennes (see Chapter III), to which the border was added for difference. Street's *History of Grantham* states:

There is an ancient military or knight's mace in the town, said to have been once in the keeping of the Corporation, along the haft of which the trefoil or ivy leaf is worked. It is an object of very great interest, a relic of ancient armoury; two feet two inches in length, and weighs between three and four pounds; made of iron, the head having seven projecting flanges, each terminating in a spike; one of these has been broken off, and the next bent, evidently by a blow. In the shaft is a hole through which passed a ring on the last link of the chain by which it was fastened to the saddle. If the trefoil was a bearing of the De Warennes, this was the mace of one of those renowned Barons.

LINCOLNSHIRE

The mace, now repaired, is still in the possession of the Corporation. The above writer's conjecture that it may have been the weapon of one of the Warennes is unsupported by heraldry, for the trefoil forms no part of the Warenne insignia. It is, however, possible that the trefoils on the mace suggested to the Corporation the emblems with which they differenced the Warenne arms to produce their own shield.

LOUTH Borough Council

Having no arms, the Corporation uses those of the family of Louth: Sable, a gold wolf, salient.

SCUNTHORPE Borough Council

ARMS: Vert, a gold chain of five links fesswise; above it, two shells (*gryphoea incurva*), and in the base a wheatsheaf, all gold.

CREST: On a wreath or and vert, the top of a blast-furnace with flames coming from it, proper.

MOTTO: *Refulget labores nostros coelum*—'The sky reflects our works.'

These were granted in 1936.

The green field and the wheatsheaf refer to Scunthorpe's agricultural past, and the chain and blast-furnace to the iron and steel industry on which its modern development has been based. The shells relate to the geological formation of the district.

The wheatsheaves also allude to the family of Sheffield which held the Manor of Kirton (of which Scunthorpe formed part); Sir Berkeley Sheffield was the Charter Mayor.

STAMFORD Borough Council

ARMS: Gules, three gold lions of England, impaling checky or and azure.

These are recorded at the College of Arms. The chequers are those of the Earls Warenne (see Chapter III) who held the manor in the thirteenth century. The Royal Arms were probably assumed in token that Stamford was a royal borough.

STAMFORD

GAINSBOROUGH Urban District Council

ARMS: Vert, a fess wavy argent charged with another azure; in chief a cog-wheel between two wheatsheaves and in base an ancient crown, all gold.

CREST: On a wreath argent and vert a gold mural crown, and thereon two gold anchors crossed saltirewise.

MOTTO: *Strive for the gain of all.*

These were granted in 1950.

The colours and emblems on the shield refer to the town's rural surroundings, the River Trent, industry, and agriculture, while the crown alludes to royal associations and the Kingdom of Mercia. The anchors recall Gainsborough's former importance as an inland port, and the mural crown, besides being an emblem of local government, refers to the castle.

GAINSBOROUGH

SLEAFORD

SPALDING

SLEAFORD Urban District Council

ARMS: Gules, on a gold chevron three estoiles sable, and on a silver chief three trefoils slipped vert.

CREST: On a wreath gold and gules an eagle proper, its wings spread and head lowered to the sinister, holding in the beak a gold ear of wheat with stalk and leaf.

These were granted in 1950.

In the lower part of the shield are the arms of the family of Carre, closely associated with the town in the sixteenth and seventeenth centuries, and founders of the local almshouses and grammar school. The trefoils on the chief are from the arms of the Herveys, Marquesses of Bristol, Lords of the Manor.

The eagle marks the town's connection with the R.A.F., particularly through the R.A.F. College at Cranwell, while the wheatear refers to agriculture.

SPALDING Urban District Council

ARMS: Azure, three wheatsheaves and in the centre an estoile all gold; on a chief or, an open book proper bound in red and edged with gold between two tulips with stalks and leaves proper.

CREST: On a wreath or and azure, a gold lymphad (ancient galley) flying pennons of St George, the sail azure charged with a lily with stalk and leaves proper.

MOTTO: *Vicinas urbes alit.*

These were granted in 1950.

The gold wheatsheaves on blue, with a star for difference, are from the arms borne by the ancient priory at Spalding, which derived them from the arms of the Earls of Chester and Lincoln. The open book symbolizes the Spalding Gentlemen's Society, the second

 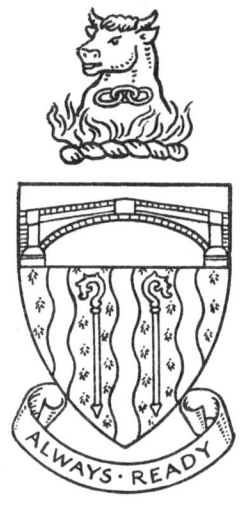 

GAINSBOROUGH R.D.C.   GLANFORD BRIGG R.D.C.   SOUTH KESTEVEN R.D.C.

oldest learned society in the kingdom. The tulips stand for the flower industry. The galley recalls the town's maritime history, and is also an emblem of St Nicholas, while the lily stands for St Mary—patron saints of the town.

The motto is usually translated, 'She nourishes the neighbouring cities.' This was adopted many years ago, probably with reference to the agricultural produce of the district.

GAINSBOROUGH Rural District Council

ARMS: Parted palewise, the dexter side barry wavy of six pieces azure and argent, and the sinister side ermine; on a gold pale a chevron vert between in chief a mitre gules charged with a gold fleur-de-lis, and in base an eagle displayed gules.

CREST: On a wreath gold and azure, a Danish dragon-ship sable, a pennon azure flying from the mast, the sail gold charged with a boar's head torn off sable with tusks and tongue gules.

MOTTO: *Trust and triumph.*

These were granted in 1952.

A note issued by the Council states:

The shield is an heraldic map of the District. The blue and white waves represent the Trent with its eagre, the ermine portion is for Ermine Street, and between these boundaries lies a rich agricultural area represented by the gold middle portion. The chevron is common to the arms of John Wycliffe, Thomas Sutton, and Admiral Lord Hawke, all having associations with the area. It is coloured green and so represents the central ridge called the Cliff. The mitre is for the ancient bishopric of Lindsey, with its head at Stow, from which the present Diocese of Lincoln descends. The fleur-de-lis is the emblem of St Mary, and in gold on red gives the present diocesan colours. The eagle represents the numerous Roman associations of the district, and also its importance as a Royal Air Force base.

[The colours of the crest-wreath] are those of the Wrays, blue and gold. The crest is the Danish dragon-ship from the Lindsey arms, recalling how Sweyn sailed up the Trent and made this district his headquarters. The boar's head alludes to his name and also to the crest of the Bacons. The motto is a quotation from *The Mill on the Floss*, written at Morton.

GLANFORD BRIGG Rural District Council

ARMS: Ermine, three palets wavy azure and between them two gold croziers back-to-back; on a chief sable, a representation of Brigg bridge proper.

CREST: On a wreath argent and azure, a Lincolnshire red shorthorn bull's head proper rising from flames and charged on the neck with a silver chain of three links.

MOTTO: *Always ready.*

These were granted in 1950.

An explanation of the bearings, contributed to the *Rural District Councils Association Journal* by Mr H. Ellis Tomlinson, states:

The ermine field is a reminder of Ermine Street, which runs through the District, and the blue waves are for the River Ancholme lying between the Trent and the southward sweep of the Humber, which form the westward and eastward boundaries. The gold croziers are found in the same position in the arms of Thornton Abbey.... They also refer to the ancient See of Lindsey, whose Bishop was seated at Kirkton-in-Lindsey. The relative positions of the waves and the croziers in the shield correspond to the geographical situation, so that a kind of heraldic map is given. The black chief, or upper portion, is from the arms of the Order of St Augustine, or Black Canons, which was represented at Thornton Curtis.

In the crest, the bull's head, representing the local strain of cattle, rises from flames standing for ironstone mining. The links, playing on the name of the County, were the device of the old Lincolnshire Sugar Company, and refer to the sugar-beet industry.

SOUTH KESTEVEN Rural District Council

ARMS: Argent, on waves of the sea in base barry wavy azure and argent, a Danish dragon-ship sable, its sail, shields, and oars gold, the sail charged with a raven proper, and from the mast-head a flag gules flying to the dexter; on a chief vert a mitre between two wheatsheaves, all gold.

CREST: On a wreath argent and vert, the battlements of a tower, and issuing therefrom a demi-savage wreathed about the loins and temples with oak leaves all proper, in his right hand a flagstaff with a flag gold fretty azure.

MOTTO: *Ora et ara*—'Pray and plough.'

These were granted in 1948.

The ship alludes to the district's historical background, and the raven is not only the emblem of the Danish invaders, but also represents the parish of Corby. The sheaves stand for agriculture, and the mitre refers to the many monastic houses in the area. In the crest, a man of the woods, recalling the ancient forest of Kesteven, maintains a banner of the arms of Willoughby, for the Earl of Ancaster, Baron Willoughby d'Eresby, and Baron Aveland.

CORBY Development Corporation

The device of the Corporation consists of a corby perched on an anvil.

LONDON

London County Council

LONDON

LONDON County Council

ARMS: Barry wavy of six pieces azure and argent, a silver chief and thereon a cross gules charged with a gold lion passant guardant.

Above the shield is placed a gold mural crown, usually depicted with turrets.

These were granted in 1914.

The blue and silver wavy bars represent the River Thames, and serve as a reminder that London is a great port. The cross of St George, besides being a national emblem, links the arms with those of the City of London. The royal lion is appropriate to the County which embraces the capital of England.

LONDON City Corporation

ARMS: Argent, a cross gules, and in the first quarter a sword erect, point upwards, also gules.

MOTTO: *Domine dirige nos*—'Lord, direct us.'

These are recorded at the College of Arms. The following are not on official record:

CREST: On a wreath argent and gules, a silver dragon's wing charged with a cross gules.

SUPPORTERS: Two silver dragons with wings spread, charged on the wings with a cross gules.

The shield combines the cross of St George with the emblem of the City's patron, St Paul, the sword having been the instrument of his martyrdom. St Paul, holding a sword in his right hand and supporting with his left a banner bearing the lions of England, appears on a thirteenth-century seal. The tradition that the weapon in the arms is the dagger with which Sir William Walworth killed Wat Tyler is inconsistent with the fact that the arms were in use before Tyler's death.

City of London

The origin of the crest and supporters is to be found in a sixteenth-century Corporation seal which shows above the shield a helmet with fan-shaped top painted with a cross as in the arms. Apparently the fan came to be mistaken for a dragon's wing crest, and early in the seventeenth century the Corporation invented a pair of dragon supporters to match it.

The crest and supporters are, therefore, based on an error. Moreover, they are subject to those variations which frequently occur in heraldry of which there is no official record; for instance, the crest is sometimes shown as consisting of a pair of wings, and the cross on the wings varies in form.

The Mayoral Seal made in 1380 contains, below the figures of St Peter and St Paul, the arms of the City supported by two lions.

BATTERSEA Borough Council

The Borough has adopted an unauthorized device consisting of a shield indented palewise blue and silver; with as crest, a dove holding in its beak an olive branch, in natural colours. The motto is *Non mihi, non tibi, sed nobis*—'Not for me, nor for thee, but for us.'

The blue and white shield is probably intended to denote Battersea's riverside position and to recall the time when it was an island—either Badric's-ey or Peter's-ey; and if the latter, perhaps so called because it belonged to the Abbey of St Peter at Westminster. The dove and olive branch, associated with the Biblical story of the Flood, may also have been selected with a view to Battersea's insular origin.

BATTERSEA

BERMONDSEY

CAMBERWELL

BERMONDSEY Borough Council

ARMS: Quarterly azure and gules, in chief a lion passant guardant supporting a crozier erect and flanked by two letters B, all gold; in the third quarter a battle-axe erect, its haft encircled by a crown, both gold; and in the fourth an ancient three-masted ship of gold, its sails spread and pennons flying.

CREST: On a wreath gold and azure, a lion passant guardant gules charged on the shoulder with a gold letter B and holding erect a gold crozier.

MOTTO: *Prosunt gentibus artes*—'Arts benefit the people.'

These were granted in 1901.

The crown and battle-axe are emblems of the Saint-King Olaf who was summoned by Ethelred to help him resist the Danes, and destroyed the old fortified bridge over the Thames to attack the Danish camp at Southwark. This is the exploit of which children still tell in the words of an ancient minstrel:

> London Bridge is broken down—
> Gold is won, and bright renown.

To St Olaf was dedicated the church in what is now Tooley Street, a corruption of St Olaf's Street.

The lion and crozier refer to the ancient Abbey of Bermondsey, which enjoyed royal favour, having been endowed by William Rufus with the Manor of Bermondsey. The ship is an allusion to the Borough's old shipbuilding industry.

BETHNAL GREEN Borough Council

The Borough has no arms. The seal contains the figures of 'the seely blind beggar of Bednall-greene,' and his daughter, the subjects of a popular ballad of Elizabethan days. 'Prettye Bessee,' the blind beggar's daughter, was 'of bewty most bright,' but suitors grew cold when they learned of her parentage. However, one young knight 'weighed not true love by the weight of his purse,' and sought her in marriage. At the wedding the blind beggar revealed himself as Henry de Montfort (eldest son of the famous Simon) who, contrary to general belief, had escaped from the battle of Evesham with his life, but having lost his sight. Unfortunately for a picturesque tradition there seems to be no doubt that Simon de Montfort's eldest son fell beside him.

CAMBERWELL Borough Council

ARMS: Quarterly gules and argent, a cross counter-changed; in the first and fourth quarters a silver well; in the second a chevron, cut short at the ends, and three cinquefoils, all gules; and in the third a lion rampant gules.

CREST: On a wreath argent and gules, a silver hind sprinkled with drops of blood and pierced through the neck by an arrow sable, lodged in front of a crozier erect gules.

MOTTO: *All's well.*

These were granted in 1901.

Camberwell is said to mean the well of crooked folk, or cripples, who flocked to the medicinal springs to be cured; hence the wells in its shield and the punning motto. Hence, too, the dedication of the parish church to St Giles, the patron of cripples, commemorated by the crest—the wounded hind in defence of which the Saint received the injury which lamed him.

The chevron and cinquefoils are from the arms of Edward Alleyn who, early in the seventeenth century, held the Manor of Dulwich, and founded the college of God's Gift.

The lion represents Peckham, which probably derived it from Robert of Gloucester, an illegitimate son of Henry I.

CHELSEA Borough Council

ARMS: Gules, a gold cross voided (i.e. in outline, the part enclosed by the gold lines being the red of the field) and therein a gold crozier erect; in the first quarter a winged bull argent; in the second, a lion rampant reguardant argent; in the third, a sword, point downwards proper, with a gold pommel and hilt, between two silver boars' heads cut off at the neck; and in the fourth a gold stag's face and antlers.

MOTTO: *Nisi Dominus frustra.*

These were granted in 1903.

The crozier alludes to the Abbot of Westminster, Lord of the Manor of Chelsea in the reign of Edward the Confessor. The winged bull is the emblem of St Luke, patron saint of the parish. The lion represents Lord Cadogan, Lord of the Manor, whose ancestor derived it by marriage with a daughter of Sir Hans Sloane, from whose arms the sword and boars' heads are taken. Another daughter of Sir Hans married into the Stanley family, whence the stag's head. The motto is a contraction of Psalm cxxvii. i: 'Except the Lord keep the city, the watchman waketh but in vain.'

LONDON

DEPTFORD Borough Council

The Borough has no arms but makes use of a device consisting of a quartered shield, flanked by dolphins, ensigned by a mural crown, and with a pair of tridents crossed behind it. The first quarter of the shield is silver with three black Cornish choughs; the second is blue with a gold ship on stocks; the third is blue with a representation of Peter the Great, of Russia, seated on a log and wielding a shipwright's adze; and the fourth bears the white horse of Kent on red.

The Cornish choughs are said to stand for Surrey, but the reason for their selection is obscure; they are, in fact, the arms attributed to Thomas Becket, and it seems probable that Deptford took them from the shield of Canterbury, capital city of Kent.

The ship on the stocks denotes the Dockyard, and the effigy of Peter the Great recalls that the Czar came to Deptford in 1698 to learn practical shipbuilding. The tridents and dolphins are obvious emblems of the sea.

CHELSEA

FINSBURY

FINSBURY Borough Council

ARMS: Gules, on a silver cross a roundel barry wavy argent and azure between on the vertical limb two roundels gules each charged with a silver crescent, and on the horizontal limb two red rings; on a gold embattled chief a gateway with two towers gules.

CREST: On a wreath argent and gules, a right forearm proper, the hand holding a silver shield charged with a red cross between four seaxes proper with gold pommels and hilts to the dexter.

SUPPORTERS: Dexter, a silver winged bull with a collar azure consisting of fleurs-de-lis, their heads alternately upwards and downwards; and sinister, a dolphin vert charged with a silver roundel, thereon a well proper.

*I

Motto: *Altiora petimus*—'We seek higher things.'

These were granted in 1931.

The following is the official explanation:

The White Cross on the lower part of the shield is the Cross of St John, the Headquarters of which Order are situated at St John's Gate in the Borough.

The fountain, or running water, may be regarded as a reference to London, as symbolized by the River Thames.

The four Red Circles, with the Crescents, indicate the Arms of Thomas Sutton, the Founder of the Charterhouse.[1]

The Embattlement has reference to the City Wall, as forming the Southern boundary of the Borough.

The two Towers and Gateway suggest the old gates opening from the City of London into the Borough, Aldersgate (for the ancient Liberty of Glasshouse Yard), Cripplegate, and Moorgate.

The Escutcheon held aloft in the Crest contains charges from the Arms used in the past for St Sepulchre.[2]

The Winged Bull is the heraldic symbol of St Luke, and the Dolphin that of St James, the badge bearing the design of the Well having special reference to the Clerks' Well (Clerkenwell).

FULHAM Borough Council

Arms: Barry wavy of ten pieces argent and azure; thereon a saltire gules charged with two crossed swords of silver, passing through a gold mitre.

Crest: On a gold mural crown with seven towers, a galley sable with oars in action and sail spread; the flags parted fesswise argent and azure, and the sail silver charged with a Tudor rose with seeds and sepals proper.

Motto: *Pro civibus et civitate*—'For the citizens and the city.'

These were granted in 1927.

The silver and blue background stands for the River Thames. The swords of St Paul on red are from the arms of the See of London whose Bishops, represented by the mitre, have held the Manor of Fulham since the end of the seventh century.

The Anglo-Saxon Chronicle, under date 879, records that 'the same year assembled a band of pirates and sat at Fulham by the Thames,' and this event is commemorated by the Danish galley in the crest.

GREENWICH Borough Council

Arms: Silver, a pale between six stars of six points, all azure, and on the pale a radiant star above an hour-glass, both silver.

Crest: On a wreath argent and azure, a ship of ancient type with one mast, the sail furled and flags flying all sable, with two gold anchors crossed saltirewise in front of it.

Motto: *Tempore utimur*—'We use time.'

These were granted in 1903.

---

[1] The arms of Thomas Sutton, now used by Charterhouse, were: Gold, a chevron between three rings all gules, and on the chevron three gold crescents.

[2] The arms used by St Sepulchre consisted of a shield parted fesswise, in the upper part three seaxes for Middlesex and in the lower part the cross of St George.

The emblems relate to the Royal Observatory, built in 1675 for the advancement of navigation and nautical astronomy. The ship and anchors forming the crest recall the Borough's close association with the Royal Navy since its old royal palace was in 1705 converted into a hospital for seamen—now a Royal Naval College.

FULHAM   GREENWICH   HACKNEY

HACKNEY Borough Council

ARMS: Parted fesswise; the lower half of the shield barry wavy of six pieces argent and azure; the upper half parted palewise, the dexter side gules with a representation of Hackney Tower proper, and the sinister side parted fesswise sable and argent with a Maltese Cross similarly parted silver and gules.

CREST: Hackney Tower, gold.

MOTTO: *Justitia turris nostra*—'Justice is our tower.'

These were granted in 1924.

The Tower is that of St Augustine's Church and is the only part of the thirteenth-century fabric that remains. This was used on the Corporation seal before arms were obtained. The Maltese Cross stands for the Knights of the Temple and the Knights of the Hospital of St John of Jerusalem, who successively held the Manor of Hackney. The Templars' cross was red on white, that of the Hospitallers white on black, and these colours are combined in the arms. The wavy white and blue bars represent the rivers and canals in and bounding the Borough. In years past the River Lea at Hackney was a much wider river than at present, as it overflowed the marshes and lowlands which are now within the Borough.

HAMMERSMITH

HAMPSTEAD

HAMMERSMITH Borough Council

ARMS: Parted palewise azure and gules, a gold chevron charged with three horseshoes azure; above the chevron two silver cross-crosslets, and below it a silver scallop shell.

CREST: On a wreath gold and azure, two crossed hammers on the battlements of a tower proper.

MOTTO: *Spectemur agendo*—'Let us be judged by our deeds.'

These were granted in 1897.

The emblems on the shield are from the arms of benefactors of the Borough. The cross-crosslets represent Edward Latymer, who died in 1626 leaving a bequest for the benefit of the poor and for the education of poor boys, and is commemorated by the schools bearing his name. The horseshoes represent Sir Nicholas Crisp (1598–1665), a prominent Royalist who contributed bricks and funds towards the building of the chapel of ease which became the parish church. The scallop shell denotes George Pring who projected the Old Bridge—the first suspension bridge to be built near London—but died in 1824 before it was finished.

The hammers, of course, refer to the name; but the name has nothing to do with hammers, being probably a development of Hame's-hythe.

LONDON

HAMPSTEAD Borough Council

ARMS: Azure, a silver cross charged with a mitre and four fleurs-de-lis all gules; a gold indented chief fretted gules.

CREST: On a wreath argent and azure, a silver stag's head with gold antlers, about the neck a holly wreath proper, from which hangs a shield gules charged with a silver fleur-de-lis.

MOTTO: *Non sibi sed toti*—'Not for self but for all.'

These were granted in 1931; a similar device was previously used without authority.

The mitre stands for the Abbey of Westminster, to which the Manor of Hampstead belonged from the end of the tenth century until 1539. The other emblems stand for later holders of the manor: the fleurs-de-lis and stag's head for Hickes, the fretty chief for Noel, and the cross for Langhorne. The holly is from the seal of the old Hampstead Vestry.

HOLBORN

HOLBORN Borough Council

ARMS: Argent, a cross gules charged with a golden hind, lodged, pierced by an arrow; on a chief sable three silver scallop shells.

CREST: Rising from a mural crown proper, a half-length figure of St Andrew in a blue robe, supporting with his left hand a silver saltire, and in his right hand an open book proper.

SUPPORTERS: Dexter, a gold lion, and sinister, a gold griffin, each with a collar gules from which hangs a shield, barry wavy of ten pieces silver and azure.

MOTTO: *Multi pertransibunt et augebitur scientia*—'Many shall pass through, and learning shall be increased.'

These were granted in 1906.

The red cross stands for the churches of St George-the-Martyr and St George, Bloomsbury; the figure of St Andrew for the parish so dedicated; and the wounded hind for St Giles-in-the-Fields, in allusion to the legend that Giles received the injury which crippled him while saving a hind from the huntsmen.

The scallop shells are from the arms of the Russells, Dukes of Bedford, whose connection with the Borough is also commemorated in the names of streets and squares.

The supporters denote the two inns of court in the Borough, the lion being that of the De Lacys, Earls of Lincoln, whose London house became Lincoln's Inn, and the griffin being from the arms of Gray's Inn. To the inns the motto, with its promise of increasing learning, also refers.

The blue and white shields worn by the supporters allude to the 'Old Bourne' from which the Borough derived its name.

ISLINGTON Borough Council

ARMS: Parted fesswise gules and argent, a cross counter-changed; in the first quarter a gold cross potent; in the second a silver lion rampant; in the third an eagle displayed sable; and in the fourth a water-bouget sable.

CREST: On a wreath argent and gules, a water-bouget sable, and in front of it a longbow fesswise and an arrow erect proper.

MOTTO: *Deus per omnia*—'God pervades all things.'

These were granted in 1901.

The following explanation of the arms was prepared by the Borough Librarian:

In the first quarter is shown the crutched cross from the arms of the Knights Hospitallers of St John of Jerusalem, a religious order instituted in the beginning of the twelfth century, who owned not only the greater part of Islington but also 'West Smethefeld, Finchesley, Kentisheton.'

The lion in the second quarter is probably taken from the crest of Sir George Colebrooke. The Manor of Highbury was alienated in the year 1723 to James Colebrooke, Esq., from whom it descended to Sir George Colebrooke, Bart. This gentleman's interest in the manor was sold 16th February 1791.

The eagle displayed in the third quarter is from the arms of Sir John Spencer, the wealthy London merchant, who came into possession of the Manor of Canonbury in 1570.

The heraldic device in the fourth quarter of the shield is known as a 'water-bouget.' Water-bougets, which are really the old form of water-bucket, were leather bags or bottles, two of which were carried on a stick over the shoulder. This device is taken from the arms of the Berners family, who came over with William the Conqueror. They became possessed of large lands in Islington, known as Bernersbury (Barnsbury) from the name of the family.

The crest above the shield consists of a water-bouget, behind a longbow and arrow, on a wreath supported on a helmet. This commemorates Islington's associations with the sports of the past.

ISLINGTON

KENSINGTON

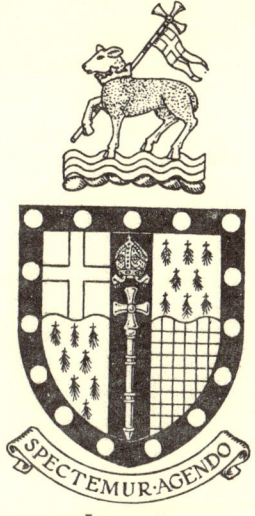
LAMBETH

KENSINGTON *Borough Council*

ARMS: Quarterly gules and gold; in the first quarter a gold celestial crown above a gold fleur-de-lis, and in the dexter chief point a silver star; in the second, a cross flory and four martlets all sable; in the third, a cross bottony and four roses gules, their stems and leaves proper; and in the fourth a gold mitre; all within a bordure quarterly or and sable.

MOTTO: *Quid nobis ardui?*—'What is hard for us?'

These arms were granted in 1901.

The celestial crown and fleur-de-lis stand for the Virgin Mary, to whom the parish church is dedicated. The other emblems refer to successive Lords of the Manor.

From the eleventh to the sixteenth century the manor was held by the De Veres, whose arms, red and gold quarters with a silver star in the first, form the basis of the Borough arms. From the De Veres part of the manor passed to the Abbey of Abingdon, which is represented by its arms in the second quarter and the mitre in the fourth quarter of the Borough shield.

In the third quarter, the roses represent Sir Walter Cope who bought the manor in 1610 (his ancestor derived the red rose from his adherence to the Lancastrian cause); and the cross bottony is taken from the arms of Sir Henry Rich, who obtained the manor by marriage with the heiress of the Copes and was raised to the peerage as Baron Kensington.

Kensington is a Royal Borough.

LAMBETH *Borough Council*

ARMS: Quarterly, the fesswise line wavy; the first quarter silver with a cross gules; the second and third ermine; the fourth chequered gold and azure; over all a pale sable charged with a gold archiepiscopal cross and above it a gold mitre; all within a border sable charged with fifteen golden roundels.

CREST: Upon a wreath argent and gules, a Holy Lamb of silver with a gold coronet about its neck, standing in water, and bearing a gold archiepiscopal cross with a silver pennon charged with a red cross.

MOTTO: *Spectemur agendo*—'Let us be judged by our works.'

These were granted in 1922.

The cross of St George is from the arms of the London C.C., and the blue and gold chequers are the arms of the Warennes, Earls of Surrey. The border denotes that a large part of the Borough belongs to the Duchy of Cornwall, having been granted by Edward III to the Black Prince (see Cornwall). The ecclesiastical emblems refer to the Archbishops of Canterbury, whose residence at Lambeth dates from the thirteenth century; and the Holy Lamb is both a religious emblem and a reference to the derivation of the name of the Borough from Lamb-hythe. The wavy fess line stands for the River Thames.

LEWISHAM

LEWISHAM Borough Council

ARMS: Parted chevronwise and in chief palewise, vert, purpure, and sable, over all a gold Saxon crown; on a chief sable a gold lion passant.

CREST: On a wreath gold and vert, a billet laid fesswise barry wavy argent and azure and thereon a raven proper.

SUPPORTERS: Dexter, a stag proper; sinister, a bear proper with a gold muzzle; each with a silver mural crown about its neck.

MOTTO: *Salus populi suprema lex*—'The welfare of the people is the highest law.'

These were granted in 1950.

The green, purple, and black divisions of the shield refer to Lee Green, Hither (Heather) Green, and Blackheath, and the crown alludes to the Saxon associations of the district.

The crest of a raven standing on a representation of water refers to the River Ravensbourne. The stag is from the arms of the Earls of Dartmouth and Viscounts Lewisham, Lords of the Manor of Lewisham, and the bear represents the Lords Northbrook, Lords of the Manor of Lee.

PADDINGTON Borough Council

ARMS: Azure, in chief two silver wolves' heads torn off at the neck; and in the base two swords proper with gold pommels and hilts, crossed saltirewise and passing through a gold mural crown.

These arms were granted in 1902.

The wolves' heads are from the arms of Sir John Aird, first Mayor of the Borough, and the swords (of St Paul) are from the arms of the See of London.

POPLAR Borough Council

The Borough has no arms, but the seal contains three shields, representing three parishes. One is blue, with a representation of the inner gate of the West India Docks, in the parish of All Saints. Above this shield is placed a ship. The second shield is red, with two gold bars each charged with a bow, and a bridge between them; this stands for St Mary's, Stratford-le-Bow. The third shield, of blue, bears the figure of a Benedictine monk in allusion to the Priory dedicated to St Leonard, in what is now the parish of Bromley-St Leonard.

ST MARYLEBONE Borough Council

ARMS: Parted chevronwise, the upper part of the shield sable, and the base barry wavy of six pieces silver and azure; on the sable, a fleur-de-lis and a rose, both gold.

CREST: On a wreath argent and sable, two bars wavy silver and azure, and standing thereon between two white lilies with green stems and leaves, the Virgin Mary, with a silver robe and a blue mantle, holding in her arms the Holy Child clad in gold, each with a gold halo about the head.

MOTTO: *Fiat secundum Verbum Tuum*—'Let it be done according to Thy Word.'

These were granted in 1901.

The Borough derives its name from an ancient Chapel founded by Barking Abbey (which held the Manor of Tyburn) and, like the Abbey, dedicated to St Mary. To distinguish it from other religious houses with the same dedication the Chapel was called St Mary-le-Bourne; and 'le bourne'—the Tyburn brook—is represented in the arms and crest by the blue and white wavy bars.

The lilies and the rose were derived from the arms of Barking Abbey, which, in reference to the legend that when the Virgin's tomb was opened it was found to contain lilies and roses, bore three white lilies and three gold roses on blue, within a red border charged with eight silver roundels.

The fleur-de-lis, besides being an emblem of the Virgin, has a secondary significance as the principal charge in the arms of the Portman family.

St Marylebone   Paddington   St Pancras

ST PANCRAS Borough Council

ARMS: Parted saltirewise sable and argent, two silver scallop shells and two elephants' heads with their trunks raised sable; on a gold chief two swords crossed saltirewise proper between two roses gules, their seeds and sepals proper.

CREST: On a wreath argent and sable the figure of St Pancras gold.

MOTTO: *With wisdom and courage.*

These were granted in 1936.

The shells are from the arms of the Duke of Bedford, whose estates cover a large part of the south of the Borough. The elephants' heads are from the heraldry of the Marquess Camden, another ground-landlord, from whom Camden Town was named. The Dean and Chapter of London, who held the Manors of Cantelows and Totenhall (or Kentish Town and Tottenham Court), are represented by the crossed swords of St Paul, emblems of his martyrdom. The swords also recall the tradition of an ancient battle at the place called Battle Bridge, now King's Cross. Different accounts make the contestants Queen Boadicea and the Romans, and King Alfred and the Danes.

St Pancras, to whom the ancient parish church was dedicated, was a young Phrygian nobleman who was martyred by Diocletian in A.D. 304. The representation of the Saint, with book and palm, forming the crest is taken from a brass at Cowfold, Sussex.

LONDON

SHOREDITCH

SOUTHWARK

SHOREDITCH Borough Council

Having no arms, the Borough makes use of those of John de Northampton, Mayor of London in 1381 and 1382 and Lord of the Manor of Shoreditch. These consist of an heraldic freak: Gules, a gold lion bi-corporate, the tails passing between the hind legs, with a crown azure. The device may alternatively be described as two lions combattant (i.e. rampant towards one another) with only one head between them.

This curious device may have been derived from the lions which supported the City of London shield on the fourteenth century Mayoral Seal (see London City Corporation).

The Borough has adopted the motto, *More light, more power*, in allusion to municipal electrical enterprise.

SOUTHWARK Borough Council

ARMS: Quarterly argent and azure, a cross quartered gules and argent; in the first quarter a red rose with seeds and sepals proper; in the second a silver lily; in the third a ring ensigned by a cross paty and interlaced with a saltire, the lower arms of which are joined, all gold; in the fourth a stag's face and antlers gules.

MOTTO: *United to serve.*

These were granted in 1902.

The quarters contain emblems of the four parishes of St Saviour (formerly St Mary Overy), St Mary Newington, St George the Martyr, and Christchurch. The curious design known as the Southwark Cross in the third quarter is the mark of the Bridge House, the headquarters of the officers connected with London Bridge, this house having anciently been situated in Southwark.

STEPNEY Borough Council

ARMS: Silver, a lymphad (ancient ship) with its sail furled sable, on water in the base of the shield; on a chief azure two silver fire-tongs erect, and between them a silver pale charged with a cross gules and in the first quarter an anchor proper.

STEPNEY   STOKE NEWINGTON

CREST: On a wreath argent and azure, the battlements of a tower proper and thereon two gold anchors saltirewise.

MOTTO: *A magnis ad maiora*—'From great things to greater.'

These were granted in 1931.

The official explanation is as follows:

The Armorial Bearings are intended to express in heraldic terms the history of the Borough of Stepney. Shipping has been its principal industry, so the main charge is an ancient sailing ship on waves of the sea. On the upper portion of the shield there has been brought in the Cross of St George with an anchor in the first quarter to difference it from the original St George's Cross. An allusion to the patron saint, St Dunstan, is shown by the two pairs of fire-tongs ... with which he was supposed to have pinched the Devil's nose. For the crest there are two anchors, again representing the port, issuant from battlements which are emblematic of the Tower of London.

In amplification of this note, it may be pointed out that the Cross of St George links the arms with those of the City of London, which Stepney adjoins, and with those of the London C.C.

STOKE NEWINGTON Borough Council

ARMS: Gules, a cross lozengy ermine and sable, over all two swords crossed saltirewise, their blades silver and pommels and hilts gold; on a chief argent a lion rampant vert, its tail forked, between two uprooted oak-trees proper with gold acorns.

CREST: On a wreath argent and gules, a demi-griffin parted chevronwise gules and gold holding a staff proper and thereon a banner ermine with a cross sable charged with five gold roundels.

MOTTO: *Respice prospice*—'Look to the past and the future.'

These were granted in 1934.

The red ground with crossed swords refer to the long connection of the Dean and Chapter of St Paul's with Stoke Newington, and the cross is from the arms of William Patten, who rebuilt the old Church of St Mary in 1550. The green lion stands for John Dudley, the griffin for Daniel Defoe, and the banner it holds for Sir Thomas Abney. The trees refer to the ancient forest lands of the vicinity.

WANDSWORTH

WOOLWICH

WANDSWORTH Borough Council

ARMS: Parted fesswise nebuly, the upper half chequered azure and gold, the gold pieces sprinkled with blue drops; the lower half sable with five gold stars; a silver border charged with eight crosslets gules.

CREST: On a wreath or and azure, a black dragon-ship with five oars in action, a gold anchor at stem and stern, five gold shields resting against the bulwarks, the flag gules, the sail azure charged with a silver wyvern within eight silver drops.

MOTTO: *We serve.*

These were granted in 1901.

The chequers are from the arms of the Warennes, Earls of Surrey. The blue drops represent the tears of the fugitive Huguenots, many of whom settled in Wandsworth. The stars stand for the five parishes united in the Borough, namely: Clapham, Putney, Streatham, Tooting, and Wandsworth. The crosses link the arms with those of the City of London and the London C.C. The nebuly party line suggests the rivers Thames and Wandle; and the dragon-ship, like that which forms the crest of Fulham, recalls the Danish inroads in the ninth century.

WESTMINSTER

WESTMINSTER City Council

ARMS: Azure, a gold portcullis; a gold chief charged with two Tudor roses and between them a pale containing the arms of Edward the Confessor, namely azure with a gold cross patonce and five gold doves.

CREST: On a wreath or and azure, a portcullis sable between two roses, that on the dexter red and the other white, each with stem and leaves proper.

LONDON

SUPPORTERS: Two lions ermine each charged on the body with a gold portcullis; the dexter lion with a gold collar charged with three red roses, and the other with a collar azure with three white roses, the roses having seeds and sepals proper.

MOTTO: *Custodi civitatem Domine*—'Keep the city, O Lord.'

The arms were first granted in 1601, and regranted with crest and supporters in 1902.

The arms are composed of the emblems of two monarchs who are particularly associated with Westminster Abbey: Edward the Confessor, who began the rebuilding of the ancient Church of St Peter; and Henry VII, who added the Chapel which bears his name. The arms of the Confessor, and the rose and portcullis, Tudor and Beaufort badges, are dealt with in Chapter II. The ermine lions, the supporters of the arms of Cecil, were adopted in token of a family which has for centuries been closely associated with Westminster, Sir William Cecil, Lord Burleigh, Lord High Treasurer in Elizabeth I's reign, having been the City's first Lord High Steward, and his descendant, the Marquess of Salisbury, holding the same civic office at the time the supporters were granted. Because of its association with Westminster, the seat of the Mother of Parliaments, the portcullis has been adopted as part of its crest by Canberra, the Federal Capital of Australia.

WOOLWICH Borough Council

ARMS: Gules, three cannon barrels palewise proper, each surmounted on the breech by a gold lion's face.

MOTTO: *Clamant nostra tela in Regis querela*—'Our weapons clash in the King's quarrel.'

These arms, granted in 1934, were used unofficially before that date. They obviously refer to the Royal Arsenal.

METROPOLITAN WATER BOARD

ARMS: Silver, on a pile vert a gold right hand issuing from a cloud and scattering eight drops of water; in the base of the shield three bars wavy azure; on a silver nebuly chief the red cross of St George charged with a gold lion passant guardant.

CREST: On a wreath argent and vert, a roundel azure charged with a gold hand issuing from clouds and scattering drops of water as in the arms.

SUPPORTERS: Dexter, Hygieia, in a white robe and blue mantle, grasping a snake; and sinister, Aquarius, in a blue cloak, pouring out water from his pot.

MOTTO: *Et plui super unam civitatem.*

These were granted in 1931.

The green pile is from the arms of Sir Hugh Myddelton, the projector of the New River. The hand—that of the Almighty—is from the seventeenth-century seal of the New River Company, which shows a hand issuing from clouds and throwing down rain on the City of London. The motto, 'And I caused it to rain upon one city' (Amos iv. 7), is from the same seal. The 'nebuly' treatment of the chief is consistent with the cloud from which the hand issues.

METROPOLITAN WATER BOARD

The chief denotes the royal recognition which has been given from time to time to the London water undertaking, and links the arms with those of the London C.C., the principal constituent authority of the Board.

The blue roundel in the crest represents the firmament. The number of the drops of rain corresponds with the number of the water companies which formed the Board. The figure of Hygieia appeared on the seal of the Grand Junction Waterworks Company, and that of Aquarius on the seals of the East London, Chelsea, Lambeth, and West Middlesex Companies.

PORT OF LONDON AUTHORITY

ARMS: Azure, a representation of the Keep of the Tower of London, silver, and rising therefrom the half-length figure of St Paul, gold, holding in his right hand a sword and in his left a scroll, also gold.

CREST: On a wreath argent and azure, an ancient ship of gold, the mainsail charged with the arms of the City of London: Silver, the cross of St George and in the first quarter the sword of St Paul gules.

SUPPORTERS: Two silver sea-lions with gold manes and fins, that on the dexter upholding the banner of King Edward II (Gules, three gold lions passant guardant); and that on the sinister upholding the banner of King Edward VII (Quarterly, 1 and 4, England; 2, Scotland; 3, Ireland).

MOTTO: *Floreat Imperii Portus*—'Let the port of Empire flourish.'

Port of London Authority

BADGE: A gold sea-lion grasping a gold trident.

STANDARD: The compartment nearest the staff is occupied by the arms; the field of the tapering part of the standard is gules, and bears a ship (like that forming the crest) between diagonal bands inscribed with the motto, and on either side the badge.

These were granted in 1909.

The achievement is remarkable for the actual representation of an existing castle, and for the inclusion of the contemporary Royal Arms.

Merioneth C.C.

MERIONETH

MERIONETH County Council

ARMS: Azure, three goats rearing on their hind legs argent, with gold horns, hoofs, tufts, and beards; on a gold chief a setting sun gules issuing from barry wavy of four pieces azure and argent.

CREST: A representation of Harlech Castle on a rock proper within a gold rim set with six gold roses (four visible).

SUPPORTERS: On a rocky ground, two dragons gules, each supporting an abbot's crozier or and charged on the wing with five gold molets.

MOTTO: *Tra Mor tra Meirion*—'While the sea lasts, so shall Merioneth.'

These were granted in 1952.

The goats and the motto formed the device of the County Council before arms were obtained. The sun setting in the sea indicates the County's westward coastline, its rocky character being shown by the ground on which the supporters stand, which also refers to Cader Idris. The gold roses in the crest allude to Edward I who built Harlech Castle. The croziers, supported by the Welsh dragons, refer to the religious foundations in the County, especially Cymmer Abbey. This lies in the parish of Llanelltyd; and to St Elltyd, an astronomer, the molets, or stars, on the dragons' wings allude.

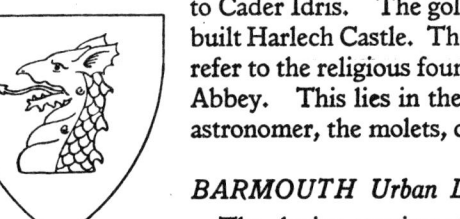

BARMOUTH

BARMOUTH Urban District Council

The device consists of the head of the Welsh dragon placed on a shield.

MIDDLESEX

Middlesex, like Essex, formerly used the arms assigned by the medieval heralds to the ancient kingdom of the Middle and East Saxons—the three notched swords, or seaxes, alluding to the theory that the Saxons derived their name from these weapons. When Middlesex C.C. obtained arms of their own, the seaxes were incorporated in them, and several local authorities in the County have one or more seaxes in their insignia in reference to the County.

MIDDLESEX C.C.

MIDDLESEX *County Council*

ARMS: Gules, three seaxes proper, hilts to the dexter, and above them a gold Saxon crown.

These arms were granted in 1910.

The Saxon crown distinguishes the arms from those assigned to the former kingdom and also from those of Essex C.C.

ACTON *Borough Council*

ARMS: Gules, an oak-tree issuing from the base proper; a chief or charged with a pale gules bearing the arms of the Middlesex C.C., between on the dexter an open book and on the sinister a cog-wheel, both proper.

CREST: In a gold mural crown, a sprig of oak proper.

MOTTO: *Floreat Actona.*

These were granted in 1921.

The oak in the arms and crest has reference to the name; the fact that Acton is 'oak town' was borne in mind when the name 'Acorn' was selected in 1929 for the automatic telephone exchange. The book is the symbol of education, and the cog-wheel represents the motor industry.

CIVIC HERALDRY

Acton

Ealing

BRENTFORD AND CHISWICK Borough Council

ARMS: Parted saltirewise silver and gules, in chief the figure of St Nicholas proper, in base two bars wavy azure, and in fess two seaxes with points upward and edges inward, their blades proper and their hilts gold.

CREST: Rising from a gold Saxon crown, a phoenix sable in flames proper.

SUPPORTERS: Two gold griffins each charged on the neck with two bars wavy azure.

MOTTO: *Firmior*—'Stronger.'

These were granted in 1932 when Brentford and Chiswick became a borough.
The arms incorporate the emblems which appeared on the seal of the former Urban

BRENTFORD AND CHISWICK

MIDDLESEX

District Council, which displayed the figure of St Nicholas in reference to the dedication of the parish church, together with the three seaxes, or 'notched swords,' of Middlesex. The phoenix represents the new Borough rising from the ashes of the old Urban District. The blue wavy bars on the shield and supporters represent the River Brent and the riverside situation of the Borough. The griffins appear to have no historic significance.

EALING Borough Council

ARMS: Parted chevronwise gules and silver, in dexter chief two crossed swords, and in sinister chief three seaxes all proper with gold pommels and hilts; and in the base an uprooted oak-tree proper.

MOTTO: *Respice prospice*—'Look backward, look forward.'

These were granted in 1902.

The crossed swords of St Paul are from the arms of the See of London, to which the manor of Ealing formerly belonged. The seaxes are from the arms of Middlesex C.C. The tree is stated to be a sign that Ealing is 'growing and flourishing.'

EDMONTON

EDMONTON Borough Council

ARMS: Parted palewise wavy sable and azure, a gold saltire charged with an open book proper bound in red and edged with gold, and in fess two silver cog-wheels.

CREST: On a wreath or and azure, flames of fire, and rising therefrom a demi-lion parted bendwise sinister sable and gold, holding in the right forepaw a sledge-hammer proper and resting the left forepaw on a cinquefoil gules.

270 CIVIC HERALDRY

SUPPORTERS: Two lions gules with gold engrailed collars and therefrom gold chains bent over their backs, each lion charged on the shoulder with a gold saltire and supporting a staff flying a banner; the dexter banner azure with an uprooted oak-tree bearing acorns proper, and the sinister banner gules with two seaxes crossed saltirewise, their blades silver and pommels and hilts gold.

MOTTO: *Faith in industry.*

These were granted in 1937.

The particoloured field represents the division of the ancient parish of Edmonton, the western portion being the district of Southgate. The saltire (repeated on the lions) refers to the Abbey of St Albans which held the Manor of Edmonton. The book alludes to the Borough's literary associations, especially with Lamb and Keats.

The lion holding a sledge-hammer symbolizes the vigour of Edmonton's industries, to which the cog-wheels also refer. The flames allude in particular to the gas industry. The lion is from the arms of the old local family of Francis, while the cinquefoil stands for the family of Charlton, sometime Lords of the Manor. The supporting lions are taken to typify courage and determination. One banner alludes to the ancient forests of the neighbourhood, and the other contains the emblems of the County.

FINCHLEY

FINCHLEY Borough Council

ARMS: Vert, a gold chevron raguly between in chief two bugle-horns with strings or, and in base a silver mitre garnished with gold; on the chevron a rose gules surmounted by another argent.

CREST: On a wreath or and vert, a finch proper resting its right claw on a gold shield charged with a fleur-de-lis gules.

SUPPORTERS: Dexter, a lion, and sinister, a stag proper, each with a collar about its neck, and suspended therefrom a bugle-horn ensigned by a ducal coronet all gold.

MOTTO: *Regnant qui serviunt*—'They rule who serve.'

These were granted in 1933.

The green field and the ragged chevron recall the oak woods for which Finchley was formerly famous, while the horns and stag stand for the hunting-ground of the Tudor monarchs, represented by the double rose. The mitre is that of the Bishops of London, who owned land in Finchley, and the lion is from the heraldry of the Countess of Pembroke, who held the manor. The finch, of course, alludes to the name.

HENDON

HENDON Borough Council

ARMS: Azure, a Holy Lamb standing on a mount proper; upon a gold chief two windmill sails sable.

CREST: On a wreath or and azure, a gold two-bladed air-screw erect with gold wings outspread.

SUPPORTERS: Dexter, a silver griffin with a mural crown gules about its neck and a molet sable on its shoulder; and sinister, a silver pegasus, also with a mural crown gules about its neck, and charged on the shoulder with an eagle displayed sable.

MOTTO: *Endeavour*.

These were granted in 1932.

The arms include emblems symbolical of the three original wards constituted in 1879, namely:

Central Hendon, represented by the Lamb, a symbol used by the Hendon U.D.C. and by its predecessor, the local Board, since 1879.

Child's Hill, the hill upon which the Lamb stands.

Mill Hill, the windmill sails.

The winged air-screw forming the crest indicates that Hendon is a centre for aviation. The griffin is a variation of the sinister supporter of Lord Powis, at one time Lord of the Manor of Hendon. The pegasus is derived from the white horse charged with black eagles which was a supporter of a former Duke of Buckingham and Chandos who owned property in the West Hendon Ward. An unfulfilled ambition of the Duke was to purchase all the property on each side of the road from Canons to London so that he might drive between his town and country residences entirely through his own property.

HESTON AND ISLEWORTH

HORNSEY

HESTON AND ISLEWORTH Borough Council

ARMS: Tierce in pairle azure, sable and gules, in chief two wings joined argent, to the dexter a gold cross bottony, and to the sinister a lion rampant guardant parted fesswise gold and silver.

MOTTO: *Unitate fortior*—'Stronger by union.'

These were granted in 1932 to the Urban District of Heston and Isleworth in anticipation of its being raised to the status of a borough.

'Tierce in pairle' means that the shield is divided into three parts, as shown in the illustration, the uppermost being coloured blue, the dexter black, and the sinister red. The three divisions are devoted respectively to Heston, Isleworth, and Hounslow.

The white (or silver) wings on blue denote Heston Air-port. The gold cross bottony, representing Isleworth, is from the seal of the Monastery of St Saviour and St Brigit of Syon, founded in 1416 and removed in 1432 to the site on which Syon House now stands. The gold and silver lion is from the arms of Hounslow Priory, founded in the thirteenth century by the Trinitarian Brothers of Redemption; the site is now occupied by Holy Trinity Church.

MIDDLESEX

HORNSEY Borough Council

ARMS: Parted chevronwise silver and gules, in chief two uprooted trees proper, and in base two crossed swords argent with gold hilts.

MOTTO: *Fortior quo paratior*—'The better prepared, the stronger.'

These were granted in 1904.

The trees recall the extensive forest which at the time of the Norman Conquest covered a large area north of London. The swords of St Paul stand for the See of London, which anciently held the Manor of Hornsey.

SOUTHALL

SOUTHALL Borough Council

ARMS: Parted fesswise gold and vert, two thorn-trees, the upper one proper and the lower gold, between two palets wavy argent each charged with another such palet azure.

CREST: Issuing from a mural crown, two flaming torches crossed saltirewise encircled by a wreath of wheat, all proper.

SUPPORTERS: Dexter, a griffin gules, and sinister, a pegasus argent with mane, tail, and hoofs azure, each with a gold Saxon crown about its neck and charged on the shoulder with a golden wheatsheaf.

MOTTO: *For all.*

These were granted in 1936.

The trees, which are thorns in allusion to the old Spelthorn Hundred, represent the 'south holt' and the 'north wood' commemorated in the name Southall-Norwood, which

K

was borne by the former Urban District. The wavy palets denote the streams running through the district. The wheat is a token of local factories concerned with the production of food, and the torches are for the gas and electricity industries.

The supporters stand for road, water, and air transport. The griffin, the emblem of the London Passenger Transport Board, indicates that London's omnibuses are made in Southall, and the motto, if put into Latin, hints at the same fact. The pegasus, coloured blue and white, was adopted to stand both for the canals which pass through Southall, and for the aerodromes in its vicinity. The Saxon crowns are from the arms of Middlesex.

SOUTHGATE

SOUTHGATE Borough Council

ARMS: Azure, issuing from the base of the shield the rising sun, gold, and on a gold chief a four-barred gate azure.

CREST: On a wreath or and azure, an oak-tree with acorns proper, and hanging therefrom a gold bugle-horn and a gold quiver of arrows.

SUPPORTERS: Two stags each with a chaplet of oak about its neck proper, and hanging from the chaplet a gold shield charged with a red rose.

MOTTO: *Ex glande quercus*—'From the acorn, the oak.'

These were granted in 1933 on Southgate's incorporation as a borough.

The emblems combine a reference to the name of the place with tokens of the oak forests which are also commemorated in the heraldry of the neighbouring Borough of Finchley. The red roses indicate that Southgate is in the Duchy of Lancaster.

TOTTENHAM

TOTTENHAM Borough Council

ARMS: Gules, a gold saltire with its limbs cut short; on a chief indented or, a helm sable between two billets azure each charged with a gold star.

CREST: Rising from a gold mural crown, a demi-lion gules supporting a silver seax with gold pommel and hilt.

SUPPORTERS: Two lions reguardant gules, each with a gold mural crown about its neck and hanging therefrom by a gold chain a roundel, that on the dexter lion ermine, and that on the sinister lion gold charged with a maunch gules.

MOTTO: *Do well and doubt not.*

These were granted in 1934 when Tottenham became a borough.

The Manor of Tottenham, held by Earl Waltheof before the Norman Conquest, passed by his daughter's marriage to David, Earl of Huntingdon, son of King Malcolm III of Scotland, and descended to William the Lion, King of Scotland. This connection with the realm of Scotland is indicated by the red lions. The Manor was next granted to William the Lion's brother, and was eventually divided between three co-heirs, Robert de Bruce, John de Baliol, and Henry de Hastings. These are represented in the arms—Bruce by the saltire and chief, Baliol by the ermine, and Hastings by the maunch—a lady's sleeve.

The stars, placed on billets (representing tiles or bricks), are from the arms of Sarah, Duchess of Somerset, founder of Tottenham Grammar School, and the helm is from those of Compton, Lord of the Manor in the sixteenth century. The crest is identical with that borne by the former Urban District Council above a shield bearing crossed swords and a hurst of seven elm-trees (the 'seven sisters'), with the motto, 'Steadfast in difficulties.'

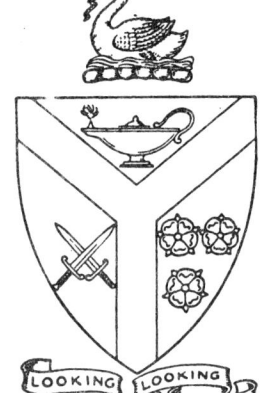

TWICKENHAM

TWICKENHAM Borough Council

ARMS: Silver, a cross-pall vert; in chief an antique lamp, lighted, proper; on the dexter side two crossed swords proper with gold hilts; and on the sinister three red roses.

CREST: On a wreath argent and vert, a swan on water holding in its beak an eel, all proper.

MOTTO: *Looking backward, looking forward.*

These were granted to the Twickenham U.D.C. in 1913. Twickenham became a borough in 1926.

The following explanation is extracted from the Official Guide:

The pall (the Y-shaped figure) not only symbolizes the name of Twickenham ('the place where the two ways meet'), but also indicates the intimate historical connection with the archiepiscopal See of Canterbury, on the arms of which the same charge appears. The antique lamp stands for Twickenham's interest in literature, the arts, and the sciences, to all of which she has given distinguished men. The crossed swords, borrowed from the arms of the See of London, refer to the earliest historical record of Twickenham, namely of land here being granted to Waldhere, Bishop of London, in 704. The three red roses are [from] the arms of our great educational pioneer, William of Wykeham, who built the tower of St Mary's Parish Church, and whose college foundation at Winchester was aided by Richard II's grant of the vicarage of Twickenham towards its endowment. The waves of the crest refer, of course, to the river which bounds the town for a distance of three miles, and the swan suggests the beautiful and tranquil character of Father Thames here as contrasted with its muddy and commercial character farther east. The eel is a delightful touch of combined humour and history, for it signifies not only the old lamprey fishing industry of Twickenham but also the famous Eel Pie Island which studs the river opposite the gardens of York House.

The distinguished men referred to in the above extract include Bacon, Clarendon, Fielding, Dickens, Tennyson, Colley Cibber, Sir John Suckling, Pope, Horace Walpole, and Turner.

WEMBLEY Borough Council

ARMS: Vert, two seaxes crossed saltirewise passing through a Saxon crown, all gold.

CREST: Within a gold Saxon crown a green mount and thereon a gold lion statant guardant.

SUPPORTERS: Two gold lions guardant each supporting a staff gules with a banner vert, the dexter banner charged with a gold balance, and the sinister banner with a gold cornucopia.

MOTTO: *Tempori parendum*—'We must move with the times.'

These were granted in 1938.

The green field symbolizes the open spaces of the Borough, and the crown and seaxes (from the arms of Middlesex) refer to the Saxon origins of the district. The lions allude

WEMBLEY

to John Lyon, founder of Harrow School, whose home was at Preston Manor, Wembley. He established a trust, of which the Borough is now beneficiary, for the maintenance of Harrow Road and Edgware Road, portions of which are within the Borough boundaries. The balance refers to the Hundred Moot of Gore, and the cornucopia symbolizes prosperity.

WILLESDEN Borough Council

ARMS: Gules, a chevron or between in chief a golden orb with a black band, ensigned with a gold cross-crosslet, and two swords saltirewise proper, their pommels and hilts gold; and in the base three lilies in a gold pot; all within a border or charged with eight roundels sable.

CREST: Issuing from a gold Saxon crown two gold wings, each charged with a cinquefoil gules.

SUPPORTERS: Two dragons azure, each with a gold Saxon crown about its neck, and charged on the shoulder with two seaxes saltirewise proper, their pommels and hilts gold.

MOTTO: *Laborare est orare*—' To work is to pray.'

These were granted in 1933 when Willesden was incorporated as a borough.

The orb is the emblem attributed to King Athelstan who, about the middle of the tenth century, granted the Manors of Neasden-cum-Willesden to the Monastery of St Arkenwold, while the eight black roundels indicate the eight Saxon manors into which Willesden was divided. The Saxon crowns and the seaxes, derived from the arms of Middlesex, represent the ancient Kingdom of the Middle Saxons. The crossed swords

WILLESDEN

are from the arms of the See of London, the Dean and Chapter of St Paul's having held the manor at the time of the Domesday Survey. The wings are taken from the crest of Archbishop Bancroft, whose family formerly occupied the Manor of Mapesbury, and the cinquefoils are from the arms of All Souls College, Oxford, which owns much land in Willesden. The lilies are the emblems of St Mary, the patron saint.

WOOD GREEN Borough Council

ARMS: Gold, on a fess azure between three uprooted yew-trees proper, a silver bar.

SUPPORTERS: Two archers in chain armour, each holding a bow proper.

MOTTO: *Nostrum viret robur.*

These were granted in 1933 when Wood Green was incorporated as a borough.

The following note was prepared by Mr Archibald G. B. Russell, Lancaster Herald:

It will be seen that ancient traditions and modern developments are here symbolized in appropriate heraldic devices. The bands of blue and silver which pass across the shield will readily be recognized as depicting in convention of line and colour the New River Cutting, which at once divides and gives strength and unity to our Borough. The yew is one of the most ancient British wild trees, and it was from its boughs that the famous longbows which loom so large in our history, whether as weapons of defence, of the chase, or of sport, were fashioned. The yew-trees with their golden backgrounds will therefore evoke bright memories of the Green or Common upon which so many generations of our forebears brought to perfection their skill with the bow. The shield is supported by two of the archers themselves, who appear at once as defenders of our arms and upholders of our traditions.

The motto inscribed upon the scroll beneath the shield embodies a play upon words, and may be interpreted either as 'Wood Green flourishes,' or 'Our strength is as a green tree.'

Wood Green

ENFIELD Urban District Council

ARMS: Gold, an enfield rampant gules; on a chief vert a bar wavy argent charged with another azure.

CREST: On a wreath or and gules, a gold buck tripping, in its mouth a red rose with green stalk and leaves.

MOTTO: *Priora cole meliora sequere*—'Cherish the past but strive for better things in the future.'

These were granted in 1946.

The enfield is a rare heraldic monster with the head of a fox, the chest of a hound, the talons of an eagle, the body of a lion, and the hindquarters and tail of a wolf. The chief represents the open spaces of the district and the New River. The buck refers to Enfield Chase, and the roses to the district's associations with the Duchy of Lancaster.

FELTHAM Urban District Council

ARMS: Parted fesswise wavy; the upper half argent with two palets sable between a Tudor rose with green stalk and leaves and a peacock with its tail spread vert; the lower half azure with two silver wings joined together and over them a gold sword erect point upwards.

CREST: On a wreath argent and azure a chaplet of hawthorn and therein a pile of gun-stones proper, and perched thereon a gold eagle with wings outspread.

MOTTO: *In unitatem coeamus*—'Let us go forward together.'

These were granted in 1945.

The arms refer to the history and modern developments of the parishes of Bedfont, Feltham, and Hanworth, which were united to form the Urban District. The wavy line

ENFIELD   FELTHAM   FRIERN BARNET

and silver-and-blue field indicate the Duke of Northumberland's River which takes the head-waters of the River Colne to Syon House, and the Longford River (also called the Queen's or Cardinal's River) which takes the Colne Waters to serve the fountain and lakes of Hampton Court.

The two black palets represent railway lines, indicating Feltham's importance in the southern portion of the British Railways system. The rose stands for the Tudor associations of Hanworth, particularly the claim that Queen Elizabeth I spent much of her early youth at Hanworth Manor. The peacock represents the topiary peacocks in the grounds of St Mary's Church, Bedfont, which are accepted as local emblems. The winged sword stands for the London Air-port and the district's close association with the aircraft industry. The sword also refers to the Royal Army Ordnance Depot, and to the ancient sword-mill marked on a seventeenth-century map. The gunstones also allude to the R.A.O.C. Depot, and to powder mills which formerly existed in the Crane Valley. The thorn-wreath refers to the Spelthorne Hundred, and the eagle is a token not only of air traffic, but also of the old Roman road to the west which passed through the district.

FRIERN BARNET Urban District Council

ARMS: Vert, a pale argent, and a gold chief dancetty charged with three fleurs-de-lis azure.

CREST: On a wreath argent and vert, a stag's face gules with gold antlers and between them a silver cross potent nowy at the centre.

MOTTO: *Ruris amator*—'Lover of the country.'

These were granted in 1938.

The pale on the green field represents the Great North Road running between grassy borders. The fleurs-de-lis indicate Barnet's royal associations in Tudor times, and the cross stands for the Knights of the Hospital of St John of Jerusalem with whom the Priory was connected. The stag's head refers to the forest land adjoining Enfield Chase.

HARROW Urban District Council

ARMS: Or, a fess arched vert; above it, a pile gules charged with a gold clarion, on the dexter side of the pile a torch sable with flames proper, and on the sinister side a quill pen sable; and in the base of the shield a hurst of trees growing on a mount vert.

CREST: Rising from a mural crown proper, a demi-lion rampant argent holding an oak-wreath proper with a silver arrow passing through it.

MOTTO: *Salus populi suprema lex*—'The welfare of the people is the highest law.'

These were granted in 1938.

The following is the official explanation of the bearings:

The shield is centrally broken by a broad horizontal green band, indicating the large proportion of open spaces in the district, and the interest of the area in the Green Belt; in the upper half of the shield appear (1) the torch of knowledge, (2) a quill, which represents heraldically the Pinner area and the eminent writers who have been associated with the district, and (3) in the centre a pile representing in shape the Gore in which were held the meetings of the Saxon Moot of the old Saxon parish of Harrow, and referring also to the present petty sessional division; the pile was also a feature of the arms of the Chandos family; in the centre of the pile is an organ rest [or clarion], which alludes to the connection of Handel with the district. In the lower half of the shield appears a clump of trees representing the Wealdstone and Harrow Weald areas which, until comparatively recently, were part of the great Weald of Middlesex; the clump of trees stand on a mound typifying the hill of Harrow-on-the-Hill. The shield is surmounted by the conventional mural crown with the heraldic figure of a lion holding a wreath through which is a silver arrow; the lion, wreath, and arrow appear also in the arms of Harrow School.

HAYES AND HARLINGTON Urban District Council

ARMS: Vert, a silver pall, its lower limb cut short, between in chief two wings joined together argent, and on each side a cog-wheel proper in front of two gold rays of lightning.

CREST: On a wreath argent and vert a circlet of brushwood, and rising therefrom a demi-stag proper supporting a seax point upwards also proper, its pommel and hilt gold, the blade encircled by a gold Saxon crown.

MOTTO: *Forward.*

These were granted in 1950.

The name 'Hayes' means a brushwood enclosure for deer; hence the stag rising from brushwood in the crest. The notched sword refers to the County, and the blade is encircled by a Saxon crown in token of the fact that in Saxon times parts of the district were royal property. In 790 King Offa granted lands in Hayes to the Archbishop of

HARROW HAYES AND HARLINGTON RUISLIP-NORTHWOOD

Canterbury, and for more than seven centuries the place was closely connected with the See. Among the Archbishops who sometimes resided at Hayes was Anselm, who is commemorated by St Anselm's Church. To mark this long association, an Archbishop's pall appears in the arms.

The three white limbs of this pall also suggest runways to those who think of the district's principal feature to-day—the London Air-port. The wings are a direct reference to this. The cog-wheels refer to modern industries in general, and the lightning flashes to the electrical industries in particular. The green of the shield refers to the district's agricultural background, and also its present-day amenities as part of London's Green Belt.

RUISLIP-NORTHWOOD Urban District Council

ARMS: Argent, a hurst of oak-trees proper growing from a green mount, and above them a roundel azure charged with a gold star of five points; on a chief gules a silver mitre between two gold fleurs-de-lis.

CREST: On a wreath argent and vert, a boar passant sable with tusks and tongue gules in front of two ears of rye slipped (i.e. with stalks) saltirewise proper.

MOTTO: *Non progredi est regredi*—'Not to go forward is to go backward.'

These were granted in 1937.

The place-name is indicated by the rye slips, and by the hurst of trees below the pole star, signifying the north wood. The mitre and fleurs-de-lis refer to the Abbey of Bec.

STAINES   SUNBURY-ON-THAMES   UXBRIDGE

STAINES Urban District Council

ARMS: Gules, a fess barry wavy of four pieces argent and azure, and thereon a representation of Staines Bridge in gold; in chief two swans proper facing one another, and in base a representation of London Stone gold between two seaxes erect, their blades silver and their pommels and hilts gold.

CREST: On a wreath argent and gules, a greyhound gules seated on the battlements of a tower or.

MOTTO: *Ad Pontes prospicimus.*

These were granted in 1951.

The cost of the grant was borne by Mr H. Scott Freeman, Clerk of the Council from 1901 to 1946. The following note was prepared by the Lancaster Herald:

The central feature consists of a representation of Staines Bridge. The white and blue wavy bands on which it is set are emblematic of water and specifically the Thames. At the base of the shield is depicted London Stone, which is, of course, a well-known feature of the district. On either side of the Stone are two seaxes—curved, one-edged swords as used by Celtic and other peoples—from the arms of the County of Middlesex. At the top are two swans facing one another, which are appropriate to the river, where they may be regarded as Royal birds, being the property of the Crown. Both the swans and the London Stone figured in the device formerly used by Staines Urban District Council.

The greyhound in the crest is an allusion to that appearing in the armorial bearings of your benefactor, Mr H. Scott Freeman.

The motto, *Ad Pontes prospicimus*, may be translated 'At the bridges we look forward.' *Ad Pontes* was the Roman name of Staines, so the symbolism conveyed is that from our ancient past we look forward to the future.

SUNBURY-ON-THAMES Urban District Council

ARMS: Parted fesswise gold and silver, a fess vert between in chief two shepherds' crooks crossed saltirewise and in base two bars wavy, all azure; and on the fess a mitre between two Saxon crowns, all gold.

CREST: On a wreath argent and vert, a seax azure, its hilt gules, lying fesswise with its point to the dexter in front of a rising sun or.

MOTTO: *Sol et pastor Deus.*

These were granted in 1948.

The sun stands for Sunbury and the crooks for Shepperton, while the motto, 'God, our sun and shepherd,' also refers to these names. The seax stands for Middlesex and the wavy bars for the River Thames.

UXBRIDGE Urban District Council

ARMS: Or, on a pile gules between two roundels barry wavy argent and azure, a gold eagle displayed.

CREST: On a wreath or and gules, a circlet composed of four chrysanthemums (three visible) with stalks and leaves proper, and rising therefrom a demi-lion gules supporting a seax point upwards, the blade proper and the pommel and hilt gold.

These were granted in 1948.

The pile is from the arms of the ancient family of Basset, and the heraldic fountains refer to the rivers in the district. The eagle is from the arms of Paget, Earl of Uxbridge, a title borne by the Marquess of Anglesey, and also alludes to the Uxbridge R.A.F. Depot and Northolt Air-port. The chrysanthemums relate particularly to horticultural nurseries in the town which specialize in these flowers, and refer generally to cultivation in the district. The national lion supports one of the notched swords of the County.

Monmouthshire C.C.

MONMOUTHSHIRE

MONMOUTHSHIRE County Council

ARMS: Parted palewise azure and sable, three gold fleurs-de-lis, and on a chief or two towers each with three turrets gules.

CREST: On a wreath gold and azure, a tower with three turrets gules charged with an escutcheon of the arms of Somerset, Marquess of Worcester, viz. Quarterly France and England within a bordure company argent and azure.

SUPPORTERS: Dexter, a gold lion guardant with a coronet of four fleurs-de-lis gules about its neck and grasping in the left forepaw a red rose with sepals, seeds, stalk, and leaves proper; and sinister, a dragon gules with a similar coronet of gold about its neck and grasping with the right forepaw a leek proper.

MOTTO: *Utrique fidelis*—'Faithful to both.'

These were granted in 1948.

The gold fleurs-de-lis upon blue and black are the arms of the old Kingdom of Gwent, and the castles refer to the many strongholds situated in this County on the borders of England and Wales. The motto declares the County faithful to both countries, and the English lion and the Welsh dragon, each holding its country's national emblem, illustrate this double allegiance. The castle forming the crest has, by the shield upon it, special allusion to Raglan Castle and its defence on behalf of King Charles I by Henry Somerset, fifth Earl and first Marquess of Worcester, a descendant of the Beaufort family and ancestor of the Duke of Beaufort.

NEWPORT County Borough Council

ARMS: Gold, a chevron reversed gules; the shield being ensigned by a cherub proper.

These were in use before 1929, when they were officially confirmed.

They are based on the red chevron on gold which formed the arms of the family De Stafford, the Earls of Stafford and Dukes of Buckingham having held the lordship of Newport in the fourteenth and fifteenth centuries. It is not known whether the cherub was intended to have any significance when it was adopted, but it is believed to be merely decorative.

ABERGAVENNY Borough Council

ARMS: Gules, a silver saltire between a rose in chief, a portcullis in base, and two fleurs-de-lis in fess, all gold.

CREST: On a wreath argent and gules an uprooted tree trunk proper, and standing thereon a black and white bull with black hoofs and a gold collar and chain, charged on the body with two gold fleurs-de-lis.

MOTTO: *Hostes nunc amici*—'Foes now friends.'

These were granted in 1901.

The arms and crest are based on the heraldry of Nevill, Marquess of Abergavenny, the saltire being from the Nevill arms, and the bull being one of their supporters. The rose and portcullis were used as badges by the Nevills to indicate their descent from Joan de Beaufort, daughter of John of Gaunt and wife of Nevill, first Earl of Westmorland. The fleurs-de-lis, royal emblems, denote the Marquess's descent, through John of Gaunt, from Edward III.

MONMOUTH

MONMOUTH Borough Council

ARMS: Azure, three gold chevrons, and over all a fess gules; the shield ensigned with a gold mural crown.

SUPPORTERS: Dexter, a lion guardant with a mural crown on its head, all gold; and sinister, a silver heraldic antelope with a gold mural crown about its neck.

MOTTO: *Monemus et munimus*—'We counsel and protect.'

These were granted in 1946, but the arms were associated with the town long before that date. They appear to be a variation of the arms of the family De Monmouth (*temp.* Henry III), which were probably based on those of De Clare.

The supporters are those of King Henry V, who was born at Monmouth, with mural crowns in substitution for royal crowns.

BLAENAVON Urban District Council

ARMS: Parted crosswise, the party lines wavy, sable and gold; in the first and fourth quarters a gold key, its ward upward and turned to the dexter, and in the second and third quarters a lozenge sable.

CREST: On a wreath gold and sable a circlet of lozenges joined together sable, and rising therefrom a right forearm in armour, the hand grasping a sword bendwise-sinister with the blade bent downwards, all proper, the hilt and pommel of the sword gold, and the forearm charged with a gold buckle.

MOTTO: *At spes non fracta*—'Yet hope is not broken.'

These were granted in 1952.

The lozenges refer to coal, the chief industry of the district, and the keys, crest, and motto are derived from the heraldry of the Kennard family, who were concerned in the formation of the Blaenavon Coal and Iron Company.

Montgomeryshire C.C.

MONTGOMERYSHIRE

MONTGOMERYSHIRE County Council

ARMS: Parted chevronwise and the chief palewise, the dexter side gold, the sinister silver, and the base azure; three lions rampant tinctured respectively gules, sable, and gold; all within a border compony sable and argent.

CREST: A swan proper rising from a mural crown gules, in its beak a sprig of oak with leaves and acorns proper.

MANTLING: Azure and gold.

SUPPORTERS: Two wyverns vert each with a gold riband about its neck and hanging therefrom by a gold ring a fleece or.

MOTTO: *Powys Paradwys Cymru*—'Powys, Paradise of Wales.'

These were granted in 1951.

Until the eleventh century, what is now Montgomeryshire was part of the principality of Powys, of which the last Prince was Bleddyn ap Cynfyn. The territory was divided between his descendants, Gwenwynwyn and Madog, who are represented in the arms by the two lions in the upper part of the shield. The third lion stands for Roger de Montgomery, Earl of Shrewsbury, a leader of the Norman invasion of Wales, from whom the town and county derived their names. The black and white of the border are the colours of Brochwel Ysgithrog, a seventh-century Prince of Powys who led the resistance to the Saxons.

In the crest, the mural crown is coloured red in allusion to Powys Castle, whose Welsh name meant 'red castle,' the seat of the Earl of Powis. The swan refers to the waterways, especially the Severn and Wye (which have their sources in the County), and the oak recalls the forests which formerly provided wood for the Royal Navy.

The supporting wyverns are from the heraldry of the Herbert family, Earls of Powis and of Pembroke and Montgomery. The fleeces refer to the former woollen industry.

LLANFYLLIN Borough Council

The Corporation has no arms. The seal bears the royal achievement of arms of the Stuart dynasty, complete with crown, supporters, and motto.

LLANIDLOES Borough Council

According to the *Municipal History of Llanidloes*, by Alderman Horsfall Turner, the witnesses reported to the Commission in 1833 that they never saw or heard of a town seal or the impression of one. There was, however, a seal soon after; it was simply a few hatched lines encircled by a ribbon bearing the name 'Llanidloes Borough.' This was superseded in 1858, when it was decided ... 'That the Town Council do forthwith order a new seal for the Corporation with the design of a ram engraved thereon surrounded with the words, Borough of Llanidloes.'

The reason for the adoption of the ram is now unknown. It was superseded in 1900, when the centre-piece of the Mayoral Chain was taken as the basis of the new design. This badge was adopted in 1887. 'Emblazoned upon it are the arms of the Borough, a composite of the arms of the chief families of Lloyd of Berthlwyd and Clochfaen. . . . It represents upon an ermine shield with border gules (red) marked with eight mullets (spur-rowels or stars) a lion rampant argent and mural crown with eight visible merlons. Its supporters, or rather ornamental figures, consist of two crossed leeks and croziers.'

MONTGOMERY Borough Council

The seal bears two crossed keys on a shield. Burke quotes: Azure, a gold lion rampant within a gold border; these are the arms attributed to Roger de Montgomery, Earl of Shrewsbury, from whom the town and county of Montgomery derived their name (see Montgomeryshire C.C.).

WELSHPOOL Borough Council

The device consists of a castle upon a shield, below which is a scroll bearing the words, *Burgus de Pola*. The place was formerly known as Pool, the word 'Welsh' being added to distinguish the town from Poole, Dorset.

NORFOLK C.C.

NORWICH

NORFOLK

NORFOLK County Council

ARMS: Parted palewise gold and sable, a bend ermine; on a chief gules a gold lion of England between two silver ostrich feathers with gold quills each ensigned by a gold prince's coronet, their pens piercing scrolls bearing the motto, *Ich dien*, as borne on the banner of King Edward III.

These arms were granted in 1904.

The lower part of the shield comprises the arms attributed to Ranulf de Guader, first Earl of Norfolk (1071–5). In the chief are royal emblems indicating the special favour in which the County which embraces Sandringham was held by Edward VII.

NORWICH City and County Borough Council

ARMS: Gules, a silver castle, and below it a gold lion passant guardant.

These arms, which appear on a fifteenth-century seal, are on record at the Heralds' College. They are sometimes surmounted by a civic fur cap, and placed between two angels in the position of supporters, but there is no authority for this practice. Fox-Davies quotes the castle as 'domed,' but the domes are sometimes omitted. The lion is said to have been granted by Edward III.

Norwich Castle was built by King Stephen on the site of a fortress erected by William I. In the fourteenth century the Castle became a prison, and in 1894 it adopted its present role of art gallery and museum.

NORFOLK

GREAT YARMOUTH KING'S LYNN NORTH WALSHAM

GREAT YARMOUTH County Borough Council

ARMS: Parted palewise gules and azure, three gold lions passant guardant halved and joined to the tail ends of three silver herrings.

MOTTO: *Rex et nostra jura*—'The King and our laws.'

These are the Royal Arms of England dimidiated with what are presumed to have been the original arms of Yarmouth, three silver herrings on blue in allusion to the fisheries on which the town was founded and its prosperity was built. The arms have a resemblance to those of the Cinque Ports (see Chapter II) to which the Yarmouth herring market was anciently subject. They appear on the stern banner of a ship in the fifteenth-century seal.

KING'S LYNN Borough Council

ARMS: Azure, three gold dragons' heads erect, each transfixed through the mouth by a gold cross-crosslet pointed at the foot.

These appear on a fifteenth-century seal, and are on record at the College of Arms. The following has been assumed by the Corporation:

CREST: On a wreath or and azure, a pelican proper.

The arms refer to the legend of St Margaret of Antioch, who has been portrayed on the seals of Lynn since the thirteenth century, and to whom the parish church is dedicated. St Margaret, the Christian daughter of a pagan priest, was imprisoned for her faith, and devoured by Satan in the form of a dragon; but a cross which she wore had power to burst the dragon open, and Margaret emerged unhurt. Her symbol is, therefore, a dragon's head pierced by a cross.

The crest has probably been adopted as a Christian emblem, for the pelican is a symbol of the Eucharist, because it was said by medieval writers to feed its young with blood drawn from its own breast.

THETFORD Borough Council

The device consists of a castle; on each of the flanking towers is a man, one holding a sword and the other blowing a horn.

DISS Urban District Council

The device consists of a shield parted palewise and barry wavy.

EAST DEREHAM Urban District Council

The device consists of a deer between three crowns.

NORTH WALSHAM Urban District Council

ARMS: Sable, a crozier between two ancient crowns all gold; on a chief dancetty or, a cross flory sable between two wheatsheaves.

CREST: On a wreath gold and sable, a griffin sable with a collar gules seated in front of the sun or.

MOTTO: *Non nobis sed omnibus*—'Not for ourselves but for all.'

These were granted in 1949.

SWAFFHAM Urban District Council

The Council makes use of an impaled shield bearing the crossed keys of St Peter on the dexter side and the crossed swords of St Paul on the sinister. The reference is to the dedication of the parish church.

Northamptonshire C.C.

NORTHAMPTONSHIRE

NORTHAMPTONSHIRE County Council

Arms: Argent, a red rose; on a chief gules a gold fetterlock between two white roses.

Crest: On a wreath argent and gules, a silver falcon with wings folded, about its neck a cord gules.

Supporters: Dexter, a white hart with an iron collar and therefrom a chain turned over the back; and sinister, a black bull guardant with a gold collar and chain similarly arranged.

Motto: *Rosa concordiae signum*—'A rose, the emblem of harmony.'

These were granted in 1939.

A rose has long been the emblem of Northamptonshire, having appeared on a seal used by the magistrates in Quarter Sessions as far back as 1665.

The emblems in the arms and crest recall Northamptonshire's associations with the houses of York and Lancaster, whose rivalry culminated in the Wars of the Roses, and whose ultimate union was symbolized by the Tudor rose.

The castle and lordship of Fotheringhay were granted by Edward III to his fifth son, Edmund Langley, Duke of York, and held by his two successors in that title, and also by Edward, Earl of March, who became Edward IV. The white roses, the falcon, and the fetterlock are Yorkist badges.

At Grafton Edward IV married Elizabeth Woodville, a member of an ancient Northamptonshire family which supported the Lancastrian cause, represented in the arms by the red rose. The rival roses were at last united in the harmony suggested by the motto when Elizabeth of York, daughter of Edward IV and Elizabeth Woodville, married the Lancastrian King Henry VII.

294 CIVIC HERALDRY

The supporters are taken from the heraldry of the Yorkist Kings, and also refer to the trade and industry of the County; the bull stands for agriculture, and the hide of both animals is used for leather and shoe-making. The hart's metal collar and chain indicates the iron and steel industry.

SOKE OF PETERBOROUGH C.C.   NORTHAMPTON   PETERBOROUGH

SOKE OF PETERBOROUGH County Council

ARMS: Barry of ten pieces argent and azure, two gold keys crossed saltirewise wards upwards.

CREST: Rising from a mural crown or, a demi-lion ermine holding in the right paw two gold stalks and ears of wheat.

MOTTO: *Cor unum.*

These were granted in 1950.

St Peter's keys, from the arms of the See and City of Peterborough, are placed on a barry field from the arms of Cecil, from whose heraldry the lion also comes. This alludes to the connection of the Marquesses of Exeter with the Council since its formation in 1889. The wheat-ears stand for agriculture. The motto is part of that of the Cecil family: *Cor unum via una*—'One heart, one way.'

NORTHAMPTON County Borough Council

ARMS: Gules, on a green mount a silver tower with three turrets, supported by two gold lions rampant guardant.

MOTTO: *Castello fortior concordia*—'Concord is stronger than a fortress.'

The arms are recorded at the Heralds' College.

Northampton Castle was built by Simon de Senlis about 1100, and was on several occasions the scene of Councils and Parliaments, including the Assize of Northampton in 1176, which provided *inter alia* for the destruction of castles which had been held against the King during the rebellion three years before, and for the future custody of castles. Northampton Castle was held for John against the barons, and for Parliament against Charles I. It stood until it was ousted by the Castle railway station, and on its demolition parts of it were re-erected on a new site.

PETERBOROUGH City Council

ARMS: Azure, two gold keys crossed saltirewise, wards upwards.

These are recorded at the Heralds' College. The keys of St Peter also appear in the arms of the See. The following have also been used as the arms of the City: Gules, two crossed keys of gold between four gold cross-crosslets pointed at the foot (the arms of the See) impaling: Azure, two crossed swords with silver blades and gold hilts, between four gold crosses paty pointed at the foot (a variation of the arms of the Deanery).

BRACKLEY Borough Council

The Borough seal bears the arms of its donor, the third Earl of Bridgewater, Lord of the Manor in the seventeenth century. These are quarterly; the first and fourth quarters silver with a lion rampant gules and three pheons sable (for Egerton); the second and third silver, on a bend azure three gold stags' heads (for Stanley). Crests: A lion rampant gules supporting a silver arrow, point downwards (for Egerton); and an eagle preying on a baby in red swaddling clothes with white bands lying on a chapeau gules turned up ermine (for Stanley).

DAVENTRY Borough Council

The seal bears the figure of a man holding an axe in one hand, and in the other, one of the branches of a tree; together with the date 1595. The derivation of the name Daventry, or Danetre, is an unsolved problem, though there are many conjectures. A popular but untrustworthy theory connects the place with the Danes. 'When the Council required a seal wherewith to conclude official agreements, the heralds of that period could evidently conceive of no better device than a rebus upon the word as generally spoken; and so we have what has been aptly described as "a savage nondescript, half Highlander, half Saracen, designed to represent a Dane, who stands with his hatchet ready to cut down a devoted and inoffensive tree"' (*Borough Hill, Daventry, and its History*, by W. Edgar).

HIGHAM FERRERS Borough Council

The seal bears a hand with the thumb and first and second fingers extended, the others being doubled in, above nine men's heads. This appears to be an ancient emblem of benediction or baptism (cf. Honiton, Devon).

KETTERING Borough Council

ARMS: Sable, a gold pelt; above it, a gold cross-crosslet pointed at the foot between two roundels barry wavy argent and azure each charged with a martlet sable.

CREST: On a wreath or and sable, flames issuing from a circlet of chain, all proper.

Kettering

SUPPORTERS: Dexter, a gold griffin reguardant with beak and claws azure and a blue chain about its neck and turned over its back; and sinister, a Negro proper wearing a blue loin-cloth, on his left wrist a blue handcuff with a broken chain azure hanging therefrom.

MOTTO: *Progressio et concordia*—'Progress and concord.'

These were granted in 1938.

Kettering's chief industry, the manufacture of boots and shoes, is represented by the hide, while the crest symbolizes the iron-ore industry. The fountains—roundels barry wavy silver and blue—refer to the formation of the Baptist Missionary Society at the Mission House at Lower Street in 1792. The birds are from the arms of the Watson family of Rockingham, who with the Montagus are Lords of the Manor of Kettering. The Montagu family is represented by the griffin. The cross is from the arms of the See of Peterborough.

The Negro with a broken chain recalls the pioneer work of William Knibb in the cause of freeing the slaves. Knibb was born at Kettering in 1803.

WELLINGBOROUGH Urban District Council

ARMS: Sable, a chevron between two lions' faces and a wheatsheaf, all gold, and on the chevron five roundels barry wavy argent and azure.

CREST: On a wreath gold and sable, issuing from flames proper a demi-bull sable, his horns and hoofs gold, having round his neck a gold ribbon from which hangs an escutcheon argent charged with a Tudor rose proper, and supporting a gold crozier.

MOTTO: *Aspice, respice*—'Look to the future and the past.'

These were granted in 1949.

WELLINGBOROUGH

BRACKLEY

NORTHAMPTON R.D.C.

The black field represents Wellingborough's industrial life, and the lions' faces refer to its royal associations, while the sheaf stands for agriculture. The chevron is from the arms of the Hatton family, and the fountains (roundels barry wavy argent and azure) stand for the five chief chalybeate springs in the district. In the crest, the bull is from the arms of Northamptonshire, and also refers to the leather industry, while the crozier stands for Crowland Abbey and the Tudor rose for Wellingborough School. The flames recall the great fire of 1738 and also represent the furnaces connected with the iron-smelting industry. The motto is taken from the inscription over the old school-house of 1620.

NORTHAMPTON Rural District Council

ARMS: Gold, a bend wavy azure between in chief a roller-bearing proper and in base a red rose with seeds and sepals proper; and a chief azure charged with three wheat-sheaves or.

CREST: On a wreath gold and azure, a representation of the Northampton Queen Eleanor memorial cross proper.

These were granted in 1952.

The roller-bearing stands for an important local industry, while the wheatsheaves are for agriculture. The rose links the arms with those of the County, and the crest shows an historic monument in the locality.

Northumberland C.C.

NORTHUMBERLAND

NORTHUMBERLAND County Council

ARMS: Parted fesswise embattled, the chief paly of eight gold and gules and the base paly of eight gules and gold.

CREST: On a wreath gold and gules, a castle proper charged with an escutcheon of the above arms, and on the towers a lion passant azure, its tail extended.

SUPPORTERS: Two gold lions each with a collar paly gold and gules and supporting a staff proper with a banner bearing the above arms.

Below the shield is the word NORTHUMBERLAND.

These were granted in 1951.

The County Council formerly used the arms attributed by the medieval heralds to the ancient Kingdom of Bernicia, the northern part of Northumbria, namely, Paly of eight pieces gold and gules. These arms may have been suggested by the Venerable Bede's reference to 'a banner made of gold and purple' which was hung over the tomb of St Oswald, the first Christian King of Northumbria.

When arms were officially granted, it was found impossible to assign to the County Council the arms attributed to Bernicia without change, and consequently the shield was divided horizontally by an embattled line, the paly design being counter-changed in the lower part of the shield. The embattlement suggests the Roman Wall and Northumberland's position as a Border county.

The crest refers to the old castle badge of the sheriffs of the County, and the blue lion is that of the Percy family, Earls and later Dukes of Northumberland, Lords Warden of the East and Middle Marches. The supporting lions are from the arms attributed to the Saint-King Oswald.

NEWCASTLE-UPON-TYNE

NEWCASTLE-UPON-TYNE City and County Borough Council

ARMS: Gules, three silver towers each with three turrets.

CREST: On a wreath argent and gules a silver tower, and thereon a gold demi-lion guardant, holding a black flagstaff with a split pennon bearing the cross of St George.

SUPPORTERS: Two silver sea-horses with gold manes and fins.

MOTTO: *Fortiter defendit triumphans*—'She bravely defends and triumphs.'

These are recorded at the College of Arms.

The term 'new castle' seems to have been applied to the stronghold erected by Robert, William I's eldest son, on the site of which Henry II raised the castle which remains to-day. In Saxon times the place was called Monkchester, the latter part of the name indicating its Roman origin as the site of one of the mile castles on Hadrian's Wall. The royal lion and pennon of St George in the crest are appropriate to a town which, on several occasions during the fourteenth century, resisted attacks by the Scots, and stood a siege in the Royalist cause during the Civil War. It is said that the motto was bestowed by Charles I. The sea-horses refer to the town's situation on a tidal river, to which it owes its prosperity.

TYNEMOUTH

TYNEMOUTH County Borough Council

The Corporation has adopted a device consisting of three gold crowns on a red shield supported by a miner and a sailor; with a three-masted ship with topsails set as crest, and the motto: *Messis ab altis*—'Harvest from the deeps.'

It has thus unconsciously appropriated the arms of the See of Ely (see Isle of Ely C.C.); but Tynemouth's crowns are not intended to commemorate the royal house of East Anglia. They are taken from the arms attributed to the Priory of Tynemouth, and are said to stand for three kings connected with the early history of the place, namely Edwin, King of Northumbria, who in the seventh century founded the priory round which the town grew; King Oswald, who rebuilt it in 634; and Oswin, King of Deira, who was buried in the Priory in 651, and became its patron saint.

BERWICK-UPON-TWEED Borough Council

The Corporation has not obtained arms, but the design on the seal has been quoted as a coat of arms, namely: Silver, on a green mount a bear with a gold collar and chain, standing against a tree proper; on either side of the tree an escutcheon bearing the former Royal Arms, France and England quarterly; on a chief azure a king in crown and robes, holding an orb and sceptre, all proper. Motto: *Victoria gloria merces*—'Victory, glory, reward' (i.e. Victory and fame are the only wages we ask).

The *bear* refers to the name. It has been conjectured that the tree is a *wych-elm,* completing the rebus. Mr Gale Pedrick (*Borough Seals*) states:

The royal figure is doubtless intended for Edward III, to whom the town surrendered after his victory at Hallidown Hill, of which event the seal may be regarded as commemorative; and the shields are also allusive to the same monarch who first quartered the arms of France with those of England.

Against this theory must be set the fact that in the Berwick seal the French coat in the Royal Arms contains only three fleurs-de-lis (France Modern) instead of an indefinite number of fleurs-de-lis (France Ancient). Edward III's arms incorporated France Ancient. France Modern only came into use in the English Royal Arms about 1405, in the reign of Henry IV: so that unless the designer of the Berwick seal anticipated a change in the style of the Royal Arms, the king is not Edward III but one of the Lancastrian or Yorkist monarchs. It is even possible that the figure is not intended for an English monarch, but for the Almighty in royal state.

BERWICK-UPON-TWEED

BLYTH Borough Council

ARMS: Parted fesswise gules and azure, a silver fess charged with three ermine spots; in chief an ancient gold crown, and in base an ancient ship proper, the mainsail set, foresail and mizzen furled, and a red pennon at each mast-head.

CREST: A mural crown sable charged with three gold miner's picks, shafts upwards, and rising therefrom a gold demi-lion holding in the right forepaw a miner's safety-lamp proper.

MOTTO: *We grow by industry*.

These were granted in 1923.

The following note is issued by the Corporation:

The crown is taken from the ancient arms used by the Priory of Tynemouth mentioned in local history in the fifteenth century.

The ermine of the fess is taken from the arms of De La Val, and a record of such name is found in local history in the year 1208. The ship is symbolical of the ship-building industry, and the crest is symbolical of the coal industry.

The lion was included as a national emblem.

MORPETH Borough Council

ARMS: Barry of ten pieces silver and gules, a gold tower with three turrets, within a border azure charged with eight gold martlets.

MOTTO: *Inter sylvas et flumina habitans*—'Dwelling 'twixt woods and rivers.'

These were granted in 1552.

The design consists of a representation of the castle of the Norman family De Merlay placed upon their arms. This is clearly stated in the grant by Norroy King-of-Arms (printed in full in Fox-Davies's *Book of Public Arms*): 'Havynge knowledge of credyble p'sones of theyre fyrst fowndac'on I could nott wtowt grett Iniury of theyre fyrst fownder Tle noble and valyaunt knyght Sir Roger De Marlay assigne unto them any other Armes Then a p'cell of his Armes for p'petuall memory of his good wyll and benevolence towardes the sayde Towne so well begon and so longe contynued, which were to his preiudyce to have it forgotten and brought into oblyvyon.'

MORPETH

BLYTH

WALLSEND

WALLSEND Borough Council

ARMS: Sable, sprinkled with gold drops, in base a gold masoned wall and standing thereon a gold eagle with wings outspread.

MOTTO: *Situ exoritur Segeduni.*

These were granted in 1902.

Here is the Roman eagle standing on a section of Hadrian's Wall, whence the town derived its name. The motto tells that Wallsend 'arose on the site of Segedunum.' The black field and the golden drops stand for the coal and copper-smelting industries.

Nottinghamshire C.C.

NOTTINGHAMSHIRE

NOTTINGHAMSHIRE County Council

ARMS: Vert, a fess wavy parted fesswise wavy argent and azure, over all a gold oak-tree bearing acorns.

CREST: Rising from a mural crown or, a gold wheatsheaf charged with a miner's shovel-blade sable.

SUPPORTERS: Dexter, a black lion with a forked tail, about its neck a gold Saxon crown; and sinister, a white greyhound collared with a Saxon crown azure, and therefrom a blue cord turned over the back.

MOTTO: *Sapienter proficiens*—'Advancing wisely.'

These were granted in 1937.

The arms represent the topographical features of the County, the tree standing in particular for Sherwood Forest. In the crest, agriculture and mining are indicated. The supporters are based on those of the Duke of Portland and the Duke of Newcastle, Lords Lieutenant of the County.

NOTTINGHAM

NOTTINGHAM City and County Borough Council

ARMS: Gules, rising from the base of the shield a ragged cross of wood proper between three open crowns of gold, the lowest encircling the bottom limb of the cross.

CREST: On a wreath gold and gules, a castle with three capped towers and an outer wall proper, the flanking towers being surmounted by a silver crescent and a golden star respectively.

SUPPORTERS: Two royal stags guardant proper, each with a gold ducal coronet about its neck and with a ragged staff beneath its hoofs.

MOTTO: *Vivit post funera virtus*—'Virtue survives death.'

BADGE: A green ragged saltire surmounted by the head of a royal stag proper.

The arms were recorded by the Heralds in 1614. The crest was granted in 1898, and at the same time supporters were added, consisting of two foresters each with a longbow; these have been replaced by the royal stags. The badge was granted, together with a standard, in 1911.

The design of the arms is similar to that of Colchester, Essex (q.v.) but there is no reason to believe that they were adopted by Nottingham in allusion to St Helena. It seems to be more probable that the ragged cross in the Nottingham arms refers to the Forest of Sherwood, to which the supporters, old and new, and the ragged staves also allude. The castle (of which little remains) commemorated by the crest was erected by William I. The significance of the star and crescent is discussed in Chapter II.

EAST RETFORD

EAST RETFORD *Borough Council*

Arms: Or, two choughs proper facing one another, their wings spread and their further legs raised with the claws interlocked.

Crest: On a wreath or and sable, a lion statant gules with a forked tail, resting its right forepaw on a gold shield charged with a deed proper with a red seal pendent therefrom.

Supporters: Two unicorns ermine with gold horns, hoofs, manes, and tufts, each with a collar sable charged with three gold scallop shells.

Motto: *Vetustas dignitatem generat*—'Age begets dignity.'

These were granted in 1940.

The facing choughs are from an old seal of the Borough. On a mace presented to the Corporation in 1679 by Sir Edward Nevile appears a lion resting its paw on a rose. On this the crest has been based, the lion's tail being forked for distinction, and the rose being replaced by a deed standing for the Borough's ancient charters, which date from the thirteenth century onwards.

The unicorns are from the heraldry of Lord Galway, whose ancestors were High Stewards of the Borough, and the shells are from the arms of the Rt Hon. F. J. Savile Foljambe, appointed High Steward in 1880.

MANSFIELD *Borough Council*

Arms: Quarterly sable and azure, a gold cross flory, in the first and fourth quarters a silver stag's face with gold antlers, and in the second and third a white cotton hank.

Crest: On a wreath gold and sable, two silver cross-crosslets pointed at the foot, set saltirewise between two gold stars in front of an oak-tree proper.

MOTTO: *Sicut quercus virescit industria*—'Industry flourishes like the oak.'
These were granted in 1892.
The cross represents Edward the Confessor (see Chapter II), in whose reign Mansfield was a royal manor. The oak stands for the Forest of Sherwood, and the cotton for industry. The stags' heads are from the arms of Cavendish-Bentinck, the crosslets from those of Howard, and the stars from those of Murray, Earl Mansfield.

MANSFIELD

NEWARK-ON-TRENT

NEWARK-ON-TRENT Borough Council

ARMS: Barry wavy of six pieces silver and azure, on a chief gules a peacock with tail spread proper between a gold fleur-de-lis and a gold lion passant guardant.

CREST: On a wreath argent and azure, a gold cormorant holding in its beak an eel proper.

SUPPORTERS: Dexter, an otter, and sinister, a beaver, both proper.

MOTTO: *Deo fretus erumpe.*

The arms were granted in 1561.

Several variations of the crest have been quoted. The bird has been described as a morfex, a seagull, and a martlet; and the eel has been called a snake. In the above description I have followed Fox-Davies.

To Newark's riverside position the wavy bars, crest, and supporters refer. The fleur-de-lis and lion are, of course, royal emblems. I supposed that the peacock alluded to the family of that name, but I am informed that they were not known in the district at the time the arms were granted, and local opinion takes the bird as the symbol of pride.

The motto is a translation of the valiant words of the Mayor, to Lord Bellasyse, during the siege of Newark by the Parliamentarians in 1646: 'Trust God, and sally.'

WORKSOP

WORKSOP Borough Council

ARMS: Silver, a cross azure charged with five gold ducal coronets; in the first quarter a lion rampant parted fesswise sable and gules; in the second, a martlet gules; in the third, a miner's shovel and pick crossed proper; and in the fourth, an uprooted oak-tree also proper.

CREST: Two squirrels proper sitting back-to-back on a gold mural crown.

SUPPORTERS: Dexter, a knight in armour proper, his right hand resting on a shield azure charged with a gold cross flory; and sinister, a forester holding a longbow proper.

MOTTO: *Sans Dieu rien*—'Nothing without God.'

These were granted in 1932.

The ducal coronets represent the five principal landowners in the 'Dukeries.' The lion rampant is from the arms of Worksop Priory, founded by a member of the Lovetoft family whose arms embodied a similar lion but with the tinctures reversed. The old Worksop family of Furnival, some members of which took part in the Crusades, is represented by the martlet from their arms and by the dexter supporter, who is portrayed in the armour of the crusading period. The cross on the knight's shield is that of St Cuthbert, to whom the Priory and Worksop College are dedicated. The coal-mining industry is indicated by the pick and shovel. The oak-tree is the Shire Oak which was at one time situated at the junction of Nottinghamshire, Derbyshire, and Yorkshire, having a bough in each of these counties. The forester denotes Sherwood, part of which lies within the Borough, and the squirrels are from the arms of the first Mayor of Worksop, Mr C. A. Longbottom.

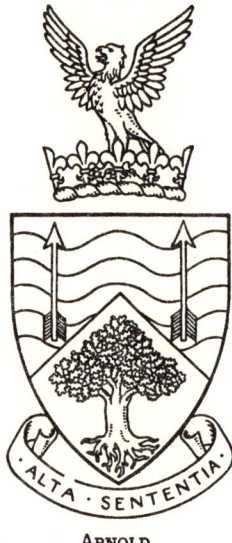

ARNOLD

EASTWOOD

ARNOLD Urban District Council

ARMS: Parted chevronwise, the chief barry wavy of six pieces argent and azure and the base gules; in chief two arrows erect, points upwards, proper, the feathers gules, and in base an uprooted oak-tree or.

CREST: On a wreath gold and gules, an eagle gules rising from a circlet of eight gold fleurs-de-lis (five visible).

MOTTO: *Alta sententia*—'With high purpose.'

These were granted in 1948.

The emblems in the shield refer to the places comprised within the district, the wavy white and blue bars standing for Daybrook, the red ground for Redhill, and the oak for Woodthorpe; while the arrows allude to the adjoining forest of Sherwood.

Arnold is referred to in Domesday Book as Ernehale, which is taken to mean 'the valley of eagles,' and to this the crest refers.

EASTWOOD Urban District Council

ARMS: Lozengy argent and sable; a chief or charged with an annulet sable between two roundels gules.

These were granted in 1951.

The 'black diamonds' stand for coal mining. The annulet represents the Plumtree family. The roundels are from the arms of the family of Grey of Codnor; they may also be taken to represent cricket balls in allusion to the fact that several well-known cricketers have come from the district.

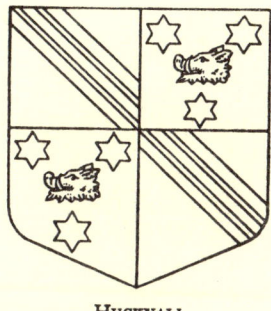

HUCKNALL

WORKSOP R.D.C.

HUCKNALL Urban District Council

Use is made of the following arms: Quarterly 1 and 4, Silver, three bendlets enhanced gules; 2 and 3, Azure, a boar's head between three six-pointed stars. The former coat is that of Byron, the family having been seated at Newstead. The second coat appears to be based on the arms of Gordon of Gight: Azure, a gold six-pointed star between three gold boars' heads. The device is therefore a variation of the arms of George Gordon, sixth Baron Byron, the poet, whose mother was Catherine Gordon of Gight.

WORKSOP Rural District Council

ARMS: Parted saltirewise vert and sable, a silver saltire between a gold wheatsheaf in chief and in base and a silver stag's face and antlers on the dexter and sinister sides, and on the saltire two tilting-spears gules, crossed with their points upwards.

CREST: On a wreath argent and sable, a lozenge sable in front of two entwined sprigs of oak bearing acorns proper, and over all a stag's face argent with antlers and tongue gules.

MOTTO: *Work supports all.*

These were granted in 1952.

The green and wheatsheaves allude to agriculture and the black to coal mining. The stags' heads are from the arms of the Duke of Portland, a local landowner, and the tilting lances refer to a former tournament field licensed by Richard I for public tourneys. In the crest, the oak and stag's head represent Sherwood Forest, and the 'black diamond' stands for coal. The motto refers to the name of the District.

Oxfordshire C.C.

OXFORDSHIRE

OXFORDSHIRE County Council

ARMS: Azure, two bends wavy argent between in chief a wheatsheaf and in base an uprooted oak-tree bearing acorns all gold, the bends surmounted in the centre point by an ox's face gules.

CREST: In a mural crown gules a mount vert, and thereon a representation of St George's Tower, Oxford Castle, proper.

SUPPORTERS: Two Oxford Down rams proper each having about its neck a collar azure charged with a bar wavy argent.

MOTTO: *Sapere aude*—'Dare to be wise.'

These were granted in 1949.

The blue of the field represents Oxford University, and the wavy bends and the ox's face play on the name Oxford in a manner rather different from the arms of Oxford City. The wheatsheaf and oak-tree refer to the agriculture and woods of the County. The crest symbolizes the close connection between the County and the Castle, which is the site both of the ancient shire hall and the modern county hall. The rams, of the famous local breed, indicate the County's connection with the wool trade for centuries. The motto is that of Lord Macclesfield, Chairman of the County Council when the arms were granted. It is taken from the First Book of Horace's *Epistles*.

OXFORD

OXFORD City and County Borough Council

ARMS: Silver, a red ox fording water barry wavy argent and azure in the base of the shield.

CREST: On a wreath argent and gules, a demi-lion guardant azure, wearing a gold royal crown and holding a Tudor rose.

SUPPORTERS: Dexter, an elephant sable ermined argent with silver ears, collar, and chain, and gold tusks; and sinister, a beaver vert, its tail azure and argent, with a gold ducal coronet about its neck and a gold chain attached thereto.

MOTTO: *Fortis est veritas*—'Strong is truth.'

These are recorded at the College of Arms.

The device on the shield, which appeared on a fourteenth-century seal, not only expresses the name, but also hints at its origin; but an alternative to the theory that the place grew up about a ford for oxen is that the syllable 'ox' is a variant of the Celtic word for water. The crest is composed of royal emblems. The significance of the elephant is unknown. The beaver probably refers to the Thames.

BANBURY Borough Council

ARMS: Azure, the sun gold, and on a chief ermine a castle of two towers between two pairs of swords crossed saltirewise with points upwards, all gules.

CREST: On a wreath gold and azure, a lady in Tudor costume proper mounted upon a white horse passant with gold and red caparisons.

BANBURY

SUPPORTERS: Two oxen gules with gold horns and hoofs, each with a silver collar charged with a bar wavy azure.

MOTTO: *Dominus nobis sol et scutum*—'The Lord is our sun and shield.'

These were granted in 1951.

The sun and motto formed the device of the Corporation before the arms were granted. The castle represents the stronghold built in 1135, which was the scene of several sieges during the Civil War, as the crossed swords denote. The crest alludes to the rhyme,

> Ride a cock-horse
> To Banbury Cross
> To see a fine lady upon a white horse.

The 'fine lady' is here shown in Tudor costume in reference to the town's charter of 1554. The supporters refer to the County.

CHIPPING NORTON Borough Council

The seal contains a castle with the letters 'I R' (for Jacobus Rex) in allusion to James I, by whom the charter of incorporation was granted.

HENLEY-UPON-THAMES Borough Council

The seal bears the letter H ensigned by a coronet beneath rays of the sun.

WOODSTOCK

WOODSTOCK Borough Council

ARMS: Gules, an uprooted tree-stock and in chief three stags' faces and antlers, all argent, within a silver border charged with eight oak leaves vert.

CREST: In a gold ducal coronet an oak-tree proper.

SUPPORTERS: Two savages, each wreathed about the temple and loins with oak leaves and bearing a club proper.

MOTTO: *Ramosa cornua cervi*—'The branching horns of the stag.'

These are recorded at the College of Arms.

The tree-stock was adopted by Edward III as one of his badges in allusion to the royal manor of Woodstock. The other emblems are also of the woodlands. The motto is from Virgil, *Eclogues*, vii, c. 30; the reference is to the horns of a stag given as an offering to Diana.

WITNEY Urban District Council

The device consists of the Holy Lamb.

Pembrokeshire C.C.

PEMBROKESHIRE

PEMBROKESHIRE County Council

ARMS: Quarterly, a cross sable; the first and fourth quarters parted fesswise gules and gold, on the gules a lion passant and on the gold two fleurs-de-lis all counter-changed; the second and third quarters argent with two bars gules; the whole within a silver bordure charged with eight martlets sable and eight ermine spots alternately.

CREST: Within a gold mural crown a rock proper, and perched thereon a gold eagle facing to the dexter with wings spread.

SUPPORTERS: Dexter, a gold lion with a collar gules and charged on the shoulder with a fleur-de-lis gules; and sinister, a dragon gules with a gold collar and charged on the shoulder with a gold fleur-de-lis.

MOTTO: *Ex unitate vires*—'Strength from unity.'

These were granted in 1937.

The County formerly used the arms of Jasper Tudor, Earl of Pembroke: Quarterly France and England within a bordure azure charged with eight gold martlets. Emblems from these arms have been included in the first and fourth quarters and the border of the arms granted to the County Council. The Tudors were closely associated with Pembrokeshire, and Henry VII was born at Pembroke Castle.

Pembrokeshire, sometimes called 'little England beyond Wales,' is inhabited by two races, the northern part being predominantly Welsh and the southern part English. The

PEMBROKESHIRE

lion and dragon represent the County's dual heritage, and the motto signifies the unity of the two elements.

The mural crown refers to the castles of Pembrokeshire, and the rock to its rugged coasts, while the eagle represents its wild life. Eagles have been seen on Ramsey Island, and the County is still noted for its falcons.

HAVERFORDWEST Borough Council

The seal bears a castle or fortified gateway with three towers, on each of the outer ones a flag, and rising from the middle one the head and shoulders of a man blowing a horn; on one side of the building is an heraldic tiger, and on the other a bird, possibly an eagle, perched on a piece of scroll work; beneath the building is a wyvern. The doors are closed. The accompanying inscription is, *O lector salve celi pateant tibi valve*—'Greeting, reader! May Heaven's doors open to thee.'

The motto suggests that the building represents the gate of Heaven; but it may originally have been intended for Haverfordwest Castle, built by Gilbert de Clare, Earl of Pembroke, about 1113.

Burke states: 'The arms are generally said to be an old man's head in profile, couped at the neck.'

PEMBROKE

PEMBROKE Borough Council

ARMS: Or, six chevrons gules within a bordure quarterly argent and azure charged with twelve martlets, gules on the argent and gold on the azure.

CREST: On a wreath gold and gules, a castle of three towers proper on a mount vert, the outer towers round and the middle one square, and in front of the portway an anchor erect sable.

SUPPORTERS: Dexter, a lion gules, and sinister, a lion argent, each with a gold naval crown about its neck, the dexter lion charged with a gold portcullis and the sinister with a Tudor rose.

MOTTO: *Ung nous servons*—'We serve as one.'

These were granted in 1950.

The chevrons are those of Gilbert de Clare, first Earl of Pembroke (so created in 1138), while in the border the red martlets on white are from the arms of William de Valence (half-brother of King Henry III), Earl of Pembroke 1251–96, and the gold martlets on blue are from the arms of Jasper Tudor who was created Earl of Pembroke in 1453. In the crest, the castle and anchor stand for Pembroke town and dock.

The red lion supporter is from the arms of William the Marshal, who was Earl of Pembroke 1199–1219, and was succeeded in the earldom by his five sons. The white lion is from the heraldry of the Herbert family, who have held the Earldom of Pembroke since 1468. The naval crowns refer to Pembroke Dock, with particular reference to the former Royal Naval Dockyard, and the portcullis and rose are badges of King Henry VII, who was born at Pembroke Castle in 1457. The motto is a variation of that of the Herbert Earls of Pembroke, *Ung je serviray*.

TENBY Borough Council

The Corporation has not obtained arms, but uses the following: Parted fesswise, the chief barry of four pieces charged with three martlets; in the base three cinquefoils. The upper part of the shield was clearly suggested by the arms of the De Valence Earls of Pembroke, who bore: Barry of ten argent and azure, an orle of martlets gules. The cinquefoils are from the arms of the See of St David's.

TENBY

RADNORSHIRE C.C.

RADNORSHIRE

RADNORSHIRE County Council

ARMS: Quarterly gules and argent, in the first and fourth quarters a gold lion rampant reguardant and in the second and third three boars' heads couped sable; all within a bordure compony gold and azure.

The shield is ensigned with a gold mural crown.

MOTTO: *Ewch yn uwch*—'Higher and higher.'

These were granted in 1950.

The lion rampant reguardant is attributed to Elystan Glodrhydd, a Prince of Wales about A.D. 1000, and the boars' heads are associated with his son Cadwgan. The bordure is from the arms of the Mortimers, Earls of March.

LLANDRINDOD WELLS Urban District Council

The seal bears the figure of Hygieia.

RUTLAND

RUTLAND County Council

RUTLAND C.C.

ARMS: Vert, strewn with gold acorns, and a horseshoe or.

CREST: On a wreath gold and vert, a gold acorn with leaves and stalk proper in front of a horseshoe or.

MOTTO: *Multum in parvo*—'Much in little.'

These were granted in 1950.

The following notes are extracted from the Oakham Official Guide:

The horseshoe represents the County's history and hunting association, and is traditionally Rutland's as witness the unique collection of horseshoes presented by royalty, peers of the realm, and noblemen passing through the County, which hang on the walls of the famous Castle Hall at Oakham.

The acorn exemplifies the former forest land which at one time covered much of the County, especially on the south side. It can also be interpreted as standing for 'smallness and importance.'

The green shield represents the County's agriculture, especially its rich pasture land, while the motto, like the acorn, bears witness to the efficiency and importance of England's smallest county.

With reference to the collection of horseshoes at Oakham, Camden states that

every baron of the realm, the first time he comes through the town of Okeham where the Ferrers seat was, shall give a horseshoe to nail on the Castle gate. If he refuse, the bailiff of the Manor has power to stop his coach and take one off the horses' feet. But mainly they give five, ten, or twenty shillings, more or less, as they please, and in proportion to the gift the shoe is made larger or smaller, with the name and title of the donor cut upon it. So it is nailed upon the gate.

This suggests that the custom had an heraldic origin in the arms of the Ferrers family—six black horseshoes (*ferres*) on silver; but there is an alternative legend that it arose from the fact that when Queen Elizabeth I passed through Oakham her horse cast a shoe.

SHROPSHIRE

SALOP C.C.

LUDLOW

SHROPSHIRE

SALOP County Council

ARMS: Gold ermined sable, three piles azure, the middle one reversed, each charged with a leopard's face or.

MOTTO: *Floreat Salopia.*

These arms were granted in 1896.

The leopards' faces are from the arms of Shrewsbury, which probably derived them from the Royal Arms of England.

BISHOP'S CASTLE Borough Council

The seal bears a domed castle with the letters 'I R' above it and the date 1609 below. The initials refer to James I. The device recalls the castle of the Bishops of Hereford whence the town takes its name.

BRIDGNORTH Borough Council

The seal bears a castle with a central domed tower, and on either side thereof a shield, one bearing the cross of St George, and the other the Royal Arms: France and England quarterly.

This seal dates from the fifteenth century. The device is sometimes used in the manner of a coat of arms, the castle, tinctured silver, being placed in a blue shield.

MOTTO: *Fidelitas urbis salus Regis*—'The faithfulness of the city is the safety of the King.'

The castle represents that built in 1098 by Robert de Belesme, Earl of Shrewsbury, who held it in rebellion against Henry I. During the Civil War the castle was besieged by the Parliamentary forces and finally demolished. The motto refers to the town's support of the Royalist cause.

LUDLOW Borough Council

ARMS: Azure, a lion couchant guardant between three roses all argent.
CREST: On a wreath argent and azure, a porcupine quarterly gold and azure.
These are recorded at the College of Arms.

Formerly the headquarters of the Welsh March, Ludlow displays the white rose and white lion of the Mortimers, Earls of March. From the Mortimers the Yorkist Plantagenets derived their legitimist title to the throne, together with the white rose by which they symbolized it (see Chapter II). The arms recall that it was at Ludlow that Richard Plantagenet, Duke of York, met the Earls of Salisbury and Warwick in 1459, to begin the campaign which resulted in his death at Wakefield in the following year.

The porcupine was probably derived from the crest of Sir Henry Sidney, President of the Welsh Marches, who died at Ludlow in 1586. The Sidney porcupine is blue with gold quills, collar, and chain.

OSWESTRY

WELLINGTON

SHREWSBURY

OSWESTRY Borough Council

'Oswald's tre' derives its name from St Oswald, first Christian King of Northumbria, who, in 642, was killed here in battle against the heathen King Penda of Mercia. The Corporation uses the arms of a monastery raised to Oswald's memory: Gules, a silver cross with the limbs cut short, between four gold lions rampant. These are a variation of the arms ascribed to Oswald himself: Azure, a gold cross and four gold lions rampant (see Durham C.C.), and it may be that in altering the colour of the field of the king's arms from blue to red, and in truncating the limbs of the cross, the designers of the monastery arms intended to symbolize Oswald's martyrdom.

The seal, which dates from the thirteenth century, bears the figure of Oswald with a sword in one hand and with the other grasping a tree.

SHROPSHIRE

SHREWSBURY Borough Council

ARMS: Azure, three gold leopards' faces.

MOTTO: *Floreat Salopia.*

The arms are on record at the Heralds' College.

They first appear on a fifteenth-century seal of the Corporation. It is probable that the leopards' faces (locally called 'loggerheads') were adopted from the Royal Arms, which appeared on a thirteenth-century seal. An alternative theory derives them from the arms of the local family of Pontisbury.

WENLOCK Borough Council

The Corporation has no arms. A fifteenth-century seal bears a Gothic canopy with three niches; in the middle one is a representation of the Holy Trinity, and in the others the Archangel Michael and St Milburga, daughter of Merwald, King of Mercia, and foundress (about 680) of a religious house which two centuries later was restored by Leofric, Earl of Mercia, and Godiva, and after the Conquest was refounded by Roger de Montgomery. Below the figures are three shields, the middle one bearing the arms of Roger de Montgomery, a lion rampant; another a hart; and the third the arms of the family of Wenlock of Much Wenlock, a chevron between three Moors' heads.

Another seal bears a rebus—a lock and the letters W E N.

WELLINGTON Urban District Council

ARMS: Argent, fretty gules, thereon a lion rampant sable; on a chief sable a silver castle between two gold fleurs-de-lis.

CREST: On a wreath argent and gules, a gold bugle-horn with strings in front of a portcullis with chains sable.

MOTTO: *Deo adjuvante*—'By the help of God.'

These were granted in 1951.

The castle and the portcullis refer to Apley Castle, which since the fourteenth century has been in the possession of the Charlton family (now represented by the Meyrick family), from whose arms the lion was taken.

The fleurs-de-lis are from the old Royal Arms in allusion to the fact that Wellington was the rendezvous of the Royalist forces in 1642, when King Charles I addressed his army here before moving to Shrewsbury. In 1644 Apley Castle and Wellington parish church were garrisoned by the Royalists, captured by the Parliamentary troops, and retaken by the Royalists.

The fret is from the arms of the old local families of Eyton and Cludde, and the horn stands for Lord Forester, who is descended from the foresters of Wellington Hay, a portion of the Wrekin Forest.

CIVIC HERALDRY

SOMERSET C.C.

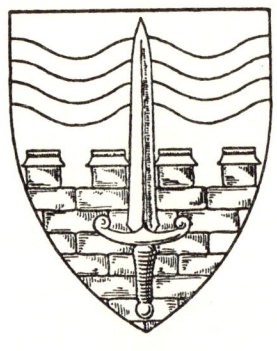

BATH

SOMERSET

SOMERSET County Council

ARMS: Gold, a red dragon rampant holding erect a mace azure.

MOTTO: *Sumorsaete ealle.*

These arms were granted in 1911.

The dragon is that of the ancient Kingdom of the West Saxons. Commonly called 'the Golden Dragon of Wessex,' this monster was sometimes described as of red gold. According to Henry of Huntingdon, writing in the twelfth century, the dragon was already the emblem of the West Saxons at the middle of the eighth century, and it seems to be likely that they had adopted it in token of their conquest of the Britons. An historical note on the British and Saxon dragons appears in Chapter II.

While Somerset bears the dragon in token of the Kingdom of Wessex, the emblem also aptly recalls that the County claims to contain King Arthur's capital, Camelot (Queen's Camel), and his place of burial, Avalon (Glastonbury).

The mace is a symbol of local government.

BATH City and County Borough Council

ARMS: The upper half of the shield is azure with two silver wavy bars; the lower half represents a battlemented stone wall of silver; over all is a sword erect, point upwards, the hilt gold and the blade gules.

The arms are on record at the Heralds' College.

The Corporation has added, as supporters, a lion and a bear, but these are unauthorized. The motto, *Floreat Bathon*, is sometimes used.

The version of the arms quoted by Burke varies the colours and places a key on the blade of the sword; it is a pity that the key has been dropped, because it completed the reference to the Abbey Church of St Peter and St Paul. The wall and water clearly illustrate the Roman baths and commemorate Bath's origin as Aquae Sulis.

BRIDGWATER

BRIDGWATER Borough Council

Arms: Gules, in base water barry wavy proper and rising therefrom the piers of a bridge of gold, and thereon a silver castle with the portcullis raised and in the portway a gold leopard's face; in chief a star of eight rays and a fleur-de-lis, both or.

Crest: On a wreath silver and gules, an ancient ship of gold, the rigging sable, flags and pennants argent and each charged with a cross gules, the sail argent charged with a chevron between three wheatsheaves all sable.

Supporters: Two gold lions guardant, each with a rope proper about its neck and an escutcheon hanging therefrom, that on the dexter lion being gules charged with two gold wavy bends, and that on the sinister lion argent charged with a trivet sable.

Motto: *Opes consilium parit*—'Wisdom begets wealth.'

These were granted in 1952.

The following note is supplied by the Corporation:

The shield carries the design of the seal, which has been used for centuries. The waves of blue in the water refer particularly to the double bore of the river, and the red field . . . may be taken as a reference to the red shield of Douai in France, whence came Walter de Douai who received the grant of the town in Norman times. The star, fleur-de-lis, and leopard's (or lion's) face are all royal emblems, and with the two royal lions which support the arms indicate the numerous royal charters, beginning with that of King John, which the town has received. The raised portcullis may be taken as an indication of the town's importance as a tourist centre.

The crest is a conventional heraldic ship of gold, representing Bridgwater's importance as a port in many periods. The sail is decorated with the arms of Admiral Blake, a native of the town, and the black chevron and sheaves may also be considered to allude to the grain and coal traffic.

CIVIC HERALDRY

The lion supporters have ropes at their necks.... The ropes allude to another local activity—the hemp industry. The two shields are those of the De Briwere and Trivet families. Bridgwater was granted to the De Briweres in the time of Henry II; Walter de Briwere founded the Hospital of St John and built the Castle. Sir Thomas Trivet, who bore punning arms of a black trivet on white, completed the bridge over the Parrett.

CHARD Borough Council

The seal bears two birds which may be peacocks.

GLASTONBURY Borough Council

The Corporation has not obtained arms, but uses the following: Azure, two gold croziers saltirewise surmounted by a gold mitre. Motto: *Floreat Ecclesia Anglicana*—'May the Church of England flourish.'

GLASTONBURY   TAUNTON   WELLS

TAUNTON Borough Council

ARMS: Azure, in chief a cherub and in base a Saxon crown, both gold.

CREST: Rising from a gold mural crown a peacock with its tail spread proper, about its neck a gold Saxon crown.

MOTTO: *Defendamus*—'Let us defend.'

These were granted in 1934.

The Borough formerly used an unauthorized device consisting of a cherub above a royal crown, based on a Corporation seal dated 1685. When application was made for this device to be granted as arms, the Heralds pointed out that they had no power to include a royal crown without a special licence from the King, and if such licence were obtained the crown would have to be placed above any other emblem in the arms. A Saxon crown was therefore substituted for the royal crown of to-day, with reference to Ine, King of the West Saxons, founder of Taunton. The cherub probably refers to the priory founded in the reign of Henry I by William Giffard, Bishop of Winchester, and the peacock was derived from an ancient seal of the Borough believed to date from about 1180.

WELLS City Council

ARMS: Silver, on a mount vert in base an ash-tree proper between three wells gules. The shield is ensigned with a mural crown.

MOTTO: *Hoc fonte derivata copia.*

These were granted in 1951, but were in earlier use as unauthorized insignia.

The present motto is a shortened form of one formerly used, namely: *Hoc fonte derivata copia in patriam populumque fluit*—'Wealth, drawn from this spring, flows forth unto our country and our people.' This is a paraphrase of a passage from Horace, Ode 6, Book III:

> *Hoc fonte derivata clades*
> *In patriam populumque fluxit;*
>
> Calamity, sprung from this source,
> Has flowed forth among our countrymen,

referring to the corruption of Roman morals by Greek influence.

WESTON-SUPER-MARE Borough Council

ARMS: Azure, on a gold fess a setting sun gules; in chief a silver sailing ship and an oak-tree proper growing on a mount vert strewn with silver billets; and in base three swimming herrings argent.

CREST: On a wreath gold and azure, a lighthouse on a rock with water at its base, and in front of the lighthouse a flying seagull, all proper.

SUPPORTERS: Dexter, a fisherman holding in his right hand a coil of rope; and sinister, an Ancient Briton with a spear in his left hand, all proper.

MOTTO: *Ever forward.*

The arms were granted in 1928 and the crest and supporters in 1937.

With emblems of fisheries and the sea are combined the setting sun, denoting the west country and the splendour of its evening skies, the tree for the local woodlands, and a figure characterizing Weston's earliest inhabitants and their settlement at Worlebury Camp.

WESTON-SUPER-MARE

YEOVIL Borough Council

The seal contains the figure of St John the Baptist, patron saint of the Church, standing under a canopy and bearing on his left arm the Holy Lamb; on either side is a tree.

CLEVEDON Urban District Council

ARMS: Gold, a pile reversed sable, its point in the form of a fleur-de-lis; in chief two roses gules and on the pile a lion rampant reguardant or.

CREST: On a wreath gold and sable, a green mount and rising therefrom a hill cleft at the summit proper.

MOTTO: *Vigilate et orate*—'Watch and pray.'

These were granted in 1933.

CREWKERNE Urban District Council

ARMS: Or, a lion rampant azure between three roundels gules; on a chief ermine a pale sable, and thereon three swords pilewise points downwards proper, their pommels and hilts gold.

CREST: On a wreath or and azure, rising from a wreath of flax in flower the mast of a ship with the pennon of St George at the head all proper, and on the mast a sail gules charged with a gold cross moline within a bordure argent sprinkled with drops gules.

MOTTO: *Keep faith.*

These were granted in 1949.

CLEVEDON   BATHAVON R.D.C.   CREWKERNE

The arms combine the lion of the Redvers Earls of Devon, the red roundels of Courtenay, and the swords of Poulett, while the ermine stands for royal associations. In the crest, the flax represents the rope industry and the sail refers to yachting and sail making. The cross on the sail is from the arms of Agnes de Monceaux who founded Crewkerne School, and the drops of blood allude to St Bartholomew, in whose name the parish church is dedicated.

KEYNSHAM *Urban District Council*

The device consists of a shield bearing six clarions.

BATHAVON *Rural District Council*

ARMS: Vert, a fess argent, thereon a bar wavy azure, and over all a gold dragon rampant.

CREST: On a wreath argent and vert, three gold wheatsheaves upon a billet sable laid fesswise.

MOTTO: *Rus Gratiis Musisque dignum*—'A countryside worthy of the Graces and Muses.'

These were granted in 1951.

The shield shows the dragon of Wessex in a green field crossed by a symbolic representation of the River Avon. In the crest, the black billet stands for the coal-mining area in the south of the district, while the wheatsheaves refer to the agricultural area in the north. The motto indicates the district's cultural and historical background.

STAFFORDSHIRE

A general emblem of the County, which occurs in the arms of the County Council and many other authorities, is the Stafford knot. This was a badge of the Earls of Stafford, and appeared in conjunction with the Bohun swan (see Buckinghamshire) on their standard. As a civic emblem it was first used by the town of Stafford, and a facetious tradition has it that the place was so infested with rogues that it was necessary to devise a noose which would enable them to be hanged three at a time.

STAFFORDSHIRE C.C.

STAFFORDSHIRE County Council

ARMS: Or, a chevron gules charged with a gold Stafford knot, and on a chief azure a gold lion passant guardant.

CREST: Above a mural crown proper, a gold Stafford knot.

SUPPORTERS: Dexter, a lion reguardant gules crowned with a gold ducal coronet; and sinister, a gold griffin, also reguardant.

MOTTO: *The knot unites.*

These were granted in 1931.

The red chevron on gold forms the arms of the family De Stafford (see Chapter III), and the knot is their badge. The supporters, also Stafford badges, are 'reguardant' (i.e. looking backwards) both for the sake of heraldic difference, and as a symbol that they look back into the past. The motto refers to the knot in the arms and indicates that the County is divided into separate administrative areas.

STAFFORDSHIRE

BURTON-UPON-TRENT   STOKE-ON-TRENT   SMETHWICK

BURTON-UPON-TRENT County Borough Council

ARMS: Barry wavy of six pieces argent and azure; a chief gules charged with a silver eagle displayed between two gold fleurs-de-lis.

CREST: Out of a gold mural crown, a right hand proper grasping a lozenge azure charged with a silver saltire.

MOTTO: *Honor alit artes*—'Honour fosters the arts.'

These were granted in 1928.

The eagle is from the arms of the Paget family (now represented by the Marquess of Anglesey), upon whom the lands of the Abbey at Burton were conferred at its dissolution; the fleurs-de-lis are from the arms of Bass, Baron Burton, and also refer to the dedication of the abbey to St Mary. The saltire in the crest alludes to a chapel of St Andrew said to have been founded at Burton by St Modwena.

SMETHWICK County Borough Council

ARMS: Or, a caduceus and a club laid saltirewise proper; on a chief azure a beacon fired between two symbols of the planet Mars, all gold.

CREST: On a wreath gold and azure, a demi-lion gules charged on the shoulder with a gold Stafford knot and holding in the paws an arrow point downwards proper.

MOTTO: *Labore et ingenio*—'By industry and ingenuity.'

These were granted in 1907.

The arms combine the caduceus of Mercury, god of commerce, the emblems of Mars for the iron and steel industry, a club from the arms of James Watt, and a beacon alluding to the part taken by William Murdoch in introducing gas-lighting. The red lion is from the crest of Sir James Timmins Chance, and the arrow represents Matthew Boulton.

STOKE-ON-TRENT City and County Borough Council

ARMS: Silver, a cross gules fretted with gold; in the first quarter a representation of the Portland vase; in the second, a kneeling camel proper charged on the body with a silver shield bearing a red cross; in the third, an eagle displayed sable; and in the fourth, a scythe proper; on a chief gules a boar's head torn off, between two Stafford knots all gold.

CREST: On a wreath argent and gules, a potter of ancient Egypt seated and working at his wheel, silver.

MOTTO: *Vis unita fortior*—'Strength is the stronger for unity.'

These were granted in 1912 after the amalgamation in one borough of Stoke-on-Trent, Burslem, Fenton, Hanley, Longton, and Tunstall.

An examination of the insignia of the former separate boroughs shows where several of the emblems in the above arms were derived.

Burslem bore arms granted in 1878, consisting of gold and red quarters with two vertical and two horizontal stripes interlaced and counter-changed; in the first and fourth quarters a Portland vase, in the second a scythe, and in the third a silver fret. Crest: A red fleur-de-lis in front of a gold wheatsheaf between two branches of laurel in proper colours. Motto: *Ready*.

Fenton had no arms, but used a device containing *inter alia* two vases.

Hanley used arms of its own invention; the shield was parted chevronwise, and the chief palewise; the first compartment was barry of six pieces gold and ermine with three blue jugs; the second was ermine with a black cross in outline between four blazing towers (perhaps furnaces); the base was red with four silver stars from the arms of the Wedgwood family. Crest: A kneeling camel charged on the body with a silver shield bearing a red cross.

Longton, having no arms, used those of Heathcote of Longton Hall, who quartered *inter alia* the arms of Sandford: Parted chevronwise black and ermine, in the chief two gold boars' heads. To the Heathcote arms Longton added the crest of the family of Moseley, an ermine eagle.

Tunstall used unauthorized arms consisting of a chevron between in chief a soup-tureen and in base a vase; on the chevron a Stafford knot and two scythes; and on a canton two furnaces.

Returning to the arms of the amalgamated borough, the gold frets on the red cross are from the arms of Burslem, and commemorate the family of Audley. The camel is from

STAFFORDSHIRE

the device of Hanley, and was taken from the crest of John Ridgway, first Mayor of that borough. The silver stars, also from the Hanley device, are from the arms of the Wedgwood family. The eagle represents Longton. The scythe (or sned), from the Burslem arms and the Tunstall device, stands for the family of Sneyd. The boar's head, from the Longton device, is from the arms of the Sandford family. The other emblems stand for the potteries and for Staffordshire.

WALSALL *County Borough Council*

The fifteenth-century seal of the Corporation bore the then Royal Arms of England (France and England quarterly), flanked by two lions seated with their backs to the shield and with their tails intertwined, and ensigned by an open crown of fleurs-de-lis. These are still used by the Corporation, with the addition of a grassy mount inside the crown, and seated thereon a bear supporting a ragged staff. The bear and ragged staff allude to Warwick 'the Kingmaker' (see Warwickshire C.C.) who held the Manor of Walsall.

WALSALL

WEST BROMWICH

WEST BROMWICH *County Borough Council*

ARMS: Azure, a stag's face and antlers argent between three gold millrinds, within a silver border charged alternately with four molets and four fleurs-de-lis all azure.

CREST: On a wreath argent and azure, in front of four feathers azure a silver stag lodged, resting its forefoot on a millrind sable.

These were granted in 1882.

Except the millrinds, which represent the iron and brass foundries, the emblems are all derived from the arms, crest, and supporters of the Earls of Dartmouth, who were formerly seated at Sandwell Hall.

WOLVERHAMPTON   BILSTON

WOLVERHAMPTON County Borough Council

ARMS: Gules, a gold cross formy between a pillar, a woolpack, and an open book, all argent, and a gold padlock.

CREST: On a wreath gold and gules, in front of a beacon sable with flames proper, two gold crossed keys, wards upwards.

MOTTO: *Out of darkness cometh light.*

These were granted in 1898.

The cross is perhaps intended to commemorate Wulfrun, sister of King Edgar, who founded a religious house at Hamton, thenceforward called Wulfrun's Hamton. The pillar is a Saxon remnant in the churchyard of St Peter's Church, and the crossed keys refer to the patron saint. The book represents the Grammar School. The woolpack stands for the wool industry, formerly the source of the town's prosperity, and the padlock is a reminder that in the eighteenth century the manufacture of locks was an important local activity, the Wolverhampton locksmiths being accredited the most ingenious in England.

Nowadays Wolverhampton is a principal town in the 'Black Country,' and the black beacon, with the apt motto, alludes to the coal and ironstone mines.

STAFFORDSHIRE

BILSTON Borough Council

ARMS: Ermine, a bend sable and thereon a gold fess between two silver martlets, and on the fess a Stafford knot gules.

CREST: On a wreath argent and sable, the rising sun, gold, in front of three oak leaves vert.

SUPPORTERS: Dexter, Faith, represented by a woman proper in a blue robe and bearing a lamp; and sinister, Industry in the guise of Vulcan, also proper, wearing a red tunic and bearing a hammer.

MOTTO: *Fidelitate et Industria stat Bilstonia*—'Bilston stands by Faith and Industry.'

These were granted in 1933 when Bilston was incorporated as a borough.

The arms are based upon those of Sir Walter de Bilston (thirteenth century) which were formerly used by the Urban District Council; the middle of the three martlets having been replaced by a Stafford knot. The sun refers to the derivation of the name from Baal or Bel's ton, the place of sun or fire worship; while the oak leaves allude to the forest in which the place was anciently situated. The supporters represent the virtues mentioned in the motto.

LICHFIELD

LICHFIELD City Council

ARMS: Checky of nine gold and ermine, in each of the gold squares a chevron gules.

SUPPORTERS: Dexter, St Chad vestured in alb and amice proper with orphreys vert embroidered in gold, a dalmatic also vert with gold embroidery, and a gold chasuble trimmed with green and embroidered with gold; his gloves white and shoes purple; in the bend of his right arm a gold pastoral staff, and in his right hand a model of Lichfield

Cathedral proper; and sinister, a Guild Master of Lichfield in fifteenth-century dress proper, carrying in his left hand a bunch of red roses with stalks and leaves proper.

MOTTO: *Salve magna parens*—'Hail, great parent.'

The arms are ancient, and the crest and supporters were granted in 1950.

The chevrons are from the arms of the Stafford family, Dukes of Buckingham and Earls of Stafford. The supporters refer to the See and the City. St Chad was the first Bishop of Lichfield (A.D. 669). The motto was Dr Samuel Johnson's choice for Lichfield, and no doubt refers to the Cathedral as the mother church of the ancient kingdom of Mercia.

NEWCASTLE-UNDER-LYME

NEWCASTLE-UNDER-LYME Borough Council

ARMS: Or, rising from a base barry wavy of four pieces argent and azure charged with three fishes swimming proper, a castle of three towers gules; on a chief azure a lion passant guardant between two fleurs-de-lis all gold.

CREST: On a wreath gold and gules, a demi-lion with a forked tail argent, charged on the shoulder with a Stafford knot gules and supporting a staff proper and thereon a banner azure charged with three gold wheatsheaves.

SUPPORTERS: Two lions guardant sable, each supporting a scythe proper.

MOTTO: *Prisca constantia*—'With ancient constancy.'

These were granted in 1951.

The castle represents the 'new castle' built in the twelfth century by the Earls of Chester, whose banner forms part of the crest. The lion and fleurs-de-lis in the shield are from the arms of the Duchy of Lancaster, while the fork-tailed lion in the crest represents Simon de Montfort.

The supporters are from the heraldry of the Sneyd family, formerly of Keele and Wolstanton (the scythes, or 'sneds,' being allusive to their name). They also stand for the new University College of North Staffordshire which is domiciled at Keele Hall, a former Sneyd residence.

ROWLEY REGIS

ROWLEY REGIS *Borough Council*

ARMS: Gules, on a pale ermine between two gold lions' faces, a human leg azure cut off at the thigh, and on a chief azure a gold lion passant.

CREST: On a wreath argent and gules a gold castle with three towers, and issuing from the battlements a demi-lion vert with a forked tail, charged on the shoulder with a gold fleur-de-lis and holding between the paws a gold anchor.

SUPPORTERS: Dexter, a smith standing in front of an anvil and holding in his right hand a hammer, its head resting on the anvil; and sinister, a miner holding in his left hand a pick resting on his shoulder, and with a safety-lamp hanging round his neck; all proper.

MOTTO: *Loyal and Industrious.*

These were granted in 1933 when Rowley Regis was incorporated as a borough.

Formerly part of the royal domain, a fact which is indicated by the lions' faces, the manor of Rowley was granted in the sixteenth century to Lord Dudley. The double-tailed lion in the crest is from the arms of Sutton, Lord Dudley, and the ermine pale in the shield is from those of Ward, the family of the present Earl of Dudley. The leg is the emblem of the family of Haden and the lion passant is that of Somery. The fleur-de-lis stands for Halesowen Priory, and the supporters and anchor refer to local industries.

STAFFORD

STAFFORD Borough Council

ARMS: Gules, a square castle with four domed towers in perspective argent, a gold pennon on each tower; in chief two Stafford knots, and in base a lion of England, all gold.

These are recorded at the College of Arms.

Stafford formerly had two castles, one belonging to the King, and the other to the Earls of Stafford. The royal castle, built by William the Conqueror, was held for the King by one Robert, called De Stafford, ancestor of the first Earl of Stafford, who, in 1348, built the second castle outside the town. Both castles have disappeared. The royal and feudal elements in Stafford's history are represented by the lion and the Stafford knots.

The arms carry on the motive of a thirteenth-century seal bearing a castle between four lions.

TAMWORTH Borough Council

The seal bears a fleur-de-lis, probably from the royal arms of Queen Elizabeth I, by whom the town was incorporated.

TIPTON Borough Council

ARMS: Gules, a castle between in chief three wheels and in base a Stafford knot all gold.

CREST: On a wreath gold and gules, a rock proper and issuing therefrom three spearheads, also proper, with gold hafts.

SUPPORTERS: Two gold lions, each holding in the mouth a strap gules and hanging therefrom a shield sable charged with a gold thunderbolt.

MOTTO: *Salus populi suprema lex*—'The welfare of the people is the highest law.'

These were granted in 1938.

TIPTON

The castle symbolizes the municipality and the knot the County, while the wheels stand for industry. The crest, consisting of spear-tips issuing from stone, alludes to the place-name, earlier Tibbingstone, or Tipstone. The shields carried by the supporting lions have black fields in allusion to the old coal mines which were responsible for the town's early growth, and are charged with thunderbolts, emblems of the present-day electrical industry. These also serve as a reminder of Captain Eyston's racing car, 'Thunderbolt,' which was made in Tipton and in 1938 set up a world land-speed record of 357 miles an hour.

WEDNESBURY Borough Council

ARMS: Sable, a fess argent between two silver lions passant each with a gold crown, and on the fess the symbol for Mars between two lozenges all sable.

CREST: On a wreath argent and sable, in front of the rising sun a tower with flames issuing from the battlements proper, the tower charged with the symbol for Mars, also sable.

MOTTO: *Arte, Marte, Vigore.*

These were granted in 1904.

The field suggests the Black Country, and the fiery tower its furnaces. The symbol for Mars represents the iron industry, and the lozenges—black diamonds—coal-mining. The lions are from the arms of the family of Heronville, upon whom the manor was bestowed by Henry II.

ALDRIDGE Urban District Council

The device consists of a beacon.

WEDNESBURY

BRIERLEY HILL

BRIERLEY HILL Urban District Council

ARMS: Or, a pale gules between two beacons sable in flames proper, and on the pale two roundels barry wavy argent and azure; on a chief gules two gold boars' heads and between them a golden roundel charged with a red rose with stalks and leaves proper.

CREST: On a wreath gold and gules, an anchor sable within and pendent from a circular chain also sable, and about the stock of the anchor a gold Stafford knot.

MOTTO: *Sine labore nihil floret*—'Nothing prospers without industry.'

These were granted in 1942.

The beacons allude to the town's principal industries of glass, iron and steel, and fireclay, while the crest refers to the manufacture of chains and anchors. The boars' heads and roundels (representing water) stand for the Manor of King's Swineford (Kingswinford), and the briar rose plays on the place-name.

CANNOCK Urban District Council

ARMS: Barry of eight pieces vert and sable, a gold stag's face and antlers between in chief an ancient crown of fleurs-de-lis, also gold, and in base a silver cross potent quadrate.

CREST: Rising from a circlet vert with flames proper issuing therefrom an oak-tree bearing acorns also proper with a gold Stafford knot about the trunk.

MOTTO: *Labor in venatu.*

These were granted in 1951.

CANNOCK COSELEY TETTENHALL

The background of the shield represents the green of Cannock Chase seamed with the black of the coalfield. The stag's head and crown recalls the old royal forest, and the cross, of the form associated with St Chad, is from the arms of the Bishoprics of Lichfield and Coventry. The Bishops of the then united See purchased the Manor of Cannock from King Richard I, and enjoyed many privileges in the Chase.

In the crest, the green circlet represents Castle Ring, and the flames allude to the industries in the area. They also represent, in conjunction with the oak-tree, the destruction of the forest for smelting before the discovery of the coal seams.

The motto, a quotation from Horace, meant in its original context 'exertion in the hunt,' but it is equally well translated as 'Work in the Chase,' which sums up Cannock's activities as an important industrial town in a former Royal Forest and Chase.

COSELEY Urban District Council

ARMS: Checky gold and azure, a chevron gules charged with a Stafford knot or; on a chief sable three gold cressets with flames proper.

CREST: Within a gold palisado crown a mount vert, and thereon a representation of Sedgley beacon-tower proper.

MOTTO: *Fellowship is life.*

These were granted in 1951.

The chequers are from the arms of the Ward family, which held the manor, while the chevron and Stafford knot are from the County insignia. The black chief alludes to the industry of the Black Country with special reference to mineral workings and tar-macadam, and the cressets are heraldic approximations to blast furnaces. Sedgley beacon-tower, which forms the crest, is a familiar landmark now owned by the Council.

DARLASTON Urban District Council

The device consists of a shield bearing a bend between two Stafford knots, and on the bend a lion passant guardant.

KIDSGROVE Urban District Council

The device consists of kids gambolling in a grove.

LEEK Urban District Council

The seal bears the rod of Mercury, symbol of commerce, among bales of goods, with the motto: *Arte favente nil desperandum*—'Supported by skill, there is no cause to despair.'

STONE Urban District Council

The Council has assumed a device of heraldic character consisting of a black shield charged with a gold chevron between in chief a wheatsheaf and a tun, both gold, and in base a shoemaker's knife and an awl crossed saltirewise proper, their handles gold; and on the chevron a Staffordshire knot proper between two black lozenges. Above the shield is a gold naval crown and issuing therefrom a silver demi-pegasus, its wings spread, holding between the hoofs a black lozenge. Below the shield is the motto: *Sit saxum firmum*—'May the stone be firm.'

The emblems in the shield refer to local industries, and the crest is a differenced form of that of the first Earl of St Vincent, who was born at Meaford and buried at Stone.

TETTENHALL Urban District Council

ARMS: Vert, a chevron engrailed between three uprooted oak-trees all gold, and on the chevron three roundels barry wavy argent and azure.

CREST: On a wreath gold and vert, a silver windmill on a green mound and in front of it two battle-axes crossed saltirewise gules.

MOTTO: *Respice aspice prospice*—'Look to the past, the present, and the future.'

These were granted in 1938.

The trees refer to the three royal forests of Kinver, Brewood, and Cannock, which met at Tettenhall, and the roundels (or heraldic fountains) denote the watershed and streams of the district, flowing into two oceans. The windmill, representing structures which were once common in the neighbourhood, stand for its windy and health-giving heights. The axes refer to the battle of Tettenhall in 910, when King Edward the Elder defeated the Danes.

STAFFORDSHIRE

UTTOXETER Urban District Council

The device on the seal consists of an escutcheon with the word *Floreat* above a Stafford knot, and the date 1896, and a fleur-de-lis in base.

WEDNESFIELD Urban District Council

The device consists of fighting men in the armour of the Saxon period, one wielding a battle-axe and the other with sword and round shield. This represents an incident in the battle at 'Woden's Field,' A.D. 910, when Edward the Elder defeated the Danes.

WILLENHALL

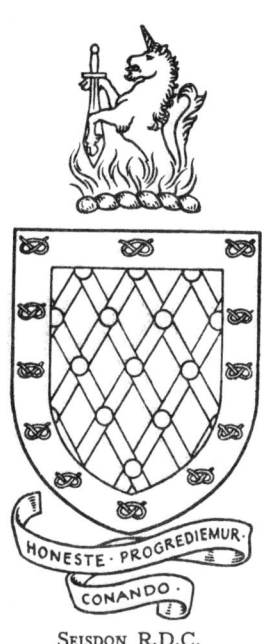

SEISDON R.D.C.

WILLENHALL Urban District Council

ARMS: Parted chevronwise azure and gules, in chief two gold padlocks, and in base a female figure representing Justice, seated and facing to the sinister, clothed in white, holding in the right hand a sword proper with gold pommel and hilt, point downwards, and in the left a gold balance; all between two gold flanches, on each a key gules, wards downwards and turned toward the centre of the shield.

CREST: On a wreath or and azure, a demi-tiger gules holding between the paws a gold Stafford knot, and in front of the tiger two gold keys crossed saltirewise.

MOTTO: *Salus populi suprema lex*—'The welfare of the people is the highest law.'

These were granted in 1935.

The locks and keys stand for the town's principal and historic industry. The figure of Justice represents the ideal of a local government authority. The lion and Stafford knot are from the arms of the County.

SEISDON Rural District Council

ARMS: Argent fretty gules with gold roundels at every point of intersection, a bordure vert charged with twelve Stafford knots or.

CREST: On a wreath argent and gules, rising from flames proper a silver demi-unicorn with gold horn, hoofs, mane, and tufts, supporting a Roman sword, point downwards, proper, its pommel and hilt gold.

MOTTO: *Honeste progrediemur conando*—'Let us progress by honest endeavour.'

These were granted in 1952.

The fretty design is from the arms of the de Tressells, or Trussels, former Lords of the Manor, while the gold roundels represent the old nail-making industry of the district. The Stafford knots link the arms with the County, and their number corresponds with the twelve parishes in the Rural District.

The unicorn in the crest is from the heraldry of the Wrottesleys and Greys. The flames refer to the old iron and smelting industry, and the sword alludes to the alleged Roman camp at Kinver.

EAST SUFFOLK C.C.

WEST SUFFOLK C.C.

SUFFOLK

EAST SUFFOLK County Council

ARMS: Sable, a cross engrailed or; on a chief ermine two gold leopards' faces, and between them a pale azure charged with an ancient galley of gold on the sea proper, the sail set and the prow to the sinister, and issuing from the sinister chief the sun, also gold.

CREST: On a wreath gold and sable a rock proper, and thereon a gold falcon with bells, its wings spread and azure on the inside, supporting with the right claw a staff bearing a banner azure charged with a gold wheatsheaf.

MOTTO: *Opus nostrum dirige*—'Direct our work.'

These were granted in 1935.

The cross is from the arms of the Uffords, ancient Earls of Suffolk, and the leopards' faces are from the arms of the De La Pole Earls and Dukes of Suffolk. The crest is a differenced form of the badge of Charles Brandon, Duke of Suffolk. The galley represents a Viking ship in token that the County is peopled largely by descendants of the Norsemen, and the rising sun denotes its easterly situation. The motto is a contraction of the Vulgate text, *Opus manuum nostrarum dirige*.

WEST SUFFOLK County Council

Use is made of the arms of Edward the Confessor: Azure, a cross patonce between five doves, all gold.

IPSWICH

IPSWICH County Borough Council

ARMS: Parted palewise; the dexter gules with a gold lion rampant guardant, the sinister azure with the stern ends of three gold ships' hulls adjoining the party line.

CREST: On a wreath gold and gules, a gold demi-lion rampant holding a three-masted ship with sails furled proper.

SUPPORTERS: Two sea-horses proper with gold fins and manes.

The arms were confirmed, and the crest and supporters granted, in 1561. The arms appear to have been based on those of the Cinque Ports (see Chapter II).

A ship appears on the thirteenth-century seal.

ALDEBURGH Borough Council

ARMS: Azure, on water in base an ancient ship of three masts in full sail with a ladder affixed amidships, all proper, the mainsail charged with a lion rampant gules and the fore and aft sails and pennons each charged with a cross gules.

This was the device on a seal granted to the Borough in 1561. It was recorded as a coat of arms, colours being assigned, in 1951.

SUFFOLK

BECCLES Borough Council

The Borough has no arms. The seal contains a building, and in the foreground animals in a pound, with the date of the town's incorporation, 1584.

BURY ST EDMUNDS

ALDEBURGH

EYE

BURY ST EDMUNDS Borough Council

ARMS: Azure, three gold crowns each pierced by two gold crossed arrows, points downwards.

CREST: On a wreath gold and azure, a wolf sitting and holding between its forepaws the crowned head of St Edmund, all proper.

MOTTO: *Sacrarium Regis cunabula Legis*—'The shrine of the King and the cradle of the Law.'

These were granted in 1609.

The arms clearly refer to the death of St Edmund, last King of the East Angles. To this realm the medieval heralds assigned arms consisting of three gold crowns on blue (identical with the arms of Sweden, whence, perhaps, the heralds assumed the East Angles to have come). In 870 King Edmund was overthrown and captured by the Danes in a battle at Hoxne. Choosing martyrdom rather than renunciation of Christianity, he was shot to death with arrows and afterwards beheaded. When his followers recovered his body they were unable to find the head until their search was directed by the dead King's voice crying, 'Here! Here!' and the head was found guarded by a wolf (cf. Southwold).

* M

EYE Borough Council

ARMS: Azure, a gold cross flory between four gold martlets (being a variation of the arms ascribed to King Edward the Confessor) and in the chief a silver eagle with a gold crown, wings outspread, perched upon two sprays of white roses with stems and leaves proper.

CREST: Above an imperial crown a golden star charged with an eye.

MOTTO: *Oculus in coelum*—'The Eye in Heaven.'

These arms were granted in 1592.

The following is an extract from the grant:

DENIQ ex officij mei Principalis Regis Armorum praedt authoritate Scutum seu Clypeum de antiquis Armorum sci Edwardi Regis Angliae Insignibus: videlicet: In Campo caeruleo Crucem floridam auream, quatuor Meruletis auibus interpositam una cum insuperiori Aquilam albam alis distensam Rosarum ramiculis cum rosis cimillimis suffultam composui et consignaui per praesentes: Et ulterius supra Cassidem pro Crista vel Trophaeo e Corona Solis Imperiali auro gemmis q' nitente Stellam Innocentiae, Jouis oculo peruigili munitam, Clamyde q' seu Paludament cum Lacynijs ab utra q' ventillantibus, et hoc Symbolo supra scripto (Oculus in Coelum) veluti hijs verbis in Clavigatione huius Dyplomatis declaravimus, et in margine depicta magis dilucide exemplificamus.

The grant explains the significance of the crest: 'Issuing from the Crown of the Imperial Sun, shining with gold and gems, the Star of Innocence furnished with the all-seeing eye of Jehovah.' Thus the eye not only is a rebus, but has a religious significance which is exemplified by the motto. The roses and eagle were probably derived from the royal emblems of Queen Elizabeth I (see Chapter II).

LOWESTOFT Borough Council

ARMS: Silver, on a chevron sable three Lowestoft china plates proper; in the chief an antique crown gules between two Tudor roses, and in the base the sun rising from the point of the shield, gold.

CREST: On a wreath argent and sable, the figure of St Margaret, half-length, holding in her hands a pearl, all proper.

MOTTO: *Point du jour*—'Daybreak.'

These were granted in 1913.

The parish church is dedicated to St Margaret; hence the representation of the saint, who is identifiable by the pearl, *margarita*. A seal of the Corporation shows St Margaret holding a shield charged with a crown and a Tudor rose, emblems which have been preserved in the arms. The antique crown tells that Lowestoft was anciently part of a royal manor, and the plates represent an old local industry. The rising sun stands for the town's modern note as a health resort and, with the motto, indicates its easterly situation.

SOUTHWOLD Borough Council

ARMS: Sable, a gold crown pierced by two gold arrows saltirewise.

CREST: On a wreath gold and sable, the half-length figure of St Edmund, King and Martyr.

SUFFOLK

MOTTO: *They ryght defend.*

These are recorded at the College of Arms. In some representations of the arms a reversed S is placed in the base of the shield.

Southwold derived its arms from Bury St Edmunds, the manor having been held by the Abbey of Bury and the parish church being dedicated to St Edmund.

LOWESTOFT   SOUTHWOLD   SUDBURY

SUDBURY Borough Council

ARMS: Sable, a silver talbot in a sitting position; on a chief gules a lion passant guardant between two fleurs-de-lis, all gold.

CREST: On a wreath argent and sable, a gold talbot's head between two silver ostrich feathers.

These were granted in 1576.

The talbot's head in the crest is sometimes represented as red and sometimes as black.

The talbot is from the arms of the family of Sudbury or Sudberry, and is stated to have been adopted in particular reference to Simon of Sudbury, in the fourteenth century successively Bishop of London, Archbishop of Canterbury, and Chancellor of England. Simon, a native of Sudbury, was a benefactor of the town, and it was natural that the townsmen should remember him when obtaining arms; but Burke credits him with a different coat, namely: Silver, on a blue cross a gold crowned M.

The other emblems are of a royal character.

FELIXSTOWE   HADLEIGH

FELIXSTOWE Urban District Council

The Urban District Council has not obtained arms, but makes use of a shield parted chevronwise and the chief palewise; the first compartment is gold with a cross gules; for Roger Bigod, Earl of Norfolk; the second contains the arms of the See of Rochester, Silver with a saltire gules charged with a gold scallop shell; and the base is barry wavy of six pieces silver and azure, with a gold mitre. In some representations, a mural crown is placed above the shield, and a mace and sword behind it.

I am indebted to the Clerk of the Council for the following note:

In White's *Suffolk* there is the following passage: 'It is said to have been called Felixstowe from Felix the Burgundian who converted the East Anglians to Christianity and became the first Bishop of Dunwich in 630. It has been conjectured that this Saint landed and for some time resided here on his arrival in this country, but the place was no doubt a part of the parish of Walton and did not receive its present name till a Priory of Black Monks dedicated to St Felix was founded here by Roger Bigod, Earl of Norfolk, who gave it as a cell to the Priory at Rochester about A.D. 1150. He endowed it with the lands taken out of his Manor of Walton which form the Manor of Felixstowe Priory.'

HADLEIGH Urban District Council

ARMS: Azure, a chevron gold ermined sable between three silver woolpacks.

CREST: On a wreath gold and azure, a mount vert, and thereon standing a silver lamb bearing a banner azure charged with a silver woolpack, the staff gold.

These were granted in 1618, the year in which Hadleigh, then famous for the manufacture of woollen cloth, was incorporated.

Its prosperity subsequently declined to such an extent that it was deprived of its charter in 1687. The arms of the former borough are now used by the Urban District Council.

NEWMARKET

GIPPING R.D.C.

NEWMARKET Urban District Council

ARMS: Vert, a horse courant argent; on a chief gules a lion rampant guardant between two Saxon crowns all gold, in each crown two silver arrows crossed saltirewise, points downwards.

MOTTO: *Respice finem*—'Look to the end.'

These were granted in 1951.

The green field represents Newmarket Heath, and the horse is an obvious reference to the town's main interest. The lion stands for its royal associations, and the arrow-pierced crowns of St Edmund refer to East Anglia.

GIPPING Rural District Council

ARMS: Azure, strewn with silver fleurs-de-lis, a bend wavy argent between two ears of wheat with stalks and leaves gold.

CREST: On a wreath argent and azure, an ash-tree proper growing on a mount vert and hanging from the branches by a riband azure an escutcheon sable charged with a gold leopard's face.

MOTTO: *Domini est dirigere*—'It is for the Lord to direct.'

These were granted in 1951.

The blue field and fleurs-de-lis refer to St Mary the Virgin, in whose name many parishes in the area are dedicated. The wheat ears allude to the two former rural districts of Bosmere, and Claydon and East Stow, combined in the present Rural District; and the wavy bend represents the River Gipping.

The ash-tree refers to the Ashburnham family, and the leopard's face to the Wentworth and De Saumarez families, while the latter also links the arms with those of the East Suffolk C.C.

Surrey C.C.

SURREY

SURREY County Council

ARMS: Parted palewise azure and sable, a fess likewise parted ermine and gold; in chief, an ancient crown of gold and a silver sprig of oak.

These were granted in 1934.

The blue and gold tinctures are from the arms of the Warenne Earls of Surrey (blue and gold chequers), the black is from the shields of Guildford and Godalming, and the ermine is from that of Richmond (Surrey). The crown, representing that of King Edgar, stands for Kingston-on-Thames, where several Saxon kings were crowned. The oak is an emblem of Surrey's rural parts, and is also derived from the heraldry of the Fitzalan and Howard Earls of Surrey.

CROYDON County Borough Council

ARMS: Quarterly silver and gold, a cross gules composed of two vertical and two horizontal stripes interlaced; in the first quarter three Cornish choughs proper; in the second, three crosses paty, pointed at the foot sable; in the third a cross flory azure charged with three gold roundels; and in the fourth a fess embattled gules.

CREST: On a wreath argent and gules, a gold crozier lying on a mount vert, and thereon a roundel barry wavy silver and azure in front of a tilting-spear and sword saltirewise proper, between two tufts of rye-grass springing from the mount proper and tied with gold bands.

MOTTO: *Sanitate crescamus*—'May we grow in health.'

These were granted in 1886.

The Cornish choughs are from the arms of Thomas Becket, and appear on the shield of Canterbury (q.v.). These with the three crosses in the second quarter, from the pall in the arms of the Archbishopric of Canterbury, stand for the long association between Croydon and the Archbishops; the manor was presented by William the Conqueror to Lanfranc, who built the palace where his successors resided occasionally until 1750. The emblems in the third quarter are from the arms of Archbishop Whitgift, founder of the Grammar School; and the embattled fess, suggesting a town wall, is a municipal emblem.

The blue and white roundel, or fountain, stands for the springs which issue from the chalk hill whence the place gets its name (*croie dune*); and the rye-grass is that grown on the Irrigation Farm, 'of which it is well known that Croydon grows more than any other town in the Kingdom.'

BARNES

BARNES Borough Council

ARMS: Azure, a gold saltire between four white ostrich feathers, and on the saltire two crossed oars in proper colours, the blade of that to the dexter dark blue, and the blade of the other light blue.

SUPPORTERS: Two griffins gules, each with a gold flory collar, the collar of the dexter griffin charged with four crosses paty pointed at the foot sable, and the other with four lozenges sable.

MOTTO: *Not for ourselves alone.*

These were granted on the creation of the Borough in 1932.

The ostrich feathers refer to the fact that Barnes claims as a native the then Prince of Wales (now Duke of Windsor), who was born at White Lodge, Richmond Park. The oars, in the colours of Oxford and Cambridge, allude to the University Boat Race, which ends at Mortlake. The arms are unique among English civic coats in that they contain a reference to a sporting event; and from the technical point of view it is of interest that in the official blazon the blades of the oars are described as 'dark blue' and 'light blue,' English words being used because the term 'azure' cannot be made to indicate different shades of blue.

The griffins are derived from the dexter supporter of the Earls Spencer, Lords of the Manor of Mortlake, and the crosslets are from the arms of the Archbishops of Canterbury, who anciently held the manor. The lozenges are from the arms of the Bishop of Southwark, in whose diocese Barnes lies.

CROYDON   BEDDINGTON AND WALLINGTON   EPSOM AND EWELL

BEDDINGTON AND WALLINGTON Borough Council

ARMS: Argent, a fess embattled gules between three red roses each charged with a white rose, within a bordure compony or and azure, and in the centre of the shield an escutcheon azure charged with an aeroplane proper flying above a gold sun rising from the base.

CREST: On a wreath argent and gules a right arm in armour, bent at the elbow, the hand grasping a gauntlet by the fingers, all proper.

MOTTO: *Per ardua ad summa*—'Through difficulties to the heights.'

These were granted in 1937, but were in use unofficially by the former Urban District Council from 1921.

The embattled fess refers to the Roman town of Noviomagus which is believed to have been sited in that part of modern Wallington called Woodcote. The border is in the colours of the Warenne Earls of Surrey, and the Tudor roses refer to visits to Beddington by Henry VIII and Queen Elizabeth I when the Carew family was seated there.

The inescutcheon refers to the great air-port which grew out of a flying-ground established at South Beddington during the 1914–18 War. This is the first instance of the introduction of a complete aeroplane in civic heraldry.

The crest of a mailed hand holding a gauntlet ready to be cast down refers to the fact that the Manor of Wallington was formerly held by the Dymock family, whose head (as holder of the Manor of Scrivelsby, in Lincolnshire) is the Hereditary Champion of England.

EPSOM AND EWELL Borough Council

ARMS: Parted chevronwise vert and argent, in chief two gold horses' heads torn off at the neck, and in base two bars wavy azure.

MOTTO: *None Such.*

These were granted in 1937.

The following descriptive note was written by the Rev. E. E. Dorling:

The colours green and white (or silver) which have been chosen for the surface, or as it is called in heraldry 'the field,' of the coat of arms are intended to symbolize the verdure and the chalk of the Downs, which may surely be taken as typical of our countryside. In the green may also be seen a hint at this tree-embowered neighbourhood. Was it not Cobbett who said that he was not sure if Epsom should be described as a town in a wood or as a wood in a town?

It was felt . . . that the shield of the new Borough must contain some reference to the 'leading industry' of the neighbourhood. Within the bounds of the Borough is the best-known race-course of the world. On the Downs the most famous horse-race of the year is run. Epsom is the centre of a highly important training industry, and the prosperity of the town is based largely upon it and the employment that it gives to many of its inhabitants. Hence the introduction of the golden horses' heads which are placed upon the green of the field.

The blue wavy bars represent Ewell with its streams and wells, and the motto recalls the old royal palace of Nonsuch, of which the park remains as the property of the Borough.

GODALMING Borough Council

ARMS: Parted palewise gules and sable, a silver woolpack; on a chief argent a red rose with seeds and sepals proper between two escutcheons, one gules with a silver fess dancetty between two silver crosses paty, and the other gules with three pears, lying bendwise, proper.

CREST: On a wreath argent and gules, a ram standing on a mount vert and holding in its mouth a pear, all proper; suspended by a red ribbon from the ram's neck, a gold shield charged with a pair of shears, points upwards, proper.

MOTTO: *Libera deinde fidelis*—'Free, therefore faithful.'

These arms were granted in 1893.

I am indebted to the Town Clerk for the following notes:

The arms of the Borough of Godalming have the woolpack in the centre of the field to indicate the subsistence of the Town upon the woollen industry for several hundreds of years.

The rose indicates the fact that the first Borough Charter was granted in the days of the Tudor sovereigns, viz. in the seventeenth year of Queen Elizabeth I.

The shield on the dexter chief indicates the connection of the Manor of Godalming with its first Lord after the same passed out of royal hands, i.e. Sir George More, to whom it was granted in 1601. The shield on the sinister chief indicates the connection of the Borough with its first Warden, named Perrier, 1574.

The crest also refers to Perrier and the woollen industry.

GODALMING

GUILDFORD

GUILDFORD Borough Council

ARMS: Sable, on a mount vert a silver castle, the two outer towers with spires and the middle tower with three turrets; on the middle tower a shield, quarterly France and England, and below the battlements two gold roses; in the portway a gold portcullis and a gold key, and on the mount in front of the castle a gold lion couchant guardant; the castle placed between two silver woolpacks, and at the base of the shield water.

The above is a description of the arms as they are used, and tallies with the device on the seal on which they are based, but a record in the College of Arms tinctures the castle gold, omits the roses and the shield bearing the Royal Arms, and makes the lion passant guardant.

The ruins of the Norman Castle at Guildford stand in a public park. The woolpacks represent what was anciently the town's staple trade.

KINGSTON-UPON-THAMES Borough Council

ARMS: Azure, three salmon swimming barwise argent with fins and tails gules.

These are on record at the College of Arms. Kingston was the coronation place of several Saxon kings, and is a Royal Borough. Its fisheries were of importance at an early date.

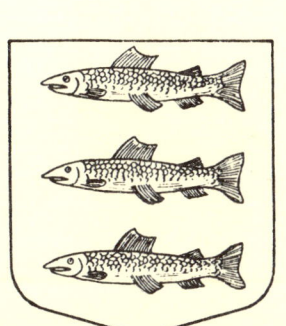

KINGSTON-UPON-THAMES   MALDEN AND COOMBE   MITCHAM

MALDEN AND COOMBE Borough Council

ARMS: Ermine, a chevron vert between two chevronels parted palewise, the upper one azure and gules and the lower one gules and azure; and on the chevron a gold cross formy.

CREST: On a wreath argent and vert, a chaplet of bay proper banded with gold, and rising therefrom a demi-stag proper with a gold ducal coronet about its neck, holding between the forefeet a roundel barry wavy argent and azure.

MOTTO: *Ducit amor oppidi*—'The love of our town leads us.'

These were granted in 1936 on the incorporation of the Borough.

The green chevron charged with a cross refers to the name Malden—*Maeldune*, 'the hill of the cross.' The blue and red chevrons are from the arms of Merton College, Oxford, which still owns in Malden the estates conferred in the thirteenth century by Walter de Merton on his house of scholars. The ermine field denotes Coombe's long-standing connection with the Crown. The green in the arms, torse, and mantling refers to the abundance of open spaces and sports grounds in the area. Among these is part of Richmond Park, whence the stag, while the heraldic fountain which it holds indicates the brooks and streams whence Cardinal Wolsey obtained water for Hampton Court.

The bay-wreath, a symbol of honour in ancient Rome, was included in token of Malden's note in Romano-British times, and the coronet refers to the Duke of Cambridge, formerly the chief landowner in Coombe.

MITCHAM Borough Council

ARMS: Or, a pale vert between two sprigs of lavender each with three stalks in flower proper; and on the pale a fess wavy argent charged with a bar wavy azure, between in chief two keys crossed saltirewise and surmounted by a sword erect point downwards, all gold, and in base a silver tower.

CREST: On a wreath gold and vert, three stalks of lavender in flower proper encircled by a gold mural crown.

These were granted in 1934 when Mitcham became a borough.

The green pale refers to Mitcham Green, and the wavy fess to Witford or Waterford, as the upper part of the town was formerly called; while the name Mitcham, or Mitchelham, 'the great dwelling,' is represented by the tower. The keys and sword are those of St Peter and St Paul, the Borough's Patron Saints, and the lavender is a product for which the district has long been famous.

REIGATE

REIGATE Borough Council

ARMS: Checky azure and gold; a chief wavy sable and thereon two crosses potent quadrate gules edged with silver, and between them on a mount an embattled gateway, with portcullis raised, in front of an oak-tree, all argent, and hanging from the tree above the gateway an escutcheon checky azure and gold.

CREST: On a wreath gold and azure, a silver demi-lion with a mural crown gules about its neck, supporting with the paws a cross-crosslet pointed at the foot also gules.

SUPPORTERS: Two pilgrims each holding a staff and having scallop shells in his hat, all proper.

MOTTO: *Never wonne ne never shall.*

These were granted in 1951.

The Corporation formerly used a device consisting of a castle gateway in front of an oak-tree from which hung the chequered shield of the Warenne Earls of Surrey. This device now forms a charge in the arms, while the Warenne chequers are the ground of the shield.

The black of the chief links the arms with those of Surrey C.C., and also Guildford, the former county town, while the wavy line represents the outline of the Surrey hills. The crosses potent and quadrate are from the arms of the priory of Austin Canons founded at Reigate by William de Warenne in the thirteenth century. The crest consists of emblems from the heraldry of Howard, with particular reference to William, Lord Howard of Effingham, who obtained from the Crown a grant of Reigate Priory in 1541.

The supporters represent Reigate's historic importance as a town on the ancient Pilgrims' Way.

RICHMOND Borough Council

ARMS: Parted fesswise gules and azure, on a fess ermine a representation of the ancient palace of Richmond proper, between two red roses; in the chief a gold lion of England between two gold portcullises, and in the base a white swan on water proper.

CREST: On a wreath argent and gules, a mount and standing thereon a stag, looking backwards, proper, holding in its mouth a spray of two roses, one white and the other red, and supporting a gold escutcheon charged with a garland of oak vert.

MOTTO: *A Deo et Rege*—'From God and the King.'

These were granted in 1891.

The roses, portcullises, and lion allude to Richmond's royal associations, and in particular to Henry VII, from whose Earldom of Richmond, in Yorkshire, the Surrey town (formerly Sheen) derived its name in 1500. The stag denotes the Old Deer Park and Richmond Park, and the swan stands for the River Thames.

RICHMOND

SURBITON

SURBITON Borough Council

ARMS: Azure, an elm-tree proper in front of a gold sun, both rising from the base of the shield.

CREST: On a wreath gold and azure, a bridge of one arch and thereon a winged lion couchant resting its right forepaw on a closed book, all or.

SUPPORTERS: Two stags, each resting the further hind foot on a charred tree-stock, all proper.

MOTTO: *Consilio et animis*—'By wisdom and courage.'

The former Urban District Council used as a device the lion of St Mark, which has been retained in the crest granted to the Borough. The bridge on which it rests symbolizes the railway, to which Surbiton owes its development, and with the elm-tree in the arms alludes to the Elmbridge Hundred in which the place lay. The rising sun refers to the newly formed Borough, and the stags are from the arms of Messrs Coutts, the bankers, benefactors of the town.

SUTTON AND CHEAM Borough Council

ARMS: Azure, a pale argent between two roundels, that to the dexter gold charged with a key azure, and that to the sinister silver with a key gules, the wards of the keys being upwards and turned outwards; and on the pale four crosses formy, the lower limbs pointed sable.

CREST: On a wreath argent and azure, a popinjay proper with a collar gules, holding in the right claw a cross formy, the lower limb pointed sable.

MOTTO: *Serve God and be cheerful.*

These were granted in 1934 when Sutton and Cheam became a borough.

The crosses are from the arms of the See of Canterbury, 'Cheyham' having been given to Christchurch, Canterbury, in 1018. The keys (for St Peter) are from the arms of the Benedictine Abbey of Chertsey to which 'Sudton' belonged from the time of the Domesday Survey until 1583. The popinjay represents the Lumley family, anciently Lords of the Manor of Cheam. The motto is that of Bishop Hacket, who was Rector of Cheam, 1624–62.

SUTTON AND CHEAM

WIMBLEDON

WIMBLEDON Borough Council

ARMS: Silver, a two-headed eagle sable with beaks and legs gules and tongues azure, charged on the right wing with a golden rose and on the left with a golden fret, all within a border company of gold and azure.

CREST: In a gold mural crown a gold wheatsheaf supported by two Cornish choughs proper.

MOTTO: *Sine labe decus*—'Honour without stain.'

These were granted in 1906.

The eagle represents Julius Caesar, whose somewhat doubtful connection with Wimbledon is locally indicated by the camp and well which bear his name. The golden rose is an old royal badge, and the fret is from the arms of the family of Spencer; these emblems stand for Lords of the Manor, anciently the Crown and now Earl Spencer. The border represents the De Warennes, Earls of Surrey (see Chapter III). Former holders of the manor are commemorated by the crest, the wheatsheaf standing for the Cecil family, and the choughs for Thomas Cromwell, Earl of Essex. Cromwell derived these

CIVIC HERALDRY

birds from the arms of Cardinal Wolsey (see Esher U.D.C.) who in his turn took them from the arms of Thomas Becket (see Canterbury). It is curious that Thomas Cromwell should have borne emblems from Becket's arms in view of the fact that it was he who despoiled Becket's tomb at Canterbury.

BANSTEAD Urban District Council

The device consists of a woolpack.

CARSHALTON

EGHAM

CARSHALTON Urban District Council

ARMS: Or, a chevron gules between in chief two lions rampant facing one another gules and in base a greyhound passant sable; and on the chevron a roundel barry wavy argent and azure between two silver sprigs of oak with acorns.

CREST: On a wreath gold and gules, a swan rousant, in its beak a sprig of beech, all proper, issuing from a gold mural crown, and in front of the crown a Tudor rose proper.

MOTTO: *Animo et fide*—'By courage and faith.'

These were granted in 1952.

The basic colours, gold and red, are from the arms of the Mandevilles, who held the Manor of Carshalton after the Conquest. Other families of importance in the history of the town are also represented—the Bohuns by the swan (which also stands for the rivers and springs), the Gainsfords and Scawens by the chevron, and the families of Burghersh, Hardwick, and Fellowes by the lions. The greyhound, from the Gainsford arms, is also the name and sign of an ancient inn.

SURREY

The blue and white roundel, or heraldic fountain, refers to the many springs and pools which are a feature of the town. The oak and beech sprigs (the latter alluding to the Carshalton beeches) stand for other natural amenities. The oak has further significance: it is from the arms of Surrey C.C., and it also refers to 'The Oaks' estate, now the property of the Carshalton Council and formerly of the Earls of Derby. From this estate came the name of 'The Oaks Stakes,' instituted in 1779. The Tudor rose was used as a device by the Council before arms were obtained.

DORKING Urban District Council

The device consists of a cock.

EGHAM Urban District Council

ARMS: Vert, a representation of Magna Carta with the Great Seal of King John pendent therefrom, and in chief King John's crown, all proper.

CREST: On a wreath gold and vert, water barry wavy argent and azure and thereon a swan swimming in front of a weeping willow tree, all proper.

MOTTO: *Ut homines liberi sint*—'That men may be free.'

These were granted in 1951.

The arms commemorate the sealing of Magna Carta at Runnymede on 15th June 1215, to which the motto also refers. The crest indicates Egham's present-day amenities.

ESHER Urban District Council

The Council, having no arms of its own, uses those of Cardinal Wolsey, who for some time after his fall lived in the mansion whose remains bear the name 'Wolsey's Tower.' The arms are: Sable, a silver cross engrailed, and thereon a lion passant gules and four leopards' faces azure; and a gold chief charged with a red rose between two choughs proper.

FARNHAM Urban District Council

ARMS: Vert, a gold castle with three towers; on a chief argent a mitre vert garnished with gold between a sprig of oak and a sprig of hops both vert.

CREST: On a wreath gold and vert, a stag's head full-face proper issuing from six gold ears of wheat laid fesswise, three each way, and in front of it a stone-headed axe proper and a gold pastoral staff crossed saltirewise.

MOTTO: *By worth.*

These were granted in 1950.

The castle represents the stronghold built at Farnham in the twelfth century by Henry de Blois, Bishop of Winchester, and the mitre and pastoral staff allude to the town's long associations with the Sees of Winchester and Guildford. The green field, the stag's head, and the oak refer to the parks and woodlands of the district, while the ears of wheat stand for agriculture, and the sprig of hops for produce for which Farnham was formerly famous. The stone axe alludes to the prehistoric antiquities of the district.

FARNHAM ESHER LEATHERHEAD

LEATHERHEAD Urban District Council

ARMS: Parted saltirewise vert and barry wavy of six pieces argent and azure, in chief a flame proper encircled by a gold chain of square links, and in base a gold stag's face with an open book proper with gold binding and clasps between the antlers.

CREST: On a wreath argent and vert, a chaplet of oak leaves proper, and rising therefrom a rousing swan argent charged on the left wing with a sword gules, point upwards.

MOTTO: *Service links all.*

These were granted in 1946, provision for the grant being made by the Civil Defence Services of the area, in tribute to those who died in the war and as a permanent memorial to the comradeship formed during the years 1939–45.

The sections of the shield represent the four wards joined to form a single unit. The green pieces stand for parks, recreation ground, and agricultural land. These converge on silver and blue wavy bars, representing the River Mole, and indicate the river crossing (now by bridge) which has existed from very early times and gave rise to the name of Leatherhead, 'the public riding ford.' The book stands for the schools in the district, and the stag's head refers to the ancient deer parks.

The chain containing a flame represents the Civil Defence Services, and the unity and strength which their comradeship brought to the District. To this the motto also refers.

The swan alludes both to the rivers and to the old Swan Inn, famous in coaching days. The oak in which it nests is from the arms of the Surrey C.C. The sword, from the arms of the City of London, stands for the City Freemen's School at Ashtead, and is also a reference to the war services which the arms commemorate.

SURREY

MERTON AND MORDEN   WALTON AND WEYBRIDGE   WOKING

MERTON AND MORDEN Urban District Council

ARMS: Sable, a fret or; on a gold chief two lions passant facing one another sable.

MOTTO: *In libertate vis*—'Strength in freedom.'

These were granted in 1943.

The fret is from the arms of Merton Priory, founded in 1114 and granted a charter by King Henry I in 1121. The lions are from the arms of the Garth family, Lords of the Manor and local benefactors. The motto was adopted with reference to the struggle for freedom in which the nation and its allies were engaged when the arms were granted.

WALTON AND WEYBRIDGE Urban District Council

ARMS: Or, a fess wavy azure and thereon two bars wavy argent surmounted by two gold pales; in chief two red roses each charged with a white rose, their seeds and sepals proper, and in base an eagle displayed gules.

CREST: On a wreath gold and azure, a swan's head torn off at the neck, in the beak a sprig of oak with two acorns, all proper, and about the neck a gold Saxon crown.

MOTTO: *Dum defluat amnis*—'Till the river ceases to flow' (from Horace, *Epistulae*).

These were granted in 1946.

The livery colours, blue and gold, are the colours of the Surrey C.C., derived from the gold and blue checkers of the Warenne Earls of Surrey, and were also those of the Mortimers of Walton Leigh, from whom descended Edward IV, who owned this manor.

The fess represents the Thames and its tributaries, the Mole and the Wey, and the pales on it stand for two ancient bridges and the two successive Walton bridges of modern times.

The Tudor roses allude to Oatlands Palace, a residence of Henry VIII, and Ashley Park, built by Cardinal Wolsey. They also symbolize the joining of the Manors of Walton, Walton Leigh, and Ebso, or Abbs Court, at the time of the union of York and Lancaster under Henry VII.

The eagle refers to the district's Roman associations, notably the story of Caesar's attempted crossing of the river at Cowey Stakes.

The swan's head not only alludes to the Thames, but also stands for the Bohuns who held the Manor of Walton until 1373. The crown and oak sprig are from the arms of Surrey C.C., and the oak also refers to the Howard family, and in particular Lord Howard of Effingham, Chief Ranger of the Forest in Queen Elizabeth I's reign, and Catherine Howard, who married Henry VIII at Oatlands Palace.

WOKING Urban District Council

ARMS: Quarterly gold and gules, a cross flory between in the first and fourth quarters a fleur-de-lis and in the second and third a fret, all counter-changed.

MOTTO: *Fide et Diligentia*—'By Faith and Diligence.'

These arms were granted in 1930.

The cross is that of Edward the Confessor, the fleurs-de-lis are from the arms of the Beauforts and the frets from those of the Despenser family. The colours, gold and red, are those of the Bassets.

SUSSEX

To the ancient Kingdom of the South Saxons, the medieval heralds assigned arms consisting of six gold martlets on blue. The martlet is an heraldic generalization for various kinds of birds, and in this case it probably represents the swallow, *l'hirondelle* having been suggested by the name of Arundel, the Honour which formed a large part of Sussex (see Arundel). The martlets are used by both County Councils, and also occur in the arms of some other authorities in the County.

EAST SUSSEX C.C.

WEST SUSSEX C.C.

EAST SUSSEX County Council

ARMS: Gules, six martlets and in chief a Saxon crown, all gold.

These arms were granted in 1937.

WEST SUSSEX County Council

ARMS: Azure, six martlets and a chief, all gold.

These were granted in 1889.

BRIGHTON County Borough Council

ARMS: Silver, two dolphins swimming one above the other sable, within a border azure charged with six gold martlets.

CREST: On a wreath argent and sable, two dolphins sable, head downwards, their tails crossed, between two branches of red coral.

MOTTO: *In Deo fidemus*—'We trust in God.'

These were granted in 1897.

The dolphins are appropriate to a town which has always depended upon the sea for its prosperity, originally as a fishing village and now as a famous health and pleasure resort. The martlets are from the arms of Sussex.

BRIGHTON   EASTBOURNE   HASTINGS

EASTBOURNE County Borough Council

ARMS: Silver, on a fess with double cotises gules, a golden rose between two silver stags' faces and antlers.

CREST: On a wreath argent and gules, a sea-horse with the right foot raised vert.

MOTTO: *Meliora sequimur*—'We follow better things.'

These were granted in 1928; a similar device was used before authorized arms were obtained.

The double-cotised fess is from the arms of the baronial family of Badlesmere which anciently held the manor. The stags' heads are from the arms of Cavendish, Duke of Devonshire, and the rose represents the family of Gilbert.

HASTINGS County Borough Council

ARMS: Parted palewise gules and azure, a gold lion passant guardant between two similar lions halved and joined with the stern ends of two silver ships.

These arms are on record at the Heralds' College. They are a variation of those of the Cinque Ports (see Chapter II), the one complete lion being said to indicate the status of Hastings as the chief port of the group.

ARUNDEL Borough Council

ARMS: Gold, three martlets sable, on a chief embattled gules a gold lion rampant between two silver cross-crosslets pointed at the foot.

CREST: On a wreath gold and sable, a fleur-de-lis or, and thereon a swallow proper rising to the sinister.

SUSSEX

MOTTO: *Antiqua constans virtute*—'Steadfast in ancient virtue.'

These were granted in 1939.

The martlets are from the arms of the East Sussex C.C. The embattled chief represents Arundel Castle, and the lion (of Fitzalan) and crosslets (of Howard) are from the heraldry of the Duke of Norfolk. The swallow (*hirondelle*)—an allusion to the place-name—has been the device of Arundel from time immemorial.

ARUNDEL

BEXHILL

CHICHESTER

BEXHILL Borough Council

ARMS: Ermine, a cross consisting of two vertical and two horizontal limbs interlaced gules, in the first quarter a gold mitre, in the second a gold demi-lion joined to the stern end of a ship's hull, in the third a star sable, and in the fourth a mallard proper; on a silver chief the sun (only half visible) shining on the sea proper; all within a border azure charged with eight gold martlets.

CREST: On a wreath argent and gules, a mound of sand, and thereon a Martello tower proper.

MOTTO: *Sol et salubritas*—'Sun and health.'

These were granted in 1907.

The mitre denotes the Bishops of Chichester, to whom the manor belonged from the time of the Conquest until the reign of Henry VIII, when it passed to Lord Buckhurst, ancestor of its present holder, Earl De La Warr, who is denoted by the star, derived from his crest. The lion joined to a ship's hull is from the arms of the Cinque Ports (see

Chapter II). The mallard is from the arms of the first Earl Brassey, Mayor of the Borough in 1907-8. The sun and sea stand for Bexhill's character as a health resort, and the border tells the county in which it lies (see Sussex). The crest is one of the towers built along this coast in preparation for Napoleon's anticipated invasion.

CHICHESTER City Council

ARMS: Silver, sprinkled with drops sable; on a chief indented gules a gold lion passant guardant.

These are recorded at the Heralds' College.

HOVE

LEWES

HOVE Borough Council

ARMS: Parted chevronwise, and the chief parted palewise gold and gules; on the gold a silver saltire edged with azure; on the gules two pairs of gold leg-irons interlaced, one chevronwise and the other reversed; the base chequered azure and or with three gold martlets; all within a border ermine charged with six gold martlets.

CREST: On a wreath gold and gules, a mound of shingle, and thereon an ancient ship proper, with a sail azure strewn with gold cross-crosslets, and a banner gules charged with a gold martlet.

SUSSEX

Motto: *Floreat Hova.*

These were granted in 1899.

The saltire is that of St Andrew, to whom the old parish church is dedicated, and the leg-irons are the emblem of St Leonard, patron of the parish church of Aldrington. The chequers are from the arms of the De Warennes, and here represent the Rape of Lewes (see Lewes); and the birds thereon are from the device used by the town before it obtained arms. The border charged with martlets represents Sussex and is comparable with the borders to the shields of Brighton and Bexhill.

The ship, which is ashore on a shingle beach, represents a sixteenth-century French galley, and commemorates French attacks on the coasts of Hove and Brighthelmston.

LEWES Borough Council

Arms: Checky gold and azure, on the sinister side a canton gules charged with a lion rampant among cross-crosslets argent.

These are recorded at the Heralds' College. They appear on a fifteenth-century seal, in which the canton occupies a quarter of the shield.

The chequers were derived from the gold and blue chequers which formed the arms of the Warennes, Earls of Surrey, who held the barony of Lewes. The arms in the canton are those of the De La Warre family, but Mr Gale Pedrick, in *Borough Seals*, puts forward the theory that the lion was that of the Mowbrays, the crosses being added in allusion to the local priory of St Pancras.

RYE Borough Council

Use is made of the arms of the Cinque Ports (see Chapter II).

WORTHING Borough Council

Arms: Barry wavy of six pieces azure and silver with three fishes proper on the azure pieces; on a gold wavy chief a cornucopia proper.

Crest: On a wreath argent and azure, the figure of a woman in a silver and blue robe grasping in both hands a snake proper.

Motto: *Ex terra copiam e mari salutem.*

These were granted in 1919, but were used without authority before that date.

The motto, 'From the land fullness and from the sea health,' explains the emblems. The figure forming the crest is probably Hygieia, though it is not so described in the grant.

BOGNOR REGIS Urban District Council

Arms: Azure, on a gold pile a Saxon crown gules, and on a gold invected chief three martlets azure.

Crest: On a wreath gold and azure, a pair of gull's wings spread azure, and between them a Saxon crown gules.

Motto: *Action.*

These were granted in 1935.

WORTHING BOGNOR REGIS HORSHAM

The blue field and the gull's wings represent the sea, and the invected chief the sea wall, while the gold pile depicts the sands. The martlets refer to the old kingdom and present county of Sussex, and the crowns commemorate both the ancient kingdom and the sojourn at Bognor of King George V during his recovery from a grave illness in 1929, when the place earned the suffix 'Regis.'

Before arms were officially obtained, the Urban District Council used a device including the arms of Sir Richard Hotham, who in the eighteenth century attempted to popularize Bognor by the name 'Hothampton.'

EAST GRINSTEAD Urban District Council

The Council uses the device which appeared on a seal presented to the old Corporation in 1572 by Thomas Cure, Member of Parliament for the Borough. This consists of five ostrich feathers, their pens surmounted by a scroll. The feathers are placed between the letters D and L, for Duchy of Lancaster, and on the scroll are the letters TC—the initials of the donor of the seal. Colours are assigned to the device, the feathers being blue with gold quills.

HORSHAM Urban District Council

ARMS: Azure, a silver lion rampant resting its right hind foot on a gold letter H.

CREST: Rising from a gold mural crown a silver demi-lion between two lilies with stalks and leaves proper placed sinister bendwise.

MOTTO: *Proudly we serve.*

These were granted in 1944, but the arms were in use long before that date, being attributed to the town of Horsham in Burke's *General Armory*, 1844.

The lion apparently refers to the families of De Braose and Mowbray, which successively held the manor, and the lilies of St Mary allude to the dedication of the parish church.

LITTLEHAMPTON

SHOREHAM-BY-SEA

LITTLEHAMPTON *Urban District Council*

ARMS: Parted chevronwise engrailed azure and argent, in chief a martlet flying between two cross-crosslets pointed at the foot, all silver, and in base an ancient galley sable on water barry wavy azure and argent.

MOTTO: *Progress.*

These were granted in 1935.

The martlet is the emblem of Sussex, and the crosslets are from the arms of the Duke of Norfolk. The ship represents the port of Littlehampton.

SEAFORD *Urban District Council*

The seal bears an ancient ship.

SHOREHAM-BY-SEA *Urban District Council*

The seal bears a shield containing a lion rampant towards the sinister among cross-crosslets. This is a variation of the arms of the family De Braose, which anciently held the Manor. They bore: Silver, a blue lion rampant among black cross-crosslets. The lion faces the sinister in the arms of the High Constable of Shoreham, in which the above coat impales the three lions of England.

CHICHESTER *Rural District Council*

ARMS: Azure, a fess wavy argent between six gold martlets within a silver bordure sprinkled with drops gules.

CREST: On a wreath argent and azure, a seal proper resting the right fore-flipper on a gold mitre.

MOTTO: *Adhuc hic hesterna*—'The things of yesterday are still with us.'

These were granted in 1948.

CHICHESTER R.D.C.

UCKFIELD R.D.C.

The wavy fess represents the River Arun and the Chichester and Arundel Canal, flowing between the Sussex martlets. The drops on the border are from the arms of the City of Chichester. The seal stands for Selsey (seal's island), and the mitre recalls that this was the first stronghold of Christianity in this part of England, before St Wilfrid's bishopric was transferred to Chichester. The mitre also refers to the priory of Boxgrove.

The motto, recalling the antiquities of the district, contains the name 'Chichester.'

UCKFIELD Rural District Council

ARMS: Silver, an oak-tree growing from a field in the base all proper, and on either side of the trunk a martlet facing inwards azure, all within a border compony azure and argent.

CREST: On a wreath argent and azure, a hog rampant sable against a flaming beacon proper.

MOTTO: *Like as the oak.*

These were granted in 1948.

The oak stands for Ashdown Forest, and, with the field in which it grows, plays on the name of the District. The martlets are emblems of Sussex, and the border, compony of the Lancastrian colours, alludes to the fact that the Forest once belonged to John of Gaunt, and was known as Lancaster Great Park. The crest represents Crowborough Beacon, the highest point of the District, where the Council Offices are situated, and the hog is the rebus of Ralph Hogge, the Buxted ironmaster who cast the first iron cannon made in England. The motto is from the poem on Pepys by Rudyard Kipling, once a resident at Crowborough.

Crawley Development Corporation

CRAWLEY Development Corporation

ARMS: Gold, a fess gules between three crows sable; on the fess three silver chevrons interlaced; all within a bordure azure charged with sixteen gold martlets.

CREST: On a wreath gold and gules, a right hand holding a trowel erect proper within a circlet of palisades or.

SUPPORTERS: Dexter, a stage coachman, and sinister, a woodman, both proper.

MOTTO: *By design and endeavour.*

These were granted in 1951.

The crows allude to Crawley, the interlaced chevrons to Three Bridges, and the surrounding martlets to the County of Sussex. The palisade represents the designated area of the new town, and the trowel indicates building. The dexter supporter refers to the coaching days, when Crawley was a stopping place on the Brighton road; and the other supporter alludes to the wooded areas of the district.

Warwickshire C.C.

WARWICKSHIRE

WARWICKSHIRE County Council

ARMS: Gules, a silver bear with a red muzzle and gold collar and chain, standing and supporting a ragged staff of silver; on a gold chief three cross-crosslets gules.

The shield is ensigned by a gold mural crown.

MOTTO: *Non sanz droict*—'Not without right.'

These arms were granted in 1931.

The bear and ragged staff have long been associated with Warwickshire. Legend attributes the badge of a ragged staff to one Gwayr, a British Earl of Warwick, and a bear to one of his successors, Arthgallus, a knight of King Arthur's Round Table. This claim to the antiquity of the emblems cannot be supported, but there is no doubt that as separate badges they were used by the Beauchamps, Earls of Warwick (1268-1449). They seem to have been first united by Richard Neville, Earl of Warwick, the 'Kingmaker' (who married the heiress of the Beauchamps), whose famous device was described by Shakespeare as 'the rampant bear chained to the ragged staff.' The cross-crosslets were derived from the Beauchamp arms, red with a gold fess between six gold cross-crosslets. The motto adopted by the County is that of its famous son, William Shakespeare.

The bear and ragged staff have been used by subsequent holders of the Earldom of Warwick, the Dudleys and Grevilles, and are borne as a crest by the present Earl.

A report prepared by a committee of the County Council when the question of the arms was under discussion dealt exhaustively with the origin of the bear and ragged staff, and pointed out that the device had by common consent come to be the recognized badge of the County:

On the establishment of the Militia and Yeomanry (presumably after the passing of the

WARWICKSHIRE

Militia Act of 1786, 26 Geo III, c. 107) a badge was naturally wanted for the County Forces; there can be no doubt that as the bear and staff was in the minds of the public the proper device for the purpose, it was adopted, and there is no evidence that anyone opposed it. This badge, however, was given up by the Warwickshire Militia when they became the 5th and 6th Battalions of the 6th Regiment of the Line whose regimental badge was the Antelope, which had been granted to them in 1751.

Again, the County Justices of the Warwick Petty Sessional Division use the device as their Court Seal, a Brewery Company in the County has it as their Trade Mark, the Bear and Baculus Inn, Warwick, displays it on a prominent signboard, and china shops sell little ornaments with the device depicted upon them.

'Baculus' in the inn name quoted above, is Latin for a staff. There is a tendency to corrupt the name into 'Bear and Bacchus.'

BIRMINGHAM

COVENTRY

BIRMINGHAM City and County Borough Council

ARMS: Quarterly, the first and fourth quarters azure with five gold lozenges joined bendwise, the second and third parted palewise indented gold and gules; over all a fess ermine charged with a gold mural crown.

CREST: On a wreath gold and azure, a gold mural crown and therein a right arm, bent at the elbow, the hand grasping a hammer, all proper.

SUPPORTERS: Dexter, Industry, represented by a smith with hammer and anvil, proper; and sinister, Art, a woman in a white robe with a wreath of laurel about her temples, a red-bound book in her right hand, and a gold palette and brushes in her left hand.

MOTTO: *Forward.*

These were granted in 1889.

The arms in the quarters of the shield are two distinct coats used by the family De Bermingham who held the manor in the thirteenth century (and perhaps from the time of the Conquest) until 1527, when Edward de Bermingham was deprived of his property by John Dudley, Duke of Northumberland, by means of a false charge of riot. The bendwise lozenges appear on the shield of an effigy in St Martin's Church, believed to be William de Bermingham (*temp.* Edward I). Later members of the family seem to have quartered the two coats in one shield, but with the palewise indented coat in the first and fourth quarters. The order of the coats has been reversed by the City to difference the arms from those borne by the family; the fess has been added for further difference, and also as a note of the Calthorpes, Lords of the Manor of Edgbaston, whose arms are: Gold and blue chequers, an ermine fess.

COVENTRY City and County Borough Council

ARMS: Parted palewise gules and vert, an elephant with a castle of three domed towers on its back, all gold.

CREST: On a wreath gold and gules, a cat statant guardant proper.

MOTTO: *Camera Principis.*

These are recorded at the Heralds' College.

The following notes have been supplied by Mr W. H. Grant of Coventry:

The right to use Arms was conferred by Edward III, probably at the time of the incorporation of the City in 1345, but a corporate seal was in use prior to this date. The seal, circular in form, also showed the elephant and castle and probably had its origin as a mark for woollens, tammies, and caps exported to the East, for which, prior to this period, Coventry was famous.

The elephant as a symbol signifies strength and sagacity, while the castle signifies strength and security; but the castle has doubtless been derived from the Indian howdah.

The cat, which is sometimes described as a cat-o'-mountain, signifies watchfulness.

The motto, 'Camera Principis,' may be interpreted as Chamber (or Court) of the Prince, and probably has reference to the early part of the fourteenth century when Edward, the Black Prince, as Lord of the Manor of Cheylesmore, was closely associated with the City. It is from this Prince that the three feathers are derived which are sometimes shown in conjunction with the civic arms.

On the early seals the three feathers are shown on a banner in the centre of the tower on the elephant's back. This was allowed by the heralds at the time of their visitation in 1682, but while strictly speaking they form no part of the civic arms the right of the City to their use is undisputed and they are always shown as part of the civic symbols used by the Mayor.

LEAMINGTON Borough Council

ARMS: Parted fesswise silver and gold, a lion rampant with two tails vert, surmounted by a chevron vaire; in chief three stars gules; a border azure charged with eight gold fleurs-de-lis.

CREST: On a wreath argent and vert, between two sprays of forget-me-nots proper, a silver ragged staff, and a gold rod entwined by a serpent, set saltirewise.

MOTTO: *Sola bona quae honesta*—'Only those things that are honourable are good.'

These were granted in 1876.

NUNEATON

LEAMINGTON

RUGBY

The emblems in the shield are all derived from the arms of former Lords of the Manor. The green double-tailed lion on gold represents Dudley, Earl of Warwick; the vaire chevron stands for the Fisher family; the red stars for Willes; and the fleurs-de-lis for De Clinton. The crest combines the ragged staff of the Earls of Warwick (see Warwickshire) with the Rod of Aesculapius denoting the health-giving qualities of Royal Leamington Spa.

NUNEATON Borough Council

ARMS: Parted chevronwise, the chief silver with two lozenges sable, and the base barry wavy of six pieces azure and argent; on a chief gules a cinquefoil ermine between two gold fleurs-de-lis.

CREST: On a wreath argent and azure two lozenges sable and between them a black bear's paw, torn off, holding by the stalk a cinquefoil ermine and enfiled by a gold mural crown.

MOTTO: *Prêt d'accomplir*—'Ready to achieve.'

These were granted in 1932.

The silver and blue wavy bars, representing water, allude to the ancient name of the town, 'Eaton,' the town by the water. The black lozenges represent the coal industry. The ermine cinquefoil is from the arms of Robert de Beaumont, Earl of Leicester (cf.

Leicester and Leicestershire C.C.), who in the reign of King Stephen endowed the Priory of Nuns whence the town derived the first syllable of its name. The Priory was dedicated to the Virgin Mary, to whom the fleurs-de-lis allude. The motto not only befits a progressive town, but has an historical significance, being that of the family of Aston, formerly owners of much land in the Borough.

RUGBY Borough Council

ARMS: Parted chevronwise engrailed, azure and or, in chief a gold roundel charged with a red rose, between two gold griffins' heads torn off at the neck, and in base a black bear standing and supporting a ragged staff gules.

CREST: On a wreath gold and azure a gold thunderbolt, with flames proper, between two gold lion's forepaws, torn off, each grasping a branch of dates proper.

MOTTO: *Floreat Rugbeia.*

These were granted in 1932.

They are largely based upon the arms used by Rugby School, being those granted to its founder, Lawrence Sheriff, in 1559, namely: Azure, a gold engrailed fess between three gold griffins' heads, torn off at the neck, and on the fess a fleur-de-lis azure between two roses gules. Crest: A gold lion's paw, torn off, holding a branch of dates, the fruit gold, pods silver, stalks and leaves vert. The fleur-de-lis and roses were granted to Sheriff as a servant of Queen Elizabeth I.

The Borough arms also incorporate the bear and ragged staff (see Warwickshire C.C.). The thunderbolt, in modern heraldry the symbol of electricity, stands for the great firms of the electrical industry which are centred in Rugby, and may also be taken as a reminder of the Government wireless station.

STRATFORD-UPON-AVON Borough Council

ARMS: Gold, a chevron azure between three leopards' faces proper.

These are recorded at the Heralds' College, but without colours. As a result there has been some doubt as to the proper tinctures, but those given above have now been generally adopted. Another version made the field silver and the chevron red. The leopards' faces were probably derived from the Royal Arms (see Chapter II).

SUTTON COLDFIELD Borough Council

ARMS: Silver, on a cross sable a stag's head cut off at the neck between four doves, all silver, and in the first quarter a mitre proper; a chief vert, and thereon two gold running stags.

CREST: Issuing from a gold mural crown, a demi-stag proper holding between its forelegs two gold crossed keys, wards upwards and outwards, and a sword erect, banded with a red ribbon, all proper.

SUPPORTERS: Dexter, a gold greyhound with a red mural crown about its neck, and sinister a dragon gules with a gold mural crown about its neck; pendent from each crown by a gold chain, a silver escutcheon charged with a red rose.

These were granted in 1935.

Stratford-upon-Avon

Sutton Coldfield

The arms are based on those of Bishop Vesey, a benefactor of the town. The shield contains his mitre, and the keys and sword (for St Peter and St Paul) are from the heraldry of the See of Exeter. The stags refer to Sutton Park.

The supporters are those of the Tudors, duly differenced, in allusion to the town's charter from Henry VIII. Sutton Coldfield is entitled to the designation, 'Royal Town.'

WARWICK Borough Council

The fourteenth-century seal of the Corporation bears a castle with three towers and between them, rising from the battlements, two spires, each surmounted by a cross; on one side of the castle is the sun between two stars, and on the other the moon between two stars; on each of the flanking towers is a watchman blowing a horn, and below the battlements of the middle tower is a shield bearing a composite device: a fess between in chief three cross-crosslets (from the arms of the Beauchamp Earls of Warwick) and in base checky and a chevron (from the arms of the Newburgh Earls of Warwick). Taking the tinctures from the arms which form this coat, the field in the chief would be red, the crosslets and fess gold, the chequers gold and blue, and the chevron ermine.

The present device of the Corporation reproduces the castle but substitutes for the composite arms a shield bearing a ragged staff bendwise—a badge of the Earls of Warwick (see Chapter III). Colours are assigned to the device, the field being black, the castle silver, and the ragged staff silver on a black shield.

Another device sometimes used consists of a silver castle flanked by the sun and the moon on a red shield.

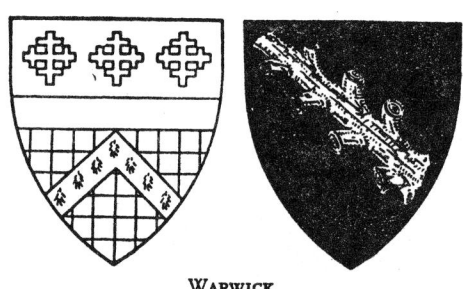

WARWICK

SOLIHULL

BEDWORTH *Urban District Council*

The device consists of an escutcheon with a border charged with stars, and the legend, 'We grow by industry.'

KENILWORTH *Urban District Council*

The device consists of a representation of Kenilworth Castle.

SOLIHULL *Urban District Council*

ARMS: Silver, a greyhound courant sable between two barrulets gules; in chief two pierced molets and in base a Saxon crown, also gules.

CREST: On a wreath argent and gules the battlements of a tower and thereon an oak-tree growing on a mount and in front of it two sickles, their hafts crossed saltirewise, all proper; the tree bearing gold acorns.

MOTTO: *Urbs in rure*—'The town in the countryside.'

These were granted in 1948.

The barrulets are from the arms of the Throgmortons, the molets from the Odingsells, and the greyhound from the Greswolds, while the crown alludes to the association of the Saxon kings with the Manor of Ulverley. The oak-tree indicates that the district was formerly part of the Forest of Arden, and the tower and sickles show that while it includes considerable residential areas parts of it are still mainly agricultural. This is also the meaning of the motto.

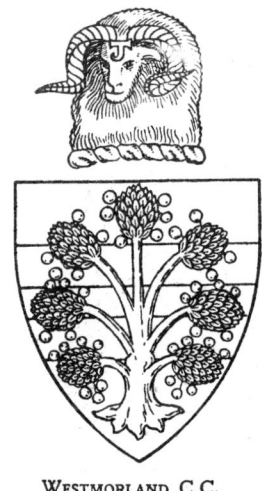

Westmorland C.C.   Kendal

WESTMORLAND

WESTMORLAND County Council

ARMS: Silver, two bars gules, and superimposed thereon a golden apple-tree with seven branches, each bearing a cluster of leaves and fruit.

CREST: On a wreath silver and gules, a Herdwick ram's head proper, charged on the forehead with a gold shearman's hook.

These were granted in 1926.

The red bars are from the arms of the De Lancaster Barons of Kendal. The County derives the apple-tree, and its distinctive form, from the thirteenth-century seal of Appleby. The ram's head refers to the staple industry of the County, and the hook connects the arms with those used by the Borough of Kendal.

'The whole,' states an official description of the arms, 'is a happy combination of North and South Westmorland, known in olden times as "the Bottom of Westmorland" (the North), and the Barony of Kendale (the South).'

APPLEBY Borough Council

The Corporation has not obtained arms, but uses the following: Gules, three crowned lions passant guardant, gold. Crest: On a mural crown a salamander in flames. Supporters: Two dragons gules. Motto: *Nec ferro nec igni*.

Though unauthorized, these form a fine and historic achievement. One result of the fact that they are not officially recorded is that there is doubt as to their customary colours, the field of the shield being sometimes quoted as blue. They were obviously based on the Royal Arms of England which appeared on a seven-branched apple-tree in the thirteenth-century seal of the Corporation, and are said to commemorate that King

APPLEBY

John gave the Borough to the burgesses. The apple-tree has become the central feature in the arms of the Westmorland C.C.

'A tradition prevails in the town,' states Berry, 'that the lions in the arms were crowned with ducal crowns in memory of some signal service performed by the burghers against the Scots.' In the absence of any record, this tradition must be accepted with reserve; but there is no doubt that the salamander—the creature reputed to be able to live in fire—refers to the town's survival of Scottish attacks, notably that of 1388, when it was sacked. The motto, too, boasts that Appleby can be destroyed 'neither by sword nor by fire.' The dragons recall the ancient British Kingdom of Cumbria.

KENDAL Borough Council

No arms are recorded at the Heralds' College, but the following have been in use since about 1629: Quarterly, gules with three wool hooks, and azure with three teazles, all proper. Motto: *Pannus mihi panis*—'Wool is my bread.'

I am informed by the Town Clerk that

the woollen industry was established in the Borough in the fourteenth century, and was for a considerable period the staple industry. Wool hooks were, and are still, used in handling the wool used at the mills; teazles were used for combing (or teasing) it. The arms have not been registered at the College of Heralds. The earliest record of them is on a tankard presented to the Corporation in 1629.

WILTSHIRE C.C.

WILTSHIRE

WILTSHIRE County Council

ARMS: Barry of eight pieces argent and vert, a silver canton charged with a dragon rampant gules.

CREST: On a wreath argent and vert, a bustard with wings spread proper.

These were granted in 1937.

The white-and-green field represents the County's chalk downs and pasture lands. The dragon is that of Wessex, of which Wilton was the capital. The bustard was chosen as the crest because it is claimed that the bird was last seen in Wiltshire; two great bustards support the arms of Cambridgeshire C.C. for a similar reason.

SALISBURY

SALISBURY City Council

ARMS: Azure, four gold bars.

SUPPORTERS: Two gold two-headed eagles with coronets azure about their necks.

The arms here quoted were recorded by the heralds in 1565. A variation was recorded in 1623, namely: Barry of eight pieces azure and or.

As to the explanation of the arms, the Controller of the Salisbury, South Wilts, and Blackmore Museum states that there are a great many theories which are negligible but romantic. One is that the four bars azure represent the four rivers which have their junction in the City. Another attributes the eagle supporters to the Bouverie family, who were great benefactors to the City; but when the arms were recorded, the Bouveries were still Huguenot refugees in the City of Canterbury, and unknown to the City of Salisbury.

CALNE

CALNE Borough Council

ARMS: Sable, a silver domed tower between two feathers argent, each piercing a gold scroll, and a third such feather in the portway.

CREST: A gold mural crown ensigned by a gold mitre with jewels proper, in front of two archiepiscopal staves crossed saltirewise proper.

SUPPORTERS: Two boars gules with gold tusks, each with a garland of silver teazles about its neck.

MOTTO: *Faith, work, service.*

The arms are ancient, and the crest and supporters were granted in 1950.

The feathers of the Heir Apparent refer to the fact that Calne was formerly part of the Duchy of Cornwall. The ecclesiastical emblems in the crest recall a disastrous meeting of the witan at Calne in 978 when (states the Anglo-Saxon Chronicle) 'all the oldest counsellors of England fell at Calne from an upper floor; but the holy Archbishop Dunstan stood alone upon a beam. Some were dreadfully bruised, and some did not escape with life.'

The boars represent Calne's present bacon industry, and the teazles its former cloth industry.

CHIPPENHAM

DEVIZES

CHIPPENHAM Borough Council

The seal contains a tree with three branches; on one side of it a shield bearing ten billets and a label of five points, and on the other a shield bearing three legs in armour. Burke describes the device as a coat of arms, giving the field as silver, the tree green, the first shield blue with silver billets and label, and the second shield gold with the legs in proper colours.

The Town Clerk informs me that the shields bear respectively the arms of Gascelyn, Lord of the Manor of Sheldon, and of Husee, Lord of the Manor of Rowdon; the tinctures quoted by Burke appear, therefore, to be erroneous, for Gascelyn bore blue billets on silver (or gold), and Husee's armoured legs are given in the *General Armory* as red with gold spurs on silver.

DEVIZES Borough Council

ARMS: Parted palewise gules and azure, a gold six-sided castle in perspective, the port flanked by two domed towers, each dome surmounted by a star sable, and another tower rising above the gate.

These are recorded at the College of Arms.

The erection of a castle at Devizes by Roger, Bishop of Salisbury, in the reign of Henry I, resulted in the town's development. Matilda made the castle her headquarters during the war with Stephen; and in the Civil War of the seventeenth century it was a Royalist stronghold, and was captured by Cromwell and dismantled.

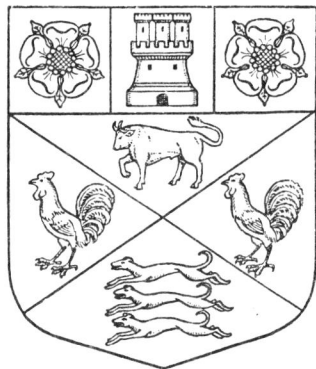

MALMESBURY MARLBOROUGH

MALMESBURY Borough Council

ARMS: Parted saltirewise argent and gules, a cross botonny between in chief a Saxon crown and in base an orb, all gold; on a chief sable a lion passant between a mitre and a crozier erect, all gold.

These were granted in 1950.

The emblems in the lower part of the shield refer to King Athelstan, from whom Malmesbury received a charter in 924. The lion, mitre, and crozier are from the insignia of Malmesbury Abbey.

MARLBOROUGH Borough Council

ARMS: Parted saltirewise gules and azure, in chief a white bull with gold horns, in base three white greyhounds with red collars and gold rings, and in fess two white capons; the chief gold charged with two red roses, and between them a pale azure and thereon a silver tower with three turrets.

These are recorded at the College of Arms. The Corporation also uses the following:

Crest: On a wreath argent and gules, a silver tower.

Supporters: Two greyhounds argent.

The original arms were a silver tower on blue; these appear in the chief of the present arms. According to Berry an explanatory note was appended to the entry of the above arms at the Visitation of 1565, stating that they were 'in commemoration of the duty and homage heretofore said and done (time out of mind) by the burgesses and community to the mayor for the time being, his aldermen and brethren of the said town, at the receiving of the oath by any burgess by them admitted, at which time they do present to the mayor a leash of white greyhounds, one white bull and two white capons.'

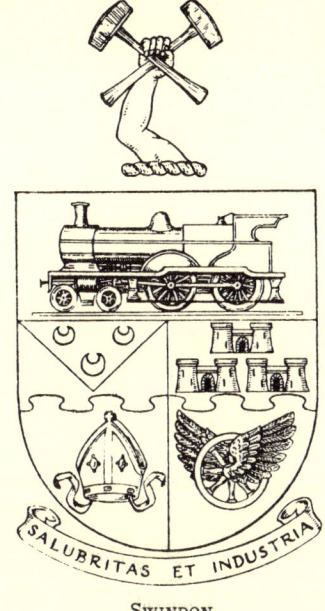

MELKSHAM   SWINDON   TROWBRIDGE

SWINDON Borough Council

ARMS: Quarterly, the fesswise line nebuly; the first quarter azure with a silver pile and thereon three crescents gules; the second gules with three silver castles; the third gules with a gold mitre; and the fourth azure with a gold winged wheel; on a chief argent a locomotive engine proper.

CREST: On a wreath argent and azure, a right arm proper, the hand grasping two gold crossed hammers.

MOTTO: *Salubritas et industria*—'Health and industry.'

These were granted in 1901.

I am indebted to the Town Clerk for an explanation of the arms. The hand holding hammers symbolizes mechanical industry, to which modern Swindon owes its position. The hammers are golden to typify the prosperity which results from all well-applied industry.

The Great Western Railway engine 'Lord of the Isles' speaks for itself as alluding to the industry to which Swindon owes its rise.

The three silver crescents are a prominent feature in the arms of the Goddard family, who have held the Manor of Swindon since the year 1560. This quarter is introduced to mark the intimate connection of the Goddard Manor with the Borough of Swindon.

The three castles are in like manner a prominent feature in the arms of the Vilett family, who for a long period held the Manor (which has now passed by inheritance into the Rolleston family) upon which a considerable portion of New Swindon is built.

After the Norman Conquest the Manor of Swindon was granted by William the Conqueror to his half-brother, Odo, Bishop of Bayeux in Normandy. 'He was one of the prime instigators of the invasion, and performed the part of a military chaplain, celebrated Mass before the Battle of Hastings, and sang their Requiems after it.' (See *Swindon and its Neighbourhood*, by the Rev. T. E. Jackson, M.A.) 'The Duke William's brother Odo, the good priest, the Bishop of Bayeux, galloped up and said to them (the Norman soldiers): Stand fast! Stand fast! Be quiet and move not. Fear nothing, for if God please we shall conquer yet. So they took courage and rested where they were, and Odo returned, galloping back to where the battle was most fierce, and was of great service on that day.' (See *Fifteen Decisive Battles of the World*, by Sir Edward Creasy, M.A.). The charge of an Episcopal Mitre symbolizes the connection of this remarkable and historic Bishop with the Manor of Swindon.

The winged wheel denotes motion, or the swiftness of railway travelling. This quarter may be taken to represent modern Swindon.

WILTON Borough Council

The fourteenth-century seal of the Corporation bears a representation of the shrine of St Edith of Wilton; above it is an angel bearing a shield charged with the three lions of England, and below it the kneeling figure of a nun.

MELKSHAM Urban District Council

ARMS: Parted palewise azure and vert, a fess dancetty of two points argent, and in chief an ancient crown of gold.

CREST: On a wreath argent and azure, a stag's head facing gules with silver antlers in front of a cog-wheel proper.

MOTTO: *Unity and progress.*

These were granted in 1948.

The blue and green of the background stands for the River Avon and the surrounding countryside, and the fess dancetty suggests both the bridge and the downs, while also forming the initial letter of the town's name. The crown refers to the fact that Melksham was part of the royal domain and a hunting-ground of the Norman and Plantagenet kings; and the stag's head alludes to the old forest lands, while the cog-wheel represents modern industries.

TROWBRIDGE Urban District Council

ARMS: Or, a fleece sable with a band gules edged with argent; a chief gules charged with a gold mural crown between two gold wheatsheaves.

CREST: On a wreath gold and sable, a gold circlet composed of six arches of a bridge (three visible), and rising therefrom a demi-lion rampant gules with gold tail and tufts.

MOTTO: *Respice prospice*—'Look to the past and to the future.'

These were granted in 1951.

The emblems in the shield refer to agriculture, the cloth industry, and local government, while the crest alludes to the bridge. The lion indicates that Trowbridge was a royal manor until Henry VIII bestowed it on his brother-in-law, Edward Seymour.

WARMINSTER   WESTBURY

WARMINSTER Urban District Council

ARMS: Gold, a man in armour mounted on a horse and riding towards the sinister, brandishing in his right hand a sword, its blade bendwise-sinister, all proper, the surcoat and shield azure lined gules, the horse sable with bardings gules lined azure.

These were granted in 1948.

They were based on an ancient seal in which the mounted figure was thought to represent Mordaunt, first Lord of Warminster.

An endorsement on the document granting the arms records the gratitude of the town of Warminster to Mr David Vesey, O.B.E., a member of the U.D.C. from 1933 to 1948, by whose gift the grant was obtained.

WESTBURY Urban District Council

Arms are not recorded at the Heralds' College, but in the *General Armory* Burke gives: Quarterly gold and azure, a cross patonce within a bordure charged with twenty lions rampant all counter-changed. The lions were probably included to denote that the manor was held by the Crown at the time of the Domesday Survey, and the cross is from the arms of the family of Paveley, to which the manor was granted by Henry II.

WORCESTERSHIRE C.C.   DUDLEY

WORCESTERSHIRE

WORCESTERSHIRE County Council

ARMS: Argent, a pear-tree proper with fruit sable, growing from a mount vert rising from water barry wavy argent and azure in base. Above the shield is a gold mural crown.

These were granted in 1947.

The pear-tree has long been an emblem of Worcestershire: see the arms of the City of Worcester.

DUDLEY County Borough Council

The Corporation has adopted a device consisting of a red shield with a silver engrailed fess; on the fess is an anchor, a trilobite, and a miner's safety-lamp; above it is a representation of Dudley Castle; and in the base is a salamander in flames. For crest, that of the Earl of Dudley, a blue lion's head, has been adopted.

The emblems on the fess stand for the iron and coal industries, and the fossils with which the Silurian limestone abounds. The salamander represents the furnaces of the Black Country.

WORCESTER City and County Borough Council

ARMS
- *Ancient*: Quarterly sable and gules, a silver tower with three turrets.
- *Modern*: Silver, a fess and three pears all sable.

Both are recorded at the College of Arms. They are sometimes combined on one shield, the modern coat (which is more than three hundred years old) being placed in a canton on the ancient arms; but the arms are usually displayed on separate shields, placed side by side.

WORCESTER

MOTTOES
- *Floreat semper fidelis civitas*—'Let the faithful city ever flourish.'
- *Civitas in bello, in pace, fidelis*—'In war and in peace, a faithful city.'
- *Semper fidelis, mutare sperno*—'Ever faithful, I scorn to change.'

The ancient arms commemorate Worcester Castle, of which nothing remains. The modern arms are said to have been adopted to mark Queen Elizabeth I's visit to Worcester, when the loyal folk transplanted a pear-tree under fruit from its orchard to the centre of the City.

The City's whole-hearted support of the Royalist cause during the Civil War justifies the assertion of fidelity in all its mottoes.

BEWDLEY Borough Council

ARMS: Silver, an anchor azure with a gold fetterlock thereon, and within the fetterlock a sword erect with gold hilt and pommel, and a red rose with a white centre.

These were recorded by the Heralds in 1634.

The anchor is a reminder that, although inland, Bewdley is a port, connected with the sea by the Severn. Formerly in the possession of the Mortimers, the manor was merged in the Crown on the accession of Edward IV, by whom it was chartered. The fetterlock and rose are badges of Edward IV, the former derived from his great-grandfather, Edmund of Langley, and the latter being the union of the roses of York and Lancaster which he effected on his marriage with Elizabeth Woodville, thereby anticipating the permanent combination of the roses carried out by Henry VII.

DROITWICH Borough Council

ARMS: Parted palewise; the dexter gules with a silver sword point downwards, surmounted by two gold lions passant; the sinister quarterly, 1 and 4 chequered silver and sable, 2 and 3 gules with two wicker moulds for salt manufacture erect argent.

These arms, which appear on a fifteenth-century seal, are recorded at the College of Arms.

Droitwich

Bewdley

Evesham

The local tradition concerning the arms is given in the Official Guide to Droitwich:

In the days of King John, that lackland monarch was fain to sell all his rights here to the burgesses for an annuity, which he disposed of next day to his brother, William of the Long Sword. The town proudly assumed for its coat of arms John's lions impaled on William's sword. For five centuries the manufacture of salt was a monopoly guarded jealously; the guild took another coat of arms showing the wicker moulds and the chequered table for their accounts.

Two lions passant were John's arms before he came to the throne (see Chapter II).

EVESHAM Borough Council

ARMS: Azure, a prince's coronet of gold between two silver ostrich feathers, their quills studded with golden roundels, and in base a gold wheatsheaf; all within a border sable charged with golden roundels.

These were recorded by the heralds in 1634.

All the emblems are from the insignia of James I's son, Henry, Prince of Wales, who caused Evesham to receive its charter of incorporation. The bezants are from the arms of the Duchy of Cornwall, and the wheatsheaf stands for the Earldom of Chester (see Chapter II).

HALESOWEN Borough Council

ARMS: Parted palewise silver and gold, a lion rampant, its tail forked, parted palewise gules and vert; a chief parted chevronwise argent and azure, with two scallop shells sable on the argent and a gold fleur-de-lis on the azure.

CREST: In a gold mural crown, an anvil sable with a gold chain about the beak and turned over the face.

SUPPORTERS: Dexter, a Canon of the Premonstratensian Order holding in his right hand a closed book; and sinister, a gentleman in the costume of the fifteenth century; both proper.

HALESOWEN

Motto: *Respice, aspice, prospice*—'Look to the past, the present, and the future.

These were granted in 1937.

The arms are made up of emblems from the heraldry of the principal owners of the Manor of Hales: Earl Roger de Montgomery (1066–94), represented by the red half of the lion; Robert Dudley, Earl of Leicester (1555), the green half of the lion; the Premonstratensian Canons (1218–1538), the fleur-de-lis and dexter supporter; and Viscount Cobham, representing the Lyttelton family, who have held the manor since 1559, signified by the scallops. The sinister supporter is intended for Sir Thomas Lyttelton, Lord Chief Justice of the Court of Common Pleas.

The crest refers to the iron and steel industry of the district, and to the chain industry of Cradley.

KIDDERMINSTER Borough Council

The Corporation has not obtained arms, but makes use of the following: Azure, two gold chevrons between three gold roundels, and on each chevron four roundels sable. Motto: *Deo adjuvante arte et industria floret*—'With God's help, it flourishes by art and industry.'

The chevrons and golden roundels are the arms of the family of Kidderminster or Kydermaster. The black roundels added for difference may have been suggested by the red roundels in the arms of the See of Worcester.

KIDDERMINSTER   OLDBURY   STOURBRIDGE

OLDBURY Borough Council

ARMS: Parted saltirewise vert and silver, two gold lions rampant on the vert and two crosses flory sable on the silver.

CREST: In a gold Saxon crown a dragon's head and wings gules.

MOTTO: *Antiquum decus floreat*—'May its ancient glory flourish.'

These were granted in 1926.

The fact that Oldbury—Ealdanbyrig—was so called by the Saxons indicates that they found an ancient British town there. The red dragon is that of the British, and the crown and crosses refer to the Saxons (see Chapter II). The gold lion upon green is from the arms of the family of Robsart.

STOURBRIDGE Borough Council

ARMS: Azure, the span of a bridge of silver, and hanging therefrom by a black chain a golden fleece; in chief two gold pears.

MOTTO: *One heart, one way.*

These were granted in 1917.

An official explanation states:

The name of the Borough and its close connection with the County of Worcester are symbolized by the Bridge and the two Pears, whilst the Fleece and the Chain suspending it are typical of the Skin and Leather Dressing and Chain Cable Industries, carried on in the Borough. The motto, 'One heart, one way,' expresses the 'singleness of mind and purpose' animating the Members of the Town Council.

MALVERN   REDDITCH   UPTON-ON-SEVERN R.D.C.

MALVERN Urban District Council

ARMS: Silver, two lions passant gules, their tails forked; on a chief gules a gold cross patonce between two roundels barry wavy argent and azure.

CREST: On a wreath argent and gules, a stag at rest in front of a pear-tree bearing fruit all proper.

MOTTO: *Levavi oculos meos in montes*—'I lifted up mine eyes unto the hills.'

These were granted in 1951.

The lions are from the arms of the Lygons, Earls Beauchamp. The cross refers to Westminster Abbey, with which the priory of Great Malvern was connected, and the roundels stand for the Malvern waters. The stag represents Malvern Chase, and the pear-tree is the County emblem.

REDDITCH Urban District Council

ARMS: Silver, a cross engrailed vert and thereon a silver needle with a golden eye and in chief an ancient crown of gold; and in the first quarter a salmon-fly proper.

CREST: On a wreath silver and vert, a half cog-wheel with a swift proper perched thereon, and in front of the cog-wheel a golden arrow.

MOTTO: *Reddite Deo.*

These were granted in 1943.

Redditch grew from a hamlet hard by the great Cistercian Abbey of Bordesley, founded in 1136 by the Empress Maud. The silver (or white) field represents the white robes of the monks, and the cross refers to the Abbey, its form and colour, suggestive of holly, being chosen because the Abbey, and the present parish church, were dedicated to St Stephen, whose festival falls within the Christmas season. The green of the cross also refers to the forest lands within which Redditch stands and the green open spaces in the Urban District, especially Feckenham, a hunting-ground and royal forest of King John. The crown alludes to both the Empress Maud and John.

The other emblems in the shield stand for Redditch's chief industries—the manufacture of needles and fishing tackle. The swift, fastest of British birds, perched on a cog-wheel, emblem of mechanical science, refers to the manufacture of aeroplane and motor-car accessories, and the arrow alludes not only to the speed and directness of modern air and road transport, but also to the River Arrow on which Redditch stands.

The motto is from the Latin version of Mark xii. 17: 'Render to Caesar the things that are Caesar's, and to God the things that are God's.' The word 'Reddite' is a play on the town's name, and the motto may thus be translated as either 'Render unto God' or 'Redditch for God.'

UPTON-ON-SEVERN *Rural District Council*

ARMS: Parted fesswise gules and sable, a fess barry wavy of six pieces argent and azure, between in chief two cross-crosslets and in base a crescent all gold, and on the fess two pales also gold, that to the dexter embattled on both sides.

CREST: On a wreath argent and azure a pear-tree proper with black pears, growing on a mount vert, and in front of the tree a gold pelican piercing its breast with its beak and drawing therefrom drops of blood gules.

Below the shield is placed a scroll bearing the name, 'Upton super Sabrinam.'

These were granted in 1948.

The crosslets are from the arms of the Beauchamps of Elmley Castle, and the crescent is from the arms of the Coventrys of Earls Croome, Earls of Coventry. The pales crossing the fess stand for the old and new bridges across the Severn. The pelican in its piety is from the heraldry of the Lechmeres of Hanley Castle, and the pear-tree refers to the County.

YORKSHIRE

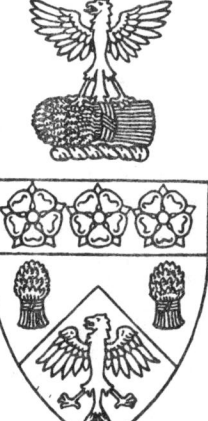
EAST RIDING C.C.

NORTH RIDING C.C.

WEST RIDING C.C.

YORKSHIRE

EAST RIDING County Council

ARMS: Parted chevronwise silver and gold, in chief two wheatsheaves proper and in base an eagle displayed azure; a chief sable charged with three white roses with seeds and sepals proper.

CREST: On a wreath argent and azure an eagle displayed azure standing on a gold wheatsheaf laid fesswise.

These were granted in 1945.

With the white roses of Yorkshire are combined wheatsheaves for agriculture, and an eagle which was used as an emblem by the County Council before arms were obtained, and was probably derived from the eagle sometimes quartered in the arms of Beverley (q.v.).

NORTH RIDING County Council

ARMS: Argent, a cross gules; a chief azure charged with three white roses with seeds and sepals proper.

These arms were granted in 1928.

Here the Yorkshire roses appear in conjunction with the cross of St George.

WEST RIDING County Council

ARMS: Ermine, a white rose set upon the sun or; and on a chief gules three white roses. all the roses with seeds and sepals proper.

The shield is ensigned by a gold mural crown.

MOTTO: *Audi consilium*—'Heed counsel.'

BADGE: A white rose with seeds and sepals proper ensigned with a gold mural crown.

The County Council has also a standard bearing the arms next to the staff, the fly gules with the badge thrice repeated, and crossed by two white bands bearing the motto.

These were granted in 1927.

The origin and historic associations of the white rose as the emblem of the Duchy of York are dealt with in Chapter II. In the West Riding arms, the rose is shown *en soleil*, a device adopted by the Yorkist king, Edward IV, when he reached the throne after the battle of Towton. It was formed by combining the York rose with the royal badge of the sun used by Richard II. Shakespeare alludes to this badge:

> Now is the winter of our discontent
> Made glorious summer by this sun of York.

The white rose-en-soleil served Edward IV well at the battle of Barnet in 1471, when it was borne as a badge by his followers. On the Lancastrian side was De Vere, Earl of Oxford, whose men were wearing his silver star. The Earl of Warwick, on the Lancastrian side, seeing through a mist De Vere's star, mistook it for Edward's shining rose, and charged—against his own supporters. The confusion which resulted lost the Lancastrians the battle.

BARNSLEY

BARNSLEY County Borough Council

ARMS: Argent, on a chevron gules, a falcon with wings spread holding a padlock all gold, between two gold boars' heads, each holding in the mouth a silver cross paty pointed at the foot; above the chevron two shuttles, and below it two crossed pickaxes proper; on a chief sable a cross paty between two covered cups all gold.

CREST: On a wreath argent and gules, a silver griffin with wings outspread sable, standing and supporting a silver shield charged with a shuttle erect sable.

SUPPORTERS: Dexter, a miner holding a pickaxe, with a pit lamp hanging round his neck; and sinister, a glass-blower holding a blowpipe with a bottle at its end, all proper.

MOTTO: *Spectemur agendo*—'Let us be judged by our works.'

The arms and crest were granted in 1869, and the supporters in 1913.

The falcon with padlock, and the boars' heads with crosses, are from the arms of the local families of Locke and Beckett, and the griffin is the crest of the Wentworths of Wentworth Woodhouse.

The emblems in the chief stand for Monk Bretton Priory, a Cluniac foundation dating from 1157; the arms of the Priory were two silver covered cups and a silver cross paty on black.

The shuttles and pickaxes, and the supporters, represent local industries.

BRADFORD City and County Borough Council

ARMS: Parted palewise gules and azure, a chevron engrailed between three buglehorns all gold, and on the chevron a well sable.

CREST: On a wreath gold and gules, a gold boar's head without tongue in front of a tree trunk with leaves sprouting therefrom proper.

SUPPORTERS: Dexter, a black ram with gold horns and with a wreath of white roses about its neck; and sinister, a white Angora goat with gold horns, wearing a collar gules charged with three white roses of York.

MOTTO: *Labor omnia vincit*—'Labour overcomes all things.'

BADGE: A silver ram's head with gold horns, crowned with a gold mural crown.

The arms and crest were granted in 1847, the supporters in 1907, and the badge in 1908.

'One blast with his horn upon St Martin's Day' was part of the service which John Northrop of Manningham owed to John of Gaunt for his lands. This service, performed in the Market Place at Bradford, became a local custom, and is commemorated by the horns in the arms.

The lands for which this service was rendered are said to have been offered as a reward to the slayer of a ravenous boar which haunted Cliffe Wood. One day when the boar was drinking at a well (later called Boar's Well, and represented in the arms) a youth shot the beast and cut out its tongue to take as evidence when claiming the reward. Shortly afterwards another man came upon the dead boar, cut off the head, and took it to put in a counter-claim. Judgment was given for him who produced the tongue, and the false claimant was punished. In allusion to this legend the boar in the crest has no tongue.

BRADFORD   DEWSBURY

The arms of the Yorkshire family named Bradford are given by Burke as a black chevron and three black bugle horns on silver, and the similarity between this coat and that of the City suggests that one was based upon the other.

The badge and supporters refer to the woollen industry.

DEWSBURY County Borough Council

ARMS: Checky gold and azure, on a chief engrailed sable a gold cross patonce between two owls argent.

CREST: On a wreath gold and azure, an owl argent standing in front of a cross patonce pointed at the foot azure.

MOTTO: *Deus noster refugium et virtus*—'God is our refuge and strength.'

These were granted in 1893.

The chequers form the arms of the Earls de Warenne (see Chapter III), the owls are from the arms of the Savile family, and as such also appear in the shield of Leeds, and the crosses represent the Copley family. The motto is from Psalm xlvi.

DONCASTER

DONCASTER County Borough Council

ARMS: Gules, a silver gateway with portcullis raised sable, between flanking towers over each of which flies a white banner, and between them a gold Saxon crown.

CREST: On a wreath argent and gules, a gold lion seated on an ermine cushion and holding a banner with gold fringe and tassels; the banner azure, charged in base with silver wavy bars, and rising therefrom a gateway, as in the arms, charged with the word *Don* in black letters.

SUPPORTERS: Two seated gold lions each holding in its mouth a white rose of York with stem and leaves proper.

MOTTO: *Comfort et Liesse* (or *Confort et Liesse*)—'Comfort and joy.'

The arms and crest were confirmed, and the supporters granted, in 1927, when Doncaster became a county borough. The unauthorized arms previously used differed from the above in that they contained a royal crown. The Saxon crown which now appears in the arms is specially appropriate inasmuch as in the reign of Edward the Confessor, Doncaster, then part of the Manor of Hexthorp, belonged to Earl Tostig. In Henry I's time it passed into the royal hands.

HALIFAX

HALIFAX *County Borough Council*

ARMS: Checky gold and azure, a man's face bearded and surrounded by a halo proper.

CREST: In a gold Saxon crown a mount vert and thereon a Paschal Lamb proper holding a gold staff with a forked pennon argent charged with a cross gules.

SUPPORTERS: Two gold lions each holding in the further forepaw a white rose with stalk, leaves, seeds, and sepals proper.

MOTTO: *Except the Lord keep the City*.

These arms, granted in 1948, were based upon an unofficial device, adopted a century earlier, in which the face on the chequered shield was placed between the words 'halez' and 'fax.'

The 'holy face'—an allusion to the name of the town—is that of St John the Baptist, to whom the parish church is dedicated. A symbol of St John the Baptist is the Holy Lamb, because it was he who hailed Jesus as 'the Lamb of God' (John i. 29). On account of this symbol, St John the Baptist became the patron saint of wool merchants. To the wool trade Halifax owed its early prosperity, and accordingly dedicated its church to the appropriate saint. The crest therefore stands both for that dedication and for the industry of which Halifax is still an important centre.

The Saxon crown denotes that the manor was held by Edward the Confessor, and the chequers are from the arms of the Earls Warenne who held it in Norman times. The supporters are British lions holding the County emblem.

The motto, from Psalm cxxvii, was previously used in its Latin form.

YORKSHIRE

HUDDERSFIELD

KINGSTON-UPON-HULL

HUDDERSFIELD County Borough Council

ARMS: Gold, a chevron between three rams passant all sable, and on the chevron three silver towers.

CREST: On a wreath gold and sable, a silver ram's head with gold horns and a collar sable, holding in the mouth a sprig of the cotton-tree proper.

MOTTO: *Juvat impigros Deus*—'God aids the diligent.'

These were granted in 1868.

They are based on the heraldry of the family of Ramsden, who have held the Manor of Huddersfield since Elizabeth I's reign, and have done much for the town's development. The crest is similar to that of Barrow-in-Furness, commemorating a member of the same family.

KINGSTON-UPON-HULL City and County Borough Council

ARMS: Azure, three open crowns of gold palewise.

These are on record at the College of Arms.

There is a tradition that these arms originated in the device of a local company of Merchant Adventurers who likened themselves to the three Kings of the East who followed the star to Bethlehem.

'A more likely origin,' states Mr Fox-Davies, 'may be found in the arms of the City of Cologne, and the habit of those who imported fine linen from that City to set up the arms thereof as indicative of the wares they dealt in.'

Still more likely is it that the crowns were adopted in token of Edward I, who, seeing its value as a port, took over the town of Wykeham-upon-Hull from the Monks of Meaux and gave it a charter, so that thereafter it was called the King's Town. This simple explanation of the arms, which seems to have been obscured owing to the fact that nowadays the town is commonly called Hull, is supported by the thirteenth-century seal which bears the figure of a king flanked by two lions and with a third at his feet.

LEEDS

LEEDS *City and County Borough Council*

ARMS: Azure, a golden fleece; on a chief sable three silver stars.

CREST: On a wreath gold and azure, an owl proper.

SUPPORTERS: Two owls proper, each with a gold crown on its head.

MOTTO: *Pro Rege et Lege*—'For King and Law.'

The arms were recorded by the heralds in 1666. The crest and supporters were added by the Corporation and confirmed by a grant in 1921.

'Leeds is rendered wealthy by its woollen manufactures,' stated Camden, writing in 1590. The fleece stands for this industry. The roses are from the arms of Thomas Danby, Mayor of Leeds in 1661. The owl is the crest of the Savile family, and as such also appears in the arms of Dewsbury. The black chief on a blue field illustrates the fact that the heraldic rule against placing colour on colour does not necessarily apply to chiefs.

MIDDLESBROUGH *County Borough Council*

ARMS: Silver, a lion rampant azure; on a chief sable three gold ships with silver sails.

CREST: On a gold mural crown charged with three anchors sable, a lion passant azure.

MOTTO: *Erimus*—'We shall be.'

These were granted in 1911.

YORKSHIRE

The blue lion is that of Robert de Brus of Skelton (see Chapter III) who, in the twelfth century, founded a priory where Middlesbrough now stands. The motto of a branch of the family of Bruce is *Fuimus*, in allusion to their notable past. This may have been in the minds of the citizens of Middlesbrough, leading them to select that motto's antithesis, and to look forward to a notable future.

MIDDLESBROUGH   ROTHERHAM

ROTHERHAM *County Borough Council*

ARMS: Vert, in base two bars wavy argent and above them a bridge of three arches proper; in chief a silver mitre between two white roses.

CREST: On a wreath argent and vert, a hand proper holding erect a gold caduceus.

SUPPORTERS: Two gold stags, each with a chain about its neck and hanging therefrom an escutcheon sable charged with a gold bee.

MOTTO: *Sic virescit industria*—'Thus industry flourishes.'

These were granted in 1947, the emblems being drawn from a device used unofficially before that date.

The green field, the mitre, and the stags are from the insignia of Thomas of Rotherham (1423–1500), Archbishop of York, who founded a college at Rotherham and built part of the Church of All Saints.

In the original device, the bridge stood for the ancient bridge at Rotherham, and also

Old Southwark Bridge, built by Rotherham ironmasters. The bridge in the arms has the added significance that it represents the invention of the Bailey bridge by a Rotherham man.

The caduceus is the staff of Mercury, the god of commerce. The bees stand for industry, the black shields on which they lie being allusive to coal mining, and the black chains to iron and brass founding. The roses represent the County.

SHEFFIELD

SHEFFIELD City and County Borough Council

ARMS: Parted fesswise azure and vert, in chief eight silver arrows saltirewise with a silver band, and in the base three gold wheatsheaves.

CREST: On a wreath argent and azure, a silver lion rampant with two circlets azure about its neck, holding an ancient shield azure charged with eight silver arrows as in the arms.

SUPPORTERS: Dexter, Thor with his hammer, and sinister, Vulcan with pincers and anvil, all proper.

MOTTO: *Deo adjuvante labor proficit*—'By God's help labour succeeds.'

The arms are recorded at the Heralds' College; the supporters were granted in 1893.

The sheaves in the green field clearly refer to the name of the town and the River Sheaf. The arrows stand for cutlery, and the supporters for the steel industry.

The lion represents the Talbots, Earls of Shrewsbury, who held the manor; one of whom founded the Shrewsbury Chapel in the parish church of St Peter.

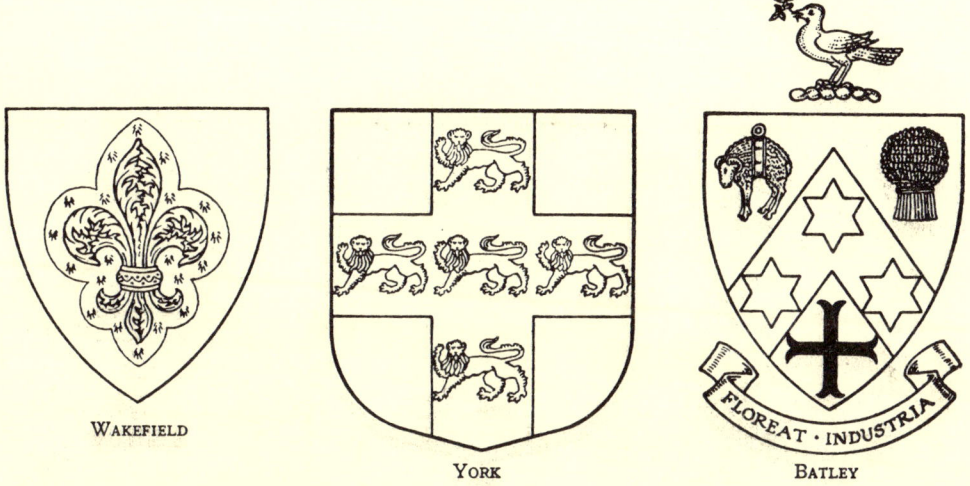

WAKEFIELD   YORK   BATLEY

WAKEFIELD City and County Borough Council

ARMS: Azure, a gold fleur-de-lis edged with ermine.

These were granted in 1932, but a device consisting of a gold fleur-de-lis on blue was previously in use for many years.

I am indebted to the Town Clerk for the following note:

Tradition runs that the City of Wakefield is entitled to the use of the fleur-de-lis by permission of Henrietta of France, Queen of Charles the First, who went over to France for the purpose of obtaining some of her crown jewels with a view to selling them and giving the proceeds to the King for war expenses. Landing at Bridlington, the Queen was followed in hot pursuit by Cromwell, who bombarded the house in which she was sleeping; but she escaped therefrom and spent the remainder of the night in a ditch. Thence in her wanderings to rejoin the King she is reputed to have reached Wakefield, where she was well treated; and as a means of showing her gratitude the Queen ordered that from that time henceforth Wakefield might use the fleur-de-lis as the arms of the town.

Upon incorporation in 1848 under the Municipal Corporations Act, 1835, arms were adopted which embodied the Corn Market, the Cattle Market, and a sheaf of wheat. Upon the creation of the Bishopric, Wakefield was by Royal Charter created a City, and the Council then adopted the fleur-de-lis, the description being: shield azure; fleur-de-lis or.

When, in 1932, the device was given official status as a coat of arms, it was necessary to make some slight addition to distinguish it from the old royal badge of a single fleur-de-lis, and this was effected by the ermine 'fimbriation,' or edging, which produced the necessary difference with the minimum change, and added to the dignity of the design.

YORK City and County Borough Council

ARMS: Silver, on a cross gules five gold lions passant guardant.

These are recorded at the College of Arms. They are often displayed with the civic sword and mace crossed behind the shield, and with a chapeau above it. The national and royal emblems are appropriate to the second city of England.

BATLEY Borough Council

The Corporation has not obtained arms, but has adopted a shield parted chevronwise blue and silver with a red chevron charged with three silver stars, above the chevron a golden fleece and a golden wheatsheaf, and below it a black cross moline. Crest: A dove holding in its beak an olive branch. Motto: *Floreat Industria*—'May industry flourish.'

The fleece and wheatsheaf refer to local industries, and the cross is that of the family of Copley, sometime of Batley Hall.

BRIDLINGTON

BEVERLEY

BRIGHOUSE

BEVERLEY Borough Council

ARMS: Silver, three bars wavy azure; on a chief azure a gold beaver with its head turned and biting at its fur.

These are recorded at the College of Arms. The tinctures have been subject to variation. In 1829 a local historian quoted the bars and chief as black, and the field and beaver as silver.

Burke in the *General Armory* quotes a quartered coat; 1 and 4, Gold, an eagle azure; 2 and 3, the above arms. This quartered shield (without tinctures) was in existence at the time of the Heralds' Visitation in 1585, and appears on waits' badges in the possession of the Corporation, and the Mayoral badge.

The Town Clerk informs me that the ancient seal of the town at the beginning of the sixteenth century bore the figure of St John of Beverley robed as an Archbishop and seated on a throne with his feet on a beaver, allusive, of course, to the name of the town.

On either side of the saint was a shield, one bearing an eagle displayed, and the other bearing the arms of the See of York impaling those of the then Archbishop, Thomas Savage.

Clearly it is from this seal that the eagle was derived, but its significance is obscure. Mere conjecture leads me to think that it may have been ascribed as arms to St John of Beverley, perhaps because the eagle was the emblem of St John the Divine.

It is probable that the eagle in the arms of the East Riding C.C. was derived from that of Beverley.

BRIDLINGTON Borough Council

ARMS: Parted palewise sable and argent, three Gothic capital letters B counterchanged; on a silver embattled chief two bars wavy azure.

CREST: A sun gules rising from a coronet consisting of eight white roses set on a gold rim.

MOTTO: *Signum salutis semper*—'Ever the sign of health.'

These were granted in 1934.

The Bs are from the arms of Bridlington Priory. The rising sun and the blue wavy bars refer to the town's position on the east coast, and the white roses, forming a 'coronet of York,' allude to the County.

BRIGHOUSE Borough Council

ARMS: Gold, on a pale sable a lion rampant or; on each side of the pale a red rose above a crescent sable.

CREST: On a wreath gold and sable, the battlements of a tower argent charged with two crescents sable, and above the battlements a silver tiger's face between two red roses with leaves and stalks proper.

MOTTO: *Labore et prudentia*—'By industry and prudence.'

These were granted in 1894.

They are based on the arms and crest of the family of Brighouse, who bore: Sable, a gold fess between three gold lions rampant, and on the fess three crescents sable. Crest: A silver tiger's head on a gold mural crown. The roses were derived from the arms of the Rastrick family.

GOOLE Borough Council

ARMS: Gold, an ancient galley sable, oars in action and flags flying gules; on a chief sable three swans argent.

SUPPORTERS: Two Vikings, each holding a spear proper.

MOTTO: *Advance.*

These were granted in 1933.

The Vikings refer to the Norse sea-rovers who settled along the Humber, and the galley stands for Goole's seafaring interests, past and present. The swans are from the arms of Selby Abbey, which was a considerable landholder in this district before its dissolution.

* o

Goole

HARROGATE Borough Council

ARMS: Quarterly argent and gules, a cross counter-changed, in the first and fourth quarters a roundel barry wavy silver and azure, and in the second and third a gold bugle-horn with gold strings; on a chief parted palewise gules and azure, a silver lion passant guardant.

CREST: On a wreath argent and gules, the battlements of a tower, and thereon a tree trunk entwined by two serpents, all proper, with a black cock with red comb and wattle perched on the trunk.

MOTTO: *Arx celebris fontibus*—'A stronghold famed for its springs.'

These were granted in 1884.

Harrogate's many springs are represented by the roundels or heraldic fountains, and the serpents stand for their healing qualities. The first to be discovered was the Tewitt well, which was found towards the close of the sixteenth century by a member of the family of Slingsby, from whose arms the bugle-horns appear to have been taken.

HEDON Borough Council

The Corporation has no arms. The seal bears a ship on water, a reminder that Hedon, now two miles from the Humber, was once connected with it by an inlet, and was a notable port. The channel has long since become dry, and Hedon's maritime prosperity has deserted it for Hull.

YORKSHIRE

KEIGHLEY

HARROGATE

MORLEY

KEIGHLEY Borough Council

ARMS: Silver, a fess sable between three stags' heads proper, and on the fess a roundel barry wavy silver and azure, all within a border embattled azure.

CREST: On a wreath argent and sable, a dragon's head gules entwined by a gold serpent and charged with a roundel as in the arms.

MOTTO: *By Worth*.

These were granted in 1883.

The fess and dragon's head are from the heraldry of the ancient family of Keighley, Lords of the Manor. In the reign of Queen Elizabeth I the heiress of the Keighleys carried the estate by marriage to the family of Cavendish, represented in the Borough arms by the serpent and the stags' heads.

The roundel, or heraldic fountain, 'refers to the situation of Keighley in a well-watered valley, the streams of which have greatly tended towards the progress of the town, being of great value for manufacturing purposes. This idea is also borne out by the motto "By Worth," that being the name of the principal stream on the banks of which Keighley is situate.... The blue embattled border surrounding the shield shows that the arms are those of an ancient town ... Keighley having obtained its original market charter in the reign of Edward I' (Burke, *General Armory*).

CIVIC HERALDRY

MORLEY Borough Council

ARMS: Silver, on a fess gules a gold shuttle; in chief a sprig of cotton proper between two roundels sable; and in base a pickaxe and spade saltirewise sable.

CREST: On a wreath argent and gules, a silver ram's head, and in front of it a shuttle proper.

MOTTO: *Industria omnia vincit*—'Industry overcomes all things.'

These were granted in 1887.

The design is wholly industrial, representing wool, cotton, and coal.

OSSETT Borough Council

The Corporation has no arms. The device consists of four medallions bearing factory buildings, a wheatsheaf, a fleece, and a pit-head, with the words: *Inutile utile ex arte*—'That which is useless is made useful through skill.'

PONTEFRACT

PUDSEY

PONTEFRACT Borough Council

ARMS: Sable, a silver quadrangular castle with four towers in perspective, and in the base water.

These were recorded by the heralds in 1584.

Pontefract Castle, where Richard II was imprisoned and done to death, was built in William I's reign by Ilbert de Lacy as part of a scheme to keep the north in subjection. It was held by the Royalists during the Civil War, and was destroyed on the death of Charles I.

PUDSEY Borough Council

ARMS: Silver, on a chevron vert, three gold spur-rowels; in chief two pairs of crossed shuttles and in base a woolpack proper; a border engrailed gules charged with eight white roses.

MOTTO: *Be just and fear not.*

These arms were granted in 1901.

The chevron and spur-rowels are from the arms of the family of Pudsey. The shuttles and woolpack denote the chief local industry. The border of white roses stands for the county in which the town lies.

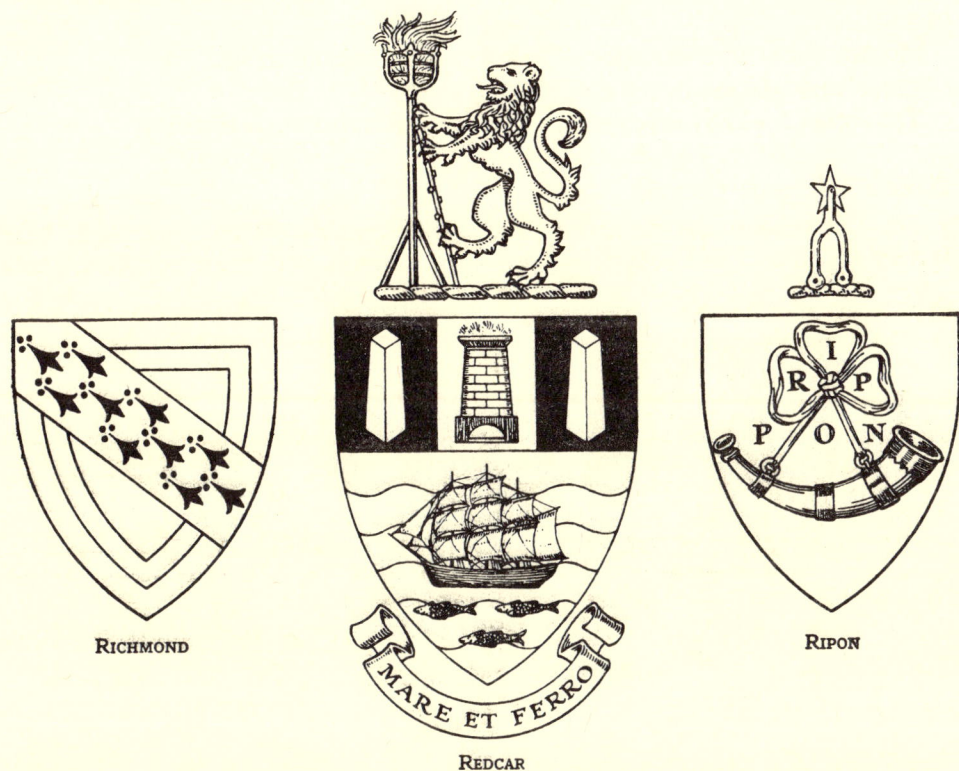

RICHMOND   REDCAR   RIPON

REDCAR Borough Council

ARMS: Barry wavy of six pieces azure and silver, thereon a ship in full sail, and below it three fish, all proper; on a chief sable two steel ingots, and between them a gold pale charged with a blast furnace, also proper.

CREST: On a wreath argent and azure, a lion rampant gules supporting a flaming beacon proper.

MOTTO: *Mare et ferro*—'By sea and steel.'

These were granted in 1922.

I am indebted to the Town Clerk for the following explanation:

The design incorporated part of the arms of Lord Zetland, the leading landowner in the Borough, and the furnace and ingot were deemed to represent the Iron and Steelworks of Messrs Dorman Long and Co., upon the prosperity of which the town greatly depends. There is also a ship, which represents the overseas trade from the River Tees, and the fishes are the emblem of our most ancient industry, which unhappily is now confined to a handful of our inshore fishermen.

Our motto, 'By Sea and Steel,' means that we profit by seaside patronage in the summer, but are dependent for our main prosperity upon the manufacture of steel.

RICHMOND Borough Council

ARMS: Gules, a silver orle surmounted by a bend ermine.

These were granted in 1665.

The orle may have been derived from the arms of Baliol of Barnard Castle. In the twelfth century the Honour of Richmond was held by the Counts and Dukes of Brittany; the arms of Brittany were simply ermine, hence the ermine bend in the Richmond shield. Burke quotes as a crest a crowned red rose but this seems to have been no more than an embellishment on the seal on which the above arms were placed, and not to have been intended as a crest.

RIPON City Council

The Corporation has not obtained arms, but makes use of the following: Gules, a gold bugle horn with the letters R I P P O N disposed about the bow in which the strings are tied. Crest: A spur. The Town Clerk writes:

The horn appears to have been used from time immemorial as the arms of Ripon, but the spur was introduced at a more recent date, probably to signify the trade of spur-making for which this City was famous in the Middle Ages. The horn refers to the Charter horn (when rights were conferred upon the City as a community in A.D. 886) and this Charter horn is carried attached to the baldrick which is worn by the Sergeant-at-Mace, who precedes the Mayor with the Mace on all ceremonial occasions. The Charter horn was never a blowing horn, but the custom of blowing a horn at the four corners of the Market Cross and in front of the Wakeman's (Mayor's) house at 9 p.m. each evening has been carried out for hundreds of years.

SCARBOROUGH Borough Council

ARMS: Parted fesswise wavy, the upper part gules and the lower barry wavy of six pieces silver and azure; in chief, issuing from the fess-line, on the dexter side an ancient galley with sail furled, and on the sinister a square tower proper; in the centre chief point a gold star.

CREST: On a wreath argent and gules, an ancient galley sable with a sail gules charged with a gold star, and in front of it three white roses.

SUPPORTERS: Two stags looking backwards gules, each with a gold chain about its neck, and pendent therefrom, on the dexter stag, a white rose, and on the sinister a gold buglehorn.

MOTTO: *Per pericula ad decus ire juvat.*

These were granted in 1935; but it appears from a record in the College of Arms that as long ago as 1585 a design was prepared for the arms though they were not actually granted.

YORKSHIRE

SCARBOROUGH

The arms are based on the town's seal dating from the thirteenth century, and clearly illustrate historic and enduring features—its harbour and castle. The lymphad and star from the ancient seal are repeated in the crest, with white roses of York.

The stags represent the forests of Pickering, Galtres, and Knaresborough, and the horn stands for a royal hunt.

THORNABY-ON-TEES Borough Council

ARMS: Barry of twelve pieces gules and silver, on a pale ermine a lion rampant azure and on a chief engrailed argent three roundels gules.

CREST: On a wreath argent and gules, the stern of a ship proper in front of two gold anchors saltirewise.

MOTTO: *Always advancing.*

These were granted in 1893.

The arms are based upon those of the family of Thornaby in the sixteenth century; the blue lion is that of the family De Brus (see Chapter III) who held the Manor of Thornaby during the Middle Ages.

TODMORDEN Borough Council

ARMS: Or, on a fess wavy azure a gold shuttle and a silver spindle; in chief a red rose, and in the base a white rose, each with green leaves and stalk.

CREST: On a wreath gold and azure, a representation of the monument called Stoodley Pike, proper.

Thornaby-on-Tees

Todmorden

MOTTO: *By industry we prosper.*

These were granted in 1896.

The fess represents the River Calder which, at the time the arms were granted, was the boundary between Yorkshire and Lancashire. The boundaries have now been altered, and the Borough lies wholly in Yorkshire, but the arms commemorate its former division between the two counties. The emblems on the fess stand for the textile industry. The obelisk forming the crest was erected to mark the Peace of Amiens.

BAILDON Urban District Council

ARMS: Vert, three chevrons and in chief a fleece, all or.

CREST: On a wreath gold and vert, a skylark holding in its beak a sprig of gorse with flowers, all proper.

MOTTO: *Surgamus ergo strenue*—'Let us arise with vigour.'

These were granted in 1952.

The emblems refer to the rearing of sheep for wool, and to the Baildon moorlands.

BINGLEY Urban District Council

Use is made of the arms of the family of Bingley: Silver, three trefoils bendwise between cotises all sable. Crest: A silver bear's head with a muzzle gules. Motto: *Opes parit industria*—'Industry begets plenty.'

The U.D.C. has added as supporters two muzzled bears.

BAILDON   CASTLEFORD   FILEY

CASTLEFORD Urban District Council

ARMS: Gules, in base water barry wavy argent and azure and rising therefrom a gold castle with three towers; in chief two white roses with seeds and sepals proper.

CREST: On a wreath gold and gules, a gold demi-eagle displayed, about its neck a collar gules and hanging therefrom a miner's lamp proper, and on each wing a Lacy knot sable.

MOTTO: *Audacter et sincere*—'Boldly and sincerely.'

These were granted in 1952.

The castle rising from water refers to the name, while the eagle alludes to the fact that Castleford stands on the site of the Roman station of Legiolum. The miner's lamp represents the chief local industry. The knots are the badge of the Lacys, Earls of Lincoln and Lords of Pontefract, the honour in which Castleford lies.

ELLAND Urban District Council

On the seal is a shield between the dates 1317, 1895, and 1937. The shield bears a bend charged with three owls, presumably the arms of the Savile family; Argent, on a bend sable three silver owls.

FILEY Urban District Council

ARMS: Parted fesswise, the chief azure with a representation of Filey Brig with the sun shining on it all proper; the base parted palewise wavy, the dexter side gold and the sinister azure with three pales wavy argent.

CREST: Within an ancient Roman crown of gold rays, a rock vert and rising therefrom a seagull holding in its beak a fish all proper.

MOTTO: *Filey et felicitas*—'Filey and felicity.'

These were granted in 1952.

The shield suggests golden sands, sea, and sunshine. The gull is an emblem of the sea and fishing, and the crown refers to the district's Roman associations.

HALTEMPRICE

HEMSWORTH

HORBURY

HALTEMPRICE Urban District Council

ARMS: Sable, a silver cross patonce and in the first quarter a white rose with seeds and sepals proper.

CREST: On a wreath silver and sable, a stag at gaze proper with a gold mural crown about its neck standing on a mount vert.

MOTTO: *Haulte emprise.*

These were granted in 1952.

The cross is from the insignia of Haltemprice Priory, and the rose is the County emblem. The crest refers to the ancient wapentake of Hart Hill which embraced the area of the present district. The mural crown alludes to royal associations.

The motto, translated as either 'High endeavour' or 'Noble undertaking,' refers to the name *Alta Prisa* given to the monastery founded in 1328 by Henry de Wake, and removed from its original situation at Cottingham to Newton, near Willerby, to ensure security of the tenure of its land.

HEMSWORTH *Urban District Council*

Use is made of the following arms: Gules, the crossed keys of St Peter and in the chief a crown surmounted by a cross, all gold, being the arms of the Province of York; impaling, Gold, three bulls' heads torn off at the neck azure, for Holgate. Above the shield is a mitre. These are the arms of Robert Holgate, Archbishop of York, 1545–55, who was a native of Hemsworth and a benefactor of the town. The Grammar School which he founded in 1546 has been removed to Barnsley, but a hospital for which he provided in his will still remains at Hemsworth.

HORBURY *Urban District Council*

Use has been made of the arms of Sir John de Horbury, Lord of the Manor of Horbury in the fourteenth century: Argent, on a bend sable three silver towers. The U.D.C. has added the motto: *Pro bono oppido*—'For a good town.'

HORSFORTH *Urban District Council*

The device is a horse.

KIRKBURTON *Urban District Council*

The device includes a long cross and a miner's shovel, with the motto, *Deo juvante*—'With God's help.'

KNARESBOROUGH *Urban District Council*

The device consists of a castle with two towers and above it a hand holding a sprig.

KNOTTINGLEY *Urban District Council*

ARMS: Azure, in base water barry wavy argent and azure, and rising therefrom a bridge of two arches proper; and in chief a gold Lacy knot between two white roses with seeds and sepals proper.

CREST: On a wreath argent and azure, a forearm, the hand holding an ancient glass bottle, all proper.

MOTTO: *Industria ditat*—'Industry enriches.'

These were granted in 1942.

The bridge stands for the ancient structure over the River Aire at Ferrybridge. The knot alludes to the name, and also to the Lacys, feudal lords of the district. The crest refers to the local glass industry.

MIRFIELD *Urban District Council*

ARMS: Azure, a chief gules, over all a ram's face between two ears of barley with stalks and blades crossed saltirewise, all gold.

CREST: On a wreath gold and azure, a demi-knight facing in steel-coloured mail and white surcoat and thereon two bars wavy sable, holding a representation of a church in gold.

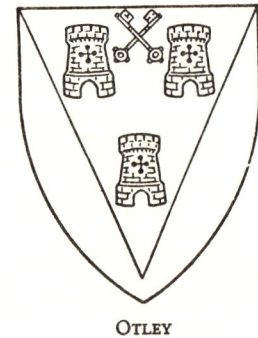

KNOTTINGLEY   MIRFIELD   OTLEY

Motto: *Fruges ecce paludis*—'Behold the fruits of the marsh.'
These were granted in 1935.
The emblems in the shield refer to the woollen and malting industries. The knight represents Sir John de Heton, whose appeal to the Pope in the thirteenth century led to the building of the parish church. The red chief on a blue field is a departure from the usual heraldic practice of not laying colour on colour.

OTLEY Urban District Council

Arms: Argent, on a pile azure three silver towers, and in the middle chief point two gold keys saltirewise, their wards upwards and inwards.
These were granted in 1951.
They were based on the arms granted in 1798 to the Otley Association.

QUEENSBURY AND SHELF Urban District Council

The device consists of a fleece suspended on a cross with forked limbs.

SALTBURN AND MARSKE-BY-THE-SEA Urban District Council

Arms: Azure, rising from waves in base a sea-gull facing proper; on a gold chief, three tridents' heads gules.
Crest: On a wreath argent and azure, water barry wavy of the same, and thereon a Roman ship proper with three pennons gules flying to the dexter, on the sail two wings joined together azure.

MOTTO: *Surgimus*—'We rise.'

These were granted in 1935.

The emblems refer to the district's seafaring interests and associations, while the gull indicates its aspirations, also expressed in the motto. The three tridents represent Saltburn, Marske, and New Marske, partners in the district, each with its place in the shield.

SALTBURN AND
MARSKE-BY-THE-SEA

SELBY

SELBY Urban District Council

The U.D.C. displays the arms of Selby Abbey: Sable, three silver swans.

SKIPTON Urban District Council

ARMS: Vert, a gold fleece and in chief two white roses with seeds and sepals proper; a chief checky gold and azure.

CREST: On a wreath gold and vert, a wyvern gules supporting a staff proper and thereon a banner barry of eight pieces gold and gules charged with a castellated gateway between two towers argent.

MOTTO: *Industria et spe*—'By industry and hope.'

These were granted in 1951.

The golden fleece in a green field refers to the importance of Skipton ('sheep town') as the chief market town in the agricultural area of Craven. The chequers and wyvern are from the heraldry of the Cliffords, who formerly held Skipton Castle, to which the towered gateway in the crest refers; and the barry banner represents the Romillys, Lords of Skipton in Norman times.

SKIPTON   SPENBOROUGH   WHITBY

SPENBOROUGH Urban District Council

ARMS: Gules, a Paschal Lamb proper and in chief three roses argent with seeds gold and sepals vert.

CREST: On a wreath argent and gules, a lion rampant purpure supporting with the left forepaw an escutcheon argent charged with a saltire gules surmounted by a label of five points azure.

MOTTO: *Industry enriches.*

These were granted in 1949.

The lamb refers to the district's woollen industry and allied trades, and the roses are County emblems. The crest consists of the lion of De Lacy, Lords of the Honour of Pontefract, supporting the shield of Neville of Liversedge.

WHITBY Urban District Council

ARMS: Barry wavy of ten pieces silver and azure, three coiled serpents proper.

CREST: On a wreath silver and azure, three white roses placed two and one in front of an anchor with a cable sable.

MOTTO: *Fuimus et sumus*—'We were and we are.'

These were granted in 1935.

The Council previously used as an unofficial device: Azure, three gold coiled serpents. Above the shield, but not on a crest-wreath, were placed a ship, a mitre, and a crozier. The arms are those attributed to St Hilda, great-niece of King Edwin of Northumbria, foundress and abbess of Whitby Abbey. Tradition states that stones in a form of coiled

YORKSHIRE

snakes found at Whitby were believed to be poisonous reptiles petrified by the prayers of St Hilda, whence the charges in her arms. The official arms retain St Hilda's serpents in conjunction with emblems of the sea and roses of York.

WOMBWELL *Urban District Council*

Use is made of the crest of the family of Wombwell: A silver unicorn's head.

MOTTO: *Secundis rebus cave.* (The family use the motto in the English form, 'In well, beware.')

KIVETON PARK R.D.C.

DONCASTER R.D.C.

WETHERBY R.D.C.

DONCASTER *Rural District Council*

ARMS: Parted palewise sable and vert, a fess wavy argent charged with another azure, and over all a silver castellated gateway with two towers each with a conical cap, with a white rose above the gateway and another below it.

These were granted in 1947.

The black-and-green field represents the district's two main industries—mining in the west and agriculture in the east. The silver-and-blue fess symbolizes the River Don and, with the castle gateway, expresses the name Doncaster. The roses are the County emblems. The arms are akin to those of Doncaster County Borough.

KIVETON PARK *Rural District Council*

ARMS: Quarterly ermine and azure, a gold cross charged in the centre with a roundel gules and thereon a white rose with seeds and sepals proper; in the first quarter a cock and a magpie combattant proper; in the second a hart trippant or; in the third a gold wheatsheaf; and in the fourth an uprooted oak-tree proper with gold acorns.

CREST: On a wreath argent and azure, a gold castle with four towers.

MOTTO: *Consilio et animis*—'By wisdom and courage.'

These were granted in 1949.

The arms are based on those of the family of Osborne of Kiveton, Earls of Danby and Dukes of Leeds. The emblems in the first quarter allude to the Cock and Pynot (magpie) Inn, Whittington Moor, where the Earl of Danby, the Duke of Devonshire, and others met to plot for the overthrow of James II.

The hart refers to Hart Hill Walk. The wheatsheaf stands for agriculture, and the rose is the County emblem. The castle represents Thorpe Castle.

WETHERBY Rural District Council

ARMS: Silver, two bars wavy azure; on a chief gules a gold wether passant between two gold ears of wheat with stalks and blades.

CREST: On a wreath argent and azure, a castle with two towers proper, on each tower a staff flying a white banner with a red cross; in front of the castle a Knight Templar holding in his right hand a battle-axe, all proper.

MOTTO: *Imperium in imperio*—'A government within another.'

These were granted in 1938.

Wetherby was the first Rural District Council to receive a grant of arms.

The wavy bars represent the River Wharfe. The wether refers to the place-name, and also, with the ears of wheat, to the agricultural character of the district.

The castle represents the old stronghold whose ruins stand near the present Council Offices. It was built by the Knights Templar in the reign of Henry III.

APPENDIX

AN ALPHABETICAL LIST OF MOTTOES OF LOCAL AUTHORITIES

A bonis ad meliora. Royston
Absque labore nihil. Darwen, Stalybridge
Action. Bognor Regis
A ddioddefws a orfu. Glamorgan C.C.
A Deo et Rege. Richmond (Surrey)
Adhuc hic hesterna. Chichester R.D.C.
Ad morem villae de Poole. Poole
Ad Pontes prospicimus. Staines
Advance. Goole
Aequo pede propera. Leigh
A good name endureth. Hornchurch
Agriculture and commerce. Maidstone
All's well. Camberwell
All things for the glory of God. Chingford
All this beauty is of God. Isle of Wight C.C.
Alta sententia. Arnold
Alte volo. Heywood
Altiora petimus. Finsbury
Altrincham en avant. Altrincham
Always advancing. Thornaby-on-Tees
Always ready. Glanford Brigg, South Shields
A magnis ad majora. Stepney
A ma puissance. Hale
Amoenitas, salubritas, urbanitas. Ryde
Amser yw'n golud. Ystradgynlais R.D.C.
Anchora spei Cereticae est in te Domine. Cardigan
Ancient and loyal. Wigan
Angliae cor. Hinckley
Animo et fide. Carshalton, Stockport
Antiqua constans virtute. Arundel
Antiqui colant Antiquum Dierum. Chester
Antiquum decus floreat. Oldbury.
Ardens fide. Brentwood
Arte et labore. Blackburn
Arte favente nil desperandum. Leek
Arte marte vigore. Wednesbury
Art, industry, contentment. Basildon

Arx celebris fontibus. Harrogate
Aspice respice. Wellingborough
At spes non fracta. Blaenavon
Audacter et sincere. Castleford
Audemus dum cavemus. Wallasey
Audentior. Watford
Audi consilium. West Riding C.C.
Auxilio Divino. Devonshire C.C.
Ave Mater Angliae. Canterbury
A vo penn bit pont. Bridgend
Awn rhagom. Cowbridge

Beau don. Bowdon
Beauty surrounds, health abounds. Morecambe and Heysham
Be just and fear not. Carlisle, Pudsey
Bene consulendo. Derbyshire C.C.
Benedicite fontes Domino. Buxton
Beware. Chorley
By concord and industry. Droylsden
By courage and faith. Seaham
By design and endeavour. Crawley
By industry and integrity. Nelson
By industry we prosper. Todmorden
By Worth. Farnham, Keighley

Cadernid, cyfiawnder, cynnydd. Barry
Cadernid Gwynedd. Caernarvonshire C.C.
Camera principis. Coventry
Caput inter nubila condit. Gateshead
Castello fortior concordia. Northampton
Cestrehunt. Cheshunt
Civitas in bello in pace fidelis. Worcester
Civitatis fortuna cives. Bebington
Clamant nostra tela in regis querela. Woolwich
Comfort (or *Confort*) *et Liesse.* Doncaster
Concilio et labore. Manchester
Consider thy purpose. Stevenage

Consilio absit discordia. Whitehaven
Consilio et animis. Kiveton Park, Surbiton
Consilio et animo. Wanstead and Woodford
Consilio et prudentia. Atherton
Constant be. Bedfordshire C.C.
Constantia basis virtutum. Andover
Copia est labor. Horwich
Cor unum. Soke of Peterborough C.C.
Courage, Humanity, Commerce. South Shields
Crede signo. Rochdale
Curandum omnium bonum. Garstang
Custodi civitatem Domine. Westminster
Cynchori er Llesiant. Penarth

De bon cuer. Walton-le-Dale
Decus et tutamen. Gravesend
Defendamus. Taunton
Deffro mae'n Ddydd. Cardiff
Dei gratia sumus quod sumus. Barking
Deo adjuvante. Wellington (Salop)
Deo adjuvante arte et industria floret. Kidderminster
Deo adjuvante labor proficit. Sheffield
Deo confidimus. West Ham
Deo fretus erumpe. Newark
Deo juvante. Kirkburton
Deus dat incrementum. Warrington
Deus nobis haec otia fecit. Liverpool
Deus noster refugium et virtus. Dewsbury
Deus per omnia. Islington
Domine dirige nos. City of London
Domini est dirige. Gipping R.D.C.
Dominus nobis sol et scutum. Banbury
Do well and doubt not. Tottenham
Do well, doubt not. Tunbridge Wells
Ducit amor appidi. Malden and Coombe
Dum cresco spero. Bromley
Dum defluat amnis. Walton and Weybridge
Duw a digon. Denbighshire C.C.

E mare ex industria. West Hartlepool
Endeavour. Hendon
En Dieu est mon esperance. Ashton-in-Makerfield
Erimus. Middlesbrough
E terra divitiae. Swadlincote
Et patribus et posteritati. Hitchin
Et plui super unam civitatem. Metropolitan Water Board

Ever forward. Weston-super-Mare
Ewch yn uwch. Radnorshire C.C.
Exaltum cornu in Deo. Truro
Except the Lord keep the city. Halifax
Ex glande quercus. Southgate
Ex terra copiam, e mari salutem. Worthing
Ex terra lucem. St Helens
Ex unitate vires. Pembrokeshire C.C.

Face the dawn. Kingswood
Faith. Billingham
Faith in industry. Edmonton
Faith, work, service. Calne
Fear God, honour the King. Wrexham
Fellowship is life. Coseley, Walthamstow
Festina lente. Audenshaw
Fiat justitia. South Molton
Fiat secundum Verbum Tuum. St Marylebone
Fide et diligentia. Woking
Fide et fortitudine. Penrith
Fide et labore. Harpenden
Fidelitas urbis salus regis. Bridgnorth
Fidelitate et Industria stat Bilstonia. Bilston
Fides et justitia. Farnborough
Fides invicta triumphat. Gloucester
Fiducia et vi. Slough
Filey et felicitas. Filey
Firma et stabilis. Kirkham
Firmior. Brentford and Chiswick
Floreat Actona. Acton
Floreat Ailesburia. Aylesbury
Floreat Bathon. Bath
Floreat Ecclesia Anglicana. Glastonbury
Floreat Etona. Eton
Floreat Hova. Hove
Floreat imperii portus. Port of London Authority
Floreat industria. Batley, Darlington
Floreat Rugbeia. Rugby
Floreat Salopia. Salop C.C., Shrewsbury
Floreat semper fidelis civitas. Worcester
Floreat Swansea. Swansea
Floret qui laborat. Mossley, Rawtenstall
Floruit floreat. Newbury
For all. Southall
For'ard, for'ard. Leicestershire C.C.
Fortior quo pariator. Hornsey
Fortis est veritas. Oxford
Fortis in arduis. Middleton

APPENDIX

Fortiter defendit triumphans. Newcastle-on-Tyne
Fortiter et recte. Crayford
Fortitudo et spes. Stockton-on-Tees
Forward. Birmingham, Hayes and Harlington
Fruges ecce paludis. Mirfield
Fuimus et sumus. Whitby

God's port our haven. Gosport
God with us. Dursley
Golud gwlad rhyddid. Cardiganshire C.C.
Gorau tarian cyfiawnder. Flintshire C.C.

Hanfod tref trefn. Ammanford
Haulte emprise. Haltemprice
Heaven's light our guide. Portsmouth
Hoc fonte derivata copia. Wells
Hold to the truth. Braintree
Home, industry, leisure. Bracknell
Honeste progrediemur conando. Seisdon R.D.C.
Honor alit artes. Burton-upon-Trent
Honor et industria. Bacup
Hostes nunc amici. Abergavenny
Hostis honori invidia. Market Harborough

Iechyd, harddwch, heddwch. Colwyn Bay
Ilfracombe potens salubritate. Ilfracombe
Imperium in imperio. Wetherby R.D.C.
In concilio consilium. Lancashire C.C.
In Deo fidemus. Brighton
Industria ditat. High Wycombe, Knottingley, Radcliffe, Widnes
Industria et spe. Skipton
Industria omnia vincit. Morley
Industria, virtus et fortitudo. Derby
Industry and prudence conquer. Accrington
Industry enriches. Spenborough.
In libertate vis. Merton and Morden
Integrity. Dukinfield
Integrity and industry. Salford
Inter sylvas et flumina habitans. Morpeth
In unitatem coeamus. Feltham
In unity progress. Ilford
Inutile utile ex arte. Ossett
In veritate victoria. Loughborough
Invicta. Kent C.C.
Invictae fidelitatis praemium. Hereford

Jewel of the Thames. Maidenhead
Judge us by our deeds. Dagenham
Jure et dignitate gladii. Cheshire C.C.
Juste nec timide. Farnworth
Justitia turris nostra. Hackney
Juvat impigros Deus. Huddersfield

Keep faith. Crewkerne
Known by their fruits. Sittingbourne

Laborare est orare. Willesden
Labore et ingenio. Smethwick
Labore et prudentia. Brighouse
Labore et scientia. Jarrow
Labore omnia florent. Eccles, Huntingdonshire C.C.
Labor in venatu. Cannock
Labor omnia vincit. Ashton-under-Lyne, Bradford, Ilkeston
Labour overcomes all things. Erith
Levavi oculos meos in montes. Malvern, Workington
Libera deinde fidelis. Godalming
Like as the oak. Uckfield R.D.C.
Looking backward, looking forward. Twickenham
Loyal and Industrious. Rowley Regis
Loyal and true. Chatham
Luck to Loyne. Lancaster
Lux et humanitas. Blackwell R.D.C.
Lux, salubritas, felicitas. Clacton

Majora, uberiora, pulchriora. Hemel Hempstead
Many minds one heart. Chelmsford
Mare ditat flores decorant. Exmouth
Mare et ferro. Redcar
Meliora sequimur. Eastbourne
Members one of another. Harlow
Messis ab altis. Tynemouth
Ministrando dignitas. Leyton
Monemus et munimus. Monmouth
Mon Mam Cymru. Anglesey C.C.
Montes unde auxilium meum. Keswick
More light more power. Shoreditch
Multi pertransibunt et augebitur scientia. Holborn
Multum in parvo. Rutland C.C.
Mutare vel timere sperno. Little Lever

APPENDIX

Ne cede malis. Herne Bay
Nec ferro nec igni. Appleby
Nec virtus nec copia desunt. Macclesfield
Never behind. Crewe
Never wonne ne never shall. Reigate
Nid cadarn ond brodyrdde. Merthyr Tydfil
Nil desperandum auspice Deo. Sunderland
Nisi Dominus frustra. Chelsea
Nobis habitatio felix. Wilmslow
None such. Epsom and Ewell
Non mihi, non tibi, sed nobis. Battersea
Non nobis sed communitati. Bexley
Non nobis sed omnibus. North Walsham
Non nobis solum. Beckenham
Non progredi est regredi. Chigwell, Ruislip-Northwood
Non sanz droict. Warwickshire C.C.
Non sibi sed toti. Hampstead
Nostrum viret robur. Wood Green
Not for ourselves alone. Barnes
Nothing without labour. Haslingden

Oculus in coelum. Eye
Omnia bona bonis. Harwich
One and all. Cornwall C.C.
One heart one way. Stourbridge
Oni heuir ni fedir. Carmarthen R.D.C.
Onward. Fleetwood, Hyde
Opes consilium parit. Bridgwater
Opes parit industria. Bingley
Opus nostrum dirige. East Suffolk C.C.
Ora et ara. South Kesteven R.D.C.
Out of darkness cometh light. Wolverhampton

Pannus mihi panis. Kendal
Per ardua ad summa. Beddington and Wallington
Perfero. Cumberland C.C.
Per mare et per terram. Boston
Per mare per ecclesiam. Southend-on-Sea
Per pericula ad decus ire iuvat. Scarborough
Perseverantia vincit. Kesteven C.C.
Persevere. Denton
Per undas per agros. Cambridgeshire C.C.
Point du jour. Lowestoft
Porta maris portus salutis. Margate
Powys Paradwys Cymru. Montgomeryshire C.C.

Praecepta non homines. Newport Pagnell
Prae salem notanda. Preesall
Prest à faire. Fareham
Pret d'accomplir. Nuneaton
Pretiumque et causa laboris. Burnley
Pride in our past, faith in our future. Hertford
Priora cole meliora sequere. Enfield
Prisca constantia. Newcastle-under-Lyme
Pro bono oppido. Horbury
Pro civibus et civitate. Fulham
Pro Deo et populo. Bishop's Stortford
Prodesse. Hindley
Progress. Blackpool, Littlehampton
Progressio cum populo. East Ham
Progressio et concordia. Kettering
Pro Hertfordae honore. Hertford (legend on standard)
Pro rege ac fide audax. Bideford
Pro rege et lege. Leeds
Prorsum semper. Gloucestershire C.C.
Pro rure pro patria. Hertford R.D.C.
Prosunt gentibus artes. Bermondsey
Proudly we serve. Horsham
Prudens futuri. Letchworth
Pugna pro patria. Aldershot
Pulchra terra Dei donum. Herefordshire C.C.
Pulchritudo et salubritas. Bournemouth

Quanti est sapere. Shardlow R.D.C.
Quid nos ardui. Kensington
Quod improbum terret probo prodest. Penzance

Ramosa cornua cervi. Woodstock
Recte fac noli timere. Prestwich
Reddite Deo. Redditch
Refulget labores nostros coelum. Scunthorpe
Regnant qui serviunt. Finchley
Respice aspice prospice. Bootle, Halesowen, Tettenhall
Respice finem. Newmarket
Respice prospice. Ealing, Stoke Newington, Trowbridge
Reviresco. Rishton
Rex et nostra jura. Great Yarmouth
Rhyddid gwerin ffyniant gwlad. Carmarthenshire C.C.
Rhyddid hedd a llwyddiant. Carmarthen
Ro an mor. Newquay
Rosa concordiae signum. Northamptonshire C.C.

Rura mihi placent. Congleton R.D.C.
Ruris amator. Friern Barnet
Rus gratiis musisque dignum. Bathavon R.D.C.

Sacrarium regis cunabula legis. Bury St Edmunds
Sal est vita. Northwich
Salubritas et eruditio. Cheltenham
Salubritas et industria. Swindon
Salus et felicitas. Sale, Torquay
Salus naufragis salus aegris. Ramsgate
Salus populi. Southport
Salus populi suprema lex. Eastleigh, Harrow, Lewisham, Lytham-St Annes, Swinton and Pendlebury, Tipton, Tonbridge, Willenhall
Salus populi suprema est lex. Urmston
Salve magna parens. Lichfield
Sanitate crescamus. Croydon
Sans Dieu rien. Worksop
Sapere aude. Oldham, Oxfordshire C.C.
Sapienter proficiens. Nottinghamshire C.C.
Scientiae et labori detur. Luton
Secundis rebus cave. Wombwell
Semper acceptus. Paignton
Semper eadem. Leicester
Semper fidelis. Exeter
Semper fidelis mutare sperno. Worcester
Semper proficimus. Leyland
Semper serio. Hatfield R.D.C.
Semper sursum. Barrow-in-Furness
Serve God and be cheerful. Sutton and Cheam
Serve with gladness. Romford
Service and Efficiency. Stretford
Service links all. Leatherhead, Lindsey C.C.
Sicut quercus virescit industria. Mansfield
Sic virescit industria. Rotherham
Sic vos non vobis. Baldock
Signum salutis semper. Bridlington
Sine labe decus. Wimbledon
Sine labore nihil floret. Brierley Hill
Sit saxum firmum. Stone
Sit Tibi sancta cohors comitum. Congleton
Situ exoritur Seguduni. Wallsend
Sola bona quae honesta. Leamington
Sol et pastor Deus. Sunbury-on-Thames
Sol et salubritas. Bexhill
Spectemur agendo. Barnsley, Chorley R.D.C., Hammersmith, Lambeth
Spe nemo ruet. Spennymoor

Stabit saxum fluet amnis. Clitheroe
Steadfast and faithful. Axminster
Steadfast in difficulties. Tottenham
Strive for the gain of all. Gainsborough
Sub cruce floreamus. Poulton-le-Fylde
Sudore non sopore. St Ives (Hunts)
Sumorsaete ealle. Somerset C.C.
Supera moras. Bolton
Surgamus ergo strenue. Baildon
Surgimus. Saltburn and Marske
Suum cuique tribuere. Wrexham R.D.C.

Tempore utimur. Greenwich
Tempori parendum. Bishop Auckland, Wembley
Tenax et Fidelis. Dartford
Terra marique. Thornton Cleveleys
The knot unites. Staffordshire C.C.
They ryght defend. Southwold
Tra mor tra Meirion. Merionethshire C.C.
True worth never fails. Failsworth
Trust and fear not. Hertfordshire C.C.
Trust and triumph. Gainsborough R.D.C.
Turris fortissima est nomen Jehovae. Plymouth

Ubi fides ibi lux et robur. Birkenhead
Undeb hedd llwyddiant. Breconshire C.C.
Ung nous servons. Pembroke
Unitate fortior. Heston and Isleworth
Unitate praestans. Preston R.D.C.
United to serve. Southwark
Unity and progress. Melksham
Urbs in rure. Solihull
Ut homines liberi sint. Egham
Utrique fidelis. Monmouthshire C.C.

Vestigia nulla retrorsum. Buckinghamshire C.C.
Vetustas dignitatem generat. East Retford
Vicinas urbes alit. Spalding
Victoria gloria merces. Berwick-upon-Tweed
Vigilantes. Cleethorpes
Vigilate et orate. Clevedon
Vincit amor patriae. Sunderland R.D.C.
Vincit omnia industria. Bury
Virtus veritas libertas. Glossop
Virtute et industria. Bristol
Vis unita fortior. Crosby, Stoke-on-Trent
Vivit post funera virtus. Nottingham

We grow by industry. Blyth
We long endure. Colne
We serve. Dartford R.D.C., Wandsworth
Who's afear'd? Dorset C.C.
With Fort and Fleet for Home and England.
  Gillingham

With wisdom and courage. St Pancras
Work supports all. Worksop R.D.C.

Y ddraig goch ddyry gychwyn. Cardiff, Prestatyn
Ymlaen Llanelli. Llanelly

INDEX

INDEX

SECTION A—PERSONS AND FAMILIES

ABERGAVENNY, MARQUESS OF, 20, 286
Abney, 261
Acland, 89
Ailesbury, De, 59
Aird, Sir John, 257
Allen, 147
Alleyn, Edward, 20, 248
Anglesey, Marquess of, 284, 329
Anlach, 56
Anne Boleyn, 30, 239
Anselm, 282
Appleyard, 240
Arbalestier, 228
Arderne, 82
Arthur, King, 17, 322
Ashawe, 229
Ashburnham, 349
Assheton, 20, 81, 207, 208, 216, 223
Aston, 378
Athelstan, King, 108, 277, 386
Atherton, 215, 222
Attwood, 123
Audley, 330
Austell, 90
Awfa ap Cynddelw, 47

Bacon, 244
Badlesmere, 366
Bailey, 406
Baldwin, 226
Baliol, 275, 414
Banastre, 230
Bancroft, 278
Banks, 196
Barri, De, 144
Barrington, 169
Bass, 20, 329
Basset, 284, 364
Beauchamp, Barons of Bedford, 20, 48, 49
——, Earls, 395
——, Earls of Warwick, 20, 374, 379
—— family, 396
Beaufort, 15, 200, 286, 364
Beaumont, 144, 232, 234, 377
Becket, Thomas, 4, 20, 24, 131, 136, 178, 249, 350, 360
Beckett, 399
Bede, the Venerable, 40, 117, 120, 298
Bedford, Barons of, 20, 48, 49
——, Dukes of, 20, 48, 254, 258

Belesme, De, 319
Bellasis, 121
Berkeley, 89, 152
Bermyngham, De, 20, 376
Berners, 254
Bexley, Lord, 179
Bigod, Roger, 348
Billingham, 121
Bilston, 333
Bingley, 416
Biscop, Benedict, 118, 120
Blake, Admiral, 323
Blanchminster, 89
Bleddyn ap Cynfyn, 288
Blois, Henry de, 158
Bohun, 20, 58, 328, 360, 364
Bold, 202
Bolitho, 88
Bootle, 20, 197
Bossard, 50
Boulton, Matthew, 330
Bourchier, 109
Bouverie, 384
Bradford, 400
Bradshaw, 215
Bramhall, 83
Brandling, 121
Brandon, 343
Braose, De, 19, 143, 144, 145, 371
Brassey, Earl, 367
Brereton, 84
Brian, De, 71
Bridgewater, Earls and Dukes of, 5, 295
Brighouse, 20, 409
Bristol, Marquess of, 242
Brittany, Dukes of, 239, 414
Briwere, De, 324
Bruce, De Brus, 19, 275, 405, 415
Brychan, 56, 70, 143
Buccleuch, Duke of, 194, 208
Buckhurst, Lord, 367
Buckingham, Dukes of, 19, 56, 58 ff., 272, 286, 334
Bulkeley, 82
Bunyan, John, 41, 48
Burghersh, 360
Burleigh, Lord, 263
Burton, Lord, 20, 329
Bussell, 226
Bute, Marquess of, 50
Butler, Boteler, 204
Byerley, 122
Byron, 20, 201, 224, 225, 309

Cadogan, 248, 317
Caesar, Julius, 17, 359, 364
Calthorpe, 376
Cambridge, Earls and Dukes of, 16, 355
Camden, Marquess, 258
Camden, Sir William, 179
Canterbury, Archbishops of, 256, 276, 281, 350
Canute, 184
Cardonell, De, 145
Carew, 352
Carlyell, De, 92
Carre, 242
Carrington, 80
Cator, 179
Cavendish, 20, 97 ff., 366, 411
Cavendish-Bentinck, 306
Cawley, Lord, 218
Cecil, 19, 127, 164, 170, 263, 294, 359
Chance, 330
Charles I, 100, 321, 407
Charlton, 270, 321
Charnock, 230
Chatham, Earl of, 20, 180
Chester, Earls of, 12, 16, 72 ff., 95, 203, 204, 236, 242, 334
Chichester, Bishops of, 367
Chorley, 20, 207, 230
Clare, De, 19, 115, 141, 142, 145, 147, 149, 164, 183, 192, 287, 315, 316
Clarendon, Lord, 165
Clayton, 223
Clifford, 421
Clifton, 216, 225
Clinton, De, 377
Cludde, 321
Cobham, Lord, 393
Cocker, 196
Coel, King, 22, 128
Colebrook, 254
Colleton, Sir John, 109
Compton, 275
Constantius, Emperor, 128
Cope, 255
Copley, 20, 400, 408
Cornwall, Earls and Dukes of, 16, 85 ff., 102 ff.
Coulson, 123
Courtauld, 135
Coutts, 358
Courtenay, 20, 158, 186, 327

P
433

INDEX

Coventry, Earl of, 396
Coverdale, Miles, 110
Craven, 204
Cripps, 147
Crisp, Sir Nicholas, 20, 252
Crompton, Samuel, 196
Cromwell, Thomas, 24, 359
Cunobelin, Cymbeline, 128
Curwen, 93

Dacre, 91
Dafydd ap Gwilym, 67
Danby, 404, 424
D'Arcy, 136
Dartmouth, Earl of, 257, 332
David I, King of Scotland, 16, 64, 275
Davies of Llandinam, Lord, 144
Dearden, 201
Defoe, Daniel, 261
De La Pole, 12, 343
De La Val, 301
De La Warr, 367, 369
Denton, 223
Derby, Earls of, 19, 73, 79, 100, 193, 197, 361
Despenser. See Spencer.
D'Eton, 75
Devon, Earls of, 327
Devonshire, Dukes of, 20, 97 ff., 194, 366, 424
Dorman, Long & Co., 413
Douai, Walter de, 323
Drake, Sir Francis, 20, 29, 42, 102
Dudley, Earl of, 20, 335, 390
—— family, 233, 261, 335, 374 ff., 393
Dukinfield, 20, 78, 81
Dunraven, Lord, 146
Durham, Bishops of, 116, 118 ff., 215
Dursley, Viscount, 152
Dymock, 352

Eccleston, 202
Edgar, King, 11, 126, 332, 350
Edmund, Saint and King, 14, 18, 23, 345 ff.
Edmund Ironside, 184
Ednyfed Fychan, 95
Edward I, 14, 47, 95, 115, 266
Edward II, 12, 14, 264
Edward III, 13, 14, 15, 29, 57, 105, 109, 182, 187, 205, 256, 301, 313, 376
Edward IV, 14, 15, 293, 363, 391, 398
Edward VII, 264
Edward the Black Prince, 14, 15, 256, 376
Edward the Confessor, 18, 100, 132, 134, 137, 151, 154, 263, 344, 346, 364, 402
Edward the Elder, 340, 341
Edward the Martyr, 14, 25, 52

Edwin, King of Northumbria, 300, 422
Edwin of Tegeinol, 140
Egerton, 218, 295
Egfrid, King, 120
Eleanor of Castile, 115, 168
Eleanor of Provence, 14
Elizabeth I, Queen, 13, 14, 115, 151, 170, 233, 280, 318, 346, 352, 391
Elizabeth II, Queen, 208
Elizabeth Woodville, 15, 293, 391
Elletson, 228
Elystan Glodrhydd, 317
Essex, Earls of, 157, 359
Ethelred, King, 247
Exeter, Marquess of, 294
Eyston, 336
Eyton, 321

Farington, Farrington, 226, 231
Feilden, 195
Fellowes, 360
Ferrers, 19, 73, 79, 100, 193, 318
Fisher, 377
Fitton, 83
FitzAlan, 350, 367
FitzRoger, 215
Flamville, 235
Fleetwood, 20, 212, 226, 227, 228
Fletcher, 304
Fogge, 190
Foljambe, 305
Fordham, Sir H. G., 64
Forester, Lord, 321
Francis, 270
Fraunceys, 132
Freeman, 283
Furnival, 307

Gainsford, 360
Galway, Lord, 305
Gamble, Sir David, 202
Garth, 363
Gascelyn, 385
Gaveston, Piers, 213
George V, 11, 370
George VI, 164, 179
Gerard, 202, 222
Giffard, William, 325
Gilbert, 366
Gloucester, Earls and Dukes of, 19, 58, 115, 147, 149, 150
Goddard, 387
Godiva, 321
Gordon, 309
Grantmesnil, 235
Granville, 141, 145
Greathead, 117
Greg, 84
Grelley, 200, 225
Grenville, 29, 89, 105
Greswold, 380
Grey, 76, 308, 342
Grey de Radcliffe, Lord, 218
Grimsby, 237

Guader, Ranulf de, 20, 290
Gwynedd, Princes of, 72, 184, 304

Hacket, Bishop, 359
Hackworth, 122
Haden, 335
Hamilton, 230
Hampden, John, 59
Handel, 40, 281
Handforth, 84
Harborough, Earls of, 235
Hardwick, 360
Hargreaves, 207
Harold, King, 18, 134, 138
Harrington, Earl of, 101
Hastings, 233 ff., 275
Hatton, 297
Haughton, 223
Hawke, Lord, 243
Hazlerigg, 233
Heathcote, 330
Hengist and Horsa, 17, 177
Henrietta Maria, Queen, 13, 407
Henry I, 205
Henry II, 11, 178
Henry III, 14
Henry IV, 13, 233, 301
Henry V, 14, 191, 287
Henry VI, 14, 15
Henry VII, 191, 263, 293, 314, 316, 357
Henry VIII, 14, 98, 163, 170, 191, 364, 379
Herbert, 289, 316
Hereford, Bishops of, 175
Hereford, Viscount, 160
Hereward the Wake, 64, 65
Heronville, 337
Herschel, Sir William, 40, 60
Hertfordshire, Earls of, 164
Hervey, 242
Heton, 420
Heywood, 20, 213
Hickes, 253
Hogge, 372
Hoghton, 230
Holden, 213
Holgate, Robert, 419
Horbury, 419
Hornby, 195
Hotham, Sir Richard, 370
Howard, 20, 70, 99, 306, 350, 357, 364, 367, 371
Hulton, 212
Husee, 385
Hyde, 20, 79, 229

Iestyn ap Gwrgan, 141, 142
Ine, King, 325

James I, 16, 50, 168, 169, 170, 191, 312, 319
James II, 424

INDEX

John, King, 11, 39, 87, 323, 361, 392, 396
John of Gaunt, 16, 99, 153, 154, 220, 232, 286, 372, 399
Johnson, Samuel, 334
Juhell, 104, 107

Katherine of Aragon, 56, 98
Keats, 40, 270
Keighley, 20, 411
Kendal, Barons of, 381
Kennard, 287
Kensington, Lord, 20, 255
Kent, Duke of, 111
Kidderminster, Kydermaster, 393
Killigrew, 86
Kipling, Rudyard, 372
Knibb, 296
Knut, King, 83

Lacy, De, 19, 77, 95, 96, 197, 208, 209, 213, 230, 254, 412, 417, 419, 422
Laird, 74
Lamb, Charles, 39, 270
Lancaster, De, 230, 381
Lancaster, Earls and Dukes of, 14, 99, 100, 153, 154, 193 ff., 232, 372
Lanfranc, 350
Langhorne, 253
Langley, 221
Langton, 230
Latymer, Edward, 20, 252
Lechmere, 396
Leeds, Duke of, 424
Leicester, Earls of, 20, 232 ff., 377, 393
Lennox, Duke of, 184
Leofric, Earl of Mercia, 321
Leslie, Earl of Leven, 161
Lever, 77, 226
Lewisham, Viscount, 257
Lilburn, 122
Lilford, Lord, 215, 222
Lincoln, Earls of, 19, 77, 95, 96, 213, 242, 254, 417
Llewelyn, Prince, 62, 95
Lloyd, 289
Locke, 399
London, Bishops of, 24, 126, 127, 135, 167, 271, 276
Longbottom, 307
Lonsdale, Earl of, 92
Louth, 241
Lovetoft, 307
Lowther, 92
Lucy, 29, 183
Lumley, 359
Lygon, 395
Lyon, John, 39, 277
Lyttelton, 393
Lytton, 172

Macclesfield, Lord, 310

Malbank, Malbanus, 83
Malton, Lord, 305
Mandeville, 360
Mansfield, Earl, 20, 306
March, Earls of, 19, 293, 317, 320
Marchell, 56
Martin, 233
Mary I, 56
Massey, 20, 74, 76, 80, 82
Matilda, Queen, 385
Maxim, Sir Hiram, 190
Maynard, 133
Merlay, De, 302
Merton, 355
Meux, 168
Meyrick, 321
Middleton, 20, 216
Mildmay, 127
Monceaux, 327
Monk, 208
Monmouth, De, 287
Monoux, 29, 133
Montagu, 296
Montchensy, 138
Monteagle, 127
Montfichet, 20, 125, 126, 132, 169
Montfort, De, 39, 232, 235, 248, 335
Montgomery, De, 288, 321, 393
Mordaunt, 389
More, 353
Morris, William, 134
Mortimer, 15, 19, 317, 320, 363, 391
Moseley, 82, 330
Mount Edgcumbe, 104
Mowbray, 235, 369, 371
Moyer, 138
Murdoch, William, 330
Murray, 20, 306
Myddleton, Sir Hugh, 263

Nall-Cain, Sir Charles, 163
Napier, Sir Robert, 50
Nasmyth, James, 211
Nevill, 20, 286, 305, 374, 422
Newburgh, 379
Newcastle, Duke of, 303
Noel, 253
Norfolk, Earls and Dukes of, 20, 290, 348, 367, 371
Northampton, John de, 259
Northbrook, Lord, 257
Northrop, 399
Northumberland, Earls and Dukes of, 298

Odingsells, 380
Odo, Bishop of Bayeux, 179, 388
Offa, King of Mercia, 165
Olaf, King, 247
Oldham, 20, 200
Orneston, 229
Osborne, 424
Oswald, King, 18, 116, 298, 320
Oswin, King of Deira, 300

Owen, Prince of Gwynedd, 62
Owen family, 47
Oxenden, 191

Paganel, 61
Paget, 284, 329
Palmer, Sir Charles Mark, 120
Parr, 202
Patten, 261
Patti, Madam, 57
Paveley, 389
Pelham, 240
Pembroke, Earls of, 166, 271, 289, 314 ff.
Penwortham, 226, 231
Pepys, Samuel, 372
Percy, 116, 298
Perrier, 353
Peter the Great of Russia, 249
Petre, 138
Philippa, Queen, 14, 15, 187
Pillesden, or Pitlesden, 189
Pitman, Sir Isaac, 152
Pitt, 20, 180
Plumtree, 308
Plymouth, Earl of, 144
Pontisbury, 321
Portland, Duke of, 303, 309
Portman, 257
Poulett, 327
Powis, Lord, 272, 289
Powys, 222
Pring, George, 252
Pryse, 67
Pudsey, 20, 413

Radcliffe, 20, 218, 240
Ramsden, 20, 194, 403
Rashdale, 20, 201
Rastrick, 409
Redvers, 327
Rhys ap Tewdwr Mawr, 69
Rich, 20, 255
Richard I, 11, 13, 106, 154, 161
Richard II, 14, 98
Richard III, 150
Richard, Earl of Cornwall, 85, 102 ff.
Richmond, Earls and Dukes of, 239, 357, 414
Ridgway, 331
Robert of Gloucester, 248
Robin Hood, 32, 174
Robsart, 394
Romilly, 421
Rotherham, Thomas of, 21, 405
Russell, 20, 48, 254

St Alban, 165
St Andrew, 22, 77, 88, 94, 104, 226, 254, 369
St Anthony, 88
St Bartholomew, 327

INDEX

St Chad, 23, 227, 334, 339
St Clement, 23, 29, 126
St Cuthbert, 23, 116 ff., 307
St David, 67
St Dunstan, 23, 260, 385
St Edith of Wilton, 388
St I 'li, 23, 70, 143
St E.ltyd, 266
St Etheldreda, 18, 23, 25, 65, 170
St Felix, 348
St George, 12, 23, 238, 245
St Giles, 23, 248, 254
St Helena, 22, 128
St Hilda, 422
St James, 23, 29, 136, 250
St John of Beverley, 408
St John the Baptist, 22, 23, 106, 201, 326, 402
St Lawrence, 23, 126
St Leonard, 23, 369
St Luke, 24, 248, 250
St Margaret, 4, 24, 291, 346
St Mark, 358
St Martin, 12, 24, 182
St Mary the Virgin, 13, 22, 157, 158, 166, 218, 238, 243, 255, 257, 329, 349, 378
St Michael, 24, 87, 157, 167, 229, 321
St Milburga, 321
St Mildred, 189
St Modwena, 329
St Nicholas, 24, 243, 269
St Pancras, 24, 258
St Paul, 4, 24, 66, 88, 138, 158, 245 ff., 322, 356
St Pedr, 68
St Peter, 24, 66, 88, 118, 158, 294 ff., 322, 332, 356
St Stephen, 396
St Thomas. See Becket
St Tydfil, 24, 143
St Vincent, Earl of, 340
St Wilfrid, 372
Salisbury, Bishops of, 385
———, Marquess of, 164, 170, 263
Sandbach, 83
Sandford, 330
Saumarez, 349
Savage, Thomas, 409
Savile, 20, 400, 404, 417
Savoy, Counts of, 137
Scawen, 360
Seymour, 388
Shafto, 123
Shakespeare, 21, 42, 374
Sheffield, 241

Sheriff, Lawrence, 378
Shrewsbury, Earls of, 160, 288, 319, 407
Shuttleworth, 215
Sidney, Sir Henry, 320
Skevyngton, Bishop, 63
Slingsby, 410
Sloane, 248
Sneyd, 331, 335
Somerset, Duchess of, 275
——— family, 285
Somery, 61, 335
Spencer, De Spenser, 20, 234, 254, 351, 359, 364
Stafford, 19, 56, 58 ff., 286, 328 ff.
Stamford, Earl of, 76, 82, 83
Standish, 228, 230
Stanley, 20, 75, 225, 248, 295. See also Derby, Earls of
Staveley, 20, 81
Stepney, 70
Stockport, Stopford, 20, 75, 82
Sudbury, 20, 347
Suffolk, Earls and Dukes of, 20, 157, 239, 343
Surrey, Earls of, 19, 256, 262, 350 ff.
Sussex, Earl of, 240
Sutton, 243, 250
Swansea, Lord, 144

Talbot, 160, 407
Tennyson, Lord, 237
Thornaby, 20, 415
Throgmorton, 380
Tichborne, 156
Tostig, Earl, 401
Trafford, 220, 229
Tressell or Trussel, 342
Trivet, 324
Tudor, Jasper, 314
Tunstall, 217
Tyldesley, 228
Tyler, Wat, 245
Tyndale, William, 21, 152

Ufford, 343
Urmestone, 215
Uxbridge, Earl of, 284

Valence, De, 129, 316
Vere, De, 138, 255, 398
Vesey, 379, 389
Victoria, Queen, 111

Vilars, Pain de, 204
Vilett, 387

Wake, 65, 418
Wales, Princes of, 15 ff., 26, 62 ff., 70 ff., 78, 95 ff., 141 ff., 317, 351, 392
Walmsley, 202
Waltheof, Earl, 64, 275
Walton, 230
Walworth, Sir William, 245
Ward, 335, 339
Warenne, De, 12, 19, 240, 241, 256, 262, 350 ff., 400, 402
Warwick, Earls of, 20, 331, 374 ff., 398
Washington, 123
Watson, 296
Watt, James, 330
Wedgwood, 330
Wenlock, 321
Wentworth, 349, 399
Wheatley, 183
Whethamsteade, John, 50
Whitgift, Archbishop, 21, 350
Whitgreaves, 229
Wilbraham, 84
Willes, 377
William I, 51, 64, 66
William Longsword, 392
Willoughby, 244
Winchester, Bishops of, 25, 156, 158, 325, 361
———, Marquesses of, 153
Windsor, Duke of, 16, 351
Withipole, 132
Wittewronge, 168
Wolsey, Cardinal, 24, 355, 360, 361, 364
Wombwell, 423
Worcester, Earls of, 285
Worsley, 221
Wray, 244
Wrey, 109
Wrottesley, 342
Wulfrun, 332
Wycliffe, John, 243
Wykeham, William of, 21, 137, 276

Yarborough, Earl of, 240
York, Dukes of, 15 ff., 293, 320, 391, 398

Zetland, Lord, 413

INDEX

SECTION B—PLACES AND SUBJECTS

(NOTE: The Index does not include references to detailed descriptions and illustrations of arms of local authorities; these will be found in the Contents at the beginning of the book.)

ABERGAVENNY, 20
Abingdon, 25, 255
Accrington, 19, 34, 37, 41
Acton, 35, 37, 39, 42
Aesculapius, Rod of, 31
Agriculture, 33
Air transport, 35, 272, 352
Aldeburgh, 29
Aldershot, 12, 25, 42
Alnwick, 24
Altrincham, 20, 82
Anchors, 29
Anglesey, 47
Appleby, 11, 37, 39
Aquarius, 36, 264
Arbroath, 24
Arden, Forest of, 380
Arms, definition, 6
Arundel, 17, 37
Ashburton, 14, 23
Ashdown white horse, 39
Ashton-on-Mersey, 80
Ashton-under-Lyne, 20, 41
Audenshaw, 15, 20
Avalon, 322
Axminster, 39
Aylesbury, 23

Bacup, 32, 33 ff.
Badges, 8
Banbury, 39
Bangor, 24
Banners, 8
Barking, 13, 19, 25, 36, 257
Barnard Castle, 14
Barnes, 16, 24, 30
Barnet, 398
Barnsley, 25, 34, 35
Barnstaple, 26
Barrow-in-Furness, 20, 29, 33, 37, 403
Basingstoke, 24
Bath, 31
Batley, 20, 41
Battersea, 30
Beaumaris, 29
Beavers, 30
Bebington, 74
Beckenham, 32
Beddington and Wallington, 19, 35, 36
Bedford, 3, 20, 26
Bedfordshire, 20, 41, 48 ff.
Bees, 33
Berkhamstead, 16
Berkshire, 11, 32, 51 ff.
Bermondsey, 25, 29, 38
Bernicia, Kingdom of, 18, 298
Berwick, 13, 22, 37

Bethnal Green, 39
Beverley, 30, 37, 397
Bewdley, 15, 29
Bexhill, 12, 18, 27, 28, 30, 41, 369
Bexley, 32, 33
Bideford, 27, 29
Birkenhead, 20, 29
Birmingham, 20, 33, 41
Bishop's Stortford, 24
Blackburn, 30, 33
Blackpool, 13, 28, 36, 41
Blackwell, 34
Blyth, 29, 34
Bognor Regis, 11
Bolton, 25, 32, 42
Bootle, 20, 30
Boston, 10, 30, 33 ff., 236
Bournemouth, 18, 29 ff.
Bowdon, 20
Brackley, 5, 20
Bradford, 34, 39, 41
Braintree, 24
Brecknock, 20
Brentford and Chiswick, 11, 24, 30
Bridges, 27
Bridgnorth, 13, 41
Bridgwater, 27
Bridlington, 38
Bridport, 13, 26, 28
Brierley Hill, 29, 35
Brighouse, 20
Brighton, 18, 29, 369
Bristol, 26, 28 ff.
——, Rhode Island, 149
Bromley, 14, 23, 30, 37
Brunanburgh, 39, 108
Buckingham, 20
Buckinghamshire, 20, 32, 37, 39, 58 ff.
Burnley, 19, 30, 33 ff.
Burslem, 330
Burton-on-Trent, 20, 30
Bury, 33 ff., 36
Bury St Edmunds, 18, 23, 139
Buxton, 20, 31

Caernarvonshire, 15, 17, 62 ff.
Calne, 15, 26
Camberwell, 20, 23, 31
Cambridge, 15, 27, 30
Cambridgeshire, 16, 27, 30, 64 ff., 174
Camelot, 322
Canberra, 263
Canterbury, 4, 12, 20, 24, 47
Cardiff, 15, 17, 28, 30, 42
Cardigan, 26
Cardiganshire, 41, 67 ff.
Carisbrooke Castle, 175

Carlisle, 14
Carmarthen, 15
Carmarthenshire, 17, 69 ff.
Castles, 26 ff.
Charterhouse, 250
Chatham, 20, 29 ff.
Chelmsford, 24, 31, 41
Chelsea, 20, 24, 41
Cheltenham, 18, 31, 39
Chepping Wycombe. *See* High Wycombe
Cheshire, 15, 16, 33, 72 ff.
Cheshunt, 16, 35
Chester, 12, 16, 19
Chesterfield, 14
Chichester, 12, 372
Chingford, 25
Chorley, 20, 230
Christchurch, 22
Christ Church, Oxford, 225
Cinque Ports, 11, 177, 182 ff., 344, 366 ff.
Civil Defence, 362
Clacton, 23
Cleethorpes, 30, 40
Clerkenwell, 250
Clitheroe, 26
Coal mining, 34
Colchester, 18, 22, 304
Colne, 19, 38
Colwyn Bay, 17
Congleton, 19, 37
Cornwall, 15, 16, 28, 30, 34, 41, 85 ff.
——, Duchy of, 166, 256, 384, 392
Corpus Christi College, Oxford, 200
Cotton industry, 34
Coventry, 15, 25, 196
Cowbridge, 19, 27, 37
Crayford, 35
Crests, 6
Crewe, 35
Crewkerne, 36
Crondall, 156
Cross, True, 22, 129, 138
Crowns, 10 ff., 36
Croydon, 21, 24, 31, 36
Cumberland, 32, 34, 91 ff.
Cumbria, Kingdom of, 92, 382

Dagenham, 24
Darlington, 34 ff., 41
Dartford, 25, 35, 36
Dartmouth, 14
Darwen, 30, 34
Deal, 12
Deer, 34
Denbigh, 19
Denbighshire, 19, 95 ff.
Denton, 35

INDEX

Deptford, 24, 29
Derby, 14, 34
Derbyshire, 15, 20, 97 ff.
Devizes, 26
Devon, 16, 20, 28, 42, 102 ff.
Devonport, 104
Dewsbury, 19, 20, 41, 404
Dolphins, 29
Doncaster, 11, 12, 27, 30, 423
Dorchester, 13
Dorset, 17, 112 ff.
Dover, 12, 24
Dragons, 17
Droitwich, 11, 33
Droylsden, 20, 23
Dudley, 20, 29, 35
Dukinfield, 20, 37
Dulwich College, 20
Dunstable, 25
Durham C.C., 5, 18, 24, 116 ff.
Durham City, 23
Dursley, 21

Ealing, 24
East Anglia, Kingdom of, 18
Eastbourne, 20, 30
East Ham, 20, 36, 126
East Saxons, Kingdom of, 17 ff., 124 ff.
East Stonehouse, 104
Eccles, 25, 29, 30, 33, 37
Ecclesiastical emblems, 22 ff.
Edinburgh, 23
Edmonton, 39
Egham, 11, 39
Elgin, 23
Ely, Isle of, 18, 23, 25, 30, 37, 170
Enfield, 37
Erith, 29
Ermine Street, 35, 168, 170, 236, 243 ff.
Essex, 17, 124 ff.
Eton, 5, 39
—— College, 39, 61
Evesham, 15, 16
Exeter, 16, 26, 30
——, See of, 110, 111, 379
Exmouth, 29, 33
Eye, 10, 18, 37, 42

Family emblems, 19 ff.
Fareham, 24
Farnborough, 35
Farnham, 26, 39
Farnworth, 34, 36
Faversham, 11
Feltham, 35
Fenton, 330
Feudal emblems, 19 ff.
Finchley, 32, 37
Finsbury, 23, 24, 25, 27, 29 ff.
Fisheries, 29
Fleeces, 33 ff.
Fleetwood, 20, 41
Fleurs-de-lis, 13

Flint, 15, 26
Flintshire, 17, 140
Folkestone, 29
Fords, 31
Forest emblems, 32
Fruit growing, 33
Fulham, 15, 24, 28, 30

Gates, 27
Gateshead, 23, 27, 37
Gillingham, 14, 23, 29, 42
Glamorgan, 19, 141 ff.
Glanford Brigg, 35
Glastonbury, 322
Glossop, 20
Gloucester, 12, 19, 25, 34
Gloucestershire, 19, 147 ff.
Godalming, 34, 250
Godmanchester, 13
Grantham, 19
Gravesend, 26
Greenwich, 28 ff.
Grimsby, 39
Guildford, 12, 14, 26, 34, 350
Gwent, Kingdom of, 285

Hackney, 25, 30
Hadrian's Wall, 39, 91, 298 ff.
Halesowen, 35, 335
Halifax, 19, 23
Hammersmith, 20, 37
Hampshire, 153 ff.
Hampton Court, 355
Hanley, 330
Harlech, 26, 266
Harpenden, 33
Harrogate, 31
Harrow, 39, 40
Hartlepool, 37
Harwich, 27, 29
Haslingden, 19, 30, 34, 37
Hastings, 12
Hatfield, 19
Hayes and Harlington, 24, 35
Hebden Bridge, 27
Hedon, 28
Helmets, 6
Helston, 24
Hemel Hempstead, 14
Hendon, 23, 35
Heraldic tinctures, 45
Hereford, 11
Herefordshire, 34, 160 ff.
Herne Bay, 37
Hertford, 19, 31, 37, 163
Hertfordshire, 37, 163 ff.
Heston and Isleworth, 25, 35
Heywood, 20, 34
High Wycombe, 20
Hinckley, 232
Holborn, 19, 20, 22, 23, 30, 40
Holy Lamb, 22, 23
Honiton, 22
Hornchurch, 40
Hornsey, 24, 32

Horse racing, 349, 353
Horsham, 19, 38
Hospital of St John of Jerusalem, Order of, 25, 250 ff., 281
Hounslow, 272
Hove, 18 ff., 23, 28, 42
Hucknall, 20
Huddersfield, 20, 34
Hull, 9, 10
Huntingdon, 32
Huntingdonshire, 16, 37, 173 ff.
Hyde, 20, 34 ff., 41
Hygieia, 30
Hythe, 29, 36

Icknield Way, 170
Ilford, 10, 25, 31, 32
Ilfracombe, 29
Ilkeston, 34 ff., 41
Industry, emblems of, 33 ff.
Ipswich, 12, 29 ff.
Isle of Wight, 26, 175 ff.
Islington, 20, 25

Jarrow, 21, 25, 28, 30, 40
Jerusalem, Kingdom of, 25, 52

Keighley, 20, 30, 36, 42
Kendal, 34
Kensington, 13, 20, 22, 25
Kent, 12, 17, 29 ff., 177 ff.
Kesteven (Lincs), 35
Kettering, 35
King's Lynn, 4, 24
Kingston-on-Thames, 29, 38, 350
Kingston-upon-Hull, 9, 10
Kingswood, 35
Knottingley, 35

Lambeth, 16, 19, 22, 23, 24, 37, 85
Lampeter, 27
Lancashire, 15, 19, 73, 193 ff.
Lancaster, 13, 219
——, Duchy of, 274, 279, 335, 370
——, Mass., 13, 214
Launceston, 16, 26
Leatherhead, 39
Leeds, 20, 33 ff., 41
Leicester, 12, 20
Leicestershire, 16, 20, 41, 232 ff.
Leominster, 34, 160
Lewes, 19
Lewisham, 32, 41
Leyland, 35
Leyton, 20, 25
Lichfield, 19, 23
Lifeboats, 117
Lighthouses, 30
Lincoln, 13, 22, 23, 33, 236
——, Mass., 238
Lincolnshire, 236 ff.
Lindsey (Lincs), 28, 34, 37, 39, 244
Lions, 11 ff.

INDEX

Liverpool, 28, 30, 37
Llandovery, 15
Llanelly, 23, 28, 35, 143
London Bridge, 259
——, City of, 4, 23, 24, 41, 100, 362
—— C. C., 12, 23, 30, 245 ff.
——, Port of, 12, 13, 24, 26, 28, 30
——, See of, 24, 257, 261, 269, 273, 276, 278
——, Tower of, 24, 26, 260, 264
Longton, 330
Loughborough, 20
Lowestoft, 15, 24, 30, 35
Ludlow, 19
Luton, 16, 33
Lydd, 3, 25, 28
Lyme Regis, 28
Lymington, 20, 29
Lytham St Annes, 23, 24, 28, 41

Macclesfield, 19
Maces, 10, 36
Magna Carta, 11, 39, 361
Maidenhead, 23, 27, 37, 42
Maidstone, 12, 20, 30, 39
Malden and Coombe, 32, 40
Maldon, 11, 28
Malmesbury, 14
Manchester, 12, 28 ff., 33, 203
Mansfield, 18, 20, 32, 34
Mantling, 6
Margate, 12, 29 ff.
Marlborough, 26, 39
Mars, astronomical symbol of, 34
Martello tower, 27, 367
Mayor, use of civic arms, 9
Melksham, 38
Mercia, Kingdom of, 165, 241, 320, 321, 334
Mercury's Rod, 33
Merioneth, 26, 266
Mermaids, 30
Merthyr Tydfil, 24
Merton College, Oxford, 355
Metal industry, 34
Metropolitan Water Board, 36
Middle Saxons, Kingdom of, 11, 17
Middlesbrough, 19, 28 ff., 41
Middlesex, 11, 17, 124, 267 ff.
Middleton, 20, 34, 207
Mining, 34
Mitcham, 24, 33
Monmouth, 14
Monmouthshire, 17, 285 ff.
Montgomeryshire, 288 ff.
Morecambe and Heysham, 15, 29 ff.
Morley, 34
Morpeth, 26, 42
Mossley, 41
Motor transport, 35, 337
Mottoes, 7, 41 ff.
Municipal undertakings, 36
Mural crown, 36

Nasmyth steam-hammer, 33

Naval crown, 29
Nelson, 34
Neptune, 30
Neville's Cross, 39, 123
Newark, 13, 30, 41
Newbury, 27, 34, 39
Newcastle-under-Lyme, 26
Newcastle-upon-Tyne, 26, 28, 30
Newport (Mon.), 19
New Romney, 11, 185
Norfolk, 10, 15, 20, 290 ff.
Northampton, 12, 26
Northamptonshire, 15, 35, 293 ff.
Northumberland, 18, 298 ff.
Norwich, 12, 26, 41
Nottingham, 14, 27, 32, 129
Nottinghamshire, 32, 303 ff.
Nuneaton, 22, 25, 30, 34

Oakham, 39, 318
Oldbury, 18
Oldham, 20, 38
Ostrich feathers, 15
Oswestry, 18, 116
Oxford, 7, 15, 30, 31, 38, 310
Oxfordshire, 34, 310 ff.
Oxton, 74

Paddington, 21, 24
Paignton, 25
Pembrokeshire, 17, 41, 314 ff.
Penzance, 25, 29, 39
Perth, Perthshire, 17
Peterborough, City, 24
—— C.C., 19, 24
Planta genista, 14
Plymouth, 12, 23, 29
Pontefract, 26
Poole, 28 ff.
Poplar, 27
Portcullis, 15, 27
Portsmouth, 14, 41, 176
Preston, 23
Prestwich, 32
Prittlewell, 144
Pudsey, 20, 34

Queenborough, 14
Queen's Camel, 322

Radcliffe, 20
Radnorshire, 20, 317
Railways, 35, 280, 387
Ramsgate, 12, 29, 30
Rawtenstall, 32, 34, 41, 207
Reading, 3, 14, 25
Rebuses, 37 ff.
Redcar, 13, 29, 33, 41
Redditch, 35, 36, 42
Reigate, 19, 23, 27
Religious emblems, 22 ff.
Richmond (Surrey), 15, 27, 30, 350, 351, 355

Ripon, 39
River emblems, 30
Roads, 35
Rochdale, 20, 34
Rochester, 12, 23, 26, 38
——, See of, 180, 348
Roman Britain, emblems of, 16 ff., 41, 98, 191, 270
Roses, 14 ff.
Rotherham, 21, 27, 33
Royal Air Force, 35, 157, 159, 242, 243
Royal Arms, 10 ff.
Royal Crown, 10
Royal emblems, 10 ff.
Royal Marines, 181
Royal Navy, 181
Rugby, 20, 35, 39
—— School, 378
Ruislip-Northwood, 38
Runnymede, 11, 39, 361
Rutland, 39, 318
Ryde, 29, 41

St Albans, 163, 168, 171, 270
St Davids, See of, 316
St Helens, 21
St Ives (Hunts), 34
St Marylebone, 13, 22, 30
St Pancras, 20, 24
Sale, 38
Salford, 16, 34
Salop C.C., 12
Sandringham, 87
Sandwich, 12, 182, 188
——, Mass., 12
Saxon crowns, 11
Scarborough, 26
Scottish emblems, 16
Scunthorpe, 35
Sea emblems, 28 ff.
Seaham, 29
Seals, civic, 3 ff.
Seaxes, 17
Sheffield, 30, 34, 38
Sherwood Forest, 32, 303 ff.
Ships, 28 ff.
Shoreditch, 36
Shoreham-by-Sea, 19
Shrewsbury, 12, 319
Shropshire, 319 ff.
Sidmouth, 28
Sidney Sussex College, Cambridge, 240
Sittingbourne, 23, 33, 36
Slough, 20, 33, 40
Somerset, 17, 322 ff.
Southall, 32, 35
Southampton, 12, 15, 28 ff.
Southchurch, 144
Southend-on-Sea, 22 ff., 25, 30
Southgate, 32
Southport, 28 ff.
South Saxons, Kingdom of, 11, 17, 365 ff.
South Shields, 28 ff., 33

INDEX

Southwark, 22, 23, 41
—— Bridge, 27
—— Diocese, 351
Southwold, 14, 18, 23
Spalding, 16, 33, 39, 236
Spennymoor, 39, 42
Sp...gs, 31
Stafford, 12, 20, 26
Staffordshire, 13, 19, 20, 34, 42, 328 ff.
Stalybridge, 16, 20, 78, 207
Stamford, 12, 19
Standards, 8
Star and Crescent, 13
Stepney, 23, 29
Stockport, 20, 29
Stockton-on-Tees, 26
Stoke Newington, 32
Stoke-on-Trent, 20, 36
Stourbridge, 14, 27, 35
Sudbury, 13, 20
Suffolk, 18, 20, 28, 343 ff.
Sun and Moon, 13
Sunderland, 23, 24, 28, 123
Sundridge, 182
Supporters, 7
Surbiton, 32, 35
Surrey, 11, 32, 350 ff.
Sussex, 11, 17, 365 ff.
Sutton Coldfield, 14
Swansea, 19, 26, 28
Swindon, 4, 26, 35

Tamworth, 13
Taunton, 11
Templars, Order of, 25, 166, 251, 424
Tenterden, 29
Textiles, 34
Thames, 30, 245 ff., 311, 357
Thor, 34
Thornaby-on-Tees, 13, 19, 20, 29
Todmorden, 15, 30, 34

Tonbridge, 19, 27
Torquay, 27, 29
Torrington, Great, 3, 13
Totnes, 26
Tottenham, 16
Tranmere, 74
Transport emblems, 35
Trinity, emblems of, 22, 126
Truro, 30, 34
Tudor badges, 15
Tunbridge Wells, 31
Tunstall, 330
Twickenham, 21, 24, 30, 40
Tynemouth, 34

University Boat Race, 351
Uxbridge, 33

Vintners Company, 78
Vulcan, 34, 93

Wakefield, 13
Wallasey, 29 ff., 39
Wallingford, 14, 27
Wallsend, 16, 34, 35, 39, 42
Walsall, 13, 20
Walthamstow, 29
Walton and Weybridge, 17
Walton-le-Dale, 19
Wandsworth, 19, 23, 28
Wanstead and Woodford, 18
Wantage, 39
Wareham, 13
Warrington, 16
Warwick, 20
Warwickshire, 20, 21, 42, 374 ff.
Waterloo-with-Seaforth, 210
Water supply, 36
Watford, 21, 25, 30
Wednesbury, 13, 34, 35
Wells, 31
Wembley, 39

Wenlock, 22
Wessex. *See* West Saxons
West Bridgford, 27
West Bromwich, 34
West Ham, 20, 29, 125, 132
West Hartlepool, 29
Westminster, 15, 18, 19, 27
—— Abbey, 127, 246, 248, 253, 395
Westmorland, 34, 37, 381 ff.
Weston-super-Mare, 29 ff., 39
West Saxons, Wessex, Kingdom of, 17, 112, 322, 327, 383
Weymouth, 19, 29
Wheatsheaves, 33
Widnes, 35
Wigan, 11, 13, 14, 26, 37, 38
Willenhall, 36
Willesden, 24
Wiltshire, 17, 383 ff.
Wimbledon, 14, 16, 19, 20, 24
Winchester, 12, 26
Windsor, 13, 32, 51
Wirral horn, 152
Wisbech, 24
Woking, 18, 20
Wolverhampton, 24, 34 ff.
Woodstock, 14
Woolpacks, 33 ff.
Woolwich, 42
Worcester, 14, 26, 41
——, See of, 25, 149, 393
Worcestershire, 14, 390 ff.
Workington, 36, 38
Worksop, 21, 23, 25, 32
Worthing, 28, 30
Wrexham, 17, 25, 34
Wykeham-upon-Hull, 403

Yarmouth, Great, 12, 29
Yeovil, 23
York, 12, 23
Yorkshire, 15, 216, 397 ff.
Ystradgynlais, 34